Uniformity and Fragmentation of the 1999 Montreal Convention on International Air Carrier Liability

Aerospace Law and Policy Series

VOLUME 21

Editors

Pablo Mendes de Leon, Professor of Air and Space Law, and Tanja Masson-Zwaan, Assistant Professor of Space Law, Leiden University, The Netherlands.

Introduction

The *Aerospace Law and Policy Series* critically examines the fundamental changes that international aviation and space activities have undergone since the last century, growing up as mature industries while freeing themselves from traditional regulatory constraints and displaying a variety of innovative applications that call for creative legal solutions.

Objective

The objective of the Series is to make a contribution to legal thinking on public international air and space law and policy, and their implementation at the regional and national levels, responsibility and liability of public bodies and service providers, competition law, insurance law, company law, and the complex relationship between EU law and public international law.

Readership

Aviation and space lawyers, academics, representatives of governments, international organizations, and companies involved in aviation and space activities.

The titles published in this series are listed at the end of this volume.

Uniformity and Fragmentation of the 1999 Montreal Convention on International Air Carrier Liability

Cyril-Igor Grigorieff

Wolters Kluwer

Published by:
Kluwer Law International B.V.
PO Box 316
2400 AH Alphen aan den Rijn
The Netherlands
E-mail: international-sales@wolterskluwer.com
Website: www.wolterskluwer.com/en/solutions/kluwerlawinternational

Sold and distributed by:
Wolters Kluwer Legal & Regulatory U.S.
7201 McKinney Circle
Frederick, MD 21704
United States of America
E-mail: customer.service@wolterskluwer.com

ISBN 978-94-035-3732-0

e-Book: ISBN 978-94-035-3752-8
web-PDF: ISBN 978-94-035-3773-3

Uniformity and Fragmentation of the 1999 Montreal Convention on International Air Carrier Liability

Cyril-Igor Grigorieff

Wolters Kluwer

Published by:
Kluwer Law International B.V.
PO Box 316
2400 AH Alphen aan den Rijn
The Netherlands
E-mail: international-sales@wolterskluwer.com
Website: www.wolterskluwer.com/en/solutions/kluwerlawinternational

Sold and distributed by:
Wolters Kluwer Legal & Regulatory U.S.
7201 McKinney Circle
Frederick, MD 21704
United States of America
E-mail: customer.service@wolterskluwer.com

ISBN 978-94-035-3732-0

e-Book: ISBN 978-94-035-3752-8
web-PDF: ISBN 978-94-035-3773-3

About the Author

Dr Cyril-Igor Grigorieff has been a member of the Brussels Bar since 2006 and is a former member of the Paris Bar (2014-2018). He gained experience in matters relating to airline liability in a multi-jurisdictional environment, in European Union regulatory affairs and in aircraft finance in international law firms. He furthered his skills in the sector, working on secondment for a commercial airline. His work as a practising lawyer has been acknowledged by numerous accolades.

On the academic side, Cyril-Igor teaches Aviation Contract Law at Paris-Saclay University. He is the author of around forty publications in the field of air law. Notably, he has been one of the named authors in the Belgian Transportation Code since 2010 (*Code Annoté du Droit des Transports*, Larcier), and the co-editor of the first law book in French on aircraft finance (*Le droit du financement des aéronefs*, Bruylant, 2017). This book is the outcome of his doctoral study, defended in 2021 at Leiden University under the supervision of Prof. Dr Pablo Mendes de Leon and Prof. Dr Vincent Correia.

Table of Contents

List of Abbreviations

The choice of abbreviations and acronyms tends to reflect, as much as possible, those used in each jurisdiction.

AC	Law Reports, Appeal Cases (UK)
Aff'd	Affirmed
ALADA	*Asociación Latino Americana de Derecho Aeronáutico y Espacial*
All ER	All England Law Reports
ALR	Australian Law Reports
ASEAN	Association of Southeast Asian Nations
B.O.	*Boletín Oficial* (Spain)
BCCRT	British Columbia Civil Resolution Tribunal (Canada)
BCE	Before the Common Era
Bull.	*Bulletin* (France)
c.	*contre/contra* (against)
CA	*Cour d'appel* (Belgium, France, Luxembourg, Madagascar)
CAN	Canadian Dollar
Cass.	*Cour de cassation* (Belgium, France, Luxembourg)/*Corte de cassazione* (Italy)
CC	*Conseil Constitutionnel* (France)
CE	*Conseil d'Etat* (France)
CEMAC	Economic and Monetary Community of Central Africa
Cert.	*certiorari*
CF	Federal Court (Canada)
CFR	Code of Federal Regulations (USA)
CINA	*Commission Internationale de la Navigation Aérienne*
Cir.	Circuit (USA)

CISG	United Nations Convention on Contracts for the International Sale of Goods
CITEJA	*Comité International Technique d'Experts Juridiques Aériens*
Civ	Civil
CJEU/CJEC	Court of Justice of the European Union/Court of Justice of the European Community (before 2009)
CMR	Convention on the Contract for the International Carriage of Goods by Road
COTIF	Convention Concerning International Carriage by Rail
Doc	Document
E. a.	*Et alii* (and others)
ECHR	European Court of Human Rights
ECLI	European Case Law Identifier
ECR	European Court Reports
EU	European Union
EWCA	England and Wales Court of Appeal
EWHC	England and Wales High Court
F.	Federal Reporter (USA)
F. App'x	Federal Appendix (USA)
F. Supp.	Federal Supplement (USA)
Fasc.	*Fascicule* (booklet)
FCA	Federal Court of Australia
GU	Gazzetta Ufficiale (Italy)
HCA	High Court of Australia
HCCH	Hague Conference on Private International Law
HKCA	Hong Kong Court of Appeal
HP55	1955 Hague Protocol
IATA	International Air Transport Association/International Air Traffic Association (Before 1945)
ICAO	International Civil Aviation Organization
ICHR	Inter-American Court of Human Rights
ICJ	International Court of Justice
IEHC	Irish High Court
IESC	Irish Supreme Court
ILC	International Law Commission of the United Nations
JCP	*Juris-Classeur Périodique* (*Semaine Juridique*)
LNTS	League of Nations Treaty Series
MC99	1999 Montreal Convention
N.D. Tex	Northern District of Texas (USA)
NSWCA	New South Wales Court of Appeal (Australia)
NZLR	New Zealand Law Reports

ODR	Online Dispute Resolution
OHADA	Organization for the Harmonization in Africa of Business Law
OJ	Official Journal of the European Union
Ors	Others
Phil	Philippines Reports
PICAO	Provisional International Civil Aviation Organization
QB	Queen's Bench (UK)
S.D.N.Y.	Southern District of New York (USA)
s/	*sin* (without)
SARPs	Standards and Recommended Practices (of the ICAO)
SCC	Supreme Court Cases (India)
SCR	Supreme Court Report (Canada)
SDR	Special Drawing Right
t.	*Tome* (volume)
TFEU	Treaty on the Functioning of the European Union
TOSC	Tonga Supreme Court
U.S.	Supreme Court of the United States of America
UEMOA	West African Economic and Monetary Union
UK	United Kingdom
UKHL	House of Lords of the United Kingdom
UKSC	Supreme Court of the United Kingdom
UN	United Nations
UNCITRAL	United Nations Commission on International Trade Law
UNIDROIT	International Institute for the Unification of Private Law
UNTS	United Nations Treaty Series
USA	United States of America
USD	United States Dollars
VSC	Victoria Supreme Court (Australia)
WC29	1929 Warsaw Convention
WI	Supreme Court of Wisconsin (USA)
ZAWCH	High Court of South Africa, Cape of Good Hope division

Foreword

The 1999 Montreal Convention and its predecessor, the 1929 Warsaw Convention, have been guided by a utilitarian philosophy. Aviation being an international activity since its infancy, governments agreed on common legal principles governing the most important aspects of air carriers' liability. In doing so, they adopted an innovative method and progressively shifted towards a more 'cosmopolitan' approach, as they do not only prescribe obligations for States, as it is usually done in Public International Law, but also address private law issues. More importantly, these Conventions unify 'certain' aspects of the legal regime applicable to the liability of air carriers, while ensuring uniformity of rights and obligations across jurisdictions irrespective of the different legal systems and rules. Hence, they are a perfect example of 'Uniform Law', as confirmed by the famous principle of exclusivity enshrined in, respectively, Article 24 of the 1929 Warsaw Convention and Article 29 of the 1999 Montreal Convention.

Against this backdrop, and notwithstanding the fact that many specialists are familiar with these Conventions, the present book of Dr Cyril-Igor Grigorieff constitutes a *formidable* contribution to the understanding of private air law. By focusing on the objective of uniformity, which is the backbone of these Conventions, Dr Grigorieff offers a systematic and in-depth analysis of a legal regime which is nowadays threatened by fragmentation. His analysis and conclusions go way beyond the traditional appraisal of compatibility of national or regional laws or rulings with the international instruments: he identifies all of the factors causing fragmentation and suggests how to overcome these. In doing so, he not only relies on Private and Public International Law but also examines ongoing trends across several topical jurisdictions, going beyond the US and United Kingdom examples which are traditionally used in air law books. His fine and profound knowledge of litigation of the air carriers' liability, alongside with the broad scope of national jurisdictions which he has researched, contribute to challenge solutions that are sometimes taken for granted by lawyers or to highlight the major threats to the internationally agreed uniformity.

Given the increasing tendency to adopt national or regional legislations affecting contractual liability and given the fact that national Courts sometimes show less deference towards international law as they did in the past, recalling the importance of uniformity and the *pacta sunt servanda* rule forms an essential approach in this study. At the same time, it is undisputable that international law evolves through practice, interpretation, or amendments to International Conventions. Furthermore, it could be inferred from the current factors of fragmentation that they are only a demonstration of the inadequacy of the 1999 Montreal Convention to contemporary challenges and aspirations. This conclusion would militate in favour of a modification of said Convention, by adapting it to new necessities in order to ensure a better compliance.

However, the last decades demonstrated that the era of triumphant multilateralism is perhaps over. States prove to be more reluctant to conclude and adhere to such international agreements causing extensions of the process of ratification. Unfortunately, the many calls made by the academic and professional air law community in the last years were left unanswered, and this is precisely where the book of Dr Grigorieff proves extremely useful. First, through a better understanding of the reasons leading to fragmentation, most notably at the interpretation stage, the outcome of trials could be better influenced, or at least anticipated. Second, the author correctly and pragmatically evacuates solutions that, despite being the most desirable, do not appear feasible, such as the revision of the Montreal Convention or the establishment of an International Air Law Court. Therefore, he envisages more innovative solutions, taking most notably into account the promises of Artificial Intelligence and the so-called 'Big Data'. In other words, he offers a detailed diagnostic of the current legal *panorama*, as well as a thorough reflection on the somewhat simplistic solutions which are often promoted, leading to innovative proposals.

For all these reasons, we believe that this book is designed to prove extremely valuable for students, academics and professionals interested in air law: novices will greatly benefit from the didactic qualities of this book, and experienced lawyers will find new ideas to enrich their own thinking or practice. Hence, this book should be in any air law library worth of this name.

Prof. Dr Vincent Correia
Université Paris-Saclay, France

Pablo Mendes de Leon
Professor of Air and Space Law, The Hague

Acknowledgements

This book is the result of several years of practice and research. Not a single line would have been possible without the constant encouragement of many caring and incredible people.

First of all, I would like to express my deepest gratitude to my supervisors: Prof. Dr Pablo Mendes de Leon, Emeritus Professor of Air and Space Law at Leiden University; and Prof. Dr Vincent Correia, Co-director of the *Institut Droit, Espaces et Technologies* of the Paris-Saclay University, whose clear guidance and encouragement were invaluable to the process of my doctoral dissertation. My sincere gratitude also goes to the staff of the Institute of Air and Space Law, in particular Mrs Natascha Meewisse who skilfully guided me through the PhD related processes. I should also mention the outstanding members of my doctoral and opposition committees and my incredible paranymphs Charlotte Thijssen and Davinia Dusa Grigorieff.

Next, I would like first to thank my family and particularly my parents, Danielle Bloem and Ghéorghiï Vladimirovitch Grigorieff, for having taught me the importance of academic rigour, and who also initiated me from a young age to law, aviation and languages.

Further, I wish to thank all those who helped me during this extraordinary experience. Although I may not list all of them, I truly appreciated their assistance and friendship. Special thanks go to Mina Miller for her careful proofreading.

Finally, I take full responsibility for any errors, omissions or inaccuracies which may be found in this book.

CHAPTER 1
Introduction

1.1 LEGAL CONTEXT AND DEFINITIONS

1.1.1 The Emergence of Aviation and the Need for an International Air Carrier Liability Regime

In the early 20th century, travel between China and Europe took approximately eight weeks by car for the most courageous travellers,[1] six weeks by boat, and two weeks by train.[2] The emergence of aviation in that era drastically impacted our notion of distance and quickened the speed of communication. As aviation reduced the distance between people, it also brought the promise of innovation in trade, information, leisure and the military.[3]

However, aviation was still an adventure. The feeling of being a pioneer when boarding an aircraft in the 1920s unavoidably included the acceptance of risk, given the relatively low safety level of this new mode of transport.[4] Between 1925 and 1929, the ratio of fatal accidents from air travel per hundred million passengers-kilometres was 28[5] compared to 0.02 in 1999.[6]

1. Le Figaro, http://www.lefigaro.fr/histoire/archives/2017/06/09/26010-20170609ARTFIG00288-pekin-paris-en-automobile-un-prodigieux-defi-en-1907.php (accessed 28 May 2019).
2. Numa Broc, *Les voyageurs français et la connaissance de la Chine (1860-1914)*, t. 276, Fasc. 1 (559) Revue Historique 90 (Presses Universitaires Françaises, Juillet – Septembre 1986).
3. It is reported that while the American airline industry only carried 6,000 passengers in 1930, this figure rose to more than 450,000 in 1934, and up to 1,200,000 in 1938, Source: National Air and Space Museum, https://airandspace.si.edu/exhibitions/america-by-air/online/innovation/innovation15.cfm (accessed 1 September 2020).
4. Conférence Internationale de Droit Privé Aérien, 27 Octobre-6 Novembre 1925, Paris, 1926, p. 55.
5. ICAO Doc 7686, International Conference on Private Air Law, The Hague, September 1955, volume I, *Minutes*, Montreal September 1956, p. 162.
6. Statistical Abstract of the United States, volume 125, Part 2006, p. 699 quoting ICAO, Source: Civil Aviation Statistics of the World, United States Census Bureau, https://www2.census.gov/library/publications/2005/compendia/statab/125ed/tables/trans.pdf (accessed 29 May 2019).

While the general liability regime was applied in the absence of a specific regime in many jurisdictions, States such as France, Germany and Italy started to adopt specific domestic rules governing air carriers' liability, particularly in the case of death or injury to passengers.[7] The existence of various domestic regimes became problematic, however, when international carriage was involved. As noted by Professor Daniel Goedhuis in 1937, difficulties arose when the applicable regimes were particularly different across the globe.[8] A simple review of the existing applicable air carriers' liability regimes during the infancy of aviation shows the disparity between them. For example, while one domestic legislation could allow an action to be brought against the carrier on the grounds of the contract of carriage, another enabled the passenger to sue in tort.[9]

Difficulty also arose when one State legislation, such as the United Kingdom's, considered a clause in the contract of carriage exonerating the carrier from all liability to be perfectly valid, whereas another, such as France's, did not.[10] In such a context of legal disparity, a passenger who was the victim of an accident between two States could hence have a claim that could be subject, depending on the conflict of laws rules of the Court seized, alternatively or cumulatively to:

- the laws of his or her nationality;
- the laws of his or her country of residence;
- the laws of the nationality or domicile of the carrier;
- the laws where the contract of carriage was signed;
- the laws of the country of departure or arrival or where the loss occurred;[11] and so forth.

The coexistence of several liability regimes therefore created an undesirable situation that needed to be addressed. If a new era of aviation could reduce barriers to travelling, an approximation of legislations should be able to do the same for legal difficulties.

---

7. *See*, Daniel Goedhuis, *National Airlegislations and the Warsaw Convention* (Springer, 1937); Jean Constantinoff, *Le droit aérien français et étranger: droit interne et droit international* (Librairie de Jurisprudence Ancienne et Moderne, 1932); Max Litvine, *Précis élémentaire de droit aérien* (Bruylant, 1953); Conférence Internationale de Droit Privé Aérien, 27 Octobre-6 Novembre 1925, Paris, 1926, p. 28; Yvonne Blanc-Dannery, *La Convention de Varsovie et les règles du transport aérien international* 5 (Pedone, 1933).
8. *See*, Daniel Goedhuis, *National Airlegislations and the Warsaw Convention* (Springer, 1937).
9. *See*, *Ibid.*, p. 3.
10. *See*, Fernand de Visscher, *Les conflits de lois en matière de droit aérien*, 48 Recueil des cours de l'Académie de droit international 325 (1934).
11. *See*, Conférence Internationale de Droit Privé Aérien, 27 Octobre-6 Novembre 1925, Paris, 1926, p. 11.

1.1.2 Possible Techniques of Approximation of Legislations

1.1.2.1 Harmonization and Unification Techniques

(1) Preliminary Remarks

Although the literature sometimes uses unclear wording,[12] there exist two major categories of techniques of legislative approximation: *Harmonization* and *Unification*. This distinction was notably used in the United Nations Resolution 2205 (XXI) of 17 December 1966 on the Establishment of the United Nations Commission on International Trade Law (hereinafter 'UNCITRAL'),[13] and in the International Institute for the Unification of Private Law (hereinafter 'UNIDROIT') Statute.[14]

Due to the existence of several nuances, each instrument must receive an ad hoc analysis. This study will focus particularly on the distinction made between harmonization and unification, and assumes that harmonization entails changes in domestic legislations to 'produce more or less similar law in different countries',[15] while unification concerns the 'creation of identical rules'.[16]

These concepts should not, however, be confused with *codification*, which consists of a 'more precise formulation and systematization of rules of international law in fields where there already has been extensive State practice, precedent and doctrine'.[17] Codification is therefore not possible in the absence of pre-existing international law in the sector.

---

12. *See*, for example, Innocent Fetze Kamdem, *Harmonisation, unification et uniformisation en droit des contrats: plaidoyer pour un discours affiné sur les moyens d'intégration juridique*, 13 Uniform Law Review 715-716, 722 (2008); Katharina Boele-Woelki, *Unifying and Harmonizing Substantive Law and the Role of Conflict of Laws* 32 (Pocketbooks of The Hague Academy of International Law, 2010); Hans Henrik Edlund, 'The Concept of Unification and Harmonization', in Morten Fogt (ed.), *Unification and Harmonization of International Commercial Law: Interaction or Deharmonization* 7 (Wolters Kluwer, 2012); Camilla Andersen, *Defining Uniformity in Law*, 12 Uniform Law Review 5-54 (2007); Mireille Delmas-Marty, *Trois défis pour un droit mondial* 104-134 (Seuil, 1998).
13. Article 1: 'Decides to establish a United Nations Commission on International Trade Law [...], which shall have for its object the promotion of the progressive harmonization and unification of the law on international trade, [...].' The meaning of these concepts is explained on the UNCITRAL's website as follows: '"Harmonization" may conceptually be thought of as the process through which domestic laws may be modified to enhance predictability in cross-border commercial transactions. "Unification" may be seen as the adoption by States of a common legal standard governing particular aspects of international business transactions. A model law or a legislative guide is an example of a text which is drafted to harmonize domestic law, while a convention is an international instrument which is adopted by States for the unification of the law at an international level', UNCITRAL, https://uncitral.un.org/en/about/faq/mandate_composition/history (accessed 12 February 2020).
14. Article 12(1): 'Any participating Government, as well as any international institution of an official nature, shall be entitled to set before the Governing Council proposals for the study of questions relating to the unification, harmonisation or coordination of private law.'
15. Martin Gebauer, *Unification and Harmonization of Laws* para. 4 (Max Planck Encyclopedias of International Law, 2009).
16. *Ibid*.
17. *See*, Statute of the International Law Commission, Article 15.

(2) Harmonization Techniques

Harmonization of rules is a multifaceted process. In air law, the most commonly known method consists of the adoption of Standards and Recommended Practices (hereinafter the 'SARPs')[18] which are essentially organized under Articles 37, 38 and 90 of the Convention on International Civil Aviation (hereinafter the '**1944 Chicago Convention**').[19] Article 37 of the 1944 Chicago Convention sets out that each contracting State undertakes to collaborate to secure 'the highest practicable degree of uniformity' in regulations, standards, procedure and organization. The SARPs, however, are 'legally weak',[20] as they are not 'hard law'.[21] These statements stand by themselves with respect to Recommended Practices,[22] and are equally valid regarding Standards insofar as Article 38 of the 1944 Chicago Convention allows States to depart from them under certain conditions.[23]

(3) Unification Techniques

(i) Conflict of Laws Rules

The most habitual unification technique is to adopt common rules of conflict of laws in an international convention. At the end of the 19th century, the Hague Conference on Private International Law (hereinafter 'HCCH'), the first world organization for cross-border cooperation in civil and commercial matters, developed an arsenal of international conventions to set international rules of conflict of laws in various fields.[24] The application of domestic legislation determined by the common rules of

---

18. A definition can be found in ICAO Resolution A 36-13, Appendix A: 'Standard – any specification for physical characteristics, configuration, materiel, performance, personnel or procedure, the uniform application of which is recognized as necessary for the safety or regularity of air navigation and to which contracting States will conform in accordance with the convention; in the event of impossibility of compliance, notification to the Council is compulsory under Article 38 of the Convention'; 'Recommended Practice – any specification physical characteristics, configuration, materiel, performance, personnel or procedure, the uniform application of which is recognized as desirable in the interest of safety, regularity or efficiency of international air navigation and to which contracting States will endeavor to conform in accordance with the Convention.'
19. Convention on International Civil Aviation, 7 December 1944, Chicago, ICAO Doc 7300, entry in force 4 April 1947.
20. Michael Milde, *International Air Law and ICAO* 161 (Eleven International Publishing, 2008).
21. *Ibid.*, p. 164.
22. *See*, Jacques Naveau, Marc Godfroid, Pierre Fruhling, *Précis de droit aérien* 41 (2nd edition, Bruylant, 2006).
23. The domestic reception of the Annexes to the 1944 Chicago Convention, in which the SARPs are established, is subject to different views. *See*, Pablo Mendes de Leon, *Introduction to Air Law* 25 (10th edition, Wolters Kluwer, 2017); Vincent Correia, Béatrice Trigeaud, 'Transport, navigation et sources du droit international: Remarques générales', in Saïda El Bouhoudi (ed.), *Les transports au prisme du droit international public* 55 (Pedone, 2019); Federico Bergamasco, *The ITU and ICAO Regulating Aeronautical Safety Services and Related Radio Spectrum* 251-290 (Thesis, Université de Luxembourg, 2021).
24. *See*, for example, the Convention du 12 juin 1902 pour régler les conflits de lois en matière de mariage, and the Convention du 12 juin 1902 pour régler les conflits de lois et de juridictions en

conflict of laws, however, is not always convenient, as it can result in the application of a foreign law that conflicts with the core values of the seized State, or may merely be difficult to establish with certainty.

(ii) Uniform Rules

Another unification technique consists of the adoption of 'uniform rules', generally established in the form of an international convention (hereinafter '**Uniform Instruments**'). These uniform rules do not set common rules of conflict of laws but common substantive rules of private law. Professor Antonio Malintoppi compared these two techniques of unification as follows:

> C'est justement par rapport à l'unification des règles de fond que l'on préfère utiliser l'expression 'droit uniforme', bien que l'unification des règles de droit international privé donne lieu elle aussi à un droit uniforme constitué justement par des règles de droit international privé. En effet, l'adoption de règles uniformes de fond (règles matérielles) assure l'uniformité de la réglementation juridique des faits ou des rapports qui relèvent de l'activité humaine, alors que l'adoption de règles uniformes de droit international privé aboutit seulement à l'uniformité des critères visant le choix de la loi applicable sans pourtant garantir que la réglementation juridique des faits ou rapports envisagés soit elle aussi la même dans les divers systèmes juridiques intéressés. Dans ces conditions, c'est à juste titre que nous pensons devoir utiliser l'expression *droit uniforme* pour désigner les seules règles unifiées de fond.[25]

The first characteristic of these uniform rules is to eliminate the issue of determining the applicable domestic legislation, by establishing common substantive private rules.[26] The second, as pointed out by the same author, is that the effectiveness of uniform rules relies on their primacy over domestic legislation:

> [...] le droit uniforme prime toute loi nationale et entraîne l'application d'un texte de droit spécial originairement arrêté dans une convention internationale.[27]

In essence, uniform rules could be defined as substantive private law rules, distinct from rules of conflict of laws. They are jointly elaborated with a view to unify the law, are adopted in the form of an international convention, and prevail over domestic rules.

---

matière de divorces et de séparations de corps; Convention on the Law Applicable to Traffic Accidents, 4 May 1971, The Hague, UNTS, 965, I-13925, entry in force 3 June 1975; Convention on the Law Applicable to Certain Rights in Respect of Securities held with an Intermediary, 5 July 2006, The Hague, UNTS, I-54441, entry in force 1 April 2017.

25. Antonio Malintoppi, *Droit uniforme et droit international privé*, 116 Recueil des cours de l'Académie de droit international 12 (1965).
26. *See*, Massimiliano Rimaboschi, *L'unification du droit maritime: Contribution à la construction d'un ordre juridique maritime* 57 (Presses Universitaires d'Aix-Marseille, 2006).
27. Antonio Malintoppi, *Droit uniforme et droit international privé*, 116 Recueil des cours de l'Académie de droit international 59 (1965). *See also*, Laurent Chassot, *Les sources de la responsabilité du transporteur aérien international: entre conflit et complémentarité: La Convention de Montréal et son interaction avec le droit européen et national* 31-32 (Schulthess, 2012).

Uniform Instruments were initially adopted for the rail sector and later for other modes of transportation.[28] Gradually, States enacted uniform rules in multiple areas such as: agency law, the international sale of goods, illegally exported objects, and collateral.[29]

However, in light of the diversity of Uniform Instruments and in the absence of a generally agreed definition of what constitutes 'uniform rules', each Uniform Instrument must be individually assessed.

(4) Distinction with Respect to the Techniques Used in European Union Law

Despite similarities, the techniques of approximation of legislations used in an international context should not be compared to those used in European Union (hereinafter 'EU') law, through notably directives and regulations. European directives are defined particularly in Article 288 paragraph 3 of the Treaty on the Functioning of the European Union (in short the 'TFEU')[30] as follows:

> A directive shall be binding, as to the result to be achieved, upon each Member State to which it is addressed, but shall leave to the national authorities the choice of form and methods.

European directives and harmonization techniques are therefore similar in that they both modify domestic legislations while offering a certain margin of manoeuvre.[31] But, they are notably distinct insofar as European directives, unlike harmonization techniques, use autonomous concepts proper to European law, and their creation, implementation and uniform application are regulated by European Institutions.[32]

In parallel, European regulations share some common features with uniform rules as defined above. Article 288 paragraph 2 of the TFEU provides that:

28. *See*, for instance, for the rail sector: the International Convention Concerning the Carriage of Goods by Rail, 14 October 1890, Bern; International Convention Concerning the Transport of Passengers and Luggage by Rail, 23 October 1924, Bern.
29. *See*, for example, under the auspices of UNIDROIT: Convention Relating to a Uniform Law on the Formation of Contracts for the International Sale of Goods, 1 July 1964, The Hague; Convention Relating to a Uniform Law on the International Sale of Goods, 1 July 1964, The Hague; International Convention on Travel Contracts (CCV), 23 April 1970, Brussels; Convention Providing a Uniform Law on the Form of an International Will, 26 October 1973, Washington; Convention on Agency in the International Sale of Goods, 17 February 1983, Geneva; UNIDROIT Convention on International Financial Leasing, 28 May 1988, Ottawa; UNIDROIT Convention on International Factoring, 28 May 1988, Ottawa; UNIDROIT Convention on Stolen or Illegally Exported Cultural Objects, 24 June 1995, Rome; Convention on International Interests in Mobile Equipment, 16 November 2001, Cape Town.
30. Treaty on the Functioning of the European Union (2016 version), *Official Journal*, 7 June 2016, C 202/1.
31. The EU also makes a distinction between 'minimum' and 'maximum' harmonization. The latter sets the floor or ceiling of harmonization, while the former allows Member States to adopt more stringent rules. *See*, Craig Paul, Búrca (de) Gráinne, *EU Law: Text, Cases and Material* 661 (7th edition, Oxford University Press, 2020).
32. *See*, Craig Paul, Búrca (de) Gráinne, *EU Law: Text, Cases and Material* 139, 236 (7th edition, Oxford University Press, 2020).

> A regulation shall have general application. It shall be binding in its entirety and directly applicable in all Member States.

Uniform Rules and European regulations may thus contain substantive rules that should prevail over domestic legislation.[33] Nevertheless, they are different because European regulations are directly applicable in all Member States, and again, are embedded in the larger specific autonomous[34] legal framework of EU law, and their uniform application is guaranteed by the Court of Justice of the European Union (hereinafter 'CJEU').[35]

While European directives and regulations may appear at first sight similar to the approximation of legislation techniques described above, they are in reality quite distinct as they are incorporated into the specific legal system that is European law. The parallels are therefore limited.[36]

1.1.2.2 Other Techniques

Several other techniques for the approximation of legislation exist, and they vary according to their methods and results. Among these other techniques, two in particular have been used in international private air law.

One consists in 'cooperation' or 'coordination', or even 'convergence', pursuant to the terminology used. Under this approach, two or more States jointly decide not to adopt conflicting legislation and, wherever possible, each adopt compatible legislations. This approach is often found in advanced air service agreements. For example, the 2007 Agreement on air transport between the EU, its Member States, and the United States, amended in 2010, includes specific provisions in its Annex 2 on cooperation in competition issues, such as the enhancement of mutual understanding of each competition regime, the reduction of potential conflicts and the promotion of compatible regulatory approaches.[37]

---

33. *See*, CJEC, 15 July 1964, *Flaminio Costa v. E.N.E.L.*, C-6/64, ECLI:EU:C:1964:66; CJEC, 19 June 1990, *The Queen v. Secretary of State for Transport, ex parte: Factortame Ltd*, C-213/89, ECLI:EU:C:1990:257.
34. *See*, CJEC, 5 February 1963, *NV Algemene Transport en Expeditie Onderneming van Gend & Loos v. Nederlandse Administratie der Bestelingen*, C-26/62, ECLI:EU:C:1963:1.
35. *See*, CJEC, 22 October 1987, *Foto-Frost v. Hauptzollamt Lübeck-Ost*, C-314/85, ECLI:EU:C:1987:452. It should also be mentioned that the European Commission is the guardian of the treaties. *See*, Treaty on the Functioning of the European Union, Article 258.
36. The analysis of the European Union, as a sui generis organization, is outside the scope of this study. Therefore, I will not elaborate further on techniques of approximation of legislation developed in the EU.
37. Air Transport Agreement between the United States of America and the European Community and its Member States, 25-30 April 2007, Brussels and Washington, *Official Journal*, 25 May 2007, L 134/4. Annex 2, Article 2: 'The purpose of this cooperation is: 1. to enhance mutual understanding of the application by the Participants of the laws, procedures and practices under their respective competition regimes to encourage competition in the air transportation industry; 2. to facilitate understanding between the Participants of the impact of air transportation industry developments on competition in the international aviation market; 3. to reduce the potential for conflicts in the Participants' application of their respective competition regimes to agreements and other cooperative arrangements which have an impact on the transatlantic

The other method that could qualify as an 'integration' technique has notably been used by the EU. Essentially, it consists in incorporating the existing legislation of a determined State into the legal order of another State.[38] Such a mechanism of integration or 'substitution' has been used, for example, in the 1999 Agreement on air transport between Switzerland and the EU, as variously amended. In this agreement, the parties consented that specified European legislation would apply in Switzerland.[39] However, this solution does not prevent each State or jurisdiction from modifying its domestic law over time. This is why, in the case of the agreement between the EU and Switzerland,[40] in order to ensure continuing adequacy as much as possible, the agreement also provides that the European legislation listed, in the Annex thereto, which would potentially be interpreted by the CJEU after the signing of the agreement, would be communicated to a Joint Committee in order to determine whether or not the interpretation given by said Court would also apply in Switzerland.[41]

market; and 4. to promote compatible regulatory approaches to agreements and other cooperative arrangements through a better understanding of the methodologies, analytical techniques including the definition of the relevant market(s) and analysis of competitive effects, and remedies that the Participants use in their respective independent competition reviews.' *See,* Vincent Correia, *L'Union européenne et le droit international de l'aviation civile* 637-642 (Bruylant, 2013); Kate Markhvida, 'Antitrust and Competition Law', in Paul Dempsey, Ram Jakhu (eds), *Routledge Handbook of Public Aviation Law* 328 (Routledge, 2017).

38. *See,* Vincent Correia, *L'Union européenne et le droit international de l'aviation civile* 525-529, 547 (Bruylant, 2013). In the absence of clear, generally agreed-on terminology, it should be highlighted that the term 'convergence' is occasionally used to describe this technique of substitution.
39. Agreement between the European Community and the Swiss Confederation on Air Transport, 21 June 1999, Luxembourg, *Official Journal,* L 114/73 (regularly amended).
40. This is not the case for every agreement concluded by the European Union. Each agreement must receive an ad hoc analysis.
41. So far, the Joint Committee has not published any communication on this point. In parallel, the Swiss Civil Aviation Authority considers that European case law handed down after the signing of the bilateral agreement in 1999 does not bind Swiss Courts: 'These subsequent rulings and decisions can provide guidance to the Swiss federal authorities and Courts for interpreting EU aviation law, but they are not automatically binding. The independence of Swiss jurisdiction is therefore not affected', Source: Swiss Federal Office of Civil Aviation, https://www.bazl.admin.ch/bazl/en/home/good-to-know/air-passenger-rights/qestions-and-answers-pax-rights.html (accessed 5 February 2020). This position also appears to be adopted by local Courts, such as the District Court of Bülach, which, on 2 February 2016, denied the application of an interpretation of EU Regulation 261/2004 made by the Court of Justice of the European Union. *See,* Heinrich Hempel, *Keine Ausgleichsleistungen gemäss Fluggastrerechteverordnung bei Verspätung: Urteil des Bezirksgerichts Bülach vom 2. Februar 2016 mit Anmerkungen,* 148 Schweizerische Vereinigung für Luft- und Raumrecht 52-65 (2016). On 16 December 2019, a request for a preliminary ruling was lodged to the Court of Justice of the European Union by the Landgericht of Hamburg. The request concerned the scope of European case law regarding the interpretation of EU Regulation 261/2004 in the context of the agreement on air transport between Switzerland and the European Union (*See, Official Journal,* 23 March 2020, C 95/17). The reference was later withdrawn from the roll. *See,* CJEU, 11 March 2020, *GDVI Verbraucherhilfe GmbH v. Swiss International Air Lines AG,* C-918/19, ECLI:EU:C:2020:281 (Order).

1.1.3 Solutions Adopted for the International Air Carrier Liability Regime

1.1.3.1 Adopted International Conventions Governing the International Air Carriage Liability Regime

In light of previously established practice in the rail sector, several States chose to organize elements of the international air carriage liability regime by way of international conventions that would contain, among others, uniform rules.

On 12 October 1929, the Convention for the Unification of Certain Rules Relating to International Carriage by Air (hereinafter the '**1929 Warsaw Convention**' or '**WC29**') was adopted.[42] The 1929 Warsaw Convention has since then been regularly amended and supplemented by the following instruments:

- in 1955, the Protocol to Amend the Convention for the Unification of Certain Rules Relating to International Carriage by Air, signed at Warsaw on 12 October 1929 (hereinafter the '**1955 Hague Protocol**' or '**HP55**');[43]
- in 1961, the Convention Supplementary to the Warsaw Convention for the Unification of Certain Rules Relating to International Carriage by Air Performed by a Person other than the Contracting Carrier, signed at Guadalajara on 18 September 1961 (hereinafter the '**1961 Guadalajara Convention**');[44]
- in 1971, the Protocol to Amend the Convention for the Unification of Certain Rules Relating to International Carriage by Air, signed at Warsaw on 12 October 1929 as Amended by the Protocol done at The Hague on 28 September 1955 (hereinafter the '**1971 Guatemala City Protocol**');[45]
- in 1975, the Additional Protocol No 1 to Amend Convention for the Unification of Certain Rules Relating to International Carriage by Air, signed at Warsaw on 12 October 1929 (hereinafter the '**Additional Protocol No 1**');[46] the Additional Protocol No 2 to Amend Convention for the Unification of Certain Rules Relating to International Carriage by Air, signed at Warsaw on 12 October 1929, as Amended by the Protocol done at The Hague on 28 September 1955

42. Convention for the Unification of Certain Rules Relating to International Carriage by Air, 12 October 1929, Warsaw, LNTS, 137, p. 11, entry in force 13 February 1933.
43. Protocol to Amend the Convention for the Unification of Certain Rules Relating to International Carriage by Air signed at Warsaw on 12 October 1929, 28 September 1955, The Hague, ICAO Doc 7632, entry in force 1 August 1963.
44. Convention Supplementary to the Warsaw Convention for the Unification of Certain Rules Relating to International Carriage by Air Performed by a Person other than the Contracting Carrier, 18 September 1961, Guadalajara, ICAO Doc 8181, entry in force 1 May 1964.
45. Protocol to Amend the Convention for the Unification of Certain Rules Relating to International Carriage by Air signed at Warsaw on 12 October 1929 as Amended by the Protocol done at The Hague on 28 September 1955, 8 March 1971, Guatemala City, ICAO Doc 8932, not in force.
46. Additional Protocol No 1 to Amend Convention for the Unification of Certain Rules Relating to International Carriage by Air Signed at Warsaw on 12 October 1929, 25 September 1975, Montreal, ICAO Doc 9145, entry in force 15 February 1996.

(hereinafter the '**Additional Protocol No 2**');[47] the Additional Protocol No 3 to Amend Convention for the Unification of Certain Rules Relating to International Carriage by Air, signed at Warsaw on 12 October 1929, as Amended by the Protocol done at The Hague on 28 September 1955 and at Guatemala City on 8 March 1971 (hereinafter the '**Additional Protocol No 3**');[48] and the Montreal Protocol No 4 to Amend Convention for the Unification of Certain Rules Relating to International Carriage by Air, signed at Warsaw on 12 October 1929, as Amended by the Protocol done at The Hague on 28 September 1955 (hereinafter the '**Montreal Protocol No 4**').[49]

These international instruments will be collectively referred to as the '**Warsaw Instruments**'.

In addition to these international instruments, the 1929 Warsaw Convention has been amended by several private agreements, such as the IATA Intercarrier Agreement on Passenger Liability (hereinafter the '**1995 IATA Agreement**');[50] some of which were eventually incorporated into the domestic legislation of certain States, such as the Inter Carrier Montreal Agreement (hereinafter the '**1966 Montreal Agreement**').[51] These instruments, together with the Warsaw Instruments, form what will be referred to as the '**Warsaw System**'.

In 1999, the existing multilayered system was recast by the Convention for the Unification of Certain Rules for International Carriage by Air (hereinafter the '**1999 Montreal Convention**' or '**MC99**').[52] The 1999 Montreal Convention is the last adopted International Convention in force that aims particularly to regulate, at a global level, elements of carrier liability when performing international carriage by air, particularly with respect to delay, injury and death of passengers, and related matters.

Despite the fact that Article 55 of the 1999 Montreal Convention provides that it shall prevail over its predecessors,[53] there might still exist connections between at least

47. Additional Protocol No 2 to Amend Convention for the Unification of Certain Rules Relating to International Carriage by Air Signed at Warsaw on 12 October 1929, as Amended by the Protocol done at The Hague on 28 September 1955, 25 September 1975, Montreal, ICAO Doc 9146, entry in force 15 February 1996.
48. Additional Protocol No 3 to Amend Convention for the Unification of Certain Rules Relating to International Carriage by Air Signed at Warsaw on 12 October 1929, as Amended by the Protocol done at The Hague on 28 September 1955 and at Guatemala City on 8 March 1971, 25 September, ICAO Doc 9147, not in force.
49. Montreal Protocol No 4 to Amend Convention for the Unification of Certain Rules Relating to International Carriage by Air Signed at Warsaw on 12 October 1929, as Amended by the Protocol done at The Hague on 28 September 1955, 25 September 1975, Montreal, ICAO Doc 9148, entry in force 14 June 1998.
50. Also known as 1995 IIA. This Agreement was accompanied by an agreement adopted in 1996, the Agreement on Measures to Implement the IATA Intercarrier Agreement (also known as 1996 MIA), which had 116 international carriers signatories by 2020. *See*, IATA, https://www.iata.org/contentassets/b7fc716af6a94192b1889420c7d573ce/mia-signatory-list.pdf (accessed 15 April 2021).
51. 13 May 1966 Inter Carrier Montreal Agreement, also known as CAB Agreement 18900. Made mandatory under American law. *See*, US 14 CFR Part 203.
52. Convention for the Unification of Certain Rules for International Carriage by Air, 28 May 1999, Montreal, UNTS, 2242, I-39917, entry in force 4 November 2003.
53. *See*, section 1.3.1.1(2).

the 1929 Warsaw Convention and the 1999 Montreal Convention. Therefore, for the purpose of this study, the 1929 Warsaw Convention and the 1999 Montreal Convention will be collectively referred to as the '**Conventions**'.

1.1.3.2 The Topology of Conventions Governing the International Air Carrier Liability Regime

(1) Topology

A close look at the content of the Conventions shows that different categories of provisions are contained therein: final clauses, uniform rules, and referrals to domestic legislation clauses.

(2) Final Clauses

As in any international convention, final clauses are included in the Conventions. In the 1999 Montreal Convention, final clauses are mostly found in Articles 53-57. These final clauses organize questions regarding the signing, ratification, entry into force, denunciation, relationships with other instruments, territorial application and reservations. These final clauses confirm the international status of the Conventions and, as such, international law governs their interpretation and application.

(3) Uniform Rules

Uniform rules are widely spread throughout the Conventions, particularly from Articles 1 to 52 in the 1999 Montreal Convention. They are the essence of the Conventions, as they govern the liability of carriers performing international carriage by air. Chapter 2 will examine the exact nature of these uniform rules as contained in the Conventions.

(4) Referrals to Domestic Legislation Clauses

(i) The Difference Between Exclusions and *Renvois*

In addition to final clauses and uniform rules, the Conventions may also call on the application of domestic rules. This call can be divided into two subcategories: exclusions and what will be known as *renvois* in this study.

(ii) Exclusions

The subcategory pertaining to exclusion is infinite as it relates to all situations that are not governed by the Conventions. The title of the Conventions is clear in that respect, as they only concern 'the Unification of *Certain* Rules' (*italics added*). These Conventions are unambiguous on this point, confirming their ambition is not to regulate every potential air carrier's liability issues, and therefore leave undiscussed topics to domestic law.[54]

The exclusions may be explicitly stated in the Conventions: for example, Article 2(3) of the 1999 Montreal Convention provides that:

> Except as provided in paragraph 2 of this Article, the provisions of this Convention shall not apply to the carriage of postal items.

They can also be implicit, as they cover elements that are not dealt with by the Conventions. In that regard, examples of implicit exclusions can be found in the *Travaux Préparatoires*.[55] The Minutes of the 1929 Warsaw Convention confirm, for instance, that said convention does not regulate ticket assignment:

> Et puis, il y a une question qui se pose; c'est celle de savoir si le billet de passage peut être cédé ou non. Nous ne voulons pas imposer ici l'incessibilité; mais nous voulons réserver au transporteur la possibilité d'exiger que le billet soit nominatif, avec la conséquence d'être incessible.[56]

They also underscore that flight cancellation is not governed by the Convention:

> Si vous avez l'inexécution totale, il n'y a aucun intérêt à avoir une convention internationale; l'expéditeur est dans son pays, il a toujours les ressources du droit commun. Comment et pourquoi voulez-vous appliquer ici la responsabilité limitée et ses conséquences?[57]

This exclusion is repeated in the Minutes of the 1999 Montreal Convention as follows:

> [...] matters such as the non-fulfilment of a contract of carriage, denied boarding and refunds were not covered by the Warsaw Convention, [the Delegate of Sri Lanka] indicated that he would not wish it to be construed that such matters were within the ambit of the new Convention under the said Article, especially as more cases were anticipated involving matters of that nature as a result of the increased usage of codesharing and other similar arrangements.[58]

As it will be seen further on, exclusions, and particularly implicit exclusions, may be a source of confusion when exclusivity is at stake.[59]

---

54. *See*, Antonio Malintoppi, *Droit uniforme et droit international privé*, 116 Recueil des cours de l'Académie de droit international 66-67 (1965).
55. *See*, section 1.3.3 on the use of the *Travaux Préparatoires*.
56. ICAO Doc 7838, II Conférence Internationale de Droit Privé Aérien, 4-12 Octobre 1929, *Procès-Verbaux*, Varsovie, 1930, p. 101.
57. *Ibid.*, p. 52. *See also*, *Ibid.*, p. 115: 'M. Ambrosini (Italie) – La convention ne prévoit pas le cas de non-exécution du contrat de transport. La Conférence devra le prévoir. Il faut savoir si on doit appliquer la convention ou non, c'est-à-dire le régime auquel le cas de non-exécution devra être soumis. M. De Vos –Rapporteur – C'est la loi nationale qui régit ce cas'.
58. ICAO Doc 9775, International Conference on Air Law (Convention for the Unification of Certain Rules for International Carriage by Air), Montreal, 10-28 May 1999, volume I, *Minutes*, Montreal 1999, p. 235.
59. *See*, section 2.5.3.2.

(iii) *Renvois*

The second subcategory of referrals encompasses *renvois* to domestic law made by the Conventions. References to a determined domestic law can be found, for example, in the jurisdiction clause of Article 33(4) of the 1999 Montreal Convention, which sets out that: 'Questions of procedure shall be governed by the law of the court seised of the case.' Similarly, Article 35(2) provides that: 'The method of calculating that period shall be determined by the law of the court seised of the case.' Article 45, regarding the addressee of claims, states: '[...] the procedure and effects being governed by the law of the court seised of the case'. Article 28 also sets out: 'In the case of aircraft accidents resulting in death or injury of passengers, the carrier shall, if required by its national law, make advance payments [...].'

Renvois are therefore not uniform rules. Rather, they are associated with conflict of laws rules. Their function is in contradiction to uniform rules, and they were often adopted when it was impossible to agree on a uniform rule.[60]

1.1.3.3 Concluding Remarks

Chapter 2 will discuss the choice to regulate the international air carriage liability regime mostly through uniform rules. The analysis will hopefully shed light on a clearer definition of uniform rules, as envisaged by the drafters of the Conventions.

1.2 RESEARCH QUESTIONS, STUDY STRUCTURE AND INTEREST FOR LEGAL SCIENCE

1.2.1 The Formulation of Research Questions

This analysis sets out to determine whether the regime for international air carrier liability established by the 1999 Montreal Convention can be uniform, and to what extent it has achieved its aim of uniformity.

In order to better answer this question, the analysis is divided into three sub-questions:

(1) Is uniformity a predominant aim of the 1999 Montreal Convention?
(2) If so, are there factors preventing this aim from being achieved?
(3) In cases where such factors would be detected, could a higher degree of uniformity be achieved, and should it? And, if so, how?

60. *See*, for example: Conférence Internationale de Droit Privé Aérien, 27 Octobre-6 Novembre 1925, Paris, 1926, p. 57: '[...] comme il est à peu près impossible de fixer dans une formule unique les diverses conceptions juridiques des divers Etats, il a paru plus simple de préciser dans l'article 8 que les ayants-droit seraient déterminés par la loi nationale du défunt, mais que les droits de ces personnes seraient limités à la somme maximale admise à l'article 7'.

1.2.2 Study Structure

1.2.2.1 Is Uniformity a Predominant Aim of the 1999 Montreal Convention?

The first step is to determine the reasons for the adoption of uniform rules in the 1999 Montreal Convention, and to sketch the contours of these uniform rules, especially with respect to their application. In other words, the analysis will start by verifying if the 1999 Montreal Convention not only aims to have uniform rules but also expects them to be uniformly applied by Courts across ratifying States.

Chapter 2 will therefore analyse the regulatory environment that existed prior to the adoption of uniform rules, in order to determine the reasons that led governments to adopt them. If the analysis reveals the expectation of a uniform application of the Conventions, it will then search for the introduction of specific elements to facilitate this uniform application.

1.2.2.2 If So, Are There Factors Preventing This Aim from Being Achieved?

(1) Categorization

Once the aim of uniformity of the Conventions has been analysed, this study will explore whether any factors prevent or may have prevented achieving it. This question will be divided into two sub-questions. *First*, whether elements exist that might affect uniformity in the rule-making process, that is to say, from the adoption of the Conventions. These potential factors will be referred to as 'internal' factors. *Second*, whether there are factors that are likely to affect uniformity as envisaged by the respective drafters over time, after the signing of the Conventions. This second category of potential factors for fragmentation will be referred to as 'external' factors.

(2) Internal Factors

Chapter 3 will examine the internal factors. This analysis will distinguish between drafting factors and other factors that may have existed at the time of the signing of the Conventions but are not related to semantic choices.

The drafting factors will be identified on the basis of examples of terms and concepts used in the Conventions. These examples will be selected from judicial decisions and *Travaux Préparatoires* that suggest their potential power to induce fragmentation.

(3) External Factors

Chapter 4 will focus on external factors. *First*, it will discuss whether regulatory changes have affected the Conventions' envisaged aim of uniformity, and if this is the case, to what extent. The regulatory changes will be assessed in light of both revisions to the initial text and the emergence of new consumer rights at regional and domestic levels, as exemplified by the adoption in the EU in 2004 of Regulation No 261/2004 establishing common rules on compensation and assistance to passengers in the event of denied boarding and of cancellation or long delay of flights (hereinafter '**EU Regulation 261/2004**').[61]

Second, it will review the response formulated by Courts to the possible elements found in Chapter 2. The outcome of this analysis is designed to apply the interpretation principles detailed in Articles 31-33 of the 1969 Vienna Convention on the Law of Treaties (hereinafter the '**1969 Vienna Convention**')[62] to the possible aim of uniformity of the Conventions.

Third, it will assess the potential consequences of having the Conventions drafted in and translated into different languages.

1.2.2.3 Which Methods Can Enhance Uniformity?

Chapter 5 will seek to identify methods that are likely to achieve greater uniformity in the application of the 1999 Montreal Convention. The analysis will conduct a comparative examination of what is being and has been achieved in other sectors that are regulated by uniform rules, in order to determine methods that could be transposed into the framework of the 1999 Montreal Convention.

Particular attention will also be given to Artificial Intelligence mechanisms. The benefits of these new technologies, which promise to bring further uniformity to the way decisions are handed down globally in the near future, will be explored in the context of the 1999 Montreal Convention. The risks associated with these technologies will also be assessed in light of elements causing fragmentation, identified in the previous chapters. For the sake of providing context, a brief description of how Artificial Intelligence may aid the judicial decision-making process will be appended to this study. This **Appendix** will outline the concepts of Artificial Intelligence and Predictive Justice, and will offer a short illustration of how the principles of interpretations laid down in the 1969 Vienna Convention might be translated into an algorithm.

1.2.2.4 Concluding Remarks

Chapter 6 will summarize the findings of this study and will contain personal recommendations for lawyers applying the 1999 Montreal Convention; for the International Civil Aviation Organization (hereinafter 'ICAO'); for States Party to the 1999 Montreal Convention; and for designers of applications using Artificial Intelligence. These recommendations may also contribute to amendments, or the drawing up of a new convention, should such steps be required by the conclusions drawn in this study.

---

61. Regulation (EC) No 261/2004 of the European Parliament and of the Council of 11 February 2004 establishing common rules on compensation and assistance to passengers in the event of denied boarding and of cancellation or long delay of flights, and repealing Regulation (EEC) No 295/91, *Official Journal*, 17 February 2004, L 046/1.
62. Vienna Convention on the Law of Treaties 1969, 23 May 1969, Vienna, UNTS, 1155, I-18232, entry in force on 27 January 1980.

1.2.3 Interest for Legal Science

From a scientific perspective, the purpose of this study is to analyse the application of the 1999 Montreal Convention by Courts in its particularity of containing uniform rules. To achieve this, five major legal points will be discussed.

First, this study will evaluate the importance of having uniform rules governing international air carrier liability, and the need for these rules to be uniformly applied.

Second, it will seek to determine the factors that may have contributed to a fragmentation of the 1999 Montreal Convention. From an early stage, authoritative authors acknowledged the existence of fragmentation in the context of the 1929 Warsaw Convention,[63] yet no such study has been carried out with respect to the 1999 Montreal Convention, which aimed to reduce fragmentation.[64] In addition, interest in the fragmentation of international law has grown recently, but from an international public law perspective,[65] not yet in the context of international private law.

Third, the analysis aims to assess different means of enhancing uniformity in the near future, notably through a pioneering examination of the impact of Artificial Intelligence on private air law. It will present suggestions for increasing the uniformity of the 1999 Montreal Convention by adopting new interpretation measures, either by way of amendments or by the drawing up of a new convention.

Fourth, this study wishes to provide updates on topics that continue to animate the scientific literature with recent Court decisions from various jurisdictions.

Fifth, it shall assess the effectiveness of Articles 31 and 32 of the 1969 Vienna Convention with respect to the interpretation of the provisions of the 1999 Montreal Convention.

---

63. *See*, Peter Sand, *The International Unification of Air Law*, 30 Law and Contemporary Problems 400-424 (1965); Huib Drion, *Toward a Uniform Interpretation of the Private Air Law Conventions*, 19 Journal of Air Law and Commerce 423-442 (1952); Euthymene Georgiades, *De la méthodologie juridique pour l'unification du Droit aérien international privé*, Revue Française de Droit Aérien et Spatial 369-389 (1972); René Mankiewicz, *La Convention de Varsovie et le Droit Comparé*, Revue Française de Droit Aérien et Spatial 136-150 (1969); Michel Pourcelet, *A propos d'un accident d'avion: la diversité des solutions données par les tribunaux*, Revue Générale de l'Air 211 (1973).
64. ICAO Doc 9775, International Conference on Air Law (Convention for the Unification of Certain Rules for International Carriage by Air), Montreal, 10-28 May 1999, volume I, *Minutes*, Montreal 1999, p. 205: 'Since that time the Warsaw Convention had been fragmented into different protocols and into different views, interpretations and jurisdictions. The Conference was making history in consolidating, for the first time, what had been fragmented and by introducing new elements to cope with the vision for the 21st century.'
65. *See*, International Law Commission, 'Fragmentation of International Law: Difficulties Arising from the Diversification and Expansion of International Law', in *Report of the International Law Commission on the Work of Its Fifty-Eighth Session*, II(2) Yearbook of the International Law Commission 179 (2006); Anne-Charlotte Martineau, *Une analyse critique du débat sur la fragmentation du droit international* (Thesis, Université Panthéon-Sorbonne – Paris I, 2013), Archives Ouvertes, https://tel.archives-ouvertes.fr/tel-01259489 (accessed 3 February 2019).

1.3 METHODOLOGICAL FRAMEWORK

1.3.1 Legislative Instruments, International Customary Law and General Principles of Law

1.3.1.1 The 1999 Montreal Convention and the Warsaw Instruments

(1) The 1999 Montreal Convention

The analysis of the international air carrier liability regime will essentially focus on the 1999 Montreal Convention. This choice is predicated on the fact that the 1999 Montreal Convention is the most recent instrument in force governing the air carrier liability regime, and that it has been ratified by a considerable number of States and Regional Economic Integration Organizations. On 1 January 2021, 137 of them were Parties to the 1999 Montreal Convention.[66]

(2) The Warsaw Instruments

Nevertheless, to understand an analysis of the 1999 Montreal Convention, references to its predecessors are required. References will therefore also be made to the 1929 Warsaw Convention, which was also ratified by a significant number of States[67] and enjoys significant long-time application, and to its subsequent amendments.[68]

It could be argued that there is no need to analyse the previous applicable instruments, as Article 55 of the 1999 Montreal Convention stipulates that it prevails over its predecessors:

> This Convention shall prevail over any rules which apply to international carriage by air:
> 1. between States Parties to this Convention by virtue of those States commonly being Party to:
>   (a) the Convention for the Unification of Certain Rules Relating to International Carriage by Air Signed at Warsaw on 12 October 1929 (hereinafter called the Warsaw Convention);
>   (b) the Protocol to amend the Convention for the Unification of Certain Rules Relating to International Carriage by Air Signed at Warsaw on 12 October 1929, Done at The Hague on 28 September 1955 (hereinafter called The Hague Protocol);
>   (c) the Convention, Supplementary to the Warsaw Convention, for the Unification of Certain Rules Relating to International Carriage by Air Performed by a Person other than the Contracting Carrier, signed at Guadalajara on 18 September 1961 (hereinafter called the Guadalajara Convention);

66. *See*, ICAO, https://www.icao.int/secretariat/legal/lists/current%20lists%20of%20parties/allitems.aspx (accessed 1 January 2021).
67. On 1 January 2021, 152 States ratified the 1929 Warsaw Convention, Source: ICAO, https://www.icao.int/secretariat/legal/lists/current%20lists%20of%20parties/allitems.aspx (accessed 1 January 2021).
68. *See*, section 1.1.3.1.

(d) the Protocol to amend the Convention for the Unification of Certain Rules Relating to International Carriage by Air Signed at Warsaw on 12 October 1929 as amended by the Protocol Done at The Hague on 28 September 1955, Signed at Guatemala City on 8 March 1971 (hereinafter called the Guatemala City Protocol);
(e) Additional Protocol Nos. 1 to 3 and Montreal Protocol No. 4 to amend the Warsaw Convention as amended by The Hague Protocol or the Warsaw Convention as amended by both The Hague Protocol and the Guatemala City Protocol, Signed at Montreal on 25 September 1975 (hereinafter called the Montreal Protocols); or

2. within the territory of any single State Party to this Convention by virtue of that State being Party to one or more of the instruments referred to in sub-paragraphs (a) to (e) above.

However, the preamble of the 1999 Montreal Convention underlines the connections between them as follows:

> [...] modernize and consolidate the Warsaw Convention and related instruments.

Moreover, while the 1999 Montreal Convention is a deep recast of the previous instruments, an important number of its provisions mirrors those of the previous instruments.[69] The *Travaux Préparatoires* of the 1999 Montreal Convention also highlight the historical and substantive links between these instruments.[70] For these reasons, the 1999 Montreal Convention will be examined along with its predecessors.

1.3.1.2 Methodology for Treaty Interpretation

(1) Authentic Versus Judicial Interpretations

As the Conventions are regularly interpreted by Courts, the methods used to interpret the Conventions will be examined in detail throughout this study and particularly in Chapter 4. Two categories of interpretation exist: authentic and judicial. The authentic interpretations are made directly by the drafters of the texts. They are of course rather rare. One example may nevertheless be found in the Final Act of the 1955 Hague Protocol, which confirms that an air waybill may be negotiable:

> The Conference, being of the opinion that nothing in the Warsaw Convention, as now in force, prevents the issue of a negotiable air waybill, Declares that Article IX of the Protocol to Amend the Warsaw Convention has been inserted therein only for the purpose of clarification.[71]

---

69. *See*, George Tompkins, *Liability Rules Applicable to International Air Transportation as Developed by the Courts in the United States: From Warsaw 1929 to Montreal 1999* 32 (Kluwer, 2010).
70. *See*, for example, ICAO Doc 9775, International Conference on Air Law (Convention for the Unification of Certain Rules for International Carriage by Air), Montreal, 10-28 May 1999, volume I, *Minutes*, Montreal 1999, pp. 217-220.
71. ICAO Doc 7686, International Conference on Private Air Law, The Hague, September 1955, volume II, *Documents*, Montreal September 1956, pp. 29-30.

In the past, the French *Cour de cassation* considered authentic interpretation as the only acceptable interpretation:

> Et alors enfin qu'en tout état de cause la Cour d'appel a cru devoir se fonder sur une interprétation donnée par elle de la Convention de Varsovie; qu'elle était incompétente pour interpréter une convention diplomatique, acte de haute administration qui ne peut être interprété, s'il y a lieu, que par les puissances entre lesquelles elle est intervenue.[72]

After authentic interpretation, the judicial interpretation made by Courts is the most usual category of interpretations. The interpretation mechanisms are various. Among other things, they can be: literal, teleological, analogical, evolutionary, constitutionally oriented, equitable, *ad absurdum* and so forth. Each jurisdiction has its own method(s) to interpret a legal text.

The next session shall shed light on interpretation methods under international law, particularly with regard to those established by the 1969 Vienna Convention.

(2) Judicial Interpretations: Articles 31, 32 and 33 of the 1969 Vienna Convention

(i) The Scope of the 1969 Vienna Convention

As per its preamble, the 1969 Vienna Convention recognizes the increasing importance of treaties as a source of international law. As such, said convention created, but also codified, pre-existing rules of international customary law. With respect to the scope of this book, the 1969 Vienna Convention codified several pre-existing principles of treaty interpretation. Recourse to these principles, which will be covered in the following section, can therefore either be made directly from the treaty or, as recognized by the International Court of Justice (hereinafter 'ICJ') in *Guinea-Bissau v. Senegal,*[73] from international customary law.

(ii) The Principles of Interpretation

The general principles of treaty interpretation are established under Articles 31 and 32 of the 1969 Vienna Convention. Article 31 of the 1969 Vienna Convention provides that:

> 1. A treaty shall be interpreted in good faith in accordance with the ordinary meaning to be given to the terms of the treaty in their context and in the light of its object and purpose.

72. Cass., 17 May 1966, 65-92986. *See also,* Cass., 3 June 1985, 84.94-404.
73. International Court of Justice, *Arbitral Award of 31 July 1989, Judgement, I.C.J. Reports 1991,* p. 53, at 44: 'These principles are reflected in Articles 31 and 32 of the Vienna Convention on the Law of Treaties, which may in many respects be considered as a codification of existing customary international law on the point.'

2. The context for the purpose of the interpretation of a treaty shall comprise, in addition to the text, including its preamble and annexes:
   (a) Any agreement relating to the treaty which was made between all the parties in connexion with the conclusion of the treaty;
   (b) Any instrument which was made by one or more parties in connexion with the conclusion of the treaty and accepted by the other parties as an instrument related to the treaty.
3. There shall be taken into account, together with the context:
   (a) Any subsequent agreement between the parties regarding the interpretation of the treaty or the application of its provisions;
   (b) Any subsequent practice in the application of the treaty which establishes the agreement of the parties regarding its interpretation;
   (c) Any relevant rules of international law applicable in the relations between the parties.
4. A special meaning shall be given to a term if it is established that the parties so intended.

And Article 32 sets out that:

Recourse may be had to supplementary means of interpretation, including the preparatory work of the treaty and the circumstances of its conclusion, in order to confirm the meaning resulting from the application of article 31, or to determine the meaning when the interpretation according to article 31:

(a) Leaves the meaning ambiguous or obscure; or
(b) Leads to a result which is manifestly absurd or unreasonable.

The 1969 Vienna Convention also foresees the following specific provision, under its Article 33, for treaties authenticated in two or more languages:

1. When a treaty has been authenticated in two or more languages, the text is equally authoritative in each language, unless the treaty provides or the parties agree that, in case of divergence, a particular text shall prevail.
2. A version of the treaty in a language other than one of those in which the text was authenticated shall be considered an authentic text only if the treaty so provides or the parties so agree.
3. The terms of the treaty are presumed to have the same meaning in each authentic text.
4. Except where a particular text prevails in accordance with paragraph 1, when a comparison of the authentic texts discloses a difference of meaning which the application of articles 31 and 32 does not remove, the meaning which best reconciles the texts, having regard to the object and purpose of the treaty, shall be adopted.

This last provision may therefore be applicable to treaties such as the 1999 Montreal Convention which was drawn up in six authentic languages, namely: Arabic, Chinese, English, French, Russian and Spanish, and translated in several languages.

(iii) The Application of These Principles to the 1999 Montreal Convention

The application of these principles of interpretation to the 1999 Montreal Convention is confirmed by Article 1 of the 1969 Vienna Convention, which stipulates that '[it] applies to "treaties between States"'. With respect thereof, Article 2(1)(a) of said convention defines a treaty as follows:

> [...] an international agreement concluded between States in written form and governed by international law, whether embodied in a single instrument or in two or more related instruments and whatever its particular designation.

The possibility of applying the principles of interpretation of the 1969 Vienna Convention to the 1999 Montreal Convention is also acknowledged, as reproduced hereinafter, by the *Travaux Préparatoires* of the latter:

> In echoing the Delegation of Peru's concern regarding the absence of any provision regarding the amendment of the Convention, the Delegate of Bangladesh enquired as to what procedure would be followed in the event that States Parties wished to take such action. The Chairman noted that, while there was no express provision in the Convention relating to its amendment, the over-arching legal régime established by the *1969 Vienna Convention on the Law of Treaties*, which codified the rules of international law relating to international treaty-making, would govern.[74]

The authoritative literature also confirms this point. Dr Laurent Tran noted that, in the absence of specific international rules in the 1999 Montreal Convention, the principles set out in the 1969 Vienna Convention apply.[75] This view is shared by Professors Paul Dempsey and Michael Milde.[76] Dr Laurent Chassot also considers that the 1969 Vienna Convention applies to the 1999 Montreal Convention, but highlights that its methodology is not exhaustive.[77]

(iv) The Application of These Principles to the Warsaw Instruments

The application of the interpretation principles of the 1969 Vienna Convention to the Warsaw Instruments is less obvious. Pursuant to Article 4 of the 1969 Vienna Convention, its principles do not apply to treaties concluded before its entry into force:

> Without prejudice to the application of any rules set forth in the present Convention to which treaties would be subject under international law independently of the Convention, the Convention applies only to treaties which are concluded by

74. ICAO Doc 9775, International Conference on Air Law (Convention for the Unification of Certain Rules for International Carriage by Air), Montreal, 10-28 May 1999, volume I, *Minutes*, Montreal 1999, p. 237.
75. Laurent Tran, *Le régime uniforme de responsabilité du transporteur aérien de personnes* 16 (Schultess, 2013).
76. Paul Dempsey, Michael Milde, *International Air Carrier Liability: The Montreal Convention of 1999* 45 (Centre for Research in Air & Space Law, McGill University, 2005); *See also*, Richard Gardiner, *Treaty Interpretation* 21-22 (2nd edition, The Oxford International Law Library, 2017); Olivier Cachard, *Le transport international aérien de passager* 143 (Les livres de Poche de l'Académie de droit international de La Haye, 2015).
77. Laurent Chassot, *Les sources de la responsabilité du transporteur aérien international: entre conflit et complémentarité: La Convention de Montréal et son interaction avec le droit européen et national* 36-37 (Schulthess, 2012).

> States after the entry into force of the present Convention with regard to such States.

In practice, this would mean that the interpretation principles established by the 1969 Vienna Convention would only apply to treaties concluded after its entry into force on 27 January 1980.

Nevertheless, this provision only concerns the 1969 Vienna Convention as a treaty under international law. Looking at the 1969 Vienna Convention as international customary law allows for a different approach and permits reference to the interpretation principles for the Warsaw Instruments. In a case before the House of Lords regarding the interpretation of 1929 Warsaw Convention as amended by the 1955 Hague Protocol, Lord Diplock noted that despite the 1969 Vienna Convention only being applicable to treaties concluded after it came into force, it did no more than codify already existing public international law.[78] Therefore, for the purpose of this study, the principles of interpretation established under the 1969 Vienna Convention will not automatically be excluded when discussing Warsaw Instruments' judicial decisions. I have opted for the expression 'principles of interpretation' in this study to reflect that reality.

(v) Understanding Articles 31 and 32 of the 1969 Vienna Convention in the Context of the Conventions

As seen above,[79] Articles 31 and 32 of the 1969 Vienna Convention are broadly drafted in order to encompass many different sorts of international conventions. While they do specifically aim to assist in the interpretation of international conventions, it should nevertheless be pointed out that their language is not easily accessible.

This section will try to give an indication as to the meaning behind each sentence of Articles 31 and 32 of the 1969 Vienna Convention when applying the Conventions.

Article 31(1) of the 1969 Vienna Convention provides that:

> A treaty shall be interpreted in good faith in accordance with the ordinary meaning to be given to the terms of the treaty in their context and in the light of its object and purpose.

It refers to four concepts, namely: ordinary meaning, context, object and purpose. With regard to the Conventions, the 'ordinary meaning' may be a tricky concept if one considers the terms used in the Conventions as autonomous, which will be discussed in Chapter 2. The 'context' should not be understood as the *ratio legis* of the Conventions, but rather as the surrounding environment of a provision, such as its headings and the immediate words next to the concept that need to be compared and or interpreted.[80] The 'object' and 'purpose' are specific to each treaty and will also be discussed in Chapter 2.

---

78. *Fothergill v. Monarch Airlines Ltd* (1980) UKHL 6, at 88.
79. *See*, section 1.3.1.2(2)(ii).
80. *See*, Richard Gardiner, *Treaty Interpretation* 197 (2nd edition, The Oxford International Law Library, 2017).

Article 31(2) of the 1969 Vienna Convention sets out additional elements to understand the previously enumerated concept of context. It reads as follows:

> The context for the purpose of the interpretation of a treaty shall comprise, in addition to the text, including its preamble and annexes:
>
> (a) Any agreement relating to the treaty which was made between all the parties in connexion with the conclusion of the treaty;
> (b) Any instrument which was made by one or more parties in connexion with the conclusion of the treaty and accepted by the other parties as an instrument related to the treaty.

The preamble of the 1999 Montreal Convention is not free from vagueness about the purpose of the Convention and the continuity of Warsaw jurisprudence, as discussed in Chapters 2 and 4.

Point (a) is not particularly useful for the interpretation of the Conventions, as no agreement, for instance, an explanatory report, accompanies the Conventions.[81]

Point (b) may however be useful as it makes references to ratification acts and reservations,[82] which will be discussed in Chapter 3.

Article 31(3) of the 1969 Vienna Convention does not, at first glance, assist much with respect to the interpretation of uniform rules in particular, as it provides that other elements are to be taken together with the context:

> There shall be taken into account, together with the context:
>
> (a) Any subsequent agreement between the parties regarding the interpretation of the treaty or the application of its provisions;
> (b) Any subsequent practice in the application of the treaty which establishes the agreement of the parties regarding its interpretation;
> (c) Any relevant rules of international law applicable in the relations between the parties.

Point (a) refers to a subsequent agreement regarding the interpretation of the Conventions. In practice, with respect to the 1999 Montreal Convention, none have been agreed so far.[83]

Point (b) does not particularly apply in the framework of the Conventions.[84]

Point (c) triggers the question of whether an identical and constant interpretation given in different jurisdictions may eventually be considered as international custom,

---

81. *See, Ibid.*, p. 235.
82. *See, Ibid.*, pp. 239-240.
83. The 1999 Montreal Convention, however, has been used to interpret the Warsaw text. *See, Morris v. KLM Royal Dutch Airlines* (2002) UKHL 7, at 155.
84. This provision concerns, for instance, applicable permits relating to traffic rights in cases of non-scheduled flights, required by subsequent practice despite the wording of Article 5 of the 1944 Chicago Convention: 'without the necessity to obtain prior permission'. *See*, International Law Commission, *Draft conclusions on subsequent agreements and subsequent practice in relation to the interpretation of treaties, with commentaries* 39 (2018), Source: United Nations, https://legal.un.org/docs/?path=../ilc/texts/instruments/english/commentaries/1_11_2018.pdf&lang=EF (accessed 21 February 2020). *See also*, the development below on Article 32 of the 1969 Vienna Convention, regarding the value of foreign decisions.

which by application of Article 38 of the Statute of the ICJ would be considered as international law. Unfortunately, in international law, a constant interpretation is not per se an international custom.[85]

Article 31(4) provides that:

> A special meaning shall be given to a term if it is established that the parties so intended.

This provision interferes with the 'ordinary meaning' set forth in Article 31(1). This study will therefore question whether the terms used in the Conventions should be interpreted as having 'ordinary' or 'special' meaning.[86]

In accordance with the *Travaux Préparatoires* of the 1969 Vienna Convention, there is no hierarchical order between the different tools provided under Article 31. As indicated hereinafter, their interaction should be regarded as a 'single combined operation':

> The Commission, by heading the article 'General rule of interpretation' in the singular and by underlining the connexion between paragraphs 1 and 2 and again between paragraph 3 and the two previous paragraphs, intended to indicate that the application of the means of interpretation in the article [27][87] would be a single combined operation. [...] Once it is established – and on this point the Commission was unanimous – that the starting point of interpretation is the meaning of the text, logic indicates that 'the ordinary meaning to be given to the terms of the treaty in their context and in the light of its object and purpose' should be the first element to be mentioned.[88]

Article 32 supplies supplementary tools in limited circumstances:

> Recourse may be had to supplementary means of interpretation, including the preparatory work of the treaty and the circumstances of its conclusion, in order to confirm the meaning resulting from the application of article 31, or to determine the meaning when the interpretation according to article 31:
>
> (a) Leaves the meaning ambiguous or obscure; or
> (b) Leads to a result which is manifestly absurd or unreasonable.

Textually, it refers to the *Travaux Préparatoires* and the 'circumstances' of the conclusion of the Conventions, but, as underscored by the International Law Commission (hereinafter 'ILC'), Article 32 should be understood as a non-exhaustive list.[89] The

85. *See*, Patrick Daillier, Mathias Forteau, Alain Pellet, *Droit International Public* 437-439 (8th edition, LGDJ, 2009).
86. *See*, section 4.3.3.1.
87. Adopted as Article 31 with minor changes.
88. United Nations Conferences on the Law of Treaties, First and second sessions, Vienna, 26 March-24 May 1968 and 9 April-22 May 1969, Official Records, *Documents of the Conference*, United Nations, New York, 1971, pp. 39-40, Source: United Nations, https://treaties.un.org/doc/source/docs/A_CONF.39_11_Add.2-E.pdf (accessed 2 August 2019).
89. *See*, International Law Commission, *Draft conclusions on subsequent agreements and subsequent practice in relation to the interpretation of treaties, with commentaries* 6 (2018), Source: United Nations, https://legal.un.org/docs/?path=../ilc/texts/instruments/english/commentaries/1_11_2018.pdf&lang=EF (accessed 21 February 2020).

ILC[90] and authoritative authors[91] have therefore considered foreign case law as a supplementary means of interpretation. This point is disputed, however, to the extent that Court decisions may be considered as falling under Article 31(3)(b) of the 1969 Vienna Convention. The trigger point seems to be the determination of foreign case law as a practice sufficiently extensive to demonstrate a common understanding of the Parties.[92]

(vi) Domestic Recognition of These Principles

Not all Parties to the 1999 Montreal Convention ratified the 1969 Vienna Convention. Among Parties to the 1999 Montreal Convention, the United States signed the 1969 Vienna Convention, but did not ratify it;[93] France did not even sign it,[94] and the EU was not even allowed to sign it since its ratification is not open to regional organizations.[95]

As already mentioned,[96] the principles of interpretation of the 1969 Vienna Convention may nevertheless apply in these States as international customary law.

The goal of this study is not to examine if these principles are effectively applied in every single jurisdiction. However, because interpretation tools used by Courts cannot be ignored, it will touch on their application by several selected Courts.[97]

1.3.1.3 Other International Conventions

In addition to the 1999 Montreal Convention, the Warsaw Instruments, and the 1969 Vienna Convention, this study might also, when necessary or for illustration purposes, make regular references to:

- other private air law conventions such as: the Convention for the Unification of Certain Rules relating to Damage caused by Aircraft to Third Parties on the Surface (hereinafter the '**1933 Rome Convention**');[98] the Convention on

90. *See*, *Ibid.*, pp. 26-28. However, the ILC's position seems to be different p. 36.
91. *See*, for example, Olivier Corten, *Méthodologie du droit international public* 233, 249 (Editions de l'université de Bruxelles, 2017). *Contra*, suggesting that judicial decisions may be considered as falling under Article 31(3)(b) of the 1969 Vienna Convention, Olivier Dörr, Kirsten Schmakenbach (eds), *Vienna Convention on the Law of Treaties: A Commentary* 596 (2nd edition, Springer, 2018); Gilber Guillaume, *Du caractère impératif des dispositions de l'article 28 de la Convention de Varsovie*, Revue Française de Droit Aérien et Spatial 227-239 (2006).
92. *See*, Richard Gardiner, *Treaty Interpretation* 256 (2nd edition, The Oxford International Law Library, 2017).
93. United Nations, https://treaties.un.org/Pages/ViewDetailsIII.aspx?src=TREATY&mtdsg_no=XXIII-1&chapter=23&Temp=mtdsg3&clang=_en (accessed 5 September 2020).
94. *Ibid.* France was essentially opposed to the notion of *jus cogens* as established in the 1969 Vienna Convention. *See*, Olivier Deleau, *Les positions françaises à la Conférence de Vienne sur le droit des traités*, 15 Annuaire français de droit international 7-23 (1969).
95. 1969 Vienna Convention, Article 81.
96. *See*, section 1.3.1.2(2)(i).
97. *See*, section 1.3.2.3.
98. Convention for the Unification of Certain Rules Relating to Damage Caused by Aircraft to Third Parties on the Surface, 29 May 1933, Rome.

Damage Caused by Foreign Aircraft to Third Parties on the Surface (hereinafter the '**1952 Rome Convention**');[99]
- other Uniform Instruments, particularly those relating to the transport sector, such as: the International Convention concerning the Carriage of Goods by Rail (hereinafter the '**1924 Bern CIM**');[100] the International Convention concerning the Carriage of Passengers and Luggage by Rail (hereinafter the '**1924 Bern CIV**');[101] the Convention concerning International Carriage by Rail (hereinafter the '**COTIF**');[102] the Protocol for the modification of the Convention concerning International Carriage by Rail (hereinafter the '**1999 Vilnius Protocol**');[103] the Convention on the Contract for the international Carriage of Goods by Road (hereinafter the '**CMR**');[104] the Athens Convention relating to the Carriage of Passengers and their Luggage by Sea (hereinafter the '**1974 PAL**');[105] the United Nations Convention on the Carriage of Goods by Sea (hereinafter the '**Hamburg Rules**');[106] or the United Nations Convention on the Contracts for the International Carriage of Goods Wholly or Partly by Sea (hereinafter the '**Rotterdam Rules**');[107]
- and other international public law conventions, such as: the Convention Relating to the Regulation of Aerial Navigation (hereinafter the '**1919 Paris Convention**')[108] and the 1944 Chicago Convention.

1.3.1.4 Regional Legislations

This study may also use regional instruments regulating the international liability regime of air carrier and consumer rights, with particular reference to EU Regulation 261/2004, in the context of their interactions with the Conventions.

99. Convention on Damage Caused by Foreign Aircraft to Third Parties on the Surface, 7 October 1952, Rome, ICAO Doc 7364, entry in force 4 February 1958.
100. International Convention concerning the Carriage of Goods by Rail, 23 October 1924, Bern.
101. International Convention concerning the Carriage of Passengers and Luggage by Rail, 23 October 1924, Bern.
102. Convention concerning International Carriage by Rail (COTIF), 9 May 1980, Bern, UNTS, 1396, I-23353, entry in force 1 May 1985.
103. Protocol for the modification of the Convention concerning International Carriage by Rail (COTIF) of 9 May 1980 (Protocol 1999), 3 June 1999, Vilnius, UNTS, 2828, I-23353, entry in force 1 July 2006.
104. Convention on the Contract for the International Carriage of Goods by Road (CMR), 19 May 1956, Geneva, UNTS, 399, p. 189, entry in force 2 July 1961.
105. Athens Convention relating to the Carriage of Passengers and their Luggage by Sea, 13 December 1974, Athens, UNTS, 1463, I-24817, entry in force 28 April 1987.
106. United Nations Convention on the Carriage of Goods by Sea, 31 March 1978, Hamburg, UNTS, 1695, I-29215, entry in force 1 November 1992.
107. United Nations Convention on the Contracts for the International Carriage of Goods Wholly or Partly by Sea, 11 December 2008, New York, not yet in force.
108. Convention Relating to the Regulation of Aerial Navigation, 13 October 1919, Paris, LNTS, 11, p. 173, entry in force 29 March 1922.

1.3.1.5 International Customary Law and General Principles of Law

International customary law and general principles of law will also be addressed, mostly in connection with hermeneutics issues.

1.3.1.6 Domestic Legislations

References to domestic legislations are required because the Conventions occasionally proceed to *renvois* to domestic legislation. This recourse may also be justified insofar as certain domestic legislations, like regional legislations, develop consumer protection provisions that may interfere with the Conventions.

1.3.2 Judicial Decisions

1.3.2.1 Preliminary Remarks

Significant attention will be paid to international, regional and domestic judicial decisions. The importance of judicial decisions is recognized in international law by Article 38(1)(d) of the Statute of the ICJ,[109] which reads as follows:

> The Court, whose function is to decide in accordance with international law such disputes as are submitted to it, shall apply:
>
> > [...]
> > d. subject to the provisions of Article 59, judicial decisions and the teachings of the most highly qualified publicists of the various nations, as subsidiary means for the determination of rules of law.[110]

This study will thus examine the jurisprudence produced by domestic and regional Courts regarding the 1999 Montreal Convention and its previous instruments.

In order to gain as broad a set of insights as my language skills and research tools will allow, I will try to identify highly regarded decisions in the most prominent jurisdictions in the sector, as well as in jurisdictions less commented on in English.

I will also occasionally have recourse to extensive abstracts of judicial decisions, when I deem them necessary for illustration purposes, or when specific points need to be verified. As much as possible, the abstracts used across this study will be quoted in their original language, or in the official language of the Conventions, with a personal translation when required.

109. United Nations, https://legal.un.org/avl/pdf/ha/sicj/icj_statute_e.pdf (accessed 6 September 2020).
110. Statute of the International Court of Justice, Article 59: 'The decision of the Court has no binding force except between the parties and in respect of that particular case.'

1.3.2.2 Notions on the Implementation of International Conventions in Domestic Regimes

(1) A Variety of Implementation Methods

As this study will pay great attention to the interpretation of the Conventions given by Courts, it is important to highlight *ab initio* that different systems of reception of international conventions exist across the globe, and that their differences might influence the methods or the outcome of the interpretation of the terms used in the Conventions.

The signing of an international convention, or its entry into force at the international level, does not mean that the convention automatically becomes part of the legal system of a determined State.[111] The process of implementation depends on the law of each State. The national procedures vary from one State to another. Traditionally, three major systems of national reception of international instruments are considered: monist, dualist and mixed.

(2) The Monist System

In a monist system, the international rule generally becomes binding in the national legal order by a mere act of parliament or government.[112] This is the case in France and Belgium, where international conventions enter into their legal order as an international rule by a ratification Act generally consisting of only a few lines. The consequence is that the rule laid down in an international convention will retain an international dimension and will be considered superior in the hierarchy of norms to a domestic rule.[113]

In France, this principle of primacy is written into the Constitution and was upheld by the *Cour de cassation* in 1975[114] and by the *Conseil d'Etat* in 1989.[115] In Belgium, the *Cour de cassation* also confirmed this primacy in 1971.[116]

(3) The Dualist System

In a dualist system, by contrast, the international rule needs to be incorporated into a national statutory instrument for it to become binding. As a typical example, the UK required the 1999 Montreal Convention to be written into a domestic legislation

---

111. *See*, Malcolm Shaw, *International Law* 689-692 (8th edition, Cambridge University Press, 2017).
112. The possibility for nationals to rely on international conventions may, however, depend on the self-executing character of the international convention at stake. *See*, Patrick Daillier, Mathias Forteau, Alain Pellet, *Droit International Public* 753 (8th edition, LGDJ, 2009).
113. The question of the primacy of international conventions over Constitutions is disputed, however. An ad hoc analysis is required for each jurisdiction.
114. Cass., 24 May 1975, 73-13.556, Bull., 1975, No 4, p. 6.
115. CE, 20 October 1989, No 108243.
116. Cass., 27 May 1971, Pasicrisie 886 (1971), ECLI:BE:CASS:1971:ARR:19710527.16.

instrument.[117] In this system, the international rule, once accepted, becomes a domestic rule, and has no inherent superiority in the pyramid of norms.

In theory, with the exception of a few particularities, this means that the international rule may be overridden by a posterior domestic rule on the principle of *lex posterior derogat legi priori*. Consequently, in dualist systems, while a domestic legislation may technically override a pre-existing treaty, doing so would infringe on the principle of *pacta sunt servanda* established under Article 26 of the 1969 Vienna Convention.[118] Courts therefore must try to interpret the texts in a way that reconciles the two.[119]

(4) Mixed Systems

There are also mixed systems, such as the United States,[120] where in addition to treaties like the 1999 Montreal Convention, which require the advice and consent of the Senate, other types of international agreements - known as 'executive agreements' - are concluded by the executive without being submitted to the Senate. These executive agreements have a distinct significance in domestic law.[121] Unlike in the UK, the 1999 Montreal Convention was not reproduced in a domestic instrument in the United States but was incorporated into the American legal order by way of a consent to ratification by the Senate.[122]

(5) The Potential Effects of the Variety of Implementation Methods

The distinctions among systems may not be without practical significance.[123] Their potential effects will be analysed in the course of this study and particularly in Chapter 4 when discussing interpretation methodology.

1.3.2.3 Examined Jurisdictions Regarding Autonomy

(1) Preliminary Remarks

Where different mechanisms of interpretation used by Courts in the application of the Conventions must be compared to assess the contours of the autonomy of the terms

117. The Carriage by Air Acts (Implementation of the Montreal Convention 1999) Order 2002.
118. 1969 Vienna Convention, Article 26: 'Every treaty in force is binding upon the parties to it and must be performed by them in good faith.' *See also*, 1969 Vienna Convention, Article 27: 'A party may not invoke the provisions of its internal law as justification for its failure to perform a treaty. [...].'
119. *See*, American Society of International Law, https://www.asil.org/insights/volume/2/issue/5/international-agreements-and-us-law (accessed 29 May 2019).
120. *See*, Paul Dubinsky, *International Law in the Legal System of the United States*, 58(Supplement) The American Journal of Comparative Law 455-478 (2010).
121. *See*, US Senate, https://www.senate.gov/artandhistory/history/common/briefing/Treaties.htm (accessed 29 May 2019).
122. *See*, US Department of State, https://2001-2009.state.gov/r/pa/prs/ps/2003/23851.htm (accessed 4 May 2021).
123. Even though this distinction does not reflect the nuances of each and every jurisdiction.

used therein,[124] the selection of judicial decisions is narrowed to the jurisprudence of the highest Courts of six parties to the 1999 Montreal Convention,[125] namely: the *Cour of cassation* of Belgium, the *Cour of cassation* of France, the CJEU, the Supreme Court of Canada, the Supreme Court of the United Kingdom and the Supreme Court of the United States. This selection is justified in order to examine:

- jurisdictions that have ratified the 1969 Vienna Convention and those that have not;
- monist, dualist and mixed systems of domestic reception of international conventions; and
- civil law, common law and hybrid jurisdictions.

In this selection, the ambition is to try to determine whether one or several of these distinctive elements play a significant role in the interpretation of the Conventions. A brief presentation of each of these jurisdictions is required in order to understand the legal environment in which the decisions to be explored were delivered.

(2) Selected Jurisdictions

(i) Belgium

Belgium is a monist State grounded in civil law. The *Cour de cassation* is the highest Court in the country regarding civil and commercial matters. Only appeals on points of law can reach its level.

The *Cour de cassation* historically held that, to interpret a term of private law in a provision of an international treaty, judges were allowed to refer to its usual legal definition under domestic law.[126] To this end, the Court has regularly given the *Travaux Préparatoires* an important role for interpretation purposes,[127] but has not accorded a high value to the title and preamble of legal instruments.[128] However, the Court fine-tuned its position and held in a 1977 decision regarding the interpretation of the 1929 Warsaw Convention that the following principles had to be applied:

> The interpretation of an international convention the purpose of which is the unification of the law cannot be done by reference to the domestic law of one of the contracting States. If the treaty text calls for interpretation, this ought to be done on the basis of elements that actually pertain to the treaty, notably, its object, its purpose and its context, as well as its preparatory work and genesis. The purpose of drawing up an international convention designed to become a species of international legislation would be wholly frustrated, if the courts of each State

124. *See*, section 4.3.3.4.
125. ICAO, https://www.icao.int/secretariat/legal/List%20of%20Parties/Mtl99_EN.pdf (accessed 7 September 2020).
126. Cass., 4 May 1972, 1 Pasicrisie 806-820 (1972), ECLI:BE:CASS:1972:ARR.19720504.5.
127. *See*, Cass., 18 September 1978, Pasicrisie 66 (1979), ECLI:BE:CASS:1978:ARR.19780918.1.
128. *See*, Cass., 3 November 1986, Pasicrisie 285 (1987), ECLI:BE:CASS:1986:ARR.19861103.9.

were to interpret it in accordance with concepts that are specific to their own legal system.[129]

Notwithstanding the above, the *Cour de cassation* handed down in 2000 an intriguing decision regarding the application of the CMR, but which could potentially be transposed *mutatis mutandis* to the Conventions. While confirming that the interpretation principles established in the 1969 Vienna Convention should be applied - which is consistent with Belgium being bound by said convention since 1992[130] - the Court held that, in substance, the mere violation of the objective of a treaty, in this case the aim of uniformity, was not sufficient to rule against the decision of an inferior Court.[131]

(ii) Canada

Canada is a dualist State,[132] and one of the few jurisdictions that combines common law and civil law.[133] This specificity is known as Bijuralism.

In 1970, the country became party to the 1969 Vienna Convention.[134] Its application was confirmed by the Supreme Court in *Thibodeau.*[135] In this case, Justice Cromwell held that the methodology laid down in the 1969 Vienna Convention was applicable when it came to the interpretation of the 1999 Montreal Convention.

The Supreme Court of Canada has not often been seized on the interpretation of the Conventions, but three decisions notably stand out: namely, *Montreal Trust Company*, *Ludecke* and the already mentioned *Thibodeau* judgment.[136] These will be further discussed below.[137]

(iii) France

France is a monist State[138] and one of the most commented-on civil law jurisdictions.

129. Cass., 27 January 1977, 1 Pasicrisie 574 (1977), ECLI:BE:CASS:1977:ARR.19770127.2. Source of translation: Bin Cheng, *Wilful Misconduct: From Warsaw to The Hague and from Brussels to Paris*, 2 Annals Air & Space Law 61 (1977).
130. *See*, United Nations, https://treaties.un.org/Pages/ViewDetailsIII.aspx?src=TREATY&mtdsg_no=XXIII-1&chapter=23&Temp=mtdsg3&clang=_en (accessed 15 September 2020).
131. Cass., 30 March 2000, C.9.70.176.N, ECLI:BE:CASS:2000:ARR.20000330.4: 'Que la seule invocation de la violation du but visé par le traité ne saurait davantage entraîner la cassation'.
132. *See*, on the matter, Gib van Ert, *Dubious Dualism: The Reception of International Law in Canada*, 44 Valparaiso University Law Review 927-934 (2010).
133. *See*, Canada Department of Justice, https://www.justice.gc.ca/eng/csj-sjc/harmonization/bijurilex/aboutb-aproposb.html (accessed 15 September 2020).
134. *See*, United Nations, https://treaties.un.org/Pages/ViewDetailsIII.aspx?src=TREATY&mtdsg_no=XXIII-1&chapter=23&Temp=mtdsg3&clang=_en (accessed 15 September 2020).
135. *Thibodeau v. Air Canada* (2014) 3 SCR 340, at 365.
136. *Montreal Trust Company et al. v. Canadian Pacific Airlines* (1977) 2 SCR 793; *Ludecke v. Canadian Pacific Airlines* (1979) 2 SCR 63; *Thibodeau v. Air Canada* (2014) 3 SCR 340.
137. *See*, sections 4.2.1.2, 4.3.2.2 and 4.3.3.4.
138. French Constitution, Article 55.

The role of the highest Court is shared by the *Cour de cassation*, for civil and commercial law matters, the *Conseil d'Etat*[139] and the *Conseil Constitutionnel*[140] which respectively deal with administrative and constitutional law matters. As in Belgium, the *Cour de cassation* is not per se a fully competent higher degree of jurisdiction, as it can only confirm or reject an inferior decision on a point of law without creating *erga omnes* binding precedents. In order to understand the decisions of the *Cour de cassation*, a distinction should be made between *in specie* decisions (*arrêt d'espèce*) and principle decisions (*arrêt de principe*). The latter more substantially affect the law in practice.

The right to seize the *Cour de cassation* is less stringent than the right to appeal before the Supreme Court of the United States or the Supreme Court of the United Kingdom, with the consequence that approximately twenty-five thousand decisions are handed down every year by the *Cour de cassation*,[141] with more than twenty decisions handed down on the 1999 Montreal Convention.[142]

When it comes to interpretation mechanisms, there is no general guidance under French law on how to proceed except in specific cases, such as criminal or contract law.[143] In case of ambiguity, Courts generally tend to stick to the literal meaning read together with the legislator's intent. Most decisions from the *Cour de cassation* are generally rather succinct, with the hermeneutical methodology used by the judges rarely being explained in the decisions. This is a response to the fact that a decision is supposed to be a logical deduction of the law, and that the Civil Code prohibits Courts from creating law[144] and prevents them from refusing to deliver a decision on the grounds that the law is silent or unclear.[145] The concise content of the decisions, based on the *imperatoria brevitas*, has slowly been changing since 2019, as Court's decisions have progressively presented more detailed reasoning.[146]

139. Competent notably in airport contentions. *See*, for example, CE, 9 October 2019, 430538, ECLI:FR:CECHR:2019:430538.20191009.
140. Competent notably for constitutional questions. *See*, for example, in matters of carriage of alien by air, CC, 25 October 2019, No 2019-810, ECLI:FR:CC:2019:2019.810.QPC.
141. Pascale Deumier, *Les principes UNIDROIT comme cadre de référence pour l'interprétation uniforme des droits nationaux*, 24 Revue Internationale de Droit Comparé 413-430 (2019).
142. There are *circa* two hundred decisions on the Warsaw Instruments.
143. *See*, for instance, Cass., 26 April 1984, 82-12048, on the interpretation of a Groundhandling Agreement mirroring the provisions of the 1929 Warsaw Convention as amended. The Court held that a reference to the liability provisions of said convention remained a contractual agreement and therefore did not encompass its time limitations: 'Que c'est par voie d'interprétation de cette clause imprécise que la Cour d'appel a estimé qu'elle avait pour objet d'appliquer à la responsabilité du manutentionnaire la limitation de la réparation édictée au profit du transporteur aérien mais non d'étendre à la société France X ... les règles particulières à l'action née du contrat de transport aérien et à sa prescription; que le moyen n'est donc pas fondé'.
144. French Civil Code, Article 5.
145. *Ibid.*, Article 4.
146. *See*, Cour de cassation, *Rapport de la Commission Réflexion sur la Réforme de la Cour de cassation* (April 2017), Source: Cour de cassation, https://www.courdecassation.fr/IMG///Rapport%20sur%20la%20réforme%20de%20la%20Cour%20de%20cassation.pdf (accessed 22 January 2021); Cour de cassation, *Note relative à la structure des arrêts et avis et à leur motivation en forme développée* (December 2018), Source: Cour de cassation, https://www.courdecassation.fr/IMG///NOTE%20MOTIVATION%2018%2012%202018.pdf (accessed 22

Since 1991, inferior Courts can request that the *Cour de cassation* gives a non-binding opinion in the case of serious interpretation difficulties. However, so far, no opinion has ever been delivered with respect to air transport law.

Regarding the interpretation of international conventions, although France did not ratify the 1969 Vienna Convention, the *Cour de cassation* has recognized that some of its provisions were to be considered as international customary law,[147] including Article 31, as explained by Professor Gilbert Guillaume, former President of the ICJ.[148] However, the Court regularly avoids directly interpreting the Conventions itself,[149] as it would rather proceed with the analysis of procedural or contractual provisions governed by domestic law under the vague domestic concept of 'sovereign interpretation'.[150] For example, in a 2014 cargo claim, the Court was asked to determine whether a person who was not party to a contract of carriage by air, but who was mentioned on the airway bill as the consignee together with the party to the contract, could be considered as the 'destinataire'/'person entitled to delivery' pursuant to the Conventions. In this case, the *Cour de cassation*, rather than analysing the term 'destinataire', held that the Court of Appeal had rightly and sovereignly interpreted the common intentions of the parties to the contract when it determined that the final consignee was the person entitled to delivery.[151]

January 2021). Under point 15 of this last document, the Court justified this change on the grounds that once translated, its decisions could more easily be understood by foreign law professionals: 'C'est ainsi qu'en pratique, un arrêt traduit dans une langue étrangère, devrait être aisément compris. A défaut, la Cour se priverait *ipso facto* des moyens d'influer sur l'opinion des juges et des juristes étrangers, comme elle est légitime à y prétendre dans un esprit de compétition des systèmes juridiques en confrontation (dialogue des juges)'.

147. *See*, Cass., 16 October 2012, 11-13658. *See also*, Emmanuel Decaux, Olivier de Frouville, *Droit International Public* 44 (11th edition, Dalloz, 2018).

148. *See*, Guillaume Gilbert, *Du caractère impératif des dispositions de l'article 28 de la Convention de Varsovie*, Revue Française de Droit Aérien et Spatial 233 (2006). *See also*, Cass., 8 July 2003, 99-10.590.

149. As mentioned in section 1.3.1.2(1), a widespread understanding was that international conventions could only be interpreted by way of authentic interpretations.

150. The same applies in most civil jurisdiction. In a decision regarding a catastrophe at Luxembourg airport, the Court of Appeal of Luxembourg confirmed that: 'En appliquant la Convention de Varsovie à l'accident du 6 novembre 2001 et en interprétant cette convention à la lumière de la jurisprudence française en la matière pour adopter les solutions retenues par les juges français, les juges de première instance ont exhaustivement motivé leur décision et leur choix de s'aligner sur la solution retenue par la Cour de Cassation française quant à la compétence matérielle de la juridiction répressive dans le cadre de l'application de la Convention de Varsovie est l'expression de leur pouvoir souverain d'appréciation' (CA, 29 January 2013, 61/13). This case concerned, *inter alia*, the possibility that family of air disaster victims could claim compensation before Criminal Courts in Luxembourg. In the first instance, the Court held that, in line with French practice, Criminal Courts were not competent to hear their claim (*Tribunal d'arrondissement*, 27 March 2012, 1344/12). The decision was reversed by the Court of Appeal (CA, 29 January 2013, 61/13 and CA, 21 January 2014, 44/14 V) and not further appealed before the *Cour de cassation*, which, however, was seized on a time limitation issue (*see*, section 3.2.5.2).

151. Cass., 8 July 2014, ECLI:FR:CASS:CO00655: 'Mais attendu qu'après avoir relevé que le nom de la société Régional CAE figurait dans la case "destinataire" de la lettre de transport aérien sous la mention "regional c/o bax global", c'est par une interprétation souveraine de la commune intention des parties et sans méconnaitre l'objet du litige, que la cour d'appel a estimé que la société Régional CAE avait la qualité de destinataire de la marchandise; que le moyen n'est pas fondé'.

This being said, when the *Cour de cassation* cannot avoid directly interpreting the Conventions, it generally tends to stick to a purely literal interpretation. In a decision pertaining to the value to be given to the word 'avarie', in a case where four out of sixteen boxes were missing at their destination and no complaint had been made within the required time limit, the Court confirmed that the word 'avarie' used under Article 26(2) of the 1929 Warsaw Convention did not encompass 'partial loss'. The Court disregarded the arguments raised by the airline, which referred to other provisions of the text and to the fact that 'avarie' was a generic term encompassing any damage suffered.[152]

Nevertheless, there is currently a trend towards an application of interpretation methods that is more in line with those established by the 1969 Vienna Convention. Notably, the objectives of the 1999 Montreal Convention have been taken into consideration in a number of decisions. When American Courts decided to refer claims emanating from the West Caribbean Airways catastrophe to French Courts on the grounds of the doctrine of forum non conveniens, the *Cour de cassation* held that French Courts were not competent as their seizure was not made according to the wishes of the claimants. The Court justified its decision with an examination of the purposes and object of the 1999 Montreal Convention.[153] In addition, the *Cour de cassation* seems to have more and more implicit regard for foreign case law. This trend is particularly apparent in the evolution of the application of Article 17 of the Conventions.[154]

The decisions discussed below have been selected for their importance or relevance.

152. Cass., 6 October 1992, 90-19667: 'que, la même distinction étant reprise au 2e alinéa de l'article 26 de cette convention, le terme "avarie" qui y est utilisé est un terme générique s'étendant de tout dommage subi, et, ce, d'autant plus que les trois termes "avarie", "destruction", "perte" ne correspondent pas à des événements spécifiques distincts et que le destinataire est, dans les trois cas, pareillement en mesure de constater le dommage lors de la réception de la marchandise [...]'. This decision also reflects the disparity between French and English Courts. In *Fothergill*, the House of Lords was seized on approximately the same question as the French Court. While looking at the French version of the Convention, the English Court finally came to a divergent interpretation.

153. Cass., 7 December 2011, 10-30919: 'Attendu que l'option de compétence ouverte au demandeur par les textes susvisés s'oppose à ce que le litige soit tranché par une juridiction, également compétente, autre celle qu'il a choisie; qu'en effet, cette option, qui a été assortie d'une liste limitative de fors compétents afin de concilier les divers intérêts en présence, implique, pour satisfaire aux objectifs de prévisibilité, de sécurité et d'uniformisation poursuivis par la Convention de Montréal, que le demandeur dispose, et lui seul, du choix de décider devant quelle juridiction le litige sera effectivement tranché, sans que puisse lui être opposée une règle de procédure interne aboutissant à contrarier le choix impératif de celui-ci; Attendu que, pour refuser de se dessaisir du litige, l'arrêt retient, par motifs adoptés, que la juridiction de Fort-de-France tire son pouvoir de juger d'une application rigoureuse des règles de compétence de la Convention de Montréal et, par motifs propres, que, parmi les chefs de compétence résultant de cette Convention, figure le tribunal du lieu de destination du vol, soit celui de Fort-de-France, dont le titre de compétence ne saurait être remis en cause sous couvert d'un défaut de pouvoir juridictionnel; Qu'en statuant ainsi, alors que les demandeurs avaient choisi une autre juridiction compétente pour trancher le litige, la cour d'appel a violé les textes susvisés'.

154. *See*, section 3.2.2.

(iv) The United Kingdom

The UK is a dualist State,[155] where common law is applied by English Courts.

The interpretation of law is historically governed by three rules: the Mischief Rule, the Golden Rule and the Literal Rule.[156] However, even before the ratification of the 1969 Vienna Convention in 1971,[157] English Courts regularly acknowledged that principles other than domestic interpretations should be applied with respect to the 1929 Warsaw Convention.[158]

When it came to interpreting the Conventions, the House of Lords, whose judicial function was transferred to the Supreme Court in 2009,[159] regularly confirmed the

155. *See*, for the 1929 Warsaw Convention: Carriage by Air Act 1932 – with a translation in English of the 1929 Warsaw Convention in the Schedule; for the 1999 Montreal Convention: The Carriage by Air Acts (Implementation of the Montreal Convention 1999) Order 2002.
156. *See*, The Law Commission and the Scottish Law Commission, The Interpretation of Statutes, 9 June 1969, points 23-28, Source, https://www.scotlawcom.gov.uk/files/3912/7989/6877/rep11.pdf (accessed 3 July 2019): 'The classic statement of the mischief rule is that given by the Barons of the Court of Exchequer in *Heydon's Case* [(1584) 3 Co.Rep. 7a]: "And it was resolved by them, that for the sure and true interpretation of all statutes in general (be they penal or beneficial, restrictive or enlarging of the Common Law), four things are to be discerned and considered:

    1st. What was the Common Law before the making of the Act,
    2nd. What was the mischief and defect for which the Common Law did not provide,
    3rd. What remedy the Parliament hath resolved and appointed to cure the disease of the commonwealth,
    And, 4th. The true reason of the remedy; and then the office of all the Judges is always to make such construction as shall suppress the mischief, and advance the remedy, and to suppress subtle inventions and evasions for continuance of the mischief, and *pro privato commodo*, and to add force and life to the cure and remedy, according to the true intent of the makers of the Act, *pro bono publico*."

    [...]

    The judges were, however, prepared to some extent to consider Coke's "cases out of the letter of a statute" under the so-called golden rule. This rule was attributed to Lord Wensleydale by Lord Blackburn in *River Wear Commissioners v. Adamson* [(1877) 2 App. Cas. 743 at pp. 764-5] in which he said: "I believe that it is not disputed that what Lord Wensleydale used to call the golden rule is right, viz., that we are to take the whole statute together, and construe it all together, giving the words their ordinary signification, unless when so applied they produce an inconsistency, or an absurdity or inconvenience so great as to convince the Court that the intention could not have been to use them in their ordinary signification, and to justify the Court in putting on them some other signification, which, though less proper, is one which the Court thinks the words will bear." [...] There was, however, a strong current of judicial opinion in favour of an approach rather stricter than that of the golden rule; this is commonly given the label of the literal rule. [...].'
157. *See*, United Nations, https://treaties.un.org/Pages/ViewDetailsIII.aspx?src=TREATY&mtdsg_no=XXIII-1&chapter=23&Temp=mtdsg3&clang=_en (accessed 15 September 2020).
158. Prior to the adoption of the 1969 Vienna Convention, the House of Lords already ruled on the interpretation of a shipping international convention that: 'As these rules must come under the consideration of foreign Courts it is desirable in the interests of uniformity that their interpretation should not be rigidly controlled by domestic precedents of antecedent date, but rather that the language of the rules should be construed on broad principles of general acceptation' (*Stag Line Ltd v. Foscolo Mango & Co Ltd* (1932) AC 328, at 350).
159. Supreme Court of the United Kingdom, https://www.supremecourt.uk/about/history.html (accessed 5 January 2021).

application of the interpretation principles set out in the 1969 Vienna Convention. Concerning the interpretation of the 1929 Warsaw Convention, the Court notably held in *Morris* that:

> The Convention must be considered as a whole, and it should receive a purposive construction [...]. The ordinary and natural meaning of the words used in the English text in Part I of the Schedule provides the starting point. But these words must also be compared with their equivalents in the French text [...] it should not be interpreted according to the idiom of English law. What one is looking for is a meaning which can be taken to be consistent with the common intention of the states which were represented at the international conference. The exercise is not to be controlled by technical rules of English law or domestic precedent. It would not be right to search for the legal meaning of the words used, as the Convention was not based on the legal system of any of the contracting states. It was intended to be applicable in a uniform way across legal boundaries. In situations of this kind the language used should be construed on broad principles leading to a result that is generally acceptable [...]. But this does not mean that a broad construction has to be given to the words used in the Convention. [...] It is legitimate to have regard to the travaux préparatoires in order to resolve ambiguities or obscurities [...]. But caution is needed in the use of this material, as the delegates may not have shared a common view. An expression by one of them as to his own view is likely be of little value if it was met simply by silence on the part of the other delegates. It will only be helpful if, after proper analysis, the travaux clearly and indisputably point to a definite intention on the part of the delegates as to how the point at issue should be resolved. It is also legitimate to have regard to subsequent practice in the application of the Convention, if this shows that the contracting parties were in agreement as to its interpretation, when it was entered into. General guidance to this effect is given, albeit only prospectively, in the Vienna Convention on the Law of Treaties [...]. In an ideal world the Convention should be accorded the same meaning by all who are party to it. So case law provides a further potential source of evidence. Careful consideration needs to be given to the reasoning of courts of other jurisdictions which have been called upon to deal with the point at issue, particularly those which are of high standing. Considerable weight should be given to an interpretation which has received general acceptance in other jurisdictions. On the other hand a discriminating approach is required if the decisions conflict, or if there is no clear agreement between them.[160]

Adherence to these principles in light of the 1999 Montreal Convention was lastly confirmed in the *Stott* judgment by Lord Toulson:

> The question at issue is whether the claim is outside the substantive scope and/or temporal scope of the Montreal Convention, and that depends entirely on the proper interpretation of the scope of that Convention. The governing principles are those of the Vienna Convention on the Law of Treaties.[161]

The Supreme Court has been seized on the interpretation of the Conventions on a few occasions. The most highly regarded decisions are: *Fothergill*, *Sidhu*, *Herd*,

160. *Morris v. KLM Royal Dutch Airlines* (2002) UKHL 7, at 76-81.
161. *Stott v. Thomas Cook Tour Operator Ltd* (2014) UKSC 15, at 59.

Morris, *Re Deep Vein Thrombosis* and *Stott*.[162] This last one is the unique decision delivered by the Supreme Court regarding the interpretation of the 1999 Montreal Convention. I will analyse those decisions in greater detail in the next chapters.

(v) The United States

As described above, the United States employs a mixed system,[163] where common law is applied by Federal Courts. American Courts are used to handling distinct categories of law, which either spring from the Federal level or from each Federal State. Since the 1950s, the United States has also been familiar with private uniform law, such as the Uniform Commercial Code, which remains, however, within national boundaries.

The Supreme Court of the United States never attached a clear value to the Vienna hermeneutical principles,[164] despite the Federal government considering other provisions of the 1969 Vienna Convention as customary international law on the law of treaties.[165]

The Supreme Court has developed its own mechanisms of interpretation, which have slightly varied over time. The core principles can be found in *Floyd*, where the following methodology was adopted:

> When interpreting a treaty, we 'begin "with the text of the treaty and the context in which the written words are used"'. [...] 'Other general rules of construction may be brought to bear on difficult or ambiguous passages'. [...] Moreover, 'treaties are construed more liberally than private agreements, and to ascertain their meaning, we may look beyond the written words to the history of the treaty, the negotiations, and the practical construction adopted by the parties'. [...] We proceed to apply these methods in turn.[166]

Seven important decisions regarding the interpretation of the Conventions filtered up to the level of the Supreme Court: the judgments *Franklin*, *Saks*, *Chan*, *Floyd*, *Zicherman*, *Tseng* and *Husain*,[167] though none of them interpreted the 1999 Montreal Convention. In order to determine the mechanisms used by American Courts to interpret the 1999 Montreal Convention, I have therefore chosen to include in this

162. *Fothergill v. Monarch Airlines* (1980) UKHL 6; *Sidhu and Others v. British Airways Plc; Abnett (Known as Sykes) v. Same* (1996) UKHL 5; *Fellowes or Herd and another v. Clyde Helicopters Ltd* (1997) UKHL 6; *Morris v. KLM Royal Dutch Airlines* (2002) UKHL 7; *Re Deep Vein Thrombosis and Air Travel Group Litigation* (2005) UKHL 72; *Stott v. Thomas Cook Tour Operators Ltd* (2014) UKSC 15.
163. *See*, section 1.3.2.2(4).
164. *See*, Richard Gardiner, *Treaty Interpretation* 154 (2nd edition, The Oxford International Law Library, 2017).
165. United States Department of State, https://2009-2017.state.gov/s/l/treaty/faqs/70139.htm (accessed 2 July 2019).
166. *Eastern Airlines, Inc. v. Floyd et al.*, 499 U.S. 530 (1991), at 534-535.
167. *Trans World Airlines, Inc. v. Franklin Mint Corp. et. al.*, 466 U.S. 243 (1984); *Air France v. Saks*, 470 U.S. 392 (1985); *Chan et. al. v. Korean Air Lines, Ltd*, 490 U.S. 122 (1989); *Eastern Airlines, Inc. v. Floyd et al.*, 499 U.S. 530 (1991); *Zicherman, Individually and as Executrix of the Estate of Kole, et. al. v. Korean Air Lines Co, Ltd.*, 516 U.S. 217 (1996); *El Al Israel Airlines, Ltd. v. Tsui Yuan Tseng*, 525 U.S. 155 (1999); *Olympic Airways v. Husain, Individually, and as Personal Representative of the Estate of Hanson, Deceased, et al.*, 540 U.S. 644 (2004).

overview one of the most recent decisions delivered by a Circuit Court at the time of writing, that is to say, the *Doe* decision delivered by the 6th Circuit Court in 2017.[168] All of these decisions will be further explored in the next chapters.

(vi) The European Union

The EU is a Regional Economic Integration Organization. It is not bound by the 1929 Warsaw Convention,[169] but it is Party to the 1999 Montreal Convention.[170] Article 53 of said treaty indeed authorizes Regional Economic Integration Organizations such as the EU to sign, ratify, accept, approve or accede to it. The EU may therefore be considered as a 'State Party' to the 1999 Montreal Convention, with the exception of Articles 1(2); 3(1)(b); 5(b); 23; 24; 33; 46 and 57(b). The instrument of approval submitted to the ICAO by the European Community, which became the EU from 1 December 2009, contained a declaration regarding the competence of the European Community with respect to certain matters governed by the 1999 Montreal Convention.[171]

The European legislator extended the scope of application of the 1999 Montreal Convention, normally limited by its Article 1 to 'international carriage', to flights operated inside the territory of a European Member State and set out that the liability of a Community air carrier for passengers and their baggage should be governed by all provisions of the Montreal Convention relevant to such liability.[172]

The CJEU is the highest Court for interpreting EU law.[173] In contrast to decisions delivered by the French or Belgian *Cours de cassation*, those handed down by the CJEU are binding in each Court of the EU Member States, as confirmed by the CJEU itself referring to the 'authority of an interpretation' of its decisions.[174] This gives the CJEU a paramount role when it comes to the interpretation of the 1999 Montreal Convention.

168. *Doe v. Etihad Airways, P.J.S.C.*, 870 F.3d 406 (6th Cir. 2017). In 2018, the US Supreme Court denied the petition to proceed to a judicial review of the decision. *See*, US Supreme Court, https://www.supremecourt.gov/Search.aspx?FileName=/docket/docketfiles/html/public/17-977.html (accessed 5 May 2021).
169. *See*, CJEU, 22 October 2009, *Irène Bogiatzi, married name Ventouras v. Deutscher Luftpool, Société Luxair, société luxembourgeoise de navigation aérienne SA, European Communities, Grand Duchy of Luxembourg, Foyer Assurances SA*, C-301/08, ECLI:EU:C:2009:649.
170. Council Decision of 5 April 2001 on the conclusion by the European Community of the Convention for the Unification of Certain Rules for International Carriage by Air (the Montreal Convention), 2001/539/EC, *Official Journal*, 18 July 2001, L 194/38.
171. *See*, ICAO, https://www.icao.int/secretariat/legal/List%20of%20Parties/Mtl99_EN.pdf (accessed 12 September 2020).
172. Council Regulation (EC) No 2027/97 of 9 October 1997 on air carrier liability in the event of accidents, *Official Journal*, 17 October 1997, L 285/1, as amended by Regulation (EC) No 889/2002 of the European Parliament and the Council of 13 May 2002 amending Council Regulation (EC) No 2027/97 of 9 October 1997 on air carrier liability in the event of accidents, *Official Journal*, 30 May 2002, L 140/2.
173. Known before 2009 as the Court of Justice of the European Community.
174. *See*, CJEC, 27 March 1963, *Da Costa en Schaake NV, Jacob Meijer NV, Hoechst-Holland NV v. Nederlandse Belastingadministratie*, Joined Cases C-28/62, 29/62, 30/62, ECLI:EU:C:1963:6; CJEC, 5 March 1986, *Wünsche Handelsgesellschaft GmbH & Co v. Federal Republic of Germany*, C-69/85, ECLI:EU:C:1986:104 (Order). *See also*, Vincent Correia, *Air Passengers' Rights, 'Extraordinary Circumstances', and General Principles of EU Law: Some Comments after the*

The reception of the 1999 Montreal Convention can be considered as falling into the category of monist systems. However, whereas the CJEU confirmed that international conventions concluded by the Union have primacy over secondary EU legislation – such as European regulations and directives[175] – it also consistently considers that international conventions concluded by the EU form an integral part of EU law.[176] Consequently, for the CJEU, international conventions concluded by the EU bind Member States by virtue of their duties under EU law and not international law.[177]

With respect to interpretation mechanisms, the EU is not a Party to the 1969 Vienna Convention, as explained above.[178] The CJEU has nevertheless regularly considered the principles of interpretation laid down in the 1969 Vienna Convention as international customary law.[179] In *IATA*, the Court seized on the validity of EU Regulation 261/2004 with respect to the 1999 Montreal Convention confirmed, as reported below, that the principles of interpretation set out in Article 31 of the 1969 Vienna Convention and of the 1986 Vienna Convention[180] should be applied as general customary of international law:

> It is to be noted with regard to the interpretation of those articles that, in accordance with settled case-law, an international treaty must be interpreted by reference to the terms in which it is worded and in the light of its objectives. Article 31 of the Vienna Convention of 23 May 1969 on the Law of Treaties and Article 31 of the Vienna Convention of 21 March 1986 on the Law of Treaties between States and International Organisations or between International Organisations, which express, to this effect, general customary international law, state that a treaty is to

McDonagh Case, 13 Issues in Aviation Law and Policy 275 (2014); Craig Paul, Búrca (de) Gráinne, *EU Law: Text, Cases and Material* 507 (7th edition, Oxford University Press, 2020).

175. *See*, for example, CJEC, 10 July 2008, *Emirates Airlines – Direktion für Deutschland v. Diether Schenkel*, C-173/07, ECLI:EU:C:2008:400, at 43. There are explicit exceptions to this principle of primacy, but these exceptions do not stem from EU law but from the international convention itself. *See*, for instance, the Agreement between the European Union and the Intergovernmental Organisation for International Carriage by Rail on the Accession of the European Union to the Convention concerning International Carriage by Rail (COTIF) of 9 May 1980, as amended by the Vilnius Protocol of 3 June 1999, which provides under its Article 2 that: 'Without prejudice to the object and the purpose of the Convention to promote, improve and facilitate international traffic by rail and without prejudice to its full application with respect to other Parties to the Convention, in their mutual relations, Parties to the Convention which are Member States of the Union shall apply Union rules and shall therefore not apply the rules arising from that Convention except in so far as there is no Union rule governing the particular subject concerned' (*Official Journal*, 23 February 2013, L 51/8).
176. *See*, CJEC, 39 April 1974, *R. & V. Haegeman v. Belgian State*, C-181/73, ECLI:EU:C:1974:41.
177. *See*, Craig Paul, Búrca (de) Gráinne, *EU Law: Text, Cases and Material* 389 (7th edition, Oxford University Press, 2020).
178. *See*, section 1.3.1.2(2)(vi).
179. In an aviation case unrelated to the 1999 Montreal Convention, the CJEU also confirmed that the EU must respect international law, including customary international law, in the exercise of its powers. *See*, CJEU, 21 December 2011, *Air Transport Association of America e.a. v. Secretary of State for Energy and Climate Change*, C-366/10, ECLI:EU:C:2011:864.
180. Vienna Convention on the Law of Treaties between States and International Organizations or between International Organizations, 21 March 1986, Vienna.

be interpreted in good faith in accordance with the ordinary meaning to be given to its terms in their context and in the light of its object and purpose [...].[181]

An application of this was notably reaffirmed in subsequent decisions, such as in *Walz*,[182] *Sanchez*,[183] and *Niki*.[184]

So far, the CJEU has already interpreted the 1999 Montreal Convention in ten major decisions:[185] *IATA, Walz, Sanchez, Wurcher, Air Baltic Corporation, Finnair, Guaitoli, Niki, Vueling* and *Altenrhein*.[186] These decisions will be examined more in detail in the following chapters.

1.3.2.4 Judicial Decisions Made under the Warsaw Instruments

I have chosen to refer to case law made under the Warsaw Instruments in this analysis. The *Travaux Préparatoires* of the 1999 Montreal Convention show that discussions on their continuity have taken place. The United States wished, for instance, for the preamble to include the following additional clause, making express reference to existing jurisprudence:

181. CJEC, 10 January 2006, *The Queen, on the application of International Air Transport Association and European Low Fares Airline Association v. Department for Transport*, C-344/04, ECLI:EU:C:2006:10, at 40.
182. CJEU, 6 May 2010, *Axel Walz v. Clickair SA.*, C-63/09, ECLI:EU:C:2010:251, at 22 and 23: 'In those circumstances, the term "damage", contained in an international agreement, must be interpreted in accordance with the rules of interpretation of general international law, which are binding on the European Union. In that connection, Article 31 of the Convention on the Law of Treaties, signed in Vienna on 23 May 1969, which codifies rules of general international law, states that a treaty must be interpreted in good faith in accordance with the ordinary meaning to be given to its terms in their context and in the light of its object and purpose [...].'
183. CJEU, 22 November 2012, *Pedro Espada Sánchez, Alejandra Oviedo Gonzáles, Lucía Espada Oviedo, Pedro Espada Oviedo v. Iberia Líneas Aéreas de España SA*, C-410/11, ECLI:EU:C:2013:747, at 21: '[...] even though the Vienna Convention on the Law of Treaties of 23 May 1969 does not bind either the European Union or all its Member States, that convention reflects the rules of customary international law which, as such, are binding upon the EU institutions and form part of the legal order of the European Union [...]'.
184. CJEU, 19 December 2019, *GN v. ZU acting for Niki Luftfahrt*, C-532/18, ECLI:EU:C:2019:1127, at 31.
185. Several other decisions have also delimited the scope of the 1999 Montreal Convention when interpreting EU Regulation 261/2004. Certain of these decisions will be discussed in section 4.2.2.2.
186. CJEC, 10 January 2006, *The Queen, on the application of International Air Transport Association and European Low Fares Airline Association v. Department for Transport*, C-344/04, ECLI:EU:C:2006:10; CJEU, 6 May 2010, *Axel Walz v. Clickair SA.*, C-63/09, ECLI:EU:C:2010:251; CJEU, 22 November 2012, *Pedro Espada Sánchez, Alejandra Oviedo Gonzáles, Lucía Espada Oviedo, Pedro Espada Oviedo v. Iberia Líneas Aéreas de España SA*, C-410/11, ECLI:EU:C:2013:747; CJEU, 26 February 2015, *Wucher Helicopter GmbH, Euro-Aviation Versicherungs AG v. Fridolin Santer*, C-6/14, ECLI:EU:C:2015:122; CJEU, 17 February 2016, *Air Baltic Corporation AS v. Lietuvos Respublikos specialiųjų tyrimų tarnyba*, C-429/14, ECLI:EU:C:2016:88; CJEU, 12 April 2018, *Finnair Oyj v. Keskinäinen Vakuutusyhtiö Fennia*, C-258/16, ECLI:EU:C:2018:252; CJEU, 7 November 2019, *Adriano Guaitoli, e.a. v. easyJet Airline Co. Ltd*, C-213/18, ECLI:EU:C:2019:927; CJEU, 19 December 2019, *GN v. ZU acting for Niki Luftfahrt*, C-532/18, ECLI:EU:C:2019:1127; CJEU, 9 July 2020, *SL v. Vueling Airlines SA*, C-86/19, ECLI:EU:C:2020:538; CJEU, 12 May 2021, *YL v. Altenrhein Luftfahrt GmbH*, C-70/20, ECLI:EU:C:2021:379.

> [...] in recognition of the frequently-cited objective of preserving, to the extent appropriate in these circumstances, the existing jurisprudence, standards and language which had been developed from 1929 onwards through many instruments.[187]

France, however, was opposed to this additional inclusion for the following reasons:

> Firstly, it would constitute an attack on the separation of powers to indicate to the judge what direction to take in the future. Judges must be free to take their decisions on the basis of the Convention itself, without having earlier jurisprudence imposed upon them. Secondly, the fact that jurisprudence varied substantially from State to State precluded the inclusion of a general reference to jurisprudence such as the one proposed. Thirdly, as the adoption of the Convention would entail the application of new law, there would necessarily be new jurisprudence. To stipulate that reference should be made to existing jurisprudence would be tantamount to depriving the Convention of any legal force. The Courts must have the freedom to develop new jurisprudence with regard to the new legal instrument.[188]

Moreover, current jurisprudence is also divided on this point. For instance, the Supreme Court of the United Kingdom admitted in *Stott* a certain continuity with the previous case law.[189] Saugmandsgaard Øe, Advocate General to the CJEU, also opined in *Niki* that:

> [...] in spite of the differences between Article 17 of the Warsaw Convention and Article 17(1) of the Montreal Convention, I am of the view that the Montreal Convention must nonetheless also be interpreted in the light of the decisions relating to the Warsaw Convention, given the essential equivalence between them.[190]

Taking an opposing view, Courts in the United States have sometimes adopted a different approach. In *Doe*, the 6th Circuit Court held that, given that the wording of Article 17 of the 1999 Montreal Convention was slightly different from the previous text, the decisions delivered under the previous instruments should not have any legal authority:

> [...] the Montreal Convention is a new treaty that we interpret as a matter of first impression, and there is no legal authority that would require us to import *Erhlich*'s Warsaw Convention determination to govern this Montreal Convention claim.[191]

---

187. ICAO Doc 9775, International Conference on Air Law (Convention for the Unification of Certain Rules for International Carriage by Air), Montreal, 10-28 May 1999, volume I, *Minutes*, Montreal 1999, p. 218.
188. *Ibid.*, p. 220.
189. *Stott v. Thomas Cook Tour Operators Ltd* (2014) UKSC 15, at 24-28 and 63.
190. CJEU, 26 September 2019, *GN v. ZU acting for Niki Luftfahrt*, C-532/18, ECLI:EU:C:2019:788 (Opinion), at 27.
191. *Doe v. Etihad Airways, P.J.S.C.*, 870 F.3d 406 (6th Cir. 2017), at 415. That Court, however, later admitted, at 425-426, that national or foreign decisions rendered under the previous text were still valid precedent, insofar as they concerned similar provisions and were delivered before the ratification of the 1999 Montreal Convention: 'Because these Supreme Court cases analyzed

In light of the above elements, and in spite of Article 55 of the 1999 Montreal Convention,[192] as well as the discussions on the preamble,[193] the mere existence of divergent opinions in jurisprudence over continuity between the instruments calls for an analysis of the 1999 Montreal Convention that includes references to judicial decisions developed under the Warsaw Instruments.

1.3.3 *Travaux Préparatoires*

1.3.3.1 Their Relevance

As part of an analysis of the 1999 Montreal Convention, references may be made to the Working Documents or 'Travaux Préparatoires' of different international instruments. The *Travaux Préparatoires* mainly record work done prior to and during diplomatic conferences, which often leads to the adoption of international instruments. This analysis may make regular use of the *Travaux Préparatoires* of the following diplomatic conferences:

- *Conférence Internationale de Droit Privé Aérien,* held in Paris, in October and November 1925 (hereinafter the '**1925 Paris Conference**'),[194] which prepared the *II Conférence Internationale de Droit Privé Aérien,* held in Warsaw, in October 1929 (hereinafter the '**1929 Warsaw Conference**'),[195] which was concluded by the adoption of the 1929 Warsaw Convention.
- International Conference on Private Air Law, held in The Hague, in September 1955 (hereinafter the '**1955 Hague Conference**'),[196] which was concluded by the adoption of the 1955 Hague Protocol.
- International Conference on Air Law, held in Guatemala City, in February and March 1971 (hereinafter the '**1971 Guatemala City Conference**'),[197] which was concluded by the adoption of the 1971 Guatemala City Protocol.

---

aspects of the Warsaw Convention that we have no reason to believe have changed following the ratification of the Montreal Convention (and that neither party has argued have changed following the ratification of the Montreal Convention), it is reasonable to conclude that these cases form part of the "precedent" consistent with which, according to the Explanatory Note [...], the drafters expected signatories to construe Article 17(1) of the Montreal Convention. Accordingly, we have adopted *Saks*' definition of "accident", and our discussion of damages [...] will be guided by *Zicherman*'s deference to the forum jurisdiction's choice-of-law rules.'

192. *See*, section 1.3.1.1(2).
193. *See*, *Ibid.*
194. Conférence Internationale de Droit Privé Aérien, 27 Octobre-6 Novembre 1925, Paris, 1926.
195. ICAO Doc 7838, II Conférence Internationale de Droit Privé Aérien, 4-12 Octobre 1929, *Procès-Verbaux*, Varsovie, 1930.
196. ICAO Doc 7686, International Conference on Private Air Law, The Hague, September 1955, volume I, *Minutes*, Montreal September 1956; ICAO Doc 7686, International Conference on Private Air Law, The Hague, September 1955, volume II, *Documents*, Montreal September 1956.
197. ICAO Doc 9040, International Conference on Air Law, Guatemala City, February-March 1971, volume I, *Minutes*, Montreal, 1972; ICAO Doc 9040, International Conference on Air Law, Guatemala City, February-March 1971, volume II, *Documents*, Montreal, 1972.

- International Conference on Air Law, held in Montreal, in September 1975 (hereinafter the '**1975 Montreal Conference**'),[198] which was concluded by the adoption of the 1975 Additional Protocol Nos 1, 2 and 3 and the Montreal Protocol No 4.
- International Conference on Air Law, held in Montreal, in May 1999 (hereinafter the '**1999 Montreal Conference**'),[199] which was concluded by the adoption of the 1999 Montreal Convention.

As discussions at the 1925 Paris Conference and the 1929 Warsaw Conference were reported in French only, I will quote the *Travaux Préparatoires* in their original language, with an accompanying translation when required.

1.3.3.2 Their Limitations

The value of the *Travaux Préparatoires* is limited under international law. As seen earlier,[200] Article 32 of the 1969 Vienna Convention only grants them a subsidiary rank for interpretation purposes.

The reason the 1969 Vienna Convention limits their use to specific situations may stem from the fact that the *Travaux Préparatoires* are not always clear, and certainly are not exhaustive. Indeed, not all preparatory work leading to the conferences is even recorded. For the 1929 Warsaw Convention, the *Comité International Technique d'Experts Juridiques Aériens* (hereinafter the 'CITEJA') did four years of preparation work to adopt the draft text. While submitted to the 1929 Warsaw Conference, it was not recorded in full in the official *Travaux Préparatoires*. Even if the 1999 Montreal Convention's *Travaux Préparatoires* are more detailed and contain most of the preparatory work, they still are not exhaustive.

I have also noted that not every formal or informal discussion that took place during the conferences could have been recorded. For example, when the subject required long political negotiations, only the outcome of the compromise was recorded in the *Travaux Préparatoires*.[201] In addition, the work of the drafting committee established by the conferences is rarely recorded. It is particularly missing in the *Travaux Préparatoires* of the 1929 Warsaw Convention. Yet, a recording of the drafting committee's work could have provided useful insights into the choice of words, such as

198. ICAO Doc 9154, International Conference on Air Law, Montreal, September 1975, volume I, *Minutes*, Montreal, 1977; ICAO Doc 9154, International Conference on Air Law, Montreal, September 1975, volume II, *Documents*, Montreal, 1977.
199. ICAO Doc 9775, International Conference on Air Law (Convention for the Unification of Certain Rules for International Carriage by Air), Montreal, 10-28 May 1999, volume I, *Minutes*, Montreal 1999; ICAO Doc 9775, International Conference on Air Law (Convention for the Unification of Certain Rules for International Carriage by Air), Montreal, 10-28 May 1999, volume II, *Documents*, Montreal 1999; ICAO Doc 9775, International Conference on Air Law (Convention for the Unification of Certain Rules for International Carriage by Air), Montreal, 10-28 May 1999, volume III, *Preparatory Material*, Montreal 1999.
200. *See*, section 1.3.1.2(2).
201. *See*, section 3.2.4.3.

'accident'.[202] The 1999 Montreal Convention's *Travaux Préparatoires* are more exhaustive, with some of the drafting committee's discussions being made publicly available.[203] Nevertheless, there is no full record of such discussions, and this study will only highlight, when deemed necessary, the delegates' participation when they are quoted.

Additionally, the limited value of the *Travaux Préparatoires* in a legal context may be explained by the fact that the conferences were attended not only by legal experts but also by civil servants, such as diplomats. The content of the Minutes must therefore be approached with care as they may express not only legal views from experts but also political views from individuals not familiar with legal matters.

1.3.3.3 Their Importance for Research Questions

Taking into account these limitations, the *Travaux Préparatoires* still have a significant importance in this study.

First, they may occasionally provide a clear indication of the Conventions negotiators' intentions, bearing in mind that the Minutes were sometimes sent to delegations for approval prior to their publication.[204]

Second, their paramount role was acknowledged during the negotiations with respect to future interpretation of the provisions of the 1999 Montreal Convention:

> Thus whatever position the Conference arrived at with regard to the issue of mental injury, its intentions regarding the scope of liability must be made clear in the 'travaux préparatoires' of the Conference for the future interpretation of the Convention;[205]
>
> [...] it could not be left to the Courts to subsequently interpret the text of Article 16, paragraph 1, independently of the Conference's 'travaux préparatoires';[206]
>
> [...] [the Delegate of the United States] noted that the conclusion which they had reached, and which they now proposed to the Group, was that the latter put together a series of hypothetical cases to illustrate how paragraph 2, sub-paragraph (a), would work in practical terms and include them in the 'travaux préparatoires' of the Conference. The Delegate of the United States averred that

202. *See,* section 3.2.2.
203. *See,* ICAO Doc 9775, International Conference on Air Law (Convention for the Unification of Certain Rules for International Carriage by Air), Montreal, 10-28 May 1999, volume II, *Documents,* Montreal 1999.
204. *See,* for example, in the Minutes of the 1955 Hague Conference: 'The President suggested – and the Conference agreed – that the minutes of the Conference be approved by the President and that the draft minutes be sent to the various Delegates so that they might make amendments which they considered appropriate before final publication', ICAO Doc 7686, International Conference on Private Air Law, The Hague, September 1955, volume I, *Minutes,* Montreal September 1956, p. 414.
205. ICAO Doc 9775, International Conference on Air Law (Convention for the Unification of Certain Rules for International Carriage by Air), Montreal, 10-28 May 1999, volume I, *Minutes,* Montreal 1999, p. 111.
206. *Ibid.,* p. 116.

> that would be of great assistance to Courts, probably more so than if the Group were to spend several days trying to perfect the language of sub-paragraph (a).[207]

Third, because Courts have occasionally referred to them.[208]

1.3.4 Other Sources

In addition to the tools used to answer the questions posed by this study, references will also be made to the most authoritative scientific literature available. Particular care will be taken to diversify the linguistic origins of the sources to the best of my skills and the availability of sources. For consistency, references to scientific literature may not always appear according to their original system in this study, but key information allowing them to be easily retrieved are kept in a format generally admitted in the English-speaking world.

Some references will also be made to private instruments, such as the 1995 IATA Agreement, and to industry practices.

Other information may also be taken from public websites and contacts with practitioners, the ICAO, the International Air Transport Association, National Civil Aviation Authorities, UNIDROIT and developers of applications of Artificial Intelligence.

1.3.5 Concluding Remarks

A more standard presentation could have been used to describe the methodology, using Article 38(1) of the Statute of the ICJ, which provides that:

> The Court, whose function is to decide in accordance with international law such disputes as are submitted to it, shall apply:
>
> a. international conventions, whether general or particular, establishing rules expressly recognized by the contesting states;
> b. international custom, as evidence of a general practice accepted as law;
> c. the general principles of law recognized by civilized nations;
> d. subject to the provisions of Article 59, judicial decisions and the teachings of the most highly qualified publicists of the various nations, as subsidiary means for the determination of rules of law.

Despite the merits of the identification of the above sources, doing so in this study would not have allowed me to explain soon enough the close ties between the Warsaw Instruments, related judicial decisions, and the 1999 Montreal Convention.

It would also have minimized the importance of the *Travaux Préparatoires*, domestic legislations and private law commentators, which all together are essential to conduct this study.

---

207. *Ibid.*, p. 154.
208. *See*, section 4.3.3.3.

The ambition here is not to step into the shoes of an international judge. Rather, it is to determine whether the regime for international air carrier liability established by the 1999 Montreal Convention can be uniform, and if so, to what extent this aim has been achieved.

For these reasons, this methodology uses an order of presentation that might appear to some as non-standard.

CHAPTER 2

Uniformity as a Predominant Aim of the 1999 Montreal Convention

2.1 INTRODUCTION

This chapter will analyse the *ratio legis* of the 1999 Montreal Convention in order to determine to what extent uniformity is a principal aim of the Convention that must be pursued in its application.

In order to answer this essential question, I will review the situation before the adoption of the 1929 Warsaw Convention (section 2.2). This historical review will reveal the difficulties encountered in the absence of common principles, and will permit a determination on the main purposes for the creation of an international regime (section 2.3). From there, the reasons for which the drafters of the Conventions adopted techniques of unification may become clear (section 2.4). This could hopefully aid in the determination of any specific characteristics envisaged by the drafters to assist this aim (section 2.5). This exercise carried out, conclusions will be drawn on the aim of uniformity of the 1999 Montreal Convention (section 2.6).

2.2 HISTORICAL CONTEXT

As described in Chapter 1, the emergence of aviation in the early 20th century substantially reduced the notion of distance and the speed of communication. But at that time, the liability regime of air carriers in the case of fatalities was only governed by domestic legislations. The air carrier liability regime could either be regulated by general tort or contractual law or by specific air legislations such as in France.[209] As one might anticipate, none of these legal provisions were identical. Therefore, in the case

209. *See*, section 1.1.1.

of international flights, the question of applicable law was raised, with the consequence that no certainty existed as to which legislation would apply in the absence of specific international rules of conflict of laws.

In addition, not only were the rules different in each domestic legislation but also substantially varied when it came to the level of passenger protection.[210] Hence, depending on the result of the applicable rules of conflict of laws, the applicable substantive law may have offered a more protective regime for the carrier or for the passenger.

In 1922, the League of Nations expressed its concerns regarding the lack of an international air carrier liability regime:

> En ce qui touche le droit privé aérien, aucun effort international officiel ne s'est jusqu'ici exercé. Les diverses législations nationales se constituent ou sont appelées à se constituer sans aucun contact organisé les unes avec les autres; il semble qu'un tel manquement de coordination peut être préjudiciable au développement de la navigation aérienne. Si aucune action ne s'exerce dans un délai assez court, des législations et des traditions divergentes se formeront dans les différents pays, et les difficultés qui se sont présentées depuis si longtemps par suite du manque d'unification en droit maritime se reproduiront et seront peut-être très préjudiciables en navigation aérienne, par suite de l'extrême mobilité des transports aériens.[211]

There was therefore a serious international call for a rapid regulatory response with respect to international air carrier liability. As noted by Professor Daniel Goedhuis a few years later, uniformity of laws governing carriage by air was at that time an 'absolute necessity'.[212]

2.3 PURPOSES

2.3.1 A Multiplicity of Purposes

In light of the context described, the following analysis is designed to determine the purposes of the 1929 Warsaw Convention and whether the drafters of the 1999 Montreal Convention had the same purposes in mind. The *Travaux Préparatoires* will be used to inform an understanding of the establishment of these Conventions.

2.3.2 Solving the Lack of Legal Certainty

As previously mentioned,[213] the existence of different legislations across the globe regulating identical situations created an undesirable and harmful situation. In the absence of approximation of legislations, both the airlines and their customers could

210. *Ibid.*
211. Conférence Internationale de Droit Privé Aérien, 27 Octobre-6 Novembre 1925, Paris, 1926, p. 28.
212. Daniel Goedhuis, *National Airlegislations and the Warsaw Convention* 3 (Springer, 1937).
213. *See*, section 2.2.

not anticipate with any certainty which rules would apply to them in the case of international carriage. As noted during the 1925 Paris Conference, the passenger must be able to know his rights, as must the carrier in order to respectively insure their risks.[214]

This anticipation is best known in legal theory as 'legal certainty' and is considered internationally to be included in the concept of 'rule of law' as pointed out here by the United Nations:

> The 'rule of law' is a concept at the very heart of the Organization's mission. It refers to a principle of governance in which all persons, institutions and entities, public and private, including the State itself, are accountable to laws that are publicly promulgated, equally enforced and independently adjudicated, and which are consistent with international human rights norms and standards. It requires, as well, measures to ensure adherence to the principles of supremacy of law, equality before the law, accountability to the law, fairness in the application of the law, separation of powers, participation in decision-making, legal certainty, avoidance of arbitrariness and procedural and legal transparency.[215]

This principle of legal certainty has further been recognized at an international level by the ICJ in *Ahmadou Sadio Diallo*,[216] and at a regional level, by the European Court of Human Rights in its *Sunday Times*[217] decision, by the Inter-American Court of Human Rights in *Cayara*,[218] and by the Court of Justice of the European Community in *Bosch*.[219] At a national level, the importance of this concept was acknowledged in several States such as in Canada,[220] France[221] and the UK.[222] In other common law jurisdictions, the concept is covered more under the doctrine of precedent.[223]

---

214. Conférence Internationale de Droit Privé Aérien, 27 Octobre-6 Novembre 1925, Paris, 1926, p. 12: 'Il importe en effet que le voyageur et l'expéditeur puissent, au cas d'accident ou de dommage, connaître l'étendue de ses droits et le moyen d'exercer son recours, et il importe aussi que les Compagnies de navigation aérienne puissent calculer l'étendue de leur responsabilité et la faire garantir. Il serait peu logique que la solution de ces questions dépendît du pays traversé ou du tribunal saisi et que la diversité des lois modifiât la solution applicable'.
215. United Nations, *The rule of law and transitional justice in conflict and post-conflict societies*, Report of the Secretary-General (UN Doc. S/2004/616), 23 August 2004, para. 6. *See also*, International Court of Justice, Inaugural Hilding Eek Memorial Lecture by H.E. Judge Peter Tomka, President of the International Court of Justice, at the Stockholm Centre for International Law and Justice - *The Rule of Law and the Role of the International Court of Justice in Word Affairs*, 2 December 2013, Source: International Court of Justice, https://www.icj-cij.org/files/press-releases/8/17848.pdf (accessed 29 May 2019).
216. ICJ, *Ahmadou Sadio Diallo (Republic of Guinea v. Democratic Republic of the Congo), Merits, Judgements*, I.C.J. Reports 2010, p. 639.
217. ECHR, 26 April 1979, *Sunday Times v. United Kingdom (No 1)*, ECLI:CE:ECHR:1979:0426JUD000653874.
218. ICHR, 3 February 1993, *Cayara v. Perú (Excepciones Preliminares)*, Serie C No 14.
219. CJEC, 6 April 1962, *Kledingverkoopbedrijf de Geus en Uitdenbogerd v. Robert Bosch GmbH and Maatschappij tot voortzetting van de zaken der firma Willem van Rijn*, C-13/61, ECLI:EU:C:1962:11. *See also*, Jeremy Van Meerbeeck, *Le principe de sécurité juridique dans la jurisprudence de la Cour de justice de l'Union européenne: de la certitude à la confiance* (thesis, 2013), Source: UCLouvain, http://hdl.handle.net/2078.3/128500 (accessed 29 May 2019).
220. *R. v. Daoust* (2004) 1 R.C.S. 217, quoted in: Pierre-André Cote, *Le souci de la sécurité juridique dans l'interprétation de la loi au Canada*, 110 Revue du notariat 685-692 (2008).
221. CE, 24 March 2006, ECLI:FR:CEASS:2006:288460.20060324.

Despite the lack of a commonly agreed definition, it can be said that the main requirement for the law is that it must be made public, clear, understandable and predictable.[224]

The *Travaux Préparatoires* of the 1929 Warsaw Convention confirm that the goal of achieving a high level of legal certainty was of paramount importance. For instance, France voiced how important it was to have a clear regime:

> Si vous adoptez le régime prévu à l'article 22, vous aurez un régime qui permettra toutes les controverses, qui permettra à toutes les victimes d'entamer un procès. [...] Vous aurez en un mot, un régime qui ne sera pas un régime claire.[225]

The French delegation added that the upcoming regime should be without legal uncertainties:

> Le système primitif était celui des 'mesures raisonnables'; on y a substitué un régime complexe qui fait une certaine part à la faute, une certaine part au risque, qui peut être le résultat d'un compromis mais qui, pour des juristes, donne ce résultat peu satisfaisant d'une convention basée sur des principes différents et qui, pour les praticiens, laisse place à une foule d'incertitudes juridiques et ruine l'unité de droit que nous voulions établir par notre convention.[226]

Switzerland also underlined that the public should be able to predict and anticipate the rules: 'Nous devons donner au public des règles qu'il connaisse'.[227] In parallel, the Rapporteur underlined that carriers should be able to determine their financial exposure.[228]

During the 1955 Hague Conference, legal certainty was considered of equal importance by the participants. For instance, in the discussions about information to be provided to passengers, the Portuguese delegation emphasized that uncertainty should be avoided:

---

222. *See*, UK Supreme Court, https://www.supremecourt.uk/docs/speech_111011.pdf (accessed 29 May 2019); *see also*, for example, in commercial law: *Golden Straight Corporation v. Nippon YKK* (2007) UKHL 12.
223. In the United States, according to some scholars, the concept appears to have declined in favour of the concept of legal indeterminacy. *See*, James Maxeiner, *Some Realism about Legal Certainty in the Globalization of the Rule of Law*, 31 Houston Journal of International Law 27-46 (2008); *See also*, James Maxeiner, *Legal Certainty and Legal Methods: A European Alternative to American Indeterminacy?*, 15 Tulane Journal of International & Comparative Law 541-607 (2007); Offer Raban, *The Fallacy of Legal Certainty: Why Vague Legal Standards May Be Better for Capitalism and Liberalism*, 19 Public Interest Law Journal 175-191 (2010).
224. The first articulation of this concept can be dated back to the Hammurabi Code, which consists of a list of private law rules engraved on a column, *circa* 1754 BCE.
225. ICAO Doc 7838, II Conférence Internationale de Droit Privé Aérien, 4-12 Octobre 1929, *Procès-Verbaux*, Varsovie, 1930, pp. 28-29.
226. *Ibid.*, pp. 33-34.
227. *Ibid.*, p. 103.
228. *Ibid.*, p. 165: 'Quant à la limitation de responsabilité, la somme de dix mille francs-or prévue primitivement pour les voyageurs, et celle de cinq cents francs-or par colis pour les marchandises ont été remplacées respectivement par les limites de vingt-cinq mille francs-or et de cent francs-or par kilo. Cette dernière modification a été apportée au texte primitif pour permettre au transporteur de connaître exactement l'étendue de son risque par le maximum de poids qu'il peut transporter'.

> It had been said that the passenger should not be left in a state of uncertainty concerning the rules applicable to the liability of the carrier, since, if the passenger considered it to be necessary, he might take out supplementary insurance.[229]

The need for certainty in the application of the text was also raised on several occasions by the International Union of Aerospace Insurers, during discussions on the revision of limits[230] and what constituted a delay.[231] In turn, the Belgian delegation highlighted that it was particularly important for the carriers and passengers to be fully aware of what they should pay and receive.[232]

At the time of the 1999 Montreal Conference, the question of legal certainty and its corollary, predictability, remained of paramount importance in the discussions,[233] as notably reported in the Minutes as follows:

> What the Group was attempting to do was to see whether it could have a greater degree of predictability and certainty so that passengers would not be even more than they currently were the victims of uncertainties of a judicial system which might be unable to offer any predictability as to results, certain that carriers would be able to organize their activities and insurance on a basis which would also bring a greater degree of predictability.[234]

In substance, the drafters of the 1999 Montreal Convention were focused on attaining 'a degree of certainty and uniformity'.[235]

The importance of the principle of legal certainty which guided the drafting of the Conventions may also be found in the national ratification memoranda. By way of example, the Explanatory Memorandum to the Australian Civil Aviation Legislation Amendment (1999 Montreal Convention and Other Measures) Bill 2008 provides that:

---

229. ICAO Doc 7686, International Conference on Private Air Law, The Hague, September 1955, volume I, *Minutes*, Montreal September 1956, p. 63.
230. *Ibid.*, p. 178: 'The attitude of the insurers towards the problem could be summed up in a very few words. They were able and willing to insure any reasonable limits of liability that the Conference might adopt. But the cost of that insurance would depend to a large extent on the certainty of those limits. Every insurer wanted to know what he was being called upon to insure and the unfortunate stage had been reached where Article 25 had been subjected to different decisions so that there was no longer any certainty in its interpretation.'
231. *Ibid.*, p. 244: '[...] the insurers were left in position of considerable uncertainty as to what was the liability that they were called upon to insure'.
232. *Ibid.*, p. 188: 'There was a unanimous feeling in the Conference in favour of a convention which would have a broad and uniform application. What was important was not the fear to increase the present limits of the Warsaw Convention. It was not particularly important if the limits were increased even more than the limits of the Protocol, if the carriers, as well as the passengers, were fully aware of what was to be paid and received.'
233. ICAO Doc 9775, International Conference on Air Law (Convention for the Unification of Certain Rules for International Carriage by Air), Montreal, 10-28 May 1999, volume I, *Minutes*, Montreal 1999, pp. 37, 43, 66, 94, 95, 111, 129, 131, 132, 140, 141, 142, 159, 161, 165, 200, 202, 206, 221, 245; ICAO Doc 9775, International Conference on Air Law (Convention for the Unification of Certain Rules for International Carriage by Air), Montreal, 10-28 May 1999, volume III, *Preparatory Material*, Montreal 1999, p. 24.
234. ICAO Doc 9775, International Conference on Air Law (Convention for the Unification of Certain Rules for International Carriage by Air), Montreal, 10-28 May 1999, volume I, *Minutes*, Montreal 1999, p. 129.
235. *Ibid.*, p. 111.

> Australian accession to the Montreal Convention would be a step towards the uniformity of international rules relating to carriage by air. Uniformity will remove uncertainty as to the rules that apply in any particular case. It will also remove inconsistency between rules applying at different stages of international carriage, or to different passengers or cargo on the same flight (eg. where the original departure and/or ultimate destination are different). This is expected to provide the benefit to both consumers and carriers of improving efficiency and reducing litigation.[236]

Since the ratification of the Conventions, the highest Courts have regularly made references to the need of legal certainty governing the Conventions. In the United States, Justice O'Connor highlighted in *Franklin* that the purposes of the Convention were to '[...] set a stable, predictable, and internationally uniform limit [...]'.[237] In *Tseng*, the US Supreme Court confirmed that: 'Such a reading would scarcely advance the predictability that adherence to the treaty has achieved worldwide.'[238] In Canada, the Supreme Court highlighted in *Thibodeau* that the purposes of the Conventions were to respond to:

> [...] concerns that many legal regimes might apply to international carriage by air with the result that there could be no uniformity or predictability with respect to either carrier liability or the rights of passengers and others using the service. Both passengers and carriers were potentially harmed by this lack of uniformity.[239]

The CJEU also regularly referred to the principle of legal certainty in relation to air law litigation.[240] In *Guaitoli*, the European Court particularly recognized that the purpose of the 1999 Montreal Convention was to 'ensure, in the interests of both parties to the dispute, greater predictability and greater legal certainty'.[241]

236. Point 4.15 of the Explanatory Memorandum to the Australian Civil Aviation Legislation Amendment (1999 Montreal Convention and Other Measures) Bill 2008, Source: Australian Federal Register of Legislation, www.legislation.gov.au/Details.C2008B00098/Explanatory%20Memorandum/Text (accessed 19 February 2019).
237. *Trans World Airlines, Inc. v. Franklin Mint Corp. et. al.*, 466 U.S. 243 (1984), at 256.
238. *El Al Israel Airlines, Ltd. v. Tsui Yuan Tseng*, 525 U.S. 155 (1999), at 171.
239. *Thibodeau v. Air Canada* (2014) 3 SCR 340, at 41.
240. *See*, CJEC, CJEC, 10 January 2006, *The Queen, on the application of International Air Transport Association and European Low Fares Airline Association v. Department for Transport*, C-344/04, ECLI:EU:C:2006:10; CJEC, 2 July 2009, *Christopher Sturgeon, Gabriel Sturgeon and Alana Sturgeon v. Condor Flugdienst GmbH* and *Stefan Böck and Cornelia Lepuschitz v. Air France SA*, C-402/07, ECLI:EU:C:2009:416 (Opinion); CJEU, 23 October 2012, *Emeka Nelson e.a. v. Deutsche Lufthansa AG and TUI Travel plc and Others v. Civil Aviation Authority*, C-581/10 and C-629/10, ECLI:EU:C:2012:657; CJEU, 28 January 2016, *Heli Flight v. EASA*, C-61/15, ECLI:EU:C:2016:59; CJEU, 6 June 2018, *Flightright GmbH v. Iberia Express SA*, C-186/17, ECLI:EU:C:2018:399 (Opinion); CJEU, 22 November 2018, *Germanwings GmbH v. Wolfgang Pauels*, C-501/17, ECLI:EU:C:2018:945 (Opinion).
241. CJEU, 7 November 2019, *Adriano Guaitoli, e.a. v. easyJet Airline Co. Ltd*, C-213/18, ECLI:EU:C:2019:927, at 54.

2.3.3 Creating a Level Playing Field Between Different Interests and Actors

2.3.3.1 Prior to the 1999 Montreal Convention

The disparity between national legislations also raised an obstacle for the development of a level playing field between carriers,[242] or in other words, a legal environment that allowed carriers from different origins an equal opportunity to compete on the market, regardless of their financial strength.[243] The *Travaux Préparatoires* of the 1925 Paris Conference are clear on this point:

> Il serait d'autre part utile que toutes les Compagnies de transports fussent placées à ce point de vue sous un régime d'égalité.[244]

In addition, it was necessary to find an equilibrium between the rights of the carriers and their customers.[245] The task was therefore, in the absence of any pre-existing custom,[246] to agree on a set of rules that would be applied internationally to protect, through insurance mechanisms,[247] both the airlines and their passengers. In 1933, this balanced approach was recalled by Dr Yvonne Blanc-Dannery, in her study on the 1929 Warsaw Convention:

> [...] il s'agissait de niveler les différences entre les législations nationales et d'égaliser les conditions d'exploitation entre les compagnies aériennes, en posant une règle uniforme. La difficulté consistait à concilier l'intérêt du transporteur avec celui de l'usager, en évitant d'avantager l'un au détriment de l'autre, de manière à favoriser le développement d'un moyen de locomotion encore nouveau et rempli d'avenir.[248]

This point of equilibrium between industry and passengers' rights has, however, moved over time as technologies have evolved. In 1929, rules were adopted to protect passengers, but did not too heavily restrict the development of civil aviation.[249] In contrast, in 1955, the need to protect the industry started to be less important than the need for passenger compensation. This change of paradigm was highlighted in the *Travaux Préparatoires* of the 1955 Hague Protocol, as follows:

---

242. Jean-Pierre Tosi, *Responsabilité aérienne* 12 (Litec, 1978).
243. The concept of 'Level Playing Field' is regularly used in Competition Law, despite the absence of a clear legal definition. *Black's Law Dictionary* provides the following definition, which will be used in this study: 'All competitors follow the same rules to get equal opportunity to compete regardless of size or financial strength. Economic and legal environment', Source: Black's Law Dictionary, https://thelawdictionary.org/level-playing-field/ (accessed 2 September 2020).
244. Conférence Internationale de Droit Privé Aérien, 27 Octobre-6 Novembre 1925, Paris, 1926, p. 12.
245. *See*, Yvonne Blanc-Dannery, *La Convention de Varsovie et les règles du transport aérien international* 9 (Pedone, 1933).
246. *Ibid.*, p. 6.
247. *Ibid.*, p. 10; ICAO Doc 7838, II Conférence Internationale de Droit Privé Aérien, 4-12 Octobre 1929, *Procès-Verbaux*, Varsovie, 1930, p. 86.
248. Yvonne Blanc-Dannery, *La Convention de Varsovie et les règles du transport aérien international* 9 (Pedone, 1933).
249. Jean-Pierre Tosi, *Responsabilité aérienne* 8 (Litec, 1978).

> Day by day an increase is justified, because this should preserve a just balance between the protection of the passenger and the shipper within reasonable limits and the interest of the development of aviation.[250]

This evolution notwithstanding,[251] this goal of equilibrium has also regularly been acknowledged by Courts, such as in the United States by the Supreme Court in *Tseng*, where the Court underlined that:

> A complementary purpose of the Convention is to accommodate or balance the interests of passengers seeking recovery for personal injuries, and the interests of air carriers seeking to limit potential liability.[252]

Other Courts have also paid great attention to this equilibrium when interpreting the Warsaw Instruments.[253]

2.3.3.2 Under the 1999 Montreal Convention

It was only in 1999 that this purpose of balance was officially written in the fifth paragraph of the preamble of the 1999 Montreal Convention, as follows:

> Convinced that collective State action for further harmonization and codification of certain rules governing international carriage by air through a new Convention is the most adequate means of achieving an equitable balance of interests [...].

The *Travaux Préparatoires* of the 1999 Montreal Convention regularly underline the importance of reaching an acceptable balance between the rights of the different actors, as highlighted here, for example, in the Minutes:

> [...] to seek a balance between the interests of the passengers *i.e.* the users of international air transportation, the carriers, and the general public, to ensure that a great measure of equity would emerge which would command widespread and substantial support and which would enable a greater degree of uniformity and ratifiability,[254]

However, in comparison to the situation that existed beforehand, where carriers in particular needed to be protected as part of an emerging industry, the paradigm shift

250. ICAO Doc 7686, International Conference on Private Air Law, The Hague, September 1955, volume I, *Minutes*, Montreal September 1956, p. 174.
251. *See*, *Eastern Airlines, Inc. v. Floyd et al.*, 499 U.S. 530 (1991), at 546: 'Whatever may be the current view among Convention signatories, in 1929 the parties were more concerned with protecting air carriers and fostering a new industry than providing full recovery to injured passengers [...].'
252. *El Al Israel Airlines, Ltd. v. Tsui Yuan Tseng*, 525 U.S. 155 (1999), at 170.
253. *See*, for example, in the United Kingdom, *Morris v. KLM Royal Dutch Airlines* (2002) UKHL 7, at 66.
254. ICAO Doc 9775, International Conference on Air Law (Convention for the Unification of Certain Rules for International Carriage by Air), Montreal, 10-28 May 1999, volume I, *Minutes*, Montreal 1999, p. 110; *See also*, *Ibid.*, p. 94: '[...] in striking that delicate balance between the interests of the consumer, the interest of the air carrier, and the need to ensure that there were was certainty, predictability and, as far as possible, uniformity in the system, it was necessary to achieve a text which could command widespread and substantial support [...] so that it would indeed be ratifiable'.

already initiated in the 1955 Hague Protocol went even further with the appearance of consumer protection as a notion in the preamble of the 1999 Montreal Convention. The third paragraph of the preamble reads:

> Recognizing the importance of ensuring protection of the interests of consumers in international carriage by air and the need for equitable compensation based on the principle of restitution.

It is necessary to understand how the references to the importance of 'ensuring protection of the interests of consumers' (third paragraph of the preamble of MC99) and the need to achieve 'an equitable balance of interests' (fifth paragraph of the preamble of MC99) work together as they may otherwise create confusion. As translated by the fifth paragraph of its preamble, the 1999 Montreal Convention had a dual purpose of solving a lack of legal certainty and creating a level playing field between different actors and interests. In contrast, the third paragraph of the 1999 Montreal Convention merely mentions a change of paradigm since 1929. Together with the first two paragraphs of the preamble, this third paragraph essentially 'recognizes' the historicity and evolution of the previous instruments. There are, however, decisions that have recognized this third paragraph as a new, additional purpose of the 1999 Montreal Convention.[255]

2.3.4 Concluding Remarks

The analysis of the situation that existed prior to the 1929 Warsaw Convention shows that, *first*, the application of different national legislations created a situation of legal uncertainty that was harming both the airline industry and its customers; *second*, that the disparities between each domestic legislation prevented the development of a level playing field for the different carriers; and, *third*, that the substantial variations between each domestic law created an unsustainable situation, which required finding a balance between the rights of carriers and their customers.

These key issues were acknowledged by the drafters of both the 1929 Warsaw Convention and the 1999 Montreal Convention, and constitute the purposes of the Conventions.

255. *See*, for instance, CJEU, 12 April 2018, *Finnair Oyj v. Keskinäinen Vakuutusyhtiö Fennia*, C-258/16, ECLI:EU:C:2018:252, at 34: 'In addition, in the light both of the third paragraph of the preamble to the Montreal Convention, which emphasises the importance of ensuring protection of the interests of consumers in international carriage by air, and of the principle of "an equitable balance of interests" referred to in the fifth paragraph of the preamble of that convention, the requirement of being in a written form cannot have the effect of excessively limiting the specific way in which a passenger may choose to complain, provided that that passenger remains identifiable as the person who made the complaint.'

2.4 THE OBJECT OF THE CONVENTIONS: UNIFICATION OF CERTAIN RULES THROUGH UNIFORM RULES AND *RENVOIS*

2.4.1 Preliminary Remarks

There remained the question of how to address these purposes in light of the different techniques of approximation of legislation described in Chapter 1. As a reminder, codification was not possible in 1929 due to the absence of extensive State practice, precedent and doctrine.[256]

2.4.2 The Inadequacy of Most Approximation Techniques

A perusal of the *Travaux Préparatoires* shows the drafters never contemplated having recourse to harmonization techniques. The reason behind this may stem from the fact that, in 1929, there was no international organization competent enough to easily suggest specific private air law rules.[257] Indeed, the *Commission Internationale pour la Navigation Aérienne,* established by the 1919 Paris Convention, was not sufficiently competent to regulate private air law matters.[258]

Regarding the other techniques discussed above, recourse to convergence techniques would not have achieved the purposes described in section 2.3. When considering integration techniques, one can easily see how in the aftermath of World War I, it would have been extremely difficult to agree on an international application of the domestic rules of one determined State.

2.4.3 The Adoption of Unification Techniques

In light of the difficulties that other techniques may have entailed, the drafters of both the 1929 Warsaw Convention and the 1999 Montreal Convention opted to adopt certain rules relating to international carriage by air through techniques of unification.

Initially, the adoption of numerous rules of conflict of laws was contemplated by negotiators at the 1925 Paris Conference, which was organized on the initiative of the French government. Its Final Protocol anticipated, among other things, regulating international air carrier liability according to the domestic legislation of the deceased,

256. *See,* section 1.1.2.1. The technique of codification may nevertheless apply to subsequent instruments, such as the 1999 Montreal Convention.
257. *See,* Michael Milde, *International Air Law and ICAO* 266 (Eleven International Publishing, 2008).
258. *See,* Conférence Internationale de Droit Privé Aérien, 27 Octobre-6 Novembre 1925, Paris, 1926, p. 9. The 1919 Paris Convention mostly aimed to recognize the sovereignty of each State in the airspace overlying its territories and waters. *See also,* Vincent Correia, 'The Legacy of the 1919 Paris Convention Relating to the Regulation of Aerial Navigation', in Pablo Mendes de Leon, Niall Buissing (eds), *Behind and Beyond the Chicago Convention: The Evolution of Aerial Sovereignty* 3-24 (Wolters Kluwer, 2019).

subject to specific limitations.[259] However, this solution to common rules of conflict of laws was not entirely satisfactory. *First*, it would not have had the benefit of creating a fair level playing field between different interests and actors.[260] As underlined by Professor Antonio Malintoppi,[261] rules of conflict of laws could leave too much choice to the parties to the contract of carriage in the determination of the applicable law, with the consequence of a benefit to the strongest party, which was a situation that needed to be avoided.[262] *Second*, it would only have partially solved the issue of legal certainty, insofar as the applicable foreign law would not necessarily have been known to, or compatible with, the core values of the laws of the Court seized.[263]

When the preparation of an international convention was entrusted to the CITEJA,[264] it rapidly suggested adopting uniform rules.[265] As described above,[266] uniform rules require the adoption of common rules, but instead of setting common rules of conflicts of laws, common substantive rules are agreed instead.[267] The specificity of these uniform rules helps eliminate the question of determination of applicable law. Additionally, the benefits of this technique of unification through the

259. Article 8 of the 1925 Final Protocol set out: 'Au cas de décès du voyageur transporté, l'action en responsabilité pourra être exercée par les personnes auxquelles cette action appartient d'après la législation nationale du défunt mais sous réserve de la limitation de responsabilité prévue à l'Article précédent'.
260. *See*, Conférence Internationale de Droit Privé Aérien, 27 Octobre-6 Novembre 1925, Paris, 1926, p. 11: 'On atténuerait déjà beaucoup les difficultés naissant du conflit des lois si on parvenait à établir une règle commune de solution du conflit. [...] Mais une telle solution serait bien insuffisante, car tout en supprimant l'incertitude de la solution du conflit des lois, elle laisserait subsister entre les intéressés une différence de traitement tenant à la différence des lois applicables'.
261. In addition to his academic merits, Professor Antonio Malintoppi is also known for being a member of the Italian delegation to the 1955 Hague Conference.
262. Antonio Malintoppi, *Droit uniforme et droit international privé*, 116 Recueil des cours de l'Académie de droit international 9 (1965).
263. *See*, Barry Spitz, *Assessment of the Unification of Private International Air Law by Treaty*, 83 South African Law Journal 176 (1966).
264. *See*, Michel Smirnoff, *Le Comité International Technique d'Experts Juridiques Aériens (CITEJA): Son Activité – Son Organisation* (Pierre Bossuet, 1936).
265. *See*, Conférence Internationale de Droit Privé Aérien, 27 Octobre-6 Novembre 1925, Paris, 1926, p. 42; Yvonne Blanc-Dannery, *La Convention de Varsovie et les règles du transport aérien international* 9 (Pedone, 1933).
266. *See*, section 1.1.2.1(3)(ii).
267. Antonio Malintoppi, *Droit uniforme et droit international privé*, 116 Recueil des cours de l'Académie de droit international 12 (1965): 'C'est justement par rapport à l'unification des règles de fond que l'on préfère utiliser l'expression "droit uniforme", bien que l'unification des règles de droit international privé donne lieu elle aussi à un droit uniforme constitué justement par des règles de droit international privé. En effet, l'adoption de règles uniformes de fond (règles matérielles) assure l'uniformité de la réglementation juridique des faits ou des rapports qui relèvent de l'activité humaine, alors que l'adoption de règles uniformes de droit international privé aboutit seulement à l'uniformité des critères visant le choix de la loi applicable sans pourtant garantir que la réglementation juridique des faits ou rapports envisagés soit elle aussi la même dans les divers systèmes juridiques intéressés. Dans ces conditions, c'est à juste titre que nous pensons devoir utiliser l'expression *droit uniforme* pour désigner les seules règles unifiées de fond'.

adoption of uniform law had already been tested and acknowledged in the rail sector.[268]

The choice made in favour of unification is also confirmed in the title of the Conventions: 'Convention for the Unification'. Although the Conventions contain a couple of rules on the conflict of laws, most of the unification materialized with the adoption of uniform rules.[269] The preamble of the 1929 Warsaw Convention is particularly clear on this point: '[...] ayant reconnu l'utilité de régler d'une manière uniforme [...]'. The preamble of the 1999 Montreal Convention confirms that the same choice governed its adoption, although it uses a different wording: '[...] action for further harmonization and codification of certain rules [...]'. However, the use of the word 'harmonization' in the preamble of the 1999 Montreal Convention was not designed to suggest that this was the solution which ought to be adopted. Indeed, the 1999 Montreal Convention and its predecessors do replace domestic legislations on specific issues, and as such could not be considered to be harmonization tools when recalling the distinction made earlier. This unfortunate new wording may be explained by the fact that, as seen above,[270] techniques of approximation of legislations are still fluid with respect to their terminology.

2.4.4 Concluding Remarks

Given their purpose and what needed to be achieved, the drafters of the 1929 Warsaw Convention and the 1999 Montreal Convention opted for unification to the exclusion of other techniques of approximation of legislations, such as harmonization. While the Conventions essentially contain uniform rules, the drafters also had recourse to rules of conflict of laws through occasional *renvois*. These elements may be considered to be the 'object' of the Conventions when reading the principles of interpretation of the 1969 Vienna Convention.

2.5 SPECIFIC FEATURES OF THE CONVENTIONS

2.5.1 Determining the Scope of 'Uniformity'

The above being clarified and verified, one still needs to ascertain what the adoption of uniform rules entailed in the minds of their drafters. Could it be posited that, in order to fulfil the purposes and object of the Conventions, the unification contemplated demanded a uniform application of the adopted uniform rules?

There is no specific clear-cut provision for this in the Conventions, and the general definition of uniform rules described in Chapter 1 does not per se entail their uniform application.

268. Yvonne Blanc-Dannery, *La Convention de Varsovie et les règles du transport aérien international* 5 (Pedone, 1933).
269. *See*, section 1.1.3.2.
270. *See*, section 1.1.2.

The following analysis will therefore examine the *Travaux Préparatoires* of the Conventions in order to answer this question. The results of that analysis will be checked in the jurisprudence. Finally, should the answer be affirmative, the analysis will try to determine if, despite the lack of a clear provision, specific mechanisms were introduced in the Conventions to ensure their uniform application.

2.5.2 Uniform Application

2.5.2.1 Possible Approaches

The question is to determine whether the Parties' intent was only to create unification through rules that could evolve separately in each ratifying State or if, quite the opposite, in their mind their creation also entailed, as advocated by Professor Daniel Goedhuis in 1937,[271] uniformity of application. Put differently, the analysis should determine whether there was intent to see the rules evolve together into a uniform application;[272] or, similarly to different Civil Codes, they should be allowed to evolve separately despite strictly identical provisions.

2.5.2.2 Travaux Préparatoires

In 1929, particular attention was given to the wording to be used in order to avoid the already recognized potential risk of different interpretations,[273] which could lead to a lack of uniformity.[274] France, for example, voiced an opinion that was strongly in favour of adopting rules that would not automatically result in potential divergent interpretations by Courts:

271. Daniel Goedhuis, *National Airlegislations and the Warsaw Convention* 10 (Springer, 1937): 'It is, however, not sufficient to have uniformity of text but one must have certain guarantees that there also will be uniformity of application.'
272. As developed by Professor Camilla Andersen under the concept of 'jurisconsultorium' alongside the 'textual uniformity'. *See*, Camilla Andersen, *Defining Uniformity in Law*, 12 Uniform Law Review 44 (2007).
273. ICAO Doc 7838, II Conférence Internationale de Droit Privé Aérien, 4-12 Octobre 1929, *Procès-Verbaux*, Varsovie, 1930, p. 41: 'Nous allons alors être soumis à des jurisprudences différentes, si nous n'arrivons pas à assurer l'unité dans un texte obligatoire'. *See also*, ICAO Doc 7838, II Conférence Internationale de Droit Privé Aérien, 4-12 Octobre 1929, *Procès-Verbaux*, Varsovie, 1930, p. 28: 'Le plus grand reproche que j'adresse à la rédaction de l'article 22 tel qu'il est actuellement rédigé, c'est que l'usager ne saura jamais quels sont, à l'égard du transporteurs ses droits et ses recours. C'est en effet un régime très compliqué car, en vertu de l'article 22, il faudra qu'il fasse la preuve de la faute du transporteur. Le transporteur lui-même ne sera cependant pas à l'abri des différences de jurisprudence qui peuvent s'établir devant les tribunaux et les tribunaux peuvent, sous l'empire de certaines doctrines quelquefois nationales, interpréter les textes d'une manière différente. Il arrivera peut-être que ce texte de l'article 22, dans un pays aura une interprétation restrictive et, dans un autre pays, une interprétation libérale: de telle sorte que l'usager se trouvera garanti par telle législation et qu'au contraire il sera découvert dans tel autre pays'.
274. Acknowledging, however, that the interpretation of certain provisions could sometimes be acceptable, such as in the case of factual elements. *See*, section 3.2.4.

> Il y a là une chose qui me paraît impossible de préciser dans la pratique et il y aura certainement de la part de la jurisprudence tantôt une interprétation tantôt une autre. Ce que désire précisément la Délégation française, c'est éviter ces difficultés et elle désire que le vice propre disparaisse aussi bien pour les marchandises que pour les voyageurs.[275]

During the 1955 Hague Conference, while '[a]ir carriers sometimes felt restricted by the ties of that uniformity',[276] emphasis was given to the need to not undermine the existing high level of uniformity. Particular care was therefore requested when suggestions were made to amend the existing phraseology. The United States, notably, pointed out, as reported below, that ambiguity should be avoided as it could increase the risk of undesirable divergent jurisprudence:

> [...] simplification should not be achieved at the expense of clarity. The new language should not be ambiguous and raise legal issues before the courts of different countries, thus placing the entire integrity of the Convention, or of the documentary provisions, in jeopardy.[277]

This objective 'to avoid the risk of having divergent interpretations'[278] was regularly repeated in 1955.[279]

In 1999, the delegates acknowledged that many provisions received conflicting interpretations,[280] which 'did not promote unification of legal rules' and could hence

275. ICAO Doc 7838, II Conférence Internationale de Droit Privé Aérien, 4-12 Octobre 1929, *Procès-Verbaux*, Varsovie, 1930, p. 36.
276. ICAO Doc 7686, International Conference on Private Air Law, The Hague, September 1955, volume I, *Minutes*, Montreal September 1956, p. 60.
277. *Ibid.*, p. 74.
278. *Ibid.*, p. 78.
279. *See*, for example, *Ibid.*, p. 183: '[...] it had to be borne in mind that the Conference was not drawing up national legislation, but an international convention. If the Conference had only to consider Scandinavian legislation, he would consider the Norwegian proposal to be very acceptable. However, he was not convinced that this proposal would be interpreted in the same way all over the world. He feared that the proposal would leave the door open to an escape from the limits in too many countries. That was mainly due to the use of the term "recklessly". What did this term mean in other languages? Was the Conference sure that judges and juries would reach the same decisions in dealing with recklessness?' *Equally, Ibid.*, p. 194: '[The Delegation of Egypt] considered that the drafting of Article 25 of the Convention was defective, since it took into account only the national law of the courts in order to establish wilful misconduct (dol) and ignored the other international sources of law, since wilful misconduct (dol) was not defined in the same way in each one of the national legislations and the Convention applied in 44 Contracting States.' *See also*, Final Act of the 1955 Hague Conference considering uniform interpretation of the convention to be of 'vital importance'.
280. *See*, for instance, ICAO Doc 9775, International Conference on Air Law (Convention for the Unification of Certain Rules for International Carriage by Air), Montreal, 10-28 May 1999, volume I, *Minutes*, Montreal 1999, p. 49: '[...] it would be possible to avoid situations such as those faced in a number of countries where different interpretations were given to the Warsaw Convention on this question'; *Ibid.*, p. 71: 'The present draft did not promote unification of legal rules and the essential terms of the Convention were open to different interpretations that could substantially affect the victim's claim'; *Ibid.*, p. 72: 'The Delegate of Bahrain took the view that in adding mental injury, a clear definition of that notion had to be included to avoid contradictions and conflicts in the interpretation of the text.'

substantially 'affect the victim's claim'.[281] In that sense, discussions and efforts were made to modernize the text to respond to existing fragmentation.[282]

2.5.2.3 Judicial Decisions

In parallel, from an early stage, many Courts recognized the need for a uniform application of the Conventions.

In the UK, the importance of uniform application particularly emerged when the House of Lords ruled that it was 'in the interest of uniformity'[283] to change their practice and to have recourse to the *Travaux Préparatoires* of the 1929 Warsaw Convention, as it was an interpretation means used in other jurisdictions. The Court also highlighted in *Morris* that: '[the Convention] was intended to be applicable in a uniform way across legal boundaries'.[284]

In turn, the CJEU highlighted in *Walz* that given the essence of the 1999 Montreal Convention, the uniform rules should receive a uniform interpretation:

> Since the Montreal Convention does not contain any definition of the term 'damage', it must be emphasised at the outset that, in the light of the aim of that convention, which is to *unify* the rules for international carriage by air, that term must be given a *uniform and autonomous interpretation*, notwithstanding the different meanings given to that concept in the domestic laws of the States Parties to that convention[285] (*italics added*).

On the other side of the Atlantic, the same view was shared by the Supreme Court of the United States in *Franklin*:

> Construction of treaties yielding parochial variations in their implementations are anathema to the *raison d'être* of treaties, and hence to the rules of construction applicable to them.[286]

This requirement was later restated by Justice Marshall in *Floyd*, as follows:

> [...] We have no doubt that subjecting international air carriers to *strict* liability for purely mental distress would be controversial for most signatory countries. Our construction avoids this potential source of divergence.[287]

281. *Ibid.*, p. 71.
282. *Ibid.*, p. 205: 'Since that time the Warsaw Convention had been fragmented into different protocols and into different views, interpretations and jurisdictions. The Conference was making history in consolidating, for the first time, what had been fragmented and by introducing new elements to cope with the vision for the 21st century'; *Ibid.*, p. 83: 'Commenting on Article 18 *(Delay)*, the Representative of China contended that, while some States might have national laws which contained a definition of the term "delay" and jurisprudence on which an interpretation of that term might be based, the lack of a standard definition could lead to a multiplicity of interpretations'; *Ibid.*, p. 178: 'The meeting had tried to better define the concept of a "principal and permanent residence", because in fact this concept was very vague and gave rise to varying interpretations according to different countries. To leave this in the realm of the ambiguous would not be forwarding the cause of unifying international law.'
283. *Fothergill v. Monarch Airlines* (1980) UKHL 6, at 68.
284. *Morris v. KLM Royal Dutch Airlines* (2002) UKHL 7, at 77.
285. CJEU, 6 May 2010, *Axel Walz v. Clickair SA.*, C-63/09, ECLI:EU:C:2010:251, at 21.
286. *Trans World Airlines, Inc. v. Franklin Mint Corp. et. al.*, 466 U.S. 243 (1984), at 263.
287. *Eastern Airlines, Inc. v. Floyd et al.*, 499 U.S. 530 (1991), at 552.

Later, in 2004, Justice Scalia[288] held in *Husain* that:

> When we interpret a treaty, we accord the judgments of our sister signatories 'considerable weight' [...] True to that canon, our previous Warsaw Convention opinions have carefully considered foreign case law.[289]

In Canada, Justice Cromwell pointed out in *Thibodeau* that one should be: 'especially reluctant to depart from any strong international consensus that has developed in relation to its interpretation'.[290]

2.5.2.4 Concluding Remarks

Although no specific provision in the Conventions explicitly provides that they should be uniformly applied, it can legitimately be concluded from their *Travaux Préparatoires*, jurisprudence, and from this analysis of the purposes and object of the Conventions, that they should. As noted by Professor Camille Andersen in her study on uniform law:

> [...] practitioners applying any international uniform convention must recognise that they share it with colleagues in other jurisdictions, and that its development is a communal evolution requiring a unique approach very different from the (differing) applications of domestic law in varying jurisdictions.[291]

A uniform application hence entails: *first*, determining existing case law not only in one's jurisdiction but also abroad and *second*, refraining from departing from any existing internationally endorsed jurisprudence.

2.5.3 Mechanisms Used to Ensure a Uniform Application

2.5.3.1 The Selection of Mechanisms

Despite the fact that no specific provision in the Conventions clearly lays out that each of them should be uniformly applied across their ratifying States, one could wonder if any specific mechanisms were nevertheless foreseen by their drafters.

The following analysis will be dedicated to the concepts of exclusivity and autonomy that might be found in the Conventions. In order to give these concepts shape in the framework of the Conventions, I will particularly refer to their *Travaux Préparatoires*, and judicial decisions.

288. Dissenting.
289. *Olympic Airways v. Husain, Individually, and as Personal Representative of the Estate of Hanson, Deceased, et al.*, 540 U.S. 644 (2004), at 658.
290. *Thibodeau v. Air Canada* (2014) 3 SCR 340, at 50.
291. Camilla Andersen, *Defining Uniformity in Law*, 12 Uniform Law Review 44-45 (2007).

2.5.3.2 Exclusivity

(1) Introduction

The 1929 Warsaw Convention and 1999 Montreal Convention both contain provisions which aim to guarantee the exclusive application of certain of their provisions. Article 24 of the 1929 Warsaw Convention reads as follows:

> 1. In the cases covered by Articles 18 and 19 any action for damages, however founded, can only be brought subject to the conditions and limits set out in this Convention.
> 2. In the cases covered by Article 17 the provisions of the preceding paragraph also apply, without prejudice to the questions as to who are the persons who have the right to bring suit and what are their respective rights.[292]

The text was slightly amended in the 1971 Guatemala City Protocol, as set out here:

> 1. In the carriage of cargo, any action for damages, however founded, can only be brought subject to the conditions and limits set out in this Convention.
> 2. In the carriage of passengers and baggage any action for damages, however founded, whether under this Convention or in contract or in tort or otherwise, can only be brought subject to the conditions and limits of liability set out in this Convention without prejudice to the question as to who are the persons who have the right to bring suit and what are their respective rights. Such limits of liability constitute maximum limits and may not be exceeded whatever the circumstances which gave rise to the liability.[293]

It was later changed again in the 1975 Montreal Protocol No 4, as follows:

> 1. In the carriage of passengers and baggage, any action for damages, however founded, can only be brought subject to the conditions and limits set out in this Convention, without prejudice to the question as to who are the persons who have the right to bring suit and what are their respective rights.
> 2. In the carriage of cargo, any action for damages, however founded, whether under this Convention or in contract or in tort or otherwise, can only be brought subject to the conditions and limits of liability set out in this Convention without prejudice to the question as to who are the persons who have the right to bring suit and what are their respective rights. Such limits of liability constitute maximum limits and may not be exceeded whatever the circumstances which gave rise to the liability.[294]

292. In the French version: '1. Dans les cas prévus aux articles 18 et 19 toutes actions en responsabilité, à quelque titre que ce soit, ne peut être exercée que dans les conditions et limites prévues par la présente Convention. 2. Dans les cas prévus à l'article 17, s'appliquent également les dispositions de l'alinéa précédent, sans préjudice de la détermination des personnes qui ont le droit d'agir et de leurs droits respectifs'.
293. 1971 Guatemala City Protocol, Article IX.
294. 1975 Montreal Protocol No 4, Article VIII.

Finally, Article 29 of the 1999 Montreal Convention now sets out that:

> In the carriage of passengers, baggage and cargo, any action for damages, however founded, whether under this Convention or in contract or in tort or otherwise, can only be brought subject to the conditions and such limits of liability as are set out in this Convention without prejudice to the question as to who are the persons who have the right to bring suit and what are their respective rights. In any such action, punitive, exemplary or any other non-compensatory damages shall not be recoverable.

Similar provisions may also be found in various Uniform Instruments. This is the case, for example, in the 1952 Rome Convention,[295] in the CMR,[296] and in the 1974 PAL.[297] But such provisions are not found in every Uniform Instrument. For instance, no such provision was included in the Hamburg Rules or in the Rotterdam Rules. Moreover, there exist Uniform Instruments that specifically reject any automatic exclusivity to their rules, such as the United Nations Convention on Contracts for the International Sale of Goods (hereinafter the '**CISG**')[298] which, under its Article 6, provides that:

> The parties may exclude the application of this Convention or, subject to article 12, derogate from or vary the effect of any of its provisions.

The presence of such provisions in the 1929 Warsaw Convention and in the 1999 Montreal Convention therefore raises the question of their role. In other words, could it be that, in the mind of their drafters, the principle of primacy of international law over domestic legislation[299] was not deemed sufficient to achieve the aim of uniformity?

(2) Travaux Préparatoires

(i) Prior to the 1999 Montreal Convention

Whereas the Final Protocol to the 1925 Paris Conference provided under its Article 8 that:

---

295. 1952 Rome Convention, Article 9: 'Neither the operator, the owner, any person liable under Article 3 or Article 4, nor their respective servants or agents, shall be liable for damage on the surface caused by an aircraft in flight or any person or thing falling therefrom otherwise than as expressly provided in this Convention. This rule shall not apply to any such person who is guilty of a deliberate act or omission done with the intent to cause damage.'
296. CMR, Article 28: '1. In cases where, under the law applicable, loss, damage or delay arising out of carriage under this Convention gives rise to an extra-contractual claim, the carrier may avail himself of the provisions of this Convention which exclude his liability or which fix or limit the compensation due. 2. In cases where the extra-contractual liability for loss, damage or delay of one of the persons for whom the carrier is responsible under the terms of article 3 is in issue, such person may also avail himself of the provisions of this Convention which exclude the liability of the carrier or which fix or limit the compensation due.'
297. 1974 PAL, Article 14: 'No action for damages for the death of or personal injury to a passenger, or for the loss of or damage to luggage, shall be brought against a carrier or performing carrier otherwise than in accordance with this Convention.'
298. United Nations Convention on Contracts for the International Sale of Goods, 11 April 1980, Vienna, UNTS, 1489, I-25567, entry in force 1 January 1988.
299. *See*, section 2.5.3.2.

> Au cas de décès du voyageur transporté, l'action en responsabilité pourra être exercée par les personnes auxquelles cette action appartient d'après la législation nationale du défunt, mais sous réserve de la limitation de responsabilité prévue à l'Article précédent.[300]

No explicit indication on the reasons behind the adoption of such an exclusivity clause can be found in the *Travaux Préparatoires* of the 1929 Warsaw Convention.

During the 1971 Guatemala City Conference, the possibility of breaking the pecuniary limits was discussed and eventually rejected.[301] As reproduced below, the IATA Observer underscored that the new wording of Article 24 particularly aimed to prevent this situation from happening:

> He thought, however, that the Drafting Committee might consider the insertion of a clause, perhaps in Article 24, along the following lines: 'The liability of carrier as established under Articles 17 to 22 of this Convention shall be the sole and exclusive liability of carrier under all circumstances in respect of damage arising out of an event giving rise to liability for the death or injury or delay of a passenger or destruction, loss, damage or delay of baggage.'[302]

The same fear appeared during the 1975 Montreal Conference:

> The Director of the Legal Bureau, in explaining the background, said that the basic question was whether the limits should be unbreakable under all circumstances. The Legal Committee, meeting prior to the Conference at Guatemala City by which the principle of unbreakability was enshrined in the Guatemala City Protocol, had examined up to eight different formulas for consecrating the unbreakability of limits and it was concluded that the best formula was the one that appeared in the text of the Guatemala City Protocol. Consequently, the Legal Committee, in drawing up the draft text on the cargo provisions, was inspired by this solution and considered it necessary to cover all kinds of suits – in contract, or in tort or otherwise – and to maintain the last phrase in draft Article E to the effect that the limits may not be exceed 'whatever the circumstances which gave rise to the liability'.[303]

The reason behind the new formula adopted during this Conference may be found in this statement, made by the delegate of the UK as follows:

> As to the proposal made by the Delegate of the Czechoslovak Socialist Republic, its acceptance would certainly destroy the Warsaw Convention for the common law countries, because an action for loss of or damage to cargo could, at the choice of the claimant in those countries, be founded on contract, or in tort or delict. Therefore, if it were left open to the claimant to escape the provisions of the Convention by basing his action on tort or delict, then one might as well have no

300. Conférence Internationale de Droit Privé Aérien, 27 Octobre-6 Novembre 1925, Paris, 1926, p. 79.
301. ICAO Doc 9040, International Conference on Air Law, Guatemala City, February-March 1971, volume I, *Minutes*, Montreal, 1972, p. 144.
302. *Ibid.*, p. 142.
303. ICAO Doc 9154, International Conference on Air Law, Montreal, September 1975, volume I, *Minutes*, Montreal, 1977, p. 164.

> convention at all so far as the common law countries were concerned, which might also be true for some other countries.[304]

The analysis of the *Travaux Préparatoires* suggests that the reasons for such a principle of exclusivity existing may be that the respective drafters wished to ensure domestic law would not jeopardize the uniform rules, and particularly the liability limits set out in the text. It can also be deduced that they did not wish for domestic legislations to threaten the purposes of the 1929 Warsaw Convention.

(ii) Under the 1999 Montreal Convention

The *Travaux Préparatoires* of the 1999 Montreal Convention give a more detailed explanation of the *raison d'être* of this principle of exclusivity. In the Minutes, the Chairman observed that:

> [...] the Convention, which primarily addressed the liability question of limits, had been careful to provide in Article 23 (Basis of Claims) that an action for damages - however founded - could only be brought on the condition and subject to the limits of liability without prejudice to the question as to who were the persons who had the right to bring the suit and what were their respective rights. Article 23 in effect put fences around how great an exposure the carrier would be liable to, by ensuring that whatever may be the nature of the action and however brought, it was subject to the conditions of the Convention. The more delicate issues as to the persons who had the right to bring the action were not really governed as such by the Convention, but were left to national law, subject only to the provision that one remained within the limits set by the Convention and the conditions subject to which the claims may be brought.[305]

Later, he recalled that:

> The purpose behind Article 28 was to ensure that, in circumstances in which the Convention applied, it was not possible to circumvent its provisions by bringing an action for damages in the carriage of passengers, baggage and cargo in contract or in tort or otherwise. Once the Convention applied, its conditions and limits of liability were applicable.[306]

The Minutes of the 1999 Montreal Convention also confirm that the rules laid down in the Convention may be different from those established under domestic law, but in the case of competition between these rules, the uniform rules should prevail:

> The Chairman observed that it was quite true that, in domestic jurisdictions, the system of evidence which was required and the burden of proof would be provided for under national legislation. However, if the draft Convention were adopted, then its provisions would have to be applied in relation to this question. The

304. *Ibid.*, p. 165.
305. ICAO Doc 9775, International Conference on Air Law (Convention for the Unification of Certain Rules for International Carriage by Air), Montreal, 10-28 May 1999, volume I, *Minutes*, Montreal 1999, p. 189.
306. *Ibid.*, p. 235.

> provisions contained in Article 23 (*Basis of Claims*)[307] made it clear that an action which was brought for damages, however founded, whether under the new Convention or in contract or tort or otherwise, could only be brought subject to the conditions and such limits of liability as were set out in the Convention. There was indeed jurisprudence which suggested that it was exclusive. It was not possible to get around the provisions of the Convention regarding the burden of proof, etc., by bringing an action in tort or by attempting to bring an action outside the Convention, if one were a party to the Convention – it would be expected that every party, in order to implement the Convention, would introduce domestic legislation which would be applicable in its Courts. Thus whereas it was quite true that in most jurisdictions the burden of proof would lie on those who asserted claims, when the new Convention was adopted its rules would apply so as to modify whatever might be the system in domestic legislation in terms of claims which were brought under the Convention, even claims which were brought outside of the Convention, insofar as they were based on damage sustained in the carriage of passengers, which would be covered by the Convention. [...].[308]

Therefore, the principle of exclusivity may have been adopted in order to guarantee a uniform application of the international air carrier liability regime, and to ensure the primacy of the Conventions over domestic legislation.[309] But this explanation may not be sufficient, given that the risk of domestic law overriding the 1999 Montreal Convention is already partially foreseen under Article 49, which provides that:

> Any clause contained in the contract of carriage and all special agreements entered into before the damage occurred by which the parties purport to infringe the rules laid down by this Convention, whether by deciding the law to be applied, or by altering the rules as to jurisdiction, shall be null and void.

Consequently, it cannot be ruled out that application of the principle of exclusivity may also imply that the carrier liability could be limited to the situations covered by their Articles 17, 18 and/or 19,[310] provided the Conventions apply pursuant to their Article 1.[311] It would then follow that if the Conventions apply, but a claim for bodily injury, damage to cargo or even a delay does not meet each of the conditions set forth respectively in these three latter Articles, the carrier could then not be held liable,

307. Renumbered in the adopted text.
308. ICAO Doc 9775, International Conference on Air Law (Convention for the Unification of Certain Rules for International Carriage by Air), Montreal, 10-28 May 1999, volume I, *Minutes*, Montreal 1999, p. 137.
309. These provisions nevertheless leave a certain role to domestic law. Article 29 of the 1999 Montreal Convention makes a *renvoi* to domestic law with respect to the determination of persons who have the right to bring suit, for instance, the legal representative of a minor, and, regarding the extent of their rights, such as whether non-economic damages can be claimed provided the compensation does not exceed the limits established in the 1999 Montreal Convention.
310. *See*, Chapter 3.
311. 1929 Warsaw Convention, Article 1(1): 'This Convention applies to all international carriage of persons, luggage or goods performed by aircraft for reward. It applies equally to gratuitous carriage by aircraft performed by an air transport undertaking'; 1999 Montreal Convention, Article 1(1): 'This Convention applies to all international carriage of persons, baggage or cargo performed by aircraft for reward. It applies equally to gratuitous carriage by aircraft performed by an air transport undertaking.'

under the Conventions or domestic law. This 'strict application of the principle of exclusivity' may be seconded by the facts that such a principle is not found in every Uniform Instrument and that, otherwise, it would be a duplicate of Article 49 and the principle of *pacta sunt servanda*.[312] This view may also be supported by the purposes of the Conventions, which are to provide for an international air carrier liability regime that is predictable and balanced. However, it is not clear at first sight how this view may accommodate the existence of the exclusion clauses as described in Chapter 1.[313]

(3) Judicial Decisions

The exclusivity of the Conventions is a powerful protection against the risk of undesirable interferences made by Courts with domestic legislations. Such interferences could lead to a significant fragmentation of the envisaged uniform rules.

However, Courts hold divergent views on how exclusivity should be understood. This point will be explored in Chapter 4.

(4) Concluding Remarks

In light of the preceding analysis, it may be concluded that, despite the different possible readings of Article 24 of the 1929 Warsaw Convention and Article 29 of the 1999 Montreal Convention, the principle of exclusivity may have been envisaged by their drafters at least as a powerful tool to guarantee the consistency of the system and to prevent the undesirable intrusion of domestic law. Its role as a mechanism to ensure a uniform application of the Conventions may be deduced from this.

2.5.3.3 The Autonomy of the Terms Used

(1) Introduction

In legal theory, the autonomy of certain international instruments vis-à-vis the international legal order was discussed at the turn of the millennium by the ILC.[314] Among other questions was a discussion of whether 'Self-Contained Regimes'[315] did exist, and whether they were a source of fragmentation of international law. However, insofar as the 1969 Vienna Convention provides a unifying frame for every treaty, the existence of fully self-contained regimes appears unlikely. Notwithstanding the above,

---

312. 1969 Vienna Convention, Article 26.
313. *See*, section 1.1.3.2(4)(ii). *See also*, Chapter 4.
314. *See*, United Nations, 'Fragmentation of International Law: Difficulties Arising from the Diversification and Expansion of International Law', in *Report of the International Law Commission on the Work of Its Fifty-Eighth Session*, II(2) Yearbook of the International Law Commission 179 (2006).
315. Although there is no generally accepted definition of a Self-Contained regime, Professor Eckart Klein suggests that they intend to replace and, in doing so, exclude the application of general international law. *See*, Eckart Klein, *Self-Contained Regime* 2 (Max Planck Encyclopedias of International Law, 2006).

one can wonder whether the Conventions could be qualified as a *lex specialis*[316] that depart from general international law to such a degree that the terms and concepts used therein should be interpreted independently from any potential meaning under domestic law, and from any possible definition given in other international instruments, with the exception of those laid out in the 1969 Vienna Convention.

The following examination will try to determine how the drafters of the Conventions intended the terms used to be interpreted, if they were supposed to be interpreted in an autonomous manner and if so, to what extent.[317]

(2) Travaux Préparatoires

The *Travaux Préparatoires* of the 1929 Warsaw Convention show that the aim of uniformity was probably one of the most difficult tasks to achieve. It required each participant to negotiate and to settle on points of law that departed from their domestic law and to accept a common international rule. This mission of compromise was described by the Rapporteur as follows:

> Une convention n'est faite et n'existe que par des concessions mutuelles. Une convention serait absolument inutile si tous les systèmes nationaux étaient équivalents. Dès lors, le CITEJA a compris qu'en cette matière toute nouvelle les législations sont jeunes et rares, que l'on pouvait déjà rédiger des textes sans parti pris, sans vouloir faire accepter tel ou tel système juridique, mais construire une œuvre moderne, dans l'équilibre et la liberté![318]

This difficult exercise was, however, guided by the will to reach uniformity, even if this entailed a departure from domestic law and customs, as recalled by the UK in these words:

> En ce qui concerne le Gouvernement britannique, la seule raison qu'il ait d'entrer dans cette convention est le désir d'atteindre l'uniformité. [...] Le projet de convention est contraire, sur plusieurs points à nos lois et à nos coutumes, mais nous sommes décidés à faire des sacrifices pour obtenir cette uniformité de régime.[319]

In 1955, the same dynamic drove negotiations.[320] Speaking for the Netherlands, Professor Daniel Goedhuis stated that uniformity was 'vital' even if 'conflicting views

316. *See*, Vincent Correia, 'L'adage lex specialis derogat generali: Réflexions générales sur sa nature, sa raison d'être et ses conditions d'application', in Muriel Ubéda-Saillard (ed.), *La mise en œuvre de la lex specialis dans le droit international contemporain* 27-47 (Pedone, 2017).
317. *See*, for the autonomy of air law in general, Pablo Mendes de Leon, *Introduction to Air Law* 4 (10th edition, Wolters Kluwer, 2017).
318. ICAO Doc 7838, II Conférence Internationale de Droit Privé Aérien, 4-12 Octobre 1929, *Procès-Verbaux*, Varsovie, 1930, p. 14.
319. *Ibid.*, p. 25. *See also*, *Ibid.*, p. 58: 'L'objet de cette convention est d'assurer l'uniformité du droit et si on insère une clause de ce genre, il y aura quantité d'évasions de la convention qui se produiront'.
320. For example, on the discussion over the concept of contributory negligence that could sometimes lead to a reduction of liability, the United States expressed opposition to any change, since: '[...] a change requiring uniformity in the form proposed would have the effect of

have been expressed as to how the conditions of a uniform application of the rules can best be maintained'.[321] The need for an autonomous dimension of the concepts and terms used therein was notably voiced by the Portuguese delegation, as follows:

> [...] since in making reference to the notion of diligence, it destroyed, to a certain extent, the unity of the law of air transport. There were differences concerning this notion, in internal laws, particularly in the field of proof.[322]

In order to ensure the autonomous dimension, the representative for Italy set out that any reference to domestic concepts should be avoided, with the consequence that, for instance, the notion of 'dol/wilful misconduct' must be explained rather than quoted *expressis verbis*.[323] The representative for Germany also endorsed this view, arguing that: '[...] it was necessary to omit the reference to national laws in order to obtain a uniform substantive rule'.[324]

Forty-five years later, the need for uniformity had not changed. However, further efforts were requested in light of increased regime complexity in 1999, as highlighted by the President of the Council of the ICAO:

> [...] it is the shared desire of the parties involved that legal certainty and uniformity be restored, while implementing, in a globally-coordinated fashion, the long overdue modernization and consolidation for the system.[325]

changing the laws of his country', ICAO Doc 7686, International Conference on Private Air Law, The Hague, September 1955, volume I, *Minutes*, Montreal September 1956, p. 262.

321. ICAO Doc 7686, International Conference on Private Air Law, The Hague, September 1955, volume I, *Minutes*, Montreal September 1956, p. 8: '[...] there is nobody here who does not realize that, unless uniformity in the matter of the air carrier's liability can be maintained, the sound development of international aviation will be retarded. Though opinion is unanimous that uniformity is vital, conflicting views have been expressed as to how the conditions of a uniform application of the rules can best be maintained'.
322. *Ibid.*, p. 96.
323. *Ibid.*, p. 168: 'Those proposals adopted approximately the Anglo-Saxon concept of "wilful misconduct" which, in his opinion, represented a happy meeting of the Roman notions of *dol* and *faute lourde* (gross negligence) which could be compared with *dol*, that is, only the most serious cases of *faute lourde* (gross negligence). In that regard, the President of the Conference in his excellent work on the Warsaw Convention had rightly written that there should be an assimilation to *dol* only in the case where the *faute lourde* (gross negligence) gave the same impression of immorality as *dol*. Consequently, he was in principle in favour of the old text of the Warsaw Convention which referred to serious default and *dol*, however, with the deletion from Article 25 of the Convention of all reference to national laws for reasons of uniformity.' *See also*, the comments made by Spain, *Ibid.*, p. 195: 'If it succeeded in finding a formula which was sufficiently explanatory, there could be no criticism from the point of view of legislative systems, since the Conference would have succeeded in a labour of uniformity and achieved a text which national judges would have to follow whatever might be the concept which existed in their respective national legislations concerning wilful misconduct (*dol*) and gross negligence (*faute lourde*).'
324. *Ibid.*, p. 171.
325. ICAO Doc 9775, International Conference on Air Law (Convention for the Unification of Certain Rules for International Carriage by Air), Montreal, 10-28 May 1999, volume I, *Minutes*, Montreal 1999, p. 37.

The efforts to ensure that air law, as universal law, be uniform[326] required yet again a distancing from domestic laws.[327] The Chairman expressed the view that the upcoming regime had to be 'sui generis',[328] that is to say:

> [...] a unique regime, taking into account all passengers-related considerations. It was not trying to approximate, or making it equivalent to, any regime which existed in domestic jurisdictions. The draft Convention had its own regime of liability, different from domestic jurisdiction; it had its own limitations as to the time within which an action could be brought and its own defences. It was different.[329]

It results therefrom that the autonomy of the terms used in the Conventions was clearly a special feature envisaged by their drafters to encourage their uniform application.

(3) Judicial Decisions

Courts have regularly confirmed the autonomous dimension associated with the wish of uniformity of the Conventions.

In *Thibodeau*, the Supreme Court of Canada summarized the reasons for the creation of uniform rules:

> The *Warsaw Convention* (and therefore its successor the *Montreal Convention*) had three main purposes: to create uniform rules governing claims arising from international air transportation; to protect the international air carriage industry by limiting carrier liability; and to balance that protective goal with the interests of

326. *See*, *Ibid.*, p. 46.
327. A striking example of the changes entailed by the adoption of uniform rules can be found in the Chairman's speech on the possible adoption of a fifth jurisdiction and its interaction with the common law principle of forum non conveniens: '[...] it remained to be determined whether or not the principle of *forum non conveniens*, as formulated, would only be applicable to the fifth jurisdiction. One side of the coin was that it might be appropriate to codify the rather general provision in relation to the entire jurisdictional issue. To the point raised by the Delegate of the United States that the imposition of that alien concept [...] might pose jurisdictional problems, [...] the Group was involved in the process of seeking uniformity. It therefore seemed inadmissible to devise a special scheme of liability predicated on the fact that ultimately adjustments would have to be made in domestic jurisdictions. [...] the need to decide whether or not, in the search for predictability and uniformity, it was necessary to forge those bridges of understanding which would be required. It was a difficult matter, as all Delegates, in their search for common solutions, would be faced with the question of how to modify their respective domestic legislation. [...] in some jurisdictions the concept of *forum non conveniens* might not exist in a particular form, as well as that many of the elements of the Convention relating to the burden of proof, what was required to be proved and the limits of liability also did not exist in the domestic legislation of many countries, [...] it would be necessary to make adjustments to such legislation in order to achieve uniformity', *Ibid.*, pp. 159-160.
328. *Ibid.*, p. 142: 'However, in terms of the practical negotiations of what the Conference was attempting to achieve in arriving at a proposal which would command the widespread and substantial support required for a package, there was a sense of creating a regime which was *sui generis* having within it, elements which, taken in isolation, might raise even more difficult problems for the jurisprudential purity of the document, but nonetheless would satisfy the ultimate objective of ensuring that a balance would be achieved.'
329. *Ibid.*, p. 115.

> passengers and others seeking recovery. These purposes responded to concerns that many legal regimes might apply to international carriage by air with the result that there could be no uniformity or predictability with respect to either carrier liability or the rights of passengers and others using the service. Both passengers and carriers were potentially harmed by this lack of uniformity.[330]

In the UK, the House of Lords confirmed in *Morris* that: '[...] the basic concepts it employs to achieve its purpose are autonomous concepts'.[331] In *Re Deep Vein Thrombosis,* Lord Scott of Foscote pointed out that the: '[...] the language of the Convention should not be interpreted by reference to domestic law principles or domestic rules of interpretation'.[332]

In Ireland, the Supreme Court highlighted that: '[...] terms in the Convention should receive, as far as practicable, an autonomous Convention meaning'.[333]

The CJEU also recognized the specific nature of the 1999 Montreal Convention in several decisions.[334] In *Walz*, it held notably that:

> [...] in the light of the aim of that convention, which is to unify the rules for international carriage by air, that term must be given a uniform and autonomous interpretation, notwithstanding the different meanings given to that concept in the domestic laws of the States Parties to that convention.[335]

The Supreme Court of the United States, however, has not explicitly confirmed the autonomous dimension of unification rules used in the Conventions. Yet it could be implicitly deducted from the reasoning of several of its decisions such as in *Floyd*[336] or in *Tseng.*[337]

Chapter 4 will carry out a more detailed examination of the interpretation and application of 'autonomy' in judicial decisions.

(4) Concluding Remarks

This analysis indicates that the drafters of the Conventions expected that the terms used therein would receive an autonomous interpretation in order to guarantee their uniform application.

330. *Thibodeau v. Air Canada* (2014) 3 SCR 340, at 41. This decision however does not distinguish the objectives and the purposes of the Conventions as done in this study.
331. *Morris v. KLM Royal Dutch Airlines* (2002) UKHL 7, at 16.
332. *Re Deep Vein Thrombosis and Air Travel Group Litigation* (2005) UKHL 72, at 11.
333. *AHP Manufacturing B.V. t/a Wyeth Medica Ireland v. DHL Worldwide Network N.V., DHL Worldwide Express GmbH, DHL International (Ireland) Limited* (2001) IESC 71.
334. *See*, as examples, CJEU, 7 November 2019, *Adriano Guaitoli, e.a. v. easyJet Airline Co. Ltd*, C-213/18, ECLI:EU:C:2019:927, at 47; CJEU, 19 December 2019, *GN v. ZU acting for Niki Luftfahrt*, C-532/18, ECLI:EU:C:2019:1127, at 32.
335. CJEU, 6 May 2010, *Axel Walz v. Clickair SA.*, C-63/09, ECLI:EU:C:2010:251, at 21.
336. *Eastern Airlines, Inc. v. Floyd et al.*, 499 U.S. 530 (1991), at 552: 'Moreover, we believe our construction of Article 17 better accords with the Warsaw Convention's stated purpose of achieving uniformity of rules governing claims arising from international air transportation.'
337. *El Al Israel Airlines, Ltd. v. Tsui Yuan Tseng*, 525 U.S. 155 (1999), at 169: 'Given the Convention's comprehensive scheme of liability rules and its contextual emphasis on uniformity, we would be hard put to conclude that the delegates at Warsaw meant to subject air carriers to the distinct, nonuniform liability rules of the individual signatory nations.'

From this, it can be concluded that the drafters considered the liability regime of the Convention as sui generis, meaning the terms set out therein should be considered to be 'autonomous' – if we refer to the vocabulary used by the Courts – from those used in domestic law. This also confirms the fact that the origin of uniform rules should not be sought in any legal system, such as continental or common law or even in Sharia,[338] even though their drafters may have been educated in such systems.[339]

In my opinion, the fact that the *Travaux Préparatoires* described the liability regime of the Conventions as sui generis also implies that the terms used in the Conventions should not be interpreted with reference to other international instruments. This view is strengthened by the conclusions of the ILC, which indicated that the interpretation and applications of special regimes should particularly reflect their own purposes and object.[340]

2.5.3.4 The Applicability of These Mechanisms to the Rules of **Renvois**

The examination started from the postulation that exclusivity and autonomy mechanisms applied to both uniform rules and the rules of *renvois*, but is this really the case for the latter? The answer is not self-evident. Nevertheless, the purposes and object of the Conventions, together with the analysis carried out of their special features, show how much uniformity was a predominant aim for the drafters of the Conventions.

Authoritative authors confirm the autonomy of terms and concepts used in other international private law instruments containing rules of *renvois*.[341] The *Travaux Préparatoires* of the 1999 Montreal Convention also demonstrate, as quoted below, that efforts were made to provide for autonomous terms and concepts when rules of *renvois* would be at stake:

> [...] on the one hand, there had been an American notion, memorialized in prior instruments, of 'domicile' of the passenger while, on the other hand, there had been the French concept of *domicile*, which was also reflected in prior instruments. It had been apparent to all Members of the Special Group that the use of those terms in the identical location had been producing a non-uniform result. They had thus worked diligently to try to find a suitable formulation of words which was not based on nationality and which would bridge the gap between 'domicile' and *domicile*. With great good will on both sides, the Special Group had come up with

338. *See*, on this topic, Hamid Kazemi, *Carrier's Liability in Air Transport with Particular Reference to Iran* (Thesis, Universiteit Leiden, 2012).
339. *See*, Michel de Juglart, Emmanuel du Pontavice, Jacqueline Dutheil de la Rochère, Georgette Miller, *Traité de droit aérien* 942 (2nd edition, LGDJ, 1989).
340. *See*, United Nations, 'Fragmentation of International Law: Difficulties Arising from the Diversification and Expansion of International Law', in *Report of the International Law Commission on the Work of Its Fifty-Eighth Session*, II(2) Yearbook of the International Law Commission 179 (2006): '(13) *Effet of the "Speciality" of a regime*. The significance of a special regime often lies in the way its norms express a unified object and purpose. Thus, their interpretation and application should, to the extent possible, reflect that object and purpose.'
341. *See*, for example, Karine Parrot, *L'interprétation des conventions de droit international privé* (Dalloz, 2006); Richard Gardiner, *Treaty Interpretation* 33 (2nd edition, The Oxford International Law Library, 2017); François Rigaux, Marc Fallon, *Droit international privé* 185, 340 (Larcier, 2005).

'principal and permanent residence', considered by both sides at the time to be a reasonable compromise, although not an ideal solution from their respective perspectives.[342]

For these reasons, it is not unreasonable to consider that the terms and concepts used in the rules of *renvois* of the 1999 Montreal Convention must also be uniformly applied.

The question of the exclusivity of the rules of *renvois* is somewhat more delicate. At first glance, the lack of such exclusivity would result in opposing the *renvois* set out in the 1999 Montreal Convention to other rules of *renvois* foreseen in domestic legislation or another international convention. However, the wording of Article 29 of the Montreal Convention suggests the non-application of the exclusivity of its rules only with respect to 'the question as to who are the persons who have the right to bring suit and what are their respective rights'. The determination of their respective rights is, however, limited by the existence of the 1999 Montreal Convention.[343] A confirmation of this view may be found in the *Travaux Préparatoires*, where they indicate that:

> The more delicate issues as to the persons who had the right to bring the action were not really governed as such by the Convention, but were left to national law, subject only to the provision that one remained within the limits set by the Convention and the conditions subject to which the claims may be brought.[344]

Considering if exclusivity did not apply to the rules of *renvois*, it would undermine the purposes and object of the 1999 Montreal Convention, it is therefore reasonable to conclude that the exclusivity clause is a mechanism also used to guarantee the uniformity in the application of the rules of *renvois* established by the 1999 Montreal Convention.

2.6 CONCLUSIONS

The disparities between the legislations on air carrier liability that existed before the adoption of the 1929 Warsaw Convention led to a lack of legal certainty and the lack of a level playing field between the different parties involved in international air carriage. Among the different options that could have been contemplated to rectify this undesirable situation, the CITEJA and delegates to the 1929 Warsaw Conference opted for a unified regime through essentially the adoption of uniform rules.

These unification rules can be defined as particularly distinct from any harmonization rules, insofar as they do not merely adapt domestic rules but jointly create new

342. ICAO Doc 9775, International Conference on Air Law (Convention for the Unification of Certain Rules for International Carriage by Air), Montreal, 10-28 May 1999, volume I, *Minutes*, Montreal 1999, p. 153.
343. *See*, for example, Laurent Chassot, *Les sources de la responsabilité du transporteur aérien international: entre conflit et complémentarité: La Convention de Montréal et son interaction avec le droit européen et national* 133, 210 et seq. (Schulthess, 2012).
344. ICAO Doc 9775, International Conference on Air Law (Convention for the Unification of Certain Rules for International Carriage by Air), Montreal, 10-28 May 1999, volume I, *Minutes*, Montreal 1999, pp. 189-190.

rules under the form of an international convention, which prevails over domestic legislation, notably through an exclusivity clause and the use of autonomous terms. They should be considered as evolving distinctly from domestic, international or other uniform law frameworks. The sustainability of their existence is, however, dependent on their uniform application by Courts.

As has now been demonstrated, the drafters intended to provide a uniform application of the Conventions. The question that remains is whether the exclusivity clause and the principle of autonomy were sufficient to achieve this predominant aim of uniformity.

Chapters 3 and 4 will determine whether specific factors may have prevented the Conventions from being uniformly applied.

CHAPTER 3

Internal Factors of Fragmentation

3.1 INTRODUCTION

This chapter is designed to determine whether, at the time of the signing of the Conventions, specific factors already existed that may have prevented them from being uniformly applied. In order to answer this question, the analysis will examine any drafting factors that could potentially have obstructed the uniform application of the Conventions (section 3.2). The discussion will then assess whether or not other factors may have prevented the Conventions' uniform application from the moment of signing (section 3.3).

3.2 DRAFTING FACTORS

3.2.1 Preliminary Remarks

The art of writing legal texts, or *légistique* as it is called in French, is complex. Many documents explain how a bill or legal text should be written in order to avoid possible confusion, and the need for recourse to interpretation mechanisms. As the law must be clear and predictable to fulfil its role,[345] many techniques are applied during drafting.[346]

At the level of the EU, the Joint Practical Guide for persons involved in the drafting of EU legislation is a very useful kit that states:

> The drafting of a legal act must be clear, easy to understand and unambiguous; simple and concise, avoiding unnecessary elements; precise, leaving no uncertainties in the mind of the reader. This common sense principle is also an expression

345. *See*, section 2.3.2.
346. *See*, for example, in France, a more than seven-hundred-page compendium, the *Guide de Légistique* (Documentation française, 3rd edition, 2017); and in Belgium, the *Principes de techniques législatives – Guide de rédaction des textes législatifs et réglementaires* (Conseil d'Etat, 2008).

> of general principles of law, such as [...] legal certainty, in that it should be possible to foresee how the law will be applied.[347]

This Practical Guide also emphasizes the importance of an autonomous perspective to the concept of European law:

> In addition, the use of expressions and phrases – in particular legal terms – that are too specific to a particular language or national legal system will increase the risk of translation problems. [...] As regards legal terminology, terms which are too closely linked to a particular national legal system should be avoided.[348]

That being said, it is not always possible to respect these principles in every circumstance. As the rules contained in the 1999 Montreal Convention do not always speak for themselves, they sometimes need to be interpreted by Courts.

The following analysis of drafting factors may then require an analysis of the scope of certain terms and concepts of the Conventions as envisaged by their drafters, and their subsequent application by Courts. The selection of terms and concepts used in this analysis is a personal choice. The selection is mostly grounded in information obtained from the *Travaux Préparatoires* and from the diverse judicial decisions produced by these terms and concepts.

The discussions below do not aim to give an exhaustive account of the former or current controversies surrounding the selected examples. Rather, they seek to discover if specific elements, embedded in the text of the 1999 Montreal Convention since its adoption, may have prevented or limited its uniform application.

3.2.2 The Lack of Autonomous Definitions: The Example of 'Accident'

3.2.2.1 'Accident' under Article 17 of the Conventions

One of the key provisions of the Conventions regarding international air carrier liability is established under Article 17.

Article 17 of the 1929 Warsaw Convention reads:

> The carrier is liable for damage sustained in the event of the death or wounding of a passenger or any bodily injury suffered by a passenger, if the accident which caused the damage so sustained took place on board the aircraft or in the course of any of the operations of embarking or disembarking.[349]

---

347. European Union, *Joint Practical Guide of the European Parliament, the Council and the Commission for persons involved in the drafting of European Union legislation* 10 (2016), Source: Publication Office of the European Union, https://op.europa.eu/en/publication-detail/-/publication/3879747d-7a3c-411b-a3a0-55c14e2ba732 (accessed 22 December 2020).
348. *Ibid.*, p. 18.
349. In the authentic French version: 'Le transporteur est responsable du dommage survenu en cas de mort, de blessure ou de toute autre lésion corporelle subie par un voyageur lorsque l'accident qui a causé le dommage s'est produit à bord de l'aéronef ou au cours de toutes opérations d'embarquement ou de débarquement.'

This provision was slightly amended in the 1999 Montreal Convention, setting out that:

> The carrier is liable for damage sustained in case of death or bodily injury of a passenger upon condition only that the accident which caused the death or injury took place on board the aircraft or in the course of any of the operations of embarking or disembarking.

Despite the use of the term 'accident' several times in the Conventions,[350] neither the 1929 Warsaw Convention nor the 1999 Montreal Convention provide a definition of 'accident', although they do define other terms, such as, for example, 'international carriage',[351] 'commercial agreement',[352] 'principal and permanent residence'[353] and 'days'.[354]

In the absence of definition in the Conventions, the following analysis will examine if any assistance can be found in the *Travaux Préparatoires* and if Courts have succeeded in applying this term in a uniform manner.

3.2.2.2 *'Accident' in the* Travaux Préparatoires

(1) Prior to the 1929 Warsaw Conference

In the pre-Warsaw negotiation time, the text prepared by the French government prior to the 1925 Paris Conference did not make reference to the concept of 'accident',[355] merely providing that:

> Le transporteur est responsable des pertes, avaries et retards qui résultent de ses fautes personnelles et du vice propre de l'appareil.[356]

The draft text adopted at the end of the 1925 Paris Conference did, however, include the term 'accident' in the list of damages that could trigger carrier liability:

> Le transporteur est responsable des accidents, pertes, avaries et retards. Il n'est pas responsable s'il prouve avoir pris les mesures raisonnables pour éviter le dommage; cette preuve est admise même dans le cas où le dommage provient d'un vice propre de l'appareil.[357]

350. 1929 Warsaw Convention, Articles 17 and 30(2); 1999 Montreal Convention, Articles 17, 30(2) and 36(2).
351. 1999 Montreal Convention, Article 1(2).
352. *Ibid.*, Article 33(3)(a).
353. *Ibid.*, Article 33(3)(b).
354. *Ibid.*, Article 52.
355. With the exception provided in Article 8, that an action could be brought in the place where the accident occurred.
356. Conférence Internationale de Droit Privé Aérien, 27 Octobre-6 Novembre 1925, Paris, 1926, p. 12.
357. *Ibid.*, p. 79.

The draft text finally submitted to the 1929 Warsaw Conference, though, did not require an accident to occur to trigger carrier liability. At that time the core provisions read:

> Le transporteur est responsable du dommage survenu pendant le transport: a) en cas de mort, de blessure ou de tout autre lésion corporelle subie par un voyageur; [...].[358]

The word 'accident' was at that time only used in the list of possible fora as set out in the former Article 26:

> L'action en responsabilité devra être portée, au choix du demandeur, dans un des Etats Contractants soit devant le tribunal du siège principal de l'exploitation [...] soit devant le lieu de destination ou, en cas de non arrivée de l'aéronef, du lieu de l'accident; [...][359]

and in the provisions regarding successive carriage:

> [...] le voyageur ou ses ayants droit ne pourront recourir que contre le transporteur ayant effectué le transport au cours duquel l'accident s'est produit [...].[360]

The initial references lead to the presumption that an 'accident' was understood to be a significant event in which the aircraft was still on the ground or ended up on it, excluding therefore minor events.

(2) The 1929 Warsaw Conference

During the negotiations in 1929, the core discussions surrounding Article 17 concerned the time period in which liability would apply. It was only at the end of the negotiations, when the drafting committee agreed to merge and renumber several draft provisions, that it introduced the term 'accident', without leaving any evidence or hint of the reason for its inclusion.

However, it is not unreasonable to speculate that the drafting committee took inspiration from the wording of Article 28(1) of the 1924 Bern Convention CIV regarding the carriage of passengers by rail,[361] which provided that:

> La responsabilité du Chemin de fer, pour la mort d'un voyageur ou pour les blessures résultant d'un accident de train, ainsi que pour les dommages causés par le retard ou la suppression d'un train ou par le manque d'une correspondance, reste soumise aux lois et règlements de l'Etat où le fait s'est produit. [...].

---

358. ICAO Doc 7838, II Conférence Internationale de Droit Privé Aérien, 4-12 Octobre 1929, *Procès-Verbaux*, Varsovie, 1930, p. 171.
359. *Ibid.*, p. 172.
360. *Ibid.*, p. 173.
361. International Convention concerning the Carriage of Passengers and Luggage by Rail (CIV), 23d October 1924, Bern. This convention was preceded by other international conventions on carriage by rail, notably with respect to carriage of goods.

On several occasions, the *Travaux Préparatoires* indicate[362] that inspiration was taken from rail conventions.[363]

This very late inclusion of the word 'accident' in the 1929 Warsaw Convention does not therefore give us clear guidance on how to define its meaning under Article 17.

While this term is not discussed per se in the context of Article 17, it appears nevertheless more than sixty times in the *Travaux Préparatoires*. My analysis unfortunately suggests that the term was used to mean different things. Whereas in a strict grammatical sense, the word in French refers to the notion of an unexpected event;[364] an analysis of its usage and occurrence shows it may also have been used in a narrower sense as a synonym for 'crash'.

This polysemy is not surprising, given that not all delegates spoke French as their mother tongue. The French version, it is worth remembering, is the unique authentic linguistic version of the 1929 Warsaw Convention;[365] it was also the sole language used during the 1929 Warsaw Conference.[366]

At the time, nobody seemed to notice these different uses of the term 'accident', or at least no one expressed the need to properly discuss its introduction. As a matter of fact, in his remarkable work on the limitation of liability in international air law, published slightly before the adoption of the 1955 Hague Protocol, Professor Huib Drion did not even deem it necessary to analyse the meaning of 'accident' in detail.[367] This leads us to believe that, at least during the first decades following the adoption of the 1929 Warsaw Convention, the lack of definition of 'accident' did not create any difficulties.[368]

(3) The 1955 Hague Conference

During discussions leading to the adoption of the 1955 Hague Protocol, the wording of Article 17 was not modified. Still, the term 'accident' was used on a few occasions, but

362. ICAO Doc 7838, II Conférence Internationale de Droit Privé Aérien, 4-12 Octobre 1929, *Procès-Verbaux*, Varsovie, 1930, *see*, for example: pp. 78, 91, 105, 113, 116, 118, 131 and particularly p. 130 where it is clearly said that: 'La conclusion à laquelle nous sommes arrivés, c'est que nous devons nous en tenir à la Convention de Berne, parce que, autrement, il faudrait encore préciser le sens du mot valablement; [...]. Comme la Convention de Berne a déjà une expérience d'un demi-siècle, nous avons préféré reprendre la formule de la Convention de Berne: la livraison des bagages a lieu contre la remise du bulletin de bagages'.
363. *See*, section 1.1.2.1(3)(ii).
364. Larousse: 'événement fortuit qui a des effets plus ou moins dommageables pour les personnes ou pour les choses [...]'; Littré: 'Ce qui advient fortuitement [...]'; Dictionnaire de l'Académie française: 'Evènement qui arrive de manière imprévue en bien ou en mal'.
365. *See*, Article 36 of the 1929 Warsaw Convention: 'La présente Convention est rédigée en français en un seul exemplaire [...]'.
366. At that time, French was indeed the diplomatic language.
367. Huib Drion, *Limitation of Liabilities in International Air Law* (Springer, 1954).
368. With the exception of Professor Daniel Goedhuis, who rapidly foresaw the risk of divergent interpretations. *See*, Daniel Goedhuis, *National Airlegislation and the Warsaw Convention* 200 (Springer, 1937).

essentially to illustrate situations involving the death of passengers or, more basically, air crashes.[369]

An interesting element is found in the comments made by the UNIDROIT, which questioned the interest of keeping the term 'accident'. Although its comments were not discussed or retained by negotiators, it is enlightening to read that it considered that a definition would be useful:

> The texts prepared at the Brighton and San Remo meetings merely required that the damage be 'in relation with the carriage'. After considerable discussion it was decided to retain the accident concept, provided the accident was defined in the following manner: 'any factor unrelated to the person of the passenger which harms his physical or mental integrity'.[370]

However, no definition was added to the 1955 Hague Protocol.

(4) The 1971 Guatemala City Conference

In 1971, a suggestion was made to delete the word 'accident' and to replace Article 17 with the following text in the 1971 Guatemala City Protocol:

> The carrier is liable for damage sustained in case of death or personal injury of a passenger upon condition only that the *event* which caused the death or injury took place on board the aircraft or in the course of any of the operations of embarking or disembarking. However, the carrier is not liable if the death or injury resulted solely from the state of health of the passenger [...][371] (*italics added*).

As suggested by Austria, this change aimed to widen the carrier's scope of liability:

> To date, the term 'accident' has been used, from which it may be deduced that the only type of damage that should be included would be damage having a direct connection with the accident resulting from the operation of the aircraft. It is now suggested that the term 'event' be substituted for the term 'accident'. This would mean that the air carrier would also be considered liable in the event, say, of a passenger killing another passenger on board the aircraft without that event having any relation to the service itself. The exception provided for in the second clause of the new Article 17 is not a remedy when the death is not exclusively ascribable to the infirmity of the passenger.[372]

---

369. *See*, for example, ICAO Doc 7686, International Conference on Private Air Law, The Hague, September 1955, volume I, *Minutes*, Montreal September 1956, pp. 86, 94, 95, 96, 97, 98, 162; ICAO Doc 7686, International Conference on Private Air Law, The Hague, September 1955, volume II, *Documents*, Montreal September 1956, p. 96 with respect to the revision of the limits of liability: 'Another argument in support of this view was that the record of air safety had vastly improved since 1929 and therefore the carrier is now involved in lower risks than those prevailing in the earlier days of air transportation development, and consequently should be prepared to pay higher amounts on the fewer occasions of accidents.'
370. ICAO Doc 7686, International Conference on Private Air Law, The Hague, September 1955, volume II, *Documents*, Montreal September 1956, p. 193.
371. 1971 Guatemala City Protocol, Article IV.
372. ICAO Doc 9040, International Conference on Air Law, Guatemala City, February-March 1971, volume II, *Documents*, Montreal 1972, p. 144.

Nevertheless, despite efforts made, the 1971 Guatemala City Protocol never came into force.

(5) *The 1999 Montreal Conference*

As already mentioned, although the 1999 Montreal Convention slightly changed the wording of Article 17, it kept the term 'accident'.

One of the working drafts, however, opened discussions on using the words 'accident' or 'event', as testified by a draft Article 16(1):

> The carrier is liable for damage sustained in case of death or [personal] [bodily] injury of a passenger upon condition only that the event [accident] which caused the death or injury [...].[373]

As seen hereinafter, the subsequent preparatory work to the conference pointed out an emerging preference for the word 'accident', and a hope to define it:

> In consideration of the terms 'event' or 'accident', one delegation expressed a preference for the term 'accident' and suggested that this term could be defined for the purposes of this Convention. This preference for the term 'accident' was shared by a great number of other delegations. [...] The Chairman also noted a considerable degree of preference for the use of the term 'accident' and noted the suggestion made by a number of delegates to define this term in the Drafting Group. [...] In considering the use of the term 'accident' or 'event', one delegation observed that the term 'accident' had been the object of a number of judicial decisions and that this body of case law could be used to clarify the meaning of this term. Another delegate stated that the term 'accident' could be defined as a sudden, unpredictable event or occurrence. The subsequent discussion revealed a clear preference for the use of the term 'accident'.[374]

Although the final text submitted to the conference eventually maintained the use of the term 'accident',[375] no genuine discussion took place during the 1999 Montreal Conference regarding its inclusion. The delegate for the United States merely expressed the following reason for keeping the term 'accident': 'The equitable balance which had been struck between the interests of passengers and carriers was that the word "accident" be used rather than the word "event" which strongly favoured the carrier's interests.'[376]

373. ICAO Doc 9775, International Conference on Air Law (Convention for the Unification of Certain Rules for International Carriage by Air), Montreal, 10-28 May 1999, volume III, *Preparatory Material*, Montreal 1999, p. 37.
374. *Ibid.*, pp. 169-170.
375. ICAO Doc 9775, International Conference on Air Law (Convention for the Unification of Certain Rules for International Carriage by Air), Montreal, 10-28 May 1999, volume II, *Documents*, Montreal 1999, p. 18.
376. ICAO Doc 9775, International Conference on Air Law (Convention for the Unification of Certain Rules for International Carriage by Air), Montreal, 10-28 May 1999, volume I, *Minutes*, Montreal 1999, p. 119.

(6) Concluding Remarks

Without a clear definition, it was left to Courts to interpret the term 'accident'. As the following section will examine, this state of affairs created the risk of reaching divergent solutions.

3.2.2.3 The Interpretation of 'Accident' in Judicial Decisions

(1) Three Major Views

The response of Courts to the lack of definition of 'accident' has unavoidably taken different forms.[377] Three major views profiled:

(1) recourse to an 'external definition', that is to say, a definition found in other legal instruments;
(2) a damage-based approach, which avoids giving any definition of accident but rather focuses on the existence of a damage; and
(3) an autonomous approach, which tries to come up with a specific definition of the term.

These three views will be explained in the next sections.

(2) The 'External Definition' Approach

The least common response encountered consists in adopting definitions used in other instruments.[378]

For example, in Spain, despite a case-by-case assessment,[379] there was a general tendency to refer to definitions found in other instruments, such as in Annex 13 of the 1947 Chicago Convention[380] or in EU Regulation 996/2010 on the

377. *See*, for example, René Mankiewicz, *The Liability Regime of the International Air Carrier: A Commentary on the Present Warsaw Convention System* 147-149 (Kluwer, 1981); annual publication of the International Air Transport Association, *The Liability Reporter*.
378. This recourse to external definitions has notably been used by the Court of Justice of the European Union in *Walz* to define the concept of damage under the 1999 Montreal Convention, pursuant to the definition given by the Articles on Responsibility of States for Internationally Wrongful Acts drawn up by the International Law Commissions. *See*, CJEU, 6 May 2010, *Axel Walz v. Clickair SA.*, C-63/09, ECLI:EU:C:2010:251, point 27. *See also*, section 4.3.3.5(4).
379. *See*, Belén Ferrer Tapia, *El contracto de transporte aéreo de pasajeros: sujetos, estatuto y responsabilidad* 166 (Dykinson, 2013).
380. ICAO, Annex 13 to the Convention on International Civil Aviation - International Standards and Recommended Practices - Aircraft Accident and Incident Investigation, Chapter 1: '*Accident*. An occurrence associated with the operation of an aircraft which takes place between the time any person boards the aircraft with the intention of flight until such time as all such persons have disembarked, in which:

investigation and prevention of accidents and incidents in civil aviation, or even domestic rules.[381]

In Member States of the West African Economic and Monetary Union (hereinafter 'UEMOA'),[382] the regional regulation on air carrier liability[383] provides a definition of accident that is substantially in line with the one laid down in Annex 13 of the Chicago Convention and which, in the absence of definition in the uniform text, is likely be used or at least taken into consideration by Courts.

(3) The 'Damage-Based' Approach

Probably in light of the general tort law under continental law, which requires fault, damage and a connection between the two,[384] French Courts adopted a 'damage-based' approach in the past. Initially, it was not clearly necessary to demonstrate the existence of an accident. As underlined by French authoritative literature, the concept was viewed through the prism of domestic law. For example, when a passenger broke a bone while walking inside the aircraft, or was the victim of damage caused by another

---

a) a person is fatally or seriously injured as a result of:
   - being in the aircraft, or
   - direct contact with any part of the aircraft, including parts which have become detached from the aircraft, or
   - direct exposure to jet blast,

   except when the injuries are from natural causes, self-inflicted or inflicted by other persons, or when the injuries are to stowaways hiding outside the areas normally available to the passengers and crew; or

b) the aircraft sustains damage or structural failure which:
   - adversely affects the structural strength, performance or flight characteristics of the aircraft, and
   - would normally require major repair or replacement of the affected component,

   except for engine failure or damage, when the damage is limited to the engine, its cowlings or accessories; or for damage limited to propellers, wing tips, antennas, tires, brakes, fairings, small dents or puncture holes in the aircraft skin; or

c) the aircraft is missing or is completely inaccessible.'

381. Belén Ferrer Tapia, *El contracto de transporte aéreo de pasajeros: sujetos, estatuto y responsabilidad* 166 (Dykinson, 2013).
382. Benin, Burkina Faso, Guinea-Bissau, Ivory Coast, Mali, Niger, Senegal and Togo.
383. Règlement N° 02/2003/CM/UEMOA relatif à la responsabilité des transporteurs aériens en cas d'accident, fait à Ouagadougou le 20 mars 2003, *Bulletin Officiel*, n° 31, premier trimestre 2003, pp. 10-12.
384. Conférence Internationale de Droit Privé Aérien, 27 Octobre-6 Novembre 1925, Paris, 1926, p. 55: 'L'opinion générale est que, tandis que la responsabilité civile à l'égard des tiers, doit comporter l'application de la théorie du risque, en revanche, dans la responsabilité du transporteur à l'égard des passagers et des marchandises, il faut admettre la théorie de la faute. [...] Il est donc juste de ne pas imposer au transporteur une responsabilité absolue et de le dégager de toute responsabilité lorsqu'il a pris les mesures raisonnables et normales pour éviter le dommage; c'est la diligence que l'on peut exiger du bon père de famille'.

passenger, Courts deemed that the occurrence of a damage was sufficient to trigger the application of Article 17.[385]

As explained by Dr Georgette Miller,[386] given that liability limits were less important in France than in the United States, as the latter applied the 1966 Montreal Agreement,[387] liability issues were essentially judged through the mechanism of exoneration of Article 20. In other words, the focus was essentially on whether or not the carrier took all necessary measures to avoid the damage. This perception, however, evolved as it will be seen in the next section.

(4) *The Autonomous Approach*

(i) Identical Definitions?

The third approach consists in trying to give an autonomous definition[388] to the term 'accident'. To this end, Courts try to find a specific definition in line with the object and purposes of the Conventions, without copying definitions that exist in international or domestic law.

This section will examine several decisions delivered by Courts in Europe and in America, in order to determine whether this approach was successful in adopting a uniform definition of 'accident'.[389]

(ii) Common Law Jurisdictions

Among common law jurisdictions, the Supreme Court of the United States was the first to be seized on the interpretation of the term 'accident' in 1985, in its *Saks* judgment. In this case, the Court acknowledged that this term should not be interpreted with reference to the definition that existed in Annex 13 to the 1947 Chicago Convention.[390] Having recourse to several hermeneutical tools,[391] the Court concluded that, in the context of the 1929 Warsaw Convention, an 'accident' was to be interpreted 'flexibly'[392] as an 'unexpected or unusual event or happening that is external to the passenger'.[393] Nearly twenty years later, in *Husain*, the same Court fine-tuned its definitions and held that omissions could also be considered as an 'accident'.[394] These

385. *See*, Michel de Juglart, Emmanuel du Pontavice, Jacqueline Dutheil de la Rochère, Georgette Miller, *Traité de droit aérien* 1:1116 and the notes (2nd edition, LGDJ, 1989).
386. Georgette Miller, *Liability in International Air Transport* 111 (Kluwer, 1977).
387. *See*, section 1.1.3.1.
388. *See*, section 2.5.3.3.
389. The hermeneutical tools used by Courts will be analysed in Chapter 4.
390. *Air France v. Saks*, 470 U.S. 392 (1985), at 407: 'The definition in Annex 13 and the corresponding Convention expressly apply to aircraft accident *investigations*, and not to principles of liability to passengers under the Warsaw Convention.'
391. To be discussed in section 4.3.3.
392. *Air France v. Saks*, 470 U.S. 392 (1985), at 405.
393. *Ibid.*
394. *Olympic Airways v. Husain, Individually, and as Personal Representative of the Estate of Hanson, Deceased, et al.*, 540 U.S. 644 (2004).

decisions were ultimately followed in hundreds of published and reported cases in the United States, each giving a more extensive factual meaning to the definition elaborated by the Supreme Court.[395] For example, the 6th Circuit held in *Doe* that being pricked by a needle hidden in a seat pocket could be viewed as an accident.[396]

In the UK, in *Morris*[397] and *Re Deep Vein Thrombosis*,[398] the House of Lords adhered to the definition given by the American Supreme Court in *Saks*. In *Morris*, the Court furthermore acknowledged the flexible nature of this definition: '[...] it was not necessary to show that the event had any relationship with the operation of the aircraft or carriage by air [...]'.[399] Since the entry into force of the 1999 Montreal Convention, the Supreme Court of the United Kingdom has not been seized yet on the interpretation to be given to the term 'accident' under this new text.[400] The Court of Appeal, however, did in *Barclay* and confirmed the same interpretation.[401]

Despite the fact that there is a certain degree of uniformity in the autonomous interpretation adopted in common law jurisdictions, the risk of divergent decisions is not completely mitigated, as debates continue on what constitutes an 'unusual' event.[402]

---

395. *See*, for example, Lawrence Goldhirsch, *The Warsaw Convention Annotated: A Legal Handbook* (Kluwer Law International, 2000); George Tompkins, *Liability Rules Applicable to International Air Transportation as Developed by the Courts in the United States: From Warsaw 1929 to Montreal 1999* (Wolters Kluwer, 2010); Paul Dempsey, Michael Milde, *International Air Carrier Liability: The Montreal Convention of 1999* (Centre for Research in Air & Space Law, McGill University, 2005); Andrew Harakas, 'Air Carrier Liability for Passenger Injury or Death Occurring During International Carriage by Air: An Overview of the Montreal Convention of 1999', in Andrew Harakas (ed.), *Litigating The Aviation Case* 16-22 (4th edition, American Bar Association, 2017); annual publication of the International Air Transport Association, *The Liability Reporter*.
396. *See*, *Doe v. Etihad Airways, P.J.S.C.*, 870 F.3d 406 (6th Cir. 2017).
397. *Morris v. KLM Royal Dutch Airlines* (2002) UKHL 7, at 71.
398. *Re Deep Vein Thrombosis and Air Travel Group Litigation* (2005) UKHL 72, at 18.
399. *Morris v. KLM Royal Dutch Airlines* (2002) UKHL 7, at 72.
400. In *Stott*, the Court mostly focused on the interpretation to be given to the terms 'bodily injury', the exclusivity and the temporal scope of the carrier's liability. *See*, *Stott v. Thomas Cook Tour Operators Ltd* (2014) UKSC 15.
401. *Barclay v. British Airways* (2008) EWCA Civ 1419. *See also*, the subsequent decision of the Court of Appeal, *Ford v. Malaysian Airline System Berhad* (2013) EWCA Civ 1163, at 28. Later, the term 'accident' was fine-tuned by the High Court in 2019 in *Labbadia*. In this matter, the Court considered that an omission could also be understood as an 'accident', ruling that the fall of a passenger on snowy aircraft stairs was an accident insofar as the stairs were not covered by a canopy: 'the Claimant's fall was directly caused by acts and omissions by airport personnel which was an unusual or unexpected event and external to him. It was not a reaction to the normal operation of the aircraft or an immutable state of affairs'. *See*, *Labbadia v. Alitalia* (2019) EWHC 2103 (QB), at 45.
402. An example can be taken from Australia, where a passenger sought compensation for an injury she claimed stemmed from the lack of crew reaction to her four requests for water. The Supreme Court of Victoria ruled that – pursuant to its case law where: 'Interpretation should be consistent across contracting states' – the claim should be interpreted in line with the *Saks* and *Husain* decisions of the American Supreme Court, and be analysed in light of the factual elements of the case. The Australian Court finally rejected the passenger's claim on the grounds that nothing unusual or unexpected occurred: 'In this case, the way in which the plaintiff's requests were dealt with were in accordance with the usual practice of attendants and were not in disregard of or contrary to airline policy' (*Di Falco v. Emirates (No 2)* (2019) VSC 654, at 9 and 45). In another example in Turkey, the Supreme Court of Appeals overruled a decision that

(iii) Civil Law Jurisdictions

In France, as already mentioned,[403] the position of French Courts evolved from a 'damage-based' approach. In 1979, the Court of Appeal of Paris[404] looked more closely at the wording of the 1929 Warsaw Convention as amended, in this case regarding hijacking, and implicitly confirmed that an 'accident' was required for the text to be applicable. In this matter, the Court defined this term as a material and fortuitous event of a mechanical or technical order, affecting the aircraft during flight and/or trouble during the normal course of the journey that resulted from an unforeseeable intervention of badly intentioned third parties.[405] While the decision was appealed before the *Cour de cassation*, this definition was not disputed.[406] In a case regarding a pulmonary embolism, the *Cour de cassation* further added in 2007 that an 'accident' under the 1929 Warsaw Convention also had to be external to the passenger.[407] In 2014, the *Cour de cassation* implicitly admitted that an accident was an external, sudden and unforeseeable event.[408] On the same day, in another case, the Court annulled a decision of the Court of Appeal of Bordeaux that had held that the ear pain suffered by a passenger as the consequence of a flight was compensable under the 1999 Montreal Convention. According to the *Cour de cassation*, the mere existence of a causal link between the damage and the flight was not sufficient because said convention required the existence of an accident.[409]

---

had considered as an 'accident' a situation in which a pilot did not divert a flight for a medical emergency after a doctor onboard advised that there was no emergency (Supreme Court of Appeals, 11th Chamber, 19 April 2018, quoted in: International Air Transport Association, 22 *The Liability Reporter* 8 (2019)). In Italy, the *Corte de cassazione* held in 2015 that the notion of normal conditions of transportation should be taken into consideration when determining the possibility of an accident (Cass., 14 July 2015, ECLI:IT:CASS:2015:14666CIV, at 8). A parallel could be made to the potential for divergent interpretations between the 'unusual' notion and the 'inherent' one developed by the Court of Justice of the European Union regarding 'extraordinary circumstances' in EU Regulation 261/2004. On this topic, *see*, section 4.2.2.2(3).

403. *See*, section 3.2.2.3(3).
404. CA Paris, 19 June 1979, Revue Française de Droit Aérien et Spatial 327 (1979). In this matter, hijacking was considered as an accident.
405. *Ibid.*, 'Un événement matériel fortuit d'ordre technique ou mécanique affectant l'appareil pendant le vol', 'le trouble au cours normal du voyage résultant d'une intervention imprévisible de tiers mal intentionnés'.
406. Cass., 16 February 1982, 80-17009.
407. Cass., 14 June 2007, 05-17248: 'que la cour d'appel a, à cet égard, constaté qu'il ne résultait d'aucun des éléments produits que l'embolie pulmonaire, [...], puisse être imputée à un événement extérieur à la personne de Mme Y [...] Par ces motifs, rejette le pourvoi'.
408. Cass., 15 January 2014, ECLI:FR:CCASS:2014:C100011: 'Attendu que, pour retenir que la responsabilité du transporteur aérien n'était pas sérieusement contestable, l'arrêt relève que, même si la cause de la chute reste inconnue en l'état du seul témoignage de Mme X ..., cette chute constitue un accident, qui résulte forcément d'un événement extérieur, soudain et imprévisible, dès lors qu'il n'est ni allégué, ni prouvé que M. X ... aurait été victime d'un malaise emportant celle-ci; Attendu qu'en se déterminant ainsi, par des motifs impropres à caractériser l'imputabilité du dommage à un accident survenu à l'occasion des opérations d'embarquement, la cour d'appel a privé sa décision de base légale'.
409. Cass., 15 January 2014, ECLI:FR:CCASS:2014:C100009: 'Attendu que, pour retenir la responsabilité du transporteur aérien, l'arrêt, après avoir constaté que l'intéressée n'invoquait pas d'incident de vol, mais seulement des douleurs ressenties lors des phases de descente et d'atterrissage, relève que le lien de causalité entre le voyage réalisé et les atteintes auditives en

This evolution shows a tendency towards alignment with the definition initially suggested by the American Supreme Court in *Saks*. However, in contrast to the *Husain* decision in the United States,[410] the *Cour de cassation* has not interpreted that an omission could validly qualify as an accident.[411]

The flexible criterion for application of the term 'accident', suggested by the American Supreme Court in *Saks*, does not appear to have been retained in every civil law jurisdiction. For example, the respective highest Courts in Austria[412] and in Germany[413] each required a connection to a risk inherent to air transportation. This position was initially seconded by the Rapporteur of the draft submitted to the 1929 Warsaw Conference.[414] This view is shared by the modern French doctrine which contends that an 'accident' must also be in direct relation with air carriage.[415] A similar position can also be found in the Belgian doctrine, which considers that, since the fault-based regime of the 1929 Warsaw Convention was replaced by a risk-based regime in the 1999 Montreal Convention, the term 'accident' could therefore be

cause a été démontré par les consultations réalisées par celle-ci, le jour même de son arrivée à destination, auprès d'un médecin généraliste, puis, quelques jours plus tard, auprès d'un spécialiste ORL, ainsi que par deux rapports d'expertise judiciaire, le dernier ayant spécialement conclu que les causes de l'otopathie barotraumatique diagnostiquée sont dues, non pas à un éventuel état pathologique antérieur de la victime, mais aux conditions de vol, les effets combinés des conditions de climatisation, de recyclage et de circulation de l'air dans les avions, avec la répétition des phases de compression, étant des facteurs de nature à favoriser les barotraumatismes; Attendu, qu'en se déterminant ainsi, par des motifs impropres à caractériser l'imputabilité du dommage à un accident qui serait survenu lors des opérations de vol, la cour d'appel a privé sa décision de base légale'.

410. *Olympic Airways v. Husain, Individually, and as Personal Representative of the Estate of Hanson, Deceased, et al.*, 540 U.S. 644 (2004).

411. Cass., 8 October 2014, ECLI:FR:CCASS:2014:C101159: 'Attendu que [...] l'arrêt, après avoir rappelé les termes du compte-rendu d'incident, selon lesquels, en sortant de l'avion, la passagère, qui portait un bébé dans les bras, a manqué la marche, glissé et, est tombée, se blessant à la cheville droite, en déduit l'existence d'un accident au sens de la Convention de Montréal, en ce que, d'une part, cette chute n'est pas le résultat d'un malaise et, d'autre part, il ne saurait être reproché à Mme X ... une faute dès lors que, se trouvant avec un enfant dans les bras, elle ne pouvait pas forcément voir le sol et qu'il appartenait dans ce cas au personnel de bord de l'aider voire de la décharger de l'enfant pour qu'elle puisse débarquer sans encombre; Attendu qu'en statuant ainsi, par des motifs impropres à caractériser l'imputabilité du dommage à un accident qui serait survenu lors des opérations de débarquement, ce dont il résultait l'existence d'une contestation sérieuse, la cour d'appel a violé les textes susvisés'. *A contrario*, in a 2016 decision, the Court of Appeal of Amsterdam suggested a certain omission could be sufficient to trigger carrier liability. However, this decision is to be read carefully, as the Court underlined that the passenger had to demonstrate the omission. *See*, Gerechtshof Amsterdam, 3 May 2016, ECLI:NL:GHAMS:2016:1750.

412. Oberster Gerichthof, 2 July 2015, 2 Ob 58.15s.

413. Bundesgerichthof, 21 November 2017, X ZR 30/15, ECLI:DE:BGH:2017:211117IXZR30.15.0.

414. ICAO Doc 7838, II Conférence Internationale de Droit Privé Aérien, 4-12 Octobre 1929, *Procès-Verbaux*, Varsovie, 1930, p. 160: 'Comme il s'agit de la responsabilité engagée à l'occasion d'un contrat de transport *déterminé*, la Convention ne s'applique évidemment qu'aux dommages causés par le matériel affecté à *ce* transport pour l'exécution du contrat'.

415. *See*, Pascal Dupont, *Manuel de droit aérien: souveraineté et libertés dans la troisième dimension* 383 (Pedone, 2015): 'Le dommage corporel subi par un voyageur, lorsqu'il est consécutif à un accident défini comme un évènement extérieur à la personne du passager, doit être en relation directe avec le transport aérien, lequel comporte le vol proprement dit, auquel il convient d'associer les opérations d'embarquement et de débarquement'.

interpreted restrictively to exclude events which do not have any direct, or sufficiently direct, links with transportation operation.[416]

(iv) Court of Justice of the European Union

In 2019 in *Niki*,[417] the CJEU, in this section also referred to as the 'EU Court', was asked to rule on this controversial issue. Following the burning of a passenger by a hot beverage during a flight, it had to give its own view of the term 'accident'. The defendant contended that a cup of coffee falling from the folding tray table onto the passenger was not the 'materialisation of a hazard typically associated with aviation',[418] which was necessary to be considered as an 'accident' in Austria. The EU Court, seized by the highest Austrian Court, ruled in favour of an extensive interpretation, holding that an 'accident' under the 1999 Montreal Convention 'covers all situations occurring on board an aircraft in which an object used when serving passengers has caused bodily injury to a passenger, without it being necessary to examine whether those situations stem from a hazard typically associated with aviation'.[419] In doing so, the CJEU rejected the position adopted in Germany and in Austria, but did not clearly align itself with existing consensus in leading common law jurisdictions.

While the EU Court appears to have put an end to the controversy regarding the need for a direct link with hazards associated with aviation, its reasoning was nevertheless confusing. *First*, while the EU Court recalled the importance of a uniform application of the 1999 Montreal Convention,[420] it gave, with no reasoning, an initial gist of the term 'accident' that was quite distinct from the one commonly admitted in many jurisdictions. When the American Supreme Court referred to 'unexpected or unusual event or happening', the EU Court used the expression 'unforeseen, harmful and involuntary event'[421] in its reasoning, replacing the notion of 'unusual' with 'involuntary' yet kept by its Advocate General.[422] This change does not have a clear explanation and could be understood as any voluntary harmful event being outside the scope of the Convention, which would appear surprising in a uniform strict liability regime. *Second*, while there was a general view to consider that the event must be external to the passenger,[423] the EU Court, again without clear explanation, drafted its decisions in a way that could lead us to believe that death or injury resulting from the passenger's health could trigger carrier liability,[424] which in turn could only be

416. *See*, Jacques Naveau, Marc Godfroid, Pierre Fruhling, *Précis de droit aérien* 330-332 (2nd edition, Bruylant, 2006).
417. CJEU, 19 December 2019, *GN v. ZU acting for Niki Luftfahrt*, C-532/18, ECLI:EU:C:2019:1127.
418. *Ibid.*, point 17.
419. *Ibid.*, point 43.
420. *Ibid.*, point 32.
421. *Ibid.*, point 35.
422. CJEU, 26 September 2019, *GN v. ZU acting for Niki Luftfahrt*, C-532/18, ECLI:EU:C:2019:788 (Opinion), point 62.
423. *Ibid.*, point 44.
424. CJEU, 19 December 2019, *GN v. ZU acting for Niki Luftfahrt*, C-532/18, ECLI:EU:C:2019:1127, point 38.

exonerated therefrom pursuant to Articles 20 and 21 of said convention. This is particularly curious given that these last two provisions are not event-orientated provisions, but damage-related ones.[425]

Despite the hierarchical place of the EU Court, this decision only responded to the question of whether the term 'accident' *in specie* required a hazard typically associated with aviation in a situation where an object used to serve passengers had caused bodily injury to a passenger. The EU Court was not therefore asked to give a definition of the term 'accident'. Consequently, the whole jurisprudence established in each Member State is not automatically overruled by this decision, and may remain diversified, despite the aim of uniformity of the Convention, as long as no hazard typically associated with aviation be requested.

In 2021, the EU Court fine-tuned its position regarding the scope of the 'unforeseen' event in *Altenrhein*.[426] It confirmed that the unforeseeability was to be looked through the operational prism, not from the passenger's perception.

(v) Concluding Remarks

It can be concluded from this overview that, despite the existence of a tendency towards an autonomous interpretation of the term 'accident', there is still not a single interpretation shared by all Courts.

While it can easily be assumed that the interpretations given by each Court initially depended on factual elements submitted to them, and that this may have therefore justified their variations, it appears that even in jurisdictions that have been inspired by the definitions provided by the American Supreme Court in *Saks*, certain variations still exist.

A possible explanation for some of these differences may also be that, when interpreting the term 'accident', Courts may be taking into account the effect that the absence of an 'accident' may have on the claim. The interpretation of 'accident' is not totally inseparable from the reading Courts may give to the principle of exclusivity.[427] In jurisdictions such as the United States or the UK,[428] which endorse a 'strict application' of the principle of exclusivity, one may see a trend towards a broader definition of the term 'accident'.[429] In parallel, in jurisdictions where there is no such strict reading of exclusivity – with the consequence that in the absence of accident, the passengers could try to seek indemnification under domestic law – a narrower

425. *See*, Robert Lawson, *The Montreal Convention 1999 at 21: Has It Come of Age or Passed Its Sell-by Date?*, 45 Air & Space Law 271 (2020).
426. CJEU, 12 May 2021, *YL v. Altenrhein Luftfahrt GmbH*, C-70/20, ECLI:EU:C:2021:379.
427. *See*, sections 2.5.3.2 and 4.3.2.
428. *See*, section 4.3.2.2.
429. A broader definition of 'accident' could be used to avoid the consequences of a strict application of the principle of exclusivity. Several authors commented that a broader definition may, however, lead to a definition close to the one set out in the unsuccessful 1971 Guatemala City Protocol. *See*, Paul Dempsey, Michael Milde, *International Air Carrier Liability: The Montreal Convention of 1999* 211 (Centre for Research in Air & Space Law, McGill University, 2005); Elmar Giemulla, e. a., *The Montreal Convention* 29-8.1 (Supplement 9, Kluwer, 2014).

interpretation of the term 'accident' is often adopted.[430] The fact that the CJEU, which is known for rather loosely applying the principle of exclusivity,[431] adopted a broad interpretation of the term 'accident' in line with jurisdictions that recognized a strict reading may raise the question of a possible change of views on this point of the EU Court in *Niki*. However, a broad interpretation of 'accident' does not automatically entail a strict application of the principle of exclusivity. As mentioned above,[432] the CJEU often sees consumer protection as an additional purpose of the 1999 Montreal Convention and, as such, uses this purpose to guide its interpretation of that convention.

3.2.2.4 Conclusions

The above analysis illustrates the difficulty of applying autonomous terms without them being defined in the Conventions. Despite the fact that, as seen above,[433] a number of Courts rely on the definition provided by the American Supreme Court to determine whether an 'accident' occurred, there is still no common definition shared by all ratifying States. Regrettably, this situation leads to a fragmentation of the 1999 Montreal Convention.

3.2.3 The Use of Concepts Taken from Other International Instruments

After a lack of definition, another drafting element that could affect the uniform application of the Conventions may be that their drafters incorporated terms from other international instruments despite the autonomy of the Conventions.

Indeed, the 1929 Warsaw Convention was not drafted from scratch, and more than mere inspiration was taken from pre-existing international conventions, such as those from the rail sector.[434] The *Travaux Préparatoires* of the 1929 Warsaw Convention make this clear, stating that:

> Il y a une autre proposition qui consistait à prendre l'article 39 de la Convention de Berne. La commission a été d'accord pour se rallier à cette proposition.[435]

Although it was clearly established from an early stage that the terminology used in the 1929 Warsaw Convention was independent from the one encountered in other

430. *See*, Laurent Tran, *Le régime uniforme de responsabilité du transporteur aérien de personnes* 158 et seq. (Schultess, 2013); Laurent Chassot, *Les sources de la responsabilité du transporteur aérien international: entre conflit et complémentarité: La Convention de Montréal et son interaction avec le droit européen et national* 189 (Schulthess, 2012).
431. *See*, section 4.3.2.3.
432. *See*, section 2.3.3.2.
433. *See*, section 3.2.2.3(4).
434. *See*, Daniel Goedhuis, *National Airlegislation and the Warsaw Convention* (Springer, 1937).
435. ICAO Doc 7838, II Conférence Internationale de Droit Privé Aérien, 4-12 Octobre 1929, *Procès-Verbaux*, Varsovie, 1930, p. 105. *See also*, *Ibid.*, p. 130.

international transportation conventions,[436] it cannot be ignored that these would certainly have had an impact on the way the terms laid down in the 1929 Warsaw Convention have been understood and interpreted in States which were also parties to these international conventions.

Thus, it cannot be ruled out that, while interpreting certain provisions of the 1929 Warsaw Convention, Courts were likely, at least initially, to use their knowledge of how identical terms and concepts were used in other international conventions, especially when it came to other international conventions regulating transport, such as the 1924 Bern CIM and CIV, which already had a well-established jurisprudence.[437] The use of other international conventions and their related case law might have led to divergent interpretations. This divergence would be particularly apparent between States that ratified the 1924 Bern CIM and CIV and those that did not.

Knowing that rail conventions were used in the drafting process, they may offer additional interpretation tools. References to rail conventions and their successive amendments were, for instance, cautiously made in the UK while interpreting the term 'bodily injury'.[438] But such recourse raises several concerns. *First*, it questions the genuine existence of the reference to other instruments, as not all Courts develop their reasoning in detail.[439] *Second*, this should be put in perspective with the lack of ratification of rail conventions by all the Parties to the 1929 Warsaw Convention. Indeed, the rail conventions only concerned some European countries in 1929.

For these simple reasons, Courts should not transpose definitions or rely on case law developed under other instruments such as international rail conventions. While an examination of solutions adopted in other international instruments may be instructive, the sui generis nature of the liability regime established by the Conventions limits their use.[440] They could therefore only be used, after due consideration, as a supplementary means of interpretation pursuant to Article 32 of the 1969 Vienna Convention.[441]

3.2.4 The Interpretations of Terms of the 1929 Warsaw Convention and the 1999 Montreal Convention According to the *Travaux Préparatoires*

3.2.4.1 Preliminary Remarks

After the aforementioned drafting elements, the *Travaux Préparatoires* indicate that the drafters of the Conventions sometimes agreed that uniform rules, including terms

436. *Ibid.*, p. 91: 'Je tiens à faire cette déclaration, parce que je crois être une des personnes qui s'occupent le plus du droit aérien et je crois pouvoir dire que l'intérêt du droit aérien est de se développer librement, de n'être opprimé ni par le droit maritime, ni par le droit terrestre, ni par le droit des chemins de fer'.
437. *See*, Bela de Nanassy, *Le droit international des transports par chemin de fer* (Rösch, 1946).
438. *Morris v. KLM Royal Dutch Airlines* (2002) UKHL 7, at 17.
439. *See*, for example, section 1.3.2.3(2)(iii).
440. *See*, sections 2.5.3.3 and 4.3.3.5(4).
441. *See*, section 1.3.1.2(2)(ii).

encompassed therein, could be applied differently. Two main reasons have been used to justify this breach in uniform application: *first*, to permit Courts to apply rules and terms to the facts of the case; and *second*, because no common position has been reached.

3.2.4.2 Situational Application: The Example of Delay

During diplomatic conferences, it is possible that reaching a compromise produces a text that creates flexibility for interpretation by Courts. This flexibility is notably required when it is deemed that a case-by-case analysis by Courts is more practical than a fixed rule to pursue the goal of the Convention. The concept of 'delay' used under Article 19 of the Conventions[442] falls into this category.

In 1929, negotiators did not spend much time discussing Article 19. If the principle of liability in case of delay of passengers did not create difficulties, the question emerged as to when a delay would occur.[443] The delegations had noticed that some airlines contractually indicated their schedule, with the consequence that it would be clear when a delay occurred, while others did not or merely indicated that their schedules were not guaranteed.[444] In a scenario where no schedule was mentioned, it was admitted that the carrier had to fulfil his duty within a reasonable time frame. Acknowledging that no formula could always determine when a delay occurred, the Rapporteur confirmed that this question would be left to the discretion of the Courts:

> Lorsqu'aucun délai n'a été stipulé, il faut qu'il remplisse ses obligations dans un délai raisonnable. Qu'entend-on par là? Aucune formule ne peut le déterminer, il s'agit d'une question d'appréciation de fait à solutionner par le juge; [...].[445]

Despite the fact that the Polish representative claimed that such a margin of manoeuvre might not have been the best option,[446] no further discussions arose on this precise point.

In 1955, the question of liability in the case of delay focused on the amount of compensation associated with it.[447] Again, some carriers considered their timetables to not be part of the contract, with the consequence that, in their views, they should not

442. The 1929 text provides that: 'Le transporteur est responsable du dommage résultant d'un retard dans le transport aérien de voyageurs, bagages ou marchandises', translated in English as follows: 'The carrier is liable for damage occasioned by delay in the carriage by air of passengers, luggage or goods.' The 1999 version reads: 'The carrier is liable for damage occasioned by delay in the carriage by air of passengers, baggage or cargo. Nevertheless, the carrier shall not be liable for damage occasioned by delay if it proves that it and its servants and agents took all measures that could reasonably be required to avoid the damage or that it was impossible for it or them to take such measures.'

443. ICAO Doc 7838, II Conférence Internationale de Droit Privé Aérien, 4-12 Octobre 1929, *Procès-Verbaux*, Varsovie, 1930, p. 37.

444. *Ibid.*, pp. 37-39 *in fine*.

445. *Ibid.*, p. 38.

446. *Ibid.*

447. ICAO Doc 7686, International Conference on Private Air Law, The Hague, September 1955, volume I, *Minutes*, Montreal September 1956, p. 238.

be held liable for delays. At the time, this problem could be solved either by respecting contractual terms or by considering the mere existence of a liability provision in the Convention to void a 'no time tables guaranteed' contractual clause. Recognizing that this situation had created 'considerable uncertainty',[448] a proposal was made to introduce the word 'unreasonable' before the word 'delay' to give more weight to Article 19. However, following a vote, the 1955 Hague Conference expressed the view that the word 'unreasonable' should not be introduced as it was already implied. This is a rare situation in which one of the conferences gives a semi-official interpretation, the trace of which can only be found in the *Travaux Préparatoires*.[449]

This clarification did not appear to be sufficient from the perspective of the 1999 Montreal Conference, however. One of the draft texts approved by the ICAO Legal Committee provided the following suggestion as a possible definition of 'delay':

> For the purpose of this Convention, delay means the failure to carry passengers or deliver baggage or cargo to their immediate or final destination within the time which it would be reasonable to expect from a diligent carrier to do so, having regard to all the relevant circumstances.[450]

During the 1999 Montreal Conference, the Chinese representative acknowledged that the lack of a common definition jeopardized the uniform interpretation of the concept of delay:

> [...] while some States might have national laws which contained a definition of the term 'delay' and jurisprudence on which an interpretation of that term might be based, the lack of standard definition could lead to a multiplicity of interpretations. In order to ensure uniformity in its interpretation, she suggested that the definition proposed [...] be retained in the draft Convention.[451]

The Chairman responded that having a common definition would be difficult, and that the best option was to leave the matter to be determined by Courts on a case-by-case basis:

> [...] in view of the difficulty of finding a precise language which would cover all circumstances which could be characterized as 'delay', a pragmatic approach had been taken to the problem, it being decided that it was preferable to leave the term 'delay' without definition. [...] Furthermore, it would be extraordinarily difficult to arrive at a definition given the jurisprudence in the area. [...] It was considerations such as these which had led [...] to conclude that it would be better not to have a

448. *See*, the observations of the International Union of Aviation Insurers, *Ibid.*, p. 244.
449. *Ibid.*, p. 247: 'The President stated that, in the event of a negative vote on the proposal, the Conference would be understood as having stated that the word "unreasonable" was not necessary because it was already implied in Article 19 as at present drafted. The Conference rejected, by a vote of 27 to 2, the proposal of the Delegation of Greece to insert the word "unreasonable" before the word "delay" in Article 19 of the Convention.'
450. ICAO Doc 9775, International Conference on Air Law (Convention for the Unification of Certain Rules for International Carriage by Air), Montreal, 10-28 May 1999, volume III, *Preparatory Material*, Montreal 1999, p. 213.
451. ICAO Doc 9775, International Conference on Air Law (Convention for the Unification of Certain Rules for International Carriage by Air), Montreal, 10-28 May 1999, volume I, *Minutes*, Montreal 1999, p. 83.

> definition of the term 'delay' in the draft Convention and to leave the matter to be determined by the courts on a case-by-case basis.[452]

The Chairman of the drafting committee concluded that: 'The general wording of Article 18 was intended to provide sufficient signposts.'[453]

This deviation from the key feature of the uniform rules of the Conventions led to various interpretations of the concept of delay. The divergences were not only in regards to the value of the contractual clauses inserted in the conditions of carriage but also in the simple appreciation of what constituted a delay.[454] For instance, should a delay be limited to a delay upon arrival, or could it also be delay only at departure? The latter situation was, for example, examined in Germany by the District Court of Frankfurt, when an aircraft returned to the airport of departure shortly after taking off on schedule. As no information was rapidly provided as to when the flight could take off again, one of the passengers decided not to wait any further and booked a new flight with another carrier. Said passenger later claimed a refund of the price of the new ticket from the original carrier. The Court held that the claim was to be analysed as a delay under the 1929 Warsaw Convention.[455]

This flexibility may also lead to additional breaches. In light of the agreed margin of manoeuvre, it may happen that the uniform rule be interpreted pursuant to domestic concepts, in violation of their autonomous nature. Such a scenario already implicitly occurred in the jurisprudence developed by the CJEU.[456] For instance, in the *IATA* case, when the CJEU was asked to rule on the validity of EU Regulation 261/2004 in light of the 1999 Montreal Convention, it held that: 'any delay [...] may, generally speaking, cause two types of damage'.[457] The Court here assumed that the concept of delay was identical in both instruments. Since then, the concept of delay under EU Regulation

452. *Ibid.*
453. *Ibid.*
454. *See*, for a description of the different interpretations, Laurent Chassot, *Les sources de la responsabilité du transporteur aérien international: entre conflit et complémentarité: La Convention de Montréal et son interaction avec le droit européen et national* 225-245 (Schulthess, 2012); Daniel Goedhuis, *National Airlegislations and the Warsaw Convention* 206-212 (Springer, 1937); Lawrence Goldhirsch, *The Warsaw Convention Annotated: A Legal Handbook* 100-104 (Kluwer Law International, 2000); René Mankiewicz, *The Liability Regime of the International Air Carrier: A Commentary on the Present Warsaw Convention System* 217-227 (Kluwer, 1981); Georgette Miller, *Liability in International Air Transport* 154-160 (Kluwer, 1977); George Tompkins, *Liability Rules Applicable to International Air Transportation as Developed by the Courts in the United States: From Warsaw 1929 to Montreal 1999* 228-231 (Kluwer, 2010).
455. Amstgericht Frankfurt am Main, 5 September 1997, 47 Zeitschrift für Luft- und Weltraumrecht 247-249 (1998) cited in, Laurent Chassot, *Les sources de la responsabilité du transporteur aérien international: entre conflit et complémentarité: La Convention de Montréal et son interaction avec le droit européen et national* 236 (Schulthess, 2012).
456. *See*, Jae Woon Lee, Joseph Wheeler, *Air Carrier Liability for Delay: A Plea to Return to International Uniformity*, 77 Journal of Air Law and Commerce 43-103 (2012).
457. CJEC, 10 January 2006, *The Queen, on the application of International Air Transport Association and European Low Fares Airline Association v. Department for Transport*, C-344/04, ECLI:EU:C:2006:10, point 43. *See also*, section 4.2.2.2.

261/2004 has regularly been refined by the Court[458] with a further risk of contamination that cannot be ruled out.[459]

The above analysis shows that the admissibility of a margin of manoeuvre in the *Travaux Préparatoires* regarding the application of the concept of delay limits the possibility of having a uniform application of the Conventions.

3.2.4.3 An Unclear Common Position: The Example of Mental Injury

(1) Preliminary Remarks

Sometimes, the lack of common agreement leads to unfortunate situations where, despite the will to achieve a uniform position, the *Travaux Préparatoires* report what could be considered a failure in the negotiations on specific points. The case of mental injury under the 1999 Montreal Convention illustrates this situation.

While it was generally admitted in the literature that applicable domestic law governs the type of compensable damage in the case of death or injury,[460] the question of whether mental/psychological injury was covered under the concept of 'bodily injury' and could thus be compensated on the grounds of Article 17 of the Conventions was more complex.[461] The next sections will shed light on this question of compensation for 'mental injury' pursuant to the *Travaux Préparatoires* and case law developed by Courts.

---

458. *See*, CJEC, 19 November 2009, *Christopher Sturgeon, Gabriel Sturgeon and Alana Sturgeon v. Condor Flugdienst GmbH* and *Stefan Böck and Cornelia Lepuschitz v. Air France SA*, Joined Cases C-402/07 and C-432/07, ECLI:EU:C:2009:716. This decision has been confirmed in subsequent decisions. Compare this to the case where the Court ruled a flight should be considered cancelled, when, despite its having taken off, it was returned to the gate and passengers were transferred onto other flights. *See*, CJEU, 13 October 2011, *Aurora Sousa Rodríguez and Others v. Air France SA*, C-83-10, ECLI:EU:C:2011:652.
459. *See*, section 4.2.2.2.
460. *See*, Huib Drion, *Limitation of Liabilities in International Air Law* 125 (Springer, 1954); Daniel Goedhuis, *National Airlegislations and the Warsaw Convention* 269 (Springer, 1937); Georgette Miller, *Liability in International Air Transport* 125 (Kluwer, 1977); René Mankiewicz, *The Liability Regime of the International Air Carrier: A Commentary on the Present Warsaw Convention System* 187 (Kluwer, 1981). *See also*, the decision of the Supreme Court of the United States, *Zicherman, Individually and as Executrix of the Estate of Kole, et. al. v. Korean Air Lines Co, Ltd.*, 516 U.S. 217 (1996), at 225. Compare this with the European decision, CJEU, 6 May 2010, *Axel Walz v. Clickair SA.*, C-63/09, ECLI:EU:C:2010:251.
461. Article 17 of the 1929 Warsaw Convention provides that: 'The carrier is liable for damage sustained in the event of the death or wounding of a passenger or any other bodily injury suffered by a passenger [...]'; or in its authentic version: 'Le transporteur est responsable du dommage survenu en cas de mort, de blessure ou de tout autre lésion corporelle subie par un voyageur [...]'. The wording was slightly amended in the 1999 version and reads: 'The carrier is liable for damage sustained in case of death or bodily injury of a passenger [...].' Dr Yvonne Blanc-Dannery commented in 1933 that the word 'injury', which may be seen as redundant with the word 'wounding' in the 1929 text, reflected in reality the condition or aggravation that may have happened after the accident took place: 'Lorsque la blessure ou la mort sont consécutives à l'accident, il n'y a pas de difficulté. Mais si le décès ou la nécessité d'une intervention chirurgicale se produisent postérieurement, c'est-à-dire après que la période de transport aérien est terminée, la responsabilité est exactement la même. L'emploi du terme "lésion" après ceux de mort et de blessure englobe et prévoit les cas de traumatismes ou de

(2) Travaux Préparatoires

The question of compensation for mental injury was briefly discussed for the first time in the context of preparations for the 1955 Hague Protocol. During the preparatory proceedings, the UNIDROIT commented that: 'the expression "bodily injury" should be understood to mean any harm to the physical or mental integrity of the person'.[462]

During the 1955 Hague Conference, the delegation for Greece wished to make it clear whether injury not connected to physical damage, such as fear, could be compensated. He suggested the addition of the following sentence to Article 17: '... or any other mental or bodily injury suffered by a passenger ...'.[463] However, as the proposal was not seconded, it did not reach the official discussion level and was therefore ignored.

In light of emerging jurisprudence granting compensation for mental injury in certain cases, considerable discussions surrounded the topic during the preparation of the 1999 Montreal Convention.[464] In one of the draft texts approved by the ICAO Legal Committee, it was suggested that Article 17 should be rephrased as follows:

> The carrier is liable for damage sustained in case of death or bodily or mental injury of a passenger upon condition only that the accident which caused the death or injury took place on board [...].[465]

Despite this suggestion not being retained in the final draft submitted to the delegates, the fate of mental injury kept negotiators extremely busy throughout the 1999 Montreal Conference. In a joint comment, Norway and Sweden suggested the addition of the words 'or mental injury' in the draft text, noting that the exclusion of mental injury did not promote the unification of legal systems:

> The exclusion of mental injury does not promote unification of legal systems, which is one of the main objectives of this process. The reason for this is that the term 'bodily injury' is not construed in the same way in all legal systems. The present draft will therefore lead to different interpretation of the Convention in different stares. As a result the present draft may give rise to forum shopping.[466]

perturbations dont les conséquences ne se manifestent pas immédiatement dans l'organisme et dont la corrélation peut être établie avec l'accident', in Yvonne Blanc-Dannery, *La Convention de Varsovie et les règles du transport aérien international* 62 (Pedone, 1933).

462. ICAO Doc 7686, International Conference on Private Air Law, The Hague, September 1955, volume II, *Documents*, Montreal September 1956, p. 193.
463. ICAO Doc 7686, International Conference on Private Air Law, The Hague, September 1955, volume I, *Minutes*, Montreal September 1956, p. 261.
464. The 1971 Guatemala City Protocol already replaced the word 'bodily injury' with 'personal injury', but never entered into force.
465. ICAO Doc 9775, International Conference on Air Law (Convention for the Unification of Certain Rules for International Carriage by Air), Montreal, 10-28 May 1999, volume III, *Preparatory Material*, Montreal 1999, p. 92.
466. ICAO Doc 9775, International Conference on Air Law (Convention for the Unification of Certain Rules for International Carriage by Air), Montreal, 10-28 May 1999, volume II, *Documents*, Montreal 1999, pp. 97-98.

The UK also recommended inserting the following definition of mental injury:

> In this Article the term 'mental injury', in a case where there is no accompanying bodily injury, means an injury resulting in a mental impairment which has a significant adverse effect on the health of the passenger.[467]

The Minutes of the 1999 Montreal Conference report that, although in principle, adding mental injuries to the wording of the text was widely accepted, the practical repercussions were raised with serious concerns. The observer of the International Union of Aerospace Insurers noted an important risk of fraud:

> Fear of flying was a well recognized phenomenon without significant parallel in other modes of transport and could be easily construed by sympathetic medical opinion as an injury. The existence, or otherwise, of mental injury was very difficult to prove, giving rise to the possibility of fraud and expensive protracted litigation.[468]

He also emphasized that, while mental injuries were compensable in other modes of transport, these conventions established limited liability regimes,[469] contrary to the 1999 Montreal Convention.[470] Following many representatives' interventions, the Chairman observed that the *Travaux Préparatoires* should clearly indicate the common position to be agreed on, in order to avoid distinct interpretations by Courts. His words, as quoted below, are very clear on this point:

> [...] the Group had now almost begun a process of recognizing the following: that bodily injury would be covered; that bodily injury which resulted in mental injury would be covered; but that mental injury *per se* would only be covered where it had a substantial adverse effect on health. [...] One additional thing that it was necessary for the Group to do was to make sure that the records of the proceedings clearly indicated what it was that the Group agreed to; that would be vital in enabling an understanding as to what it was that the language which was being used was intended to cover; it could not be left to the Courts to subsequently interpret the text of Article 16, paragraph 1, independently of the Conference's 'travaux préparatoires'.[471]

However, the question of mental injury was later integrated into a 'draft consensus package', which included, among other things, mechanisms for compensation and limits of liability. At the end of the package discussions, the final text communicated did not contain any reference to mental injury. Given the unexpected result of the package negotiations, the Chairman concluded in a rather vague way that no clear consensus had emerged as to whether moral/psychological injury should be included in the scope of the Convention:

---

467. *Ibid.*, p. 485.
468. ICAO Doc 9775, International Conference on Air Law (Convention for the Unification of Certain Rules for International Carriage by Air), Montreal, 10-28 May 1999, volume I, *Minutes*, Montreal 1999, p. 69.
469. *Ibid.*, p. 69.
470. This point was also highlighted by Canada: '[...] the unfortunate situation was the regime of no-fault and unlimited liability which created a potential for abuse', *Ibid.*, p. 73.
471. *Ibid.*, p. 116.

> [...] a considerable degree of reservation had been expressed by some Delegations about expressing mental injury in a form in which it would be independent of bodily injury, therefore suggesting that, to the extent that that was admissible, it would be necessary to circumscribe it greatly. [...] All had recognized that under the concept of bodily injury there were circumstances in which mental injury which was associated with bodily injury would indeed be recoverable and damages paid therefor[e]. The Group had equally recognized that the jurisprudence in this area was still developing.[472]

The analysis shows that this lack of common agreement, as reported in the *Travaux Préparatoires*, may lead to a diversified jurisprudence that could jeopardize the purposes of the 1999 Montreal Convention.

(3) The 'Draft Statement' of the Conference Preparing the 1999 Montreal Convention

However, in light of recognition of the importance of the matter, the plenary session of the 1999 Montreal Conference adopted a draft Statement, which reads as follows:

> For the purpose of interpretation of the *Convention for the Unification of Certain Rules for International Carriage by Air*, adopted at Montreal on 28 May 1999, the Conference states as follows: 1. With reference to Article 16, paragraph 1, of the Convention,[473] the expression 'bodily injury' is included on the basis of the fact that in some States damages for mental injuries are recoverable under certain circumstances, that jurisprudence in this area is developing and that it is not intended to interfere with this development, having regard to jurisprudence in areas other than international carriage by air; [...].[474]

The rareness of such a draft Statement regarding the interpretation of the 1999 Montreal Convention confirms, by its very necessity, that the 1999 Montreal Conference did not succeed in adopting a clear-cut political agreement on the question of mental injuries.[475] To the author's knowledge, such a 'draft Statement' was never officially signed, with the consequence that its legal value is practically null.

(4) Declarations Made by Argentina

This being said, the instrument of accession of Argentina in 2009 contained the following declaration:

> For the Argentine Republic, the term 'bodily injury' in Article 17 of this treaty includes mental injury related to bodily injury, or any other mental injury which

472. *Ibid.*, p. 201.
473. *Id est* 17.
474. *See*, ICAO Doc 9775, International Conference on Air Law (Convention for the Unification of Certain Rules for International Carriage by Air), Montreal, 10-28 May 1999, volume I, *Minutes*, Montreal 1999, p. 243.
475. *See*, Sean Gates, *La Convention de Montréal de 1999*, Revue Française de Droit Aérien et Spatial 439-446 (1999). Sean Gates was the observer for the International Union of Aviation Insurers at the 1999 Conference.

> affects the passenger's health in such a serious and harmful way that his or her ability to perform everyday tasks is significantly impaired.[476]

The legal value of this declaration is questionable. Indeed, no such declaration was required by the 1999 Montreal Convention, and no other State made one of its kind in favour or against the admissibility of mental injury.

According to Professor Iain Cameron, declarations of interpretation should not be assimilated to reservations even though they may be used to avoid reservation prohibition.[477] Professor Donald McRae considers there to be two types of interpretative declaration: one he calls 'mere interpretation declaration' and that only informs the position of a government, but whose interpretation can be rejected by Courts; and the other, a 'qualified interpretative declaration', which is in fact a disguised reservation.[478]

As the possibility of reservations is limited in the 1999 Montreal Convention,[479] the Argentinian declarations could be regarded as being inconsistent with the treaty. To my knowledge, no Argentinian decision has yet to be published regarding the value attributed to this declaration.

(5) Judicial Decisions

(i) Preliminary Remarks

As a preliminary remark, Courts might have been inclined to avoid directly interpreting the concept of 'bodily injury', and to have had recourse to the referral to domestic law set out in Article 24 of the 1929 Warsaw Convention and Article 29 of the Montreal Convention. As a matter of fact, the distinction between 'mental injury' and 'moral damage', also referred to as 'non-material damage', is slightly blurred and has not always been clearly delineated by Courts.[480] These Courts may therefore consider that any kind of damage could be compensated pursuant to domestic law, as per the above provisions of the Conventions, without analysing whether the term 'bodily injury' also includes mental injury.

---

476. ICAO, https://www.icao.int/secretariat/legal/List%20of%20Parties/Mtl99_EN.pdf (accessed 18 August 2019).
477. Iain Cameron, *Treaties, Declarations of Interpretation* 9 (Max Planck Encyclopedias of International Law, 2007).
478. Donald McRae, *The Legal Effect of Interpretative Declarations*, 49 British Yearbook of International Law 160 (1978).
479. *See*, section 3.3.2.
480. *See*, for example, *Bassam v. American Airlines, Inc.*, 287 F. App'x 309, 317 (5th Cir. 2008), where the Court held that, under the 1999 Montreal Convention, emotional distress for the loss of items in baggage cannot be compensated. This last decision should be compared to the 2010 *Walz* decision of the Court of Justice of the European Union, which held that the term 'damage', which underpins Article 22 of the 1999 Montreal Convention, that sets the limit of an air carrier's liability for damage resulting, *inter alia*, from the loss of baggage must be interpreted as including both material and non-material damage.

The following section will only focus on the way Courts have interpreted the concept of 'bodily injury' under the 1929 Warsaw Convention and the 1999 Montreal Convention.

(ii) Prior to the 1999 Montreal Convention

Prior to the adoption of the 1999 Montreal Convention, the question of the scope of mental injury under the term 'bodily injury' was particularly discussed before American Courts.[481] Certain of these Courts admitted the inclusion of 'pure' mental injury, that is, without physical manifestation, under the term 'bodily injury'.[482] However, in *Floyd* in 1991, the Supreme Court of the United States ruled that pure mental injury could not be compensated. Said Court however expressed no view as to whether a mental injury that accompanied a physical injury could be compensated.[483] Since then, certain Courts in the United States have considered that mental injuries can be compensated provided they are caused by or flow from a physical injury.[484] A similar view was adopted in the UK by the House of Lords in *Morris*. In this case, Lord Steyn considered that, in a situation where a passenger suffered no physical injury but did suffer mental injury or illness, said passenger did not have a claim under Article 17.[485] However, he noted that, with the coming into force of the 1999 Montreal Convention, things might change:

> This is how matters stand at present. Limited progress towards the admission of claims for mental injury and illness must await the coming into operation of the Montreal Convention.[486]

This exclusion of mental injuries under the term 'bodily injury' was affirmed in other jurisdictions, such as South Africa, where the High Court sitting in the Cape of

481. *See*, René Mankiewicz, *The Application of Article 17 of the Warsaw Convention to Mental Suffering Not Related to Physical Injury*, 4 Annals of Air & Space Law 187 (1979).
482. *Husserl v. Swiss Air Transport Company Ltd.*, 388 F. Supp. 1238 (S.D.N.Y. 1975), at 1250: 'But purpose and intent analysis itself is very useful. Although the draftsmen probably had no specific intent as to whether Article 17 comprehended mental and psychosomatic injuries, they did have a general intent to effect the purpose of the treaty and apparently took some pains to make it comprehensive. That they may have neglected one area should not vitiate the purpose of the Convention. There is no evidence they intended to preclude recovery for any particular type of injury. To regulate in a uniform manner the liability of the carrier, they must have intended to be comprehensive. To effect the treaty's avowed purpose, the types of injuries enumerated should be construed expansively to encompass as many types of injury as are colorably within the ambit of the enumerated types. Mental and psychosomatic injuries are colorably within that ambit and are, therefore, comprehended by Article 17.'
483. *Eastern Airlines, Inc. v. Floyd et al.*, 499 U.S. 530 (1991).
484. *See*, for example, in *re Air Crash at Little Rock Arkansas, on June 1, 1999*, 291 F.3d 503 (8th Cir. 2002), the Court ruled that, under the Warsaw text, compensation could only be claimed for mental injuries that arose from physical injuries; in *Ehrlich v. American Airlines, Inc.*, 360 F.3d 366 (2nd Cir. 2004), the Court decided that mental injuries that accompanied, but were not caused by bodily injuries, could not be indemnified under the 1929 Warsaw Convention.
485. *Morris v. KLM Royal Dutch Airlines* (2002) UKHL 7.
486. *Ibid.*, at 31.

Good Hope denied passengers the right to any compensation after their feelings had been hurt by the crew during a flight.[487]

Taking an opposite approach, the Supreme Court of Israel held in 1984 that pure psychological injuries could be compensated under Article 17 of the 1929 Warsaw Convention.[488]

(iii) Under the 1999 Montreal Convention

Since the adoption of the 1999 Montreal Convention, Courts continue to work on this particular question.[489]

In the UK, the Supreme Court confirmed its earlier position in *Stott*:

> Bodily injury (or lésion corporelle) has been held not to include mental injury, such as post-traumatic stress disorder or depression (*Morris* [...]). The same would apply to injury to feelings.[490]

In the United States, case law continued to broaden the scope of mental injury acceptable under the umbrella of 'bodily injury'.[491] In *Doe*, the 6th Circuit Court held that mental anguish was compensable, as long as it resulted from an accident that also caused bodily injury, even though the mental anguish might not flow from such bodily injury.[492] In *Jacob*, the 11th Circuit Court underlined that subsequent physical manifestations of an earlier emotional injury were not compensable under the 1999 Montreal Convention.[493] In Australia, in a case involving Post-Traumatic Stress Disorder, the New South Wales Court of Appeal held that such a disorder could be compensable, provided that there was brain damage. However, the Court noted that a mere biochemical change was not sufficient to be considered a bodily injury.[494]

487. *Potgieter v. British Airways plc* (2005) ZAWCH 5.
488. Supreme Court, 22 October 1984, Revue Française de Droit Aérien et Spatial 232 (1985) – translated in French. The interpretation method used by the Supreme Court remains questionable insofar as the Court took into consideration existing French law and French case law to interpret the Warsaw Convention, assuming that since the Convention was drafted in French, French law could be used as guidance. *See*, section 4.3.3.5.
489. *See*, for example, Mckay Cunningham, *The Montreal Convention: Can Passengers Finally Recover for Mental Injuries?*, 41 Vanderbilt Journal of Transnational Law 1043 (2008); Nandini Paliwal, *Interpretation of the Term 'Bodily Injury' in International Air Transportation: Whether Recovery for Mental Injury Is Tenable under the Warsaw System and Montreal Convention*, 2 The Aviation & Space Journal (April 2018).
490. *Stott v. Thomas Cook Tour Operators Ltd* (2014) UKSC 15, at 28.
491. *See*, for a recent overview of American case law, Andrew Harakas, 'Air Carrier Liability for Passenger Injury or Death Occurring During International Carriage by Air: An Overview of the Montreal Convention of 1999', in Andrew J. Harakas (ed.), *Litigating the Aviation Case* 23 (4th edition, American Bar Association, 2017).
492. *Doe v. Etihad Airways, P.J.S.C.*, 870 F.3d 406 (6th Cir. 2017). *See*, David Krueger, *Mental Distress for Airlines Lawyers: The Sixth Circuit's Decision in Doe v. Etihad*, 31(2) The Air and Space Lawyer 4-7 (2018).
493. *Jacob v. Korean Air Lines Co. Ltd*, 606 F. App'x 478 (11th Cir. 2015).
494. *Pel-Air Aviation Pty v. Casey* [2017] NSWCA 32, at 52.

A notable exception to this common view comes from Spain, where the Court of Appeal of Madrid held in 2008 that pure mental injury, resulting from two aborted take-offs, fell within the concept of 'bodily injury'.[495]

(iv) Is an Evolutionary Interpretation Possible?

In light of this last decision and with regard to the 'draft Statement' prepared by the plenary of the 1999 Montreal Conference, one wonders whether Courts are indeed allowed to adopt an evolutionary interpretation of the term 'bodily injury'.[496]

The 'draft Statement' is, however, in opposition with the literal meaning, context, purposes and object of the 1999 Montreal Convention, which requires the adoption of a uniform approach in its interpretation and application.[497] It also stands in contradiction with long-standing case law in many different jurisdictions.[498]

I confirm that the choice not to include mental injury in the 1999 Montreal Convention under the term 'bodily injury' was the outcome of negotiations on the consensus package, which resulted in a series of specific liability thresholds that accommodated the need for balance between passenger and carrier rights.[499] The intention was clearly to adopt common liability thresholds, and not to include mental injuries. Should 'mental injuries' now be considered as included, the substantive rules of the Convention would have to be discussed once again, particularly with regard to the choice of a strict liability regime.

In my view, the wording of the 1999 Montreal Convention is clear. When adopting that standpoint, I also take into consideration later instruments of international law, which make a clear distinction between bodily injury and mental injury.[500]

495. Audiencia Provincial Madrid, 1 February 2008, ECLI:ES:APM:2008:10106: '[...] por lesión corporal ha de considerarse no solamente la lesión física, sino también la psíquica. De lo contrario se llegaría al contrasentido de que en base al Convenio de Montreal pudieran indemnizarse los daños morales derivados de simples lesiones físicas de muy escasa trascendencia (o de daños sufridos en el equipaje), pero quedaran sin indemnizar secuelas psíquicas (que en ocasiones pueden llegar a ser incluso invalidantes) sufridas por un pasajero como consecuencia de lo acaecido en un transporte aéreo internacional'. This decision concerned two passengers who suffered anxiety following two aborted take-offs and decided not to pursue their journey from Madrid to Edinburgh. They sought compensation for material damage (the price of their tour in Scotland and the taxi costs back home from the airport) but not for moral damage (the anxiety itself). *See*, Belén Ferrer Tapia, *El contracto de transporte aéreo de pasajeros: sujetos, estatuto y responsabilidad* 189 (Dykinson, Madrid, 2013).
496. Evolutionary concepts are generally limited to general or generic terms, such as 'modern world' or 'well-being', in opposition to specific terms. *See*, International Law Commission, *Draft conclusions on subsequent agreements and subsequent practice in relation to the interpretation of treaties, with commentaries* 50 (2018).
497. *See*, Chapter 2 and 1969 Vienna Convention, Article 31(1).
498. *See*, 1969 Vienna Convention, Article 31(3). *See also*, International Law Commission, *Draft conclusions on subsequent agreements and subsequent practice in relation to the interpretation of treaties, with commentaries* 54 and 55 point 20 (2018). The ILC refers to the exclusion of evolutionary interpretations of the term 'bodily injury' in domestic Courts.
499. *See*, Bin Cheng, *A New Era in the Law of International Carriage by Air: From Warsaw (1929) to Montreal (1999)*, 53 International & Comparative Law Quarterly 850 (2004).
500. *See*, for example, Convention on Compensation for Damage Caused by Aircraft to Third Parties, 2 May 2009, Montreal, ICAO Doc 9919, not in force; Convention on Compensation for Damage

(v) Conclusion

In short, different interpretations of the term 'bodily injury' by Courts show how a lack of precise political agreement may lead to fragmentation of the Conventions.

Excluding 'mental injury' from the scope of 'bodily injury' does not automatically entail the exclusion of moral damage, understood under domestic law. Moral damage may still be granted pursuant to domestic law, provided the accident caused bodily injury. This reading, which I believe is in line with the wording of the 1999 Montreal Convention and the intentions of its drafters, permits a more uniform application of the text.

3.2.4.4 *Concluding Remarks*

The examples of delay and bodily injury demonstrate that the lack of a common position, at least as it transpired from the *Travaux Préparatoires*, may be a source of fragmentation of the Conventions. Yet, as submitted, these Conventions were designed to create a uniform application of their provisions.

3.2.5 The Unclear Formulation of the Demarcation Between the Uniform Rules and the *Renvois* Rules: The Example of Limitation of Actions

3.2.5.1 *The Two-Year Limit to Initiating Legal Proceedings*

The formulation of a provision is another element that may have led Courts to interpret the uniform rules in distinct ways. An example can be taken from the application by Courts of the provisions regarding the limitation of actions. Looking at the 1929 Warsaw Convention, Article 29 provides that:

> 1. The right to damages shall be extinguished if an action is not brought within two years, reckoned from the date of arrival at destination, [...].
> 2. The method of calculating the period of limitation shall be determined by the law of the Court seised of the case.[501]

Article 35 of the 1999 Montreal Convention is slightly similar to the English version, as it states that:

> 1. The right to damages shall be extinguished if an action is not brought within a period of two years, reckoned from the date of arrival at destination, [...].
> 2. The method of calculating that period shall be determined by the law of the court seised of the case.

to Third Parties, Resulting from Acts of Unlawful Interference Involving Aircraft, 2 May 2009, Montreal, ICAO Doc 9920, not in force.

501. The French text reads: '1. L'action en responsabilité doit être intentée, sous peine de déchéance, dans le délai de deux ans à compter de l'arrivée à destination [...]. 2. Le mode de calcul du délai est déterminé par la loi du tribunal saisi'.

These provisions are, in fact, strictly similar in the French versions.[502]

One immediately notices that while the Conventions set out a uniform time limitation of two years for actions, they also provide that the computation method be subject to domestic law.

The following section will examine whether this formulation generated divergent interpretations of the uniform rule. To this end, references will be made to the *Travaux Préparatoires* and judicial decisions related to the 1929 Warsaw Convention and the 1999 Montreal Convention.

3.2.5.2 Prior to the 1999 Montreal Convention

(1) Travaux Préparatoires

Initially, it was foreseen in the draft text submitted to the 1929 Warsaw Conference that suspension and interruption causes would be determined by the law of the Court seized of the case.[503] But, during said conference, the Italian delegation suggested changing this paradigm in favour of an unbreakable two-year limit.[504] As cited below, before the adoption of this amendment, the French delegate, while seconding the Italian proposal, voiced that the *renvoi* to domestic law concerned the manner of seizing the Court within the indicated time frame. He noted that in certain jurisdictions a preliminary conciliation was requested, while this was not the case in other jurisdictions:

> Il faudrait tout de même indiquer que c'est la loi du tribunal saisi qui fixera comment, dans le délai de deux ans, le tribunal sera saisi, parce que dans tous les pays du monde les actions ne sont pas exercées de la même façon. [...] En France, il y a le préliminaire de conciliation; dans d'autres pays le renvoi au tribunal civil est indispensable; mais je suis bien d'avis qu'il faut supprimer l'interruption de la prescription et je me rallie à la proposition Italienne.[505]

It stands to reason, then, from the *Travaux Préparatoires* of the 1929 Warsaw Convention, that the time limit to be established would be unbreakable, with the consequence that no suspension or interruption would be allowed.

(2) Judicial Decisions

A substantial number of Courts acknowledged this principle and considered the time limit established to be unbreakable, and that it therefore was not supposed to be suspended or interrupted.[506]

---

502. Which, with respect to the Warsaw text, is the only authentic version.
503. ICAO Doc 7838, II Conférence Internationale de Droit Privé Aérien, 4-12 Octobre 1929, *Procès-Verbaux*, Varsovie, 1930, p. 173: 'Le mode de calcul de la prescription, ainsi que les causes de suspension et d'interruption de la prescription sont déterminés par la loi du tribunal saisi'.
504. *Ibid.*, p. 75.
505. *Ibid.*, p. 76.
506. *See*, for example, in the following States: Argentina: Supreme Court of Justice, 16 October 2002, *Natasi Grace Jane E. c. Aerolineas Argentinas S.A. s/ Daños y Perjuicios*, N. 148. XXXVII. REX;

However, certain Courts have argued that the second paragraph of Article 29 of the 1929 Warsaw Convention authorized them to adapt this limit pursuant to their domestic procedural law.[507] This is particularly the case in France, where the *Cour de cassation* held in 1977[508] that, despite having considered the contents of the *Travaux Préparatoires*, nothing in the text of the Convention expressly indicated that the two-year limit could not be suspended or interrupted pursuant to domestic law.[509] This position was reaffirmed on several occasions.[510]

What may be considered as an unclear structure supposed to establish a demarcation between the uniform rule and the rule of *renvoi* also led to less variant decisions that nevertheless had a very low degree of predictability. This is particularly the case in Luxembourg, where the *Cour de cassation* decided in 2015 that, even though the two-year limit could not be suspended or interrupted, Article 29 of the 1929 Warsaw Convention would not be infringed upon in the situation where several claims were introduced two years after the crash of an aircraft, but within domestic law limits, insofar as at least one claim was lodged in the specified time frame.[511] One argument raised on this point was that the limit established in the 1929 Warsaw Convention was essentially aimed at unequivocally informing the carrier in a short time period of its duty to indemnify.

Belgium: CA Bruxelles, 2 May 1984, Journal des Tribunaux 550 (1984), ECLI:BE:CA-BRL:1984:19840502.2; Germany: Bundesgerichtshof, 2 April 1974, European Transport Law 777 (1974); Israel: Supreme Court, 22 October 1984, Revue Française de Droit Aérien et Spatial 232 (1985); Madagascar: CA Tananarive, 9 March 1972, Revue Française de Droit Aérien et Spatial 325 (1972); United Kingdom: *Laroche v. Spirit of Adventure (UK) Limited* (2009) EWCA Civ 12, at 70; United States: *Fishman v. Delta Air Lines Inc*, 132 F. 3d 138 (1998); Switzerland: Federal Court, 10 May 1982, Revue Française de Droit Aérien et Spatial 365 (1983).

507. *See*, for a description of the different nature of the time limitation set forth in the Conventions under domestic legislation, Laurent Chassot, *Les sources de la responsabilité du transporteur aérien international: entre conflit et complémentarité: La Convention de Montréal et son interaction avec le droit européen et national* 324-327 (Schulthess, 2012).

508. In a previous decision, with respect to a non-international flight, the *Cour de cassation* already ruled that the limit established by the Convention only governed contractual claim before civil jurisdictions, with the consequence that the two-year limit did not apply in the case of criminal proceedings. *See*, Cass., 17 May 1966, 65-92986.

509. Cass., 14 January 1977, 74-15061: 'Attendu que, pour déclarer irrecevable comme tardive l'action en réparation engagée [...] au nom de son fils mineur [...] l'arrêt attaqué énonce que le délai de deux ans imparti sous peine de déchéance par l'article 2 de la loi du 2 mars 1957 comme par l'article 29 de la Convention de Varsovie pour intenter l'action en responsabilité contre le transporteur aérien est un délai préfix et que ce caractère résulte sinon de l'expression sous peine de déchéance, qui ne lui confère pas nécessairement, du moins de la finalité du texte telle que la révèle l'intention du législateur français qui s'est expressément référé aux seules dispositions de la Convention de Varsovie dont les travaux préparatoires expriment nettement l'intention de ses auteurs de ne soumettre le délai à aucune cause de suspension; Attendu, cependant, que si la Convention de Varsovie du 12 octobre 1929, [...], prévoit que l'action en responsabilité doit être intentée à peine de déchéance dans un délai de deux ans, il n'existe dans ces textes aucune disposition expresse selon laquelle, par dérogation aux principes du droit interne français, ce délai ne serait susceptible ni d'interruption, ni de suspension [...]; Par ces motifs casse et annule'.

510. *See*, for instance, Cass., 1 July 1977, 75-15443; Cass., 26 April 1984, 82-12048; Cass., 24 May 2018,16-26.200.

511. Cass., 21 May 2015, 27/2015.

3.2.5.3 *Under the 1999 Montreal Convention*

(1) Travaux Préparatoires

Despite only minor changes to the English wording of this provision in the 1999 Montreal Convention, its *Travaux Préparatoires* unfortunately shed more ambiguity on this facet. While the Preparatory Material makes it clear that: 'To avoid different interpretations, it may be appropriate to clarify that this provision does not entitle a Court in any circumstances to interrupt or suspend the two-year period',[512] the Minutes do not reflect this point clearly. The delegate for Greece expressed this concern as follows:

> [...] the limitation period of two years stipulated in Article 29 had caused problems in jurisprudence in the past. If this was a statute of limitations which could be suspended by national domestic legislation, [he] believed this should be clarified so as not to leave such an ambiguity in the scope of the Convention.[513]

The delegate for Namibia hence suggested that:

> [...] a provision be inserted in Article 29 to make that point clear, i.e. that nothing contained in a preceding paragraph would affect the power inherent in a court seized of the case, to condone non-compliance with the time-limit referred to in paragraph 1 of that article.[514]

The Chairman responded that domestic law could indeed interfere in the computation method:

> [...] the method of calculating the period would be determined by the law of the court seized of the case, and that it may well be that a court seized of the case, in determining its method of calculation, would in fact interpret it to mean that insofar as there had been some act which would prevent the normal period of calculation being done, by virtue of fraud or otherwise, it would be the relevant law of the forum to make that determination.[515]

This situation, in his opinion, could occur under certain circumstances, such as imprisonment of the claimant, but would not be different from the previous practice.[516]

512. ICAO Doc 9775, International Conference on Air Law (Convention for the Unification of Certain Rules for International Carriage by Air), Montreal, 10-28 May 1999, volume III, *Preparatory Material*, Montreal 1999, p. 71.
513. ICAO Doc 9775, International Conference on Air Law (Convention for the Unification of Certain Rules for International Carriage by Air), Montreal, 10-28 May 1999, volume I, *Minutes*, Montreal 1999, p. 188.
514. *Ibid.*, pp. 188-189.
515. *Ibid.*, p. 189.
516. *Ibid.*, p. 236: '[...] it related to the exercise in jurisdictions to deal with time limits on the basis that there might be aspects which would render it fraudulent or inequitable. [...] many Courts did indeed exercise that jurisdiction. In terms of private international law, in terms of limitations of action, the matter was viewed as a procedural one, as a classification to be determined by *lex fori*. It was not without significance that that language had been used for the last seventy years in Article 29 of the Warsaw Convention, as well as in its successors. [...] no doubt that, if any action came up before a Court under circumstances where the claimant had

(2) *Judicial Decisions*

Minor changes in the English version do not seem to have been considered sufficient reason to re-examine in depth case law developed earlier in certain jurisdictions. For example, in 2018, the Federal Court of Australia confirmed pre-existing case law established under the 1929 Warsaw Convention, and held that the time limits of the 1999 Montreal Convention were unbreakable.[517] Similar decisions can be found in other jurisdictions, such as in the United States[518] and in Russia.[519]

However, the possibility of suspending or interrupting the two-year limit is still discussed in certain jurisdictions. In Spain, for example, the question arose of whether this provision was to be considered as falling within the category of 'prescripción' or 'caducidad'.[520] Although the highest Court has not officially put an end to this controversy, the Court of Appeal of Madrid held in 2015 that – in light of the foreign Warsaw and Montreal jurisprudence, the doctrine, and hopes of achieving uniformity – the time limit established by Article 35 was unbreakable.[521] This view was shared by the Court of Appeal of Tarragona in 2018.[522]

---

been precluded from bringing suit as a result of imprisonment, kidnapping or matters of that kind, then a Court, in the exercise of its inherent jurisdiction, in exercise of *lex fori*, would come to the conclusion that time did not begin to run until the claimant were free to be available'.

517. *See*, *Bhatia v. Malaysian Airline System Berhad* (2018) FCA 1471.
518. *See*, for example, *Dickinson v. American Airlines, Inc.*, 685 F. Supp. 2d 623 (N.D. Tex. 2010); *Narayanan v. British Airways*, 747 F.3d 1125 (9th Cir. 2014); *Von Schoenebeck v. Koninklijke Luchtvaart Maatschappij N.V.*, 659 F. App'x 392 (9th Cir. 2016), appeal before the Supreme Court denied.
519. Moscow City Court (Московский городской суд), 15 May 2017, N 4Г/ 10-1239/2017, cited in: International Air Transport Association, 21 *The Liability Reporter* 21 (2018). It is interesting to note that the Moscow City Court, acting as a cassation instance, adopted a literal interpretation of the provisions, in total opposition to the decision of the French *Cour de cassation* of 14 January 1977 detailed above. The Russian Court pointed out that if the suspension or interruption were allowed, the Conventions would have explicitly indicated it: 'Варшавская и Монреальская конвенции в императивной форме предусматривают максимальные сроки предъявления иска. Оснований для приостановления и перерыва срока исковой давности, равно как и возможности его восстановления, Конвенции не содержат. Если бы намерение было иным, то на это прямо было бы указано в названных Конвенциях'. It is worth mentioning that the Court gave consideration to the goal of uniformity of the Conventions to decline the application of domestic legislation: 'Из изложенного следует, что в целях интересов перевозчика и стабильности гражданского оборота, установлен единый срок исковой давности, который не может произвольно продлеваться по правилам внутреннего законодательства государств-участников, так как цели унификации норм ориентируют на нежелательность применения норм национального права, особенно в случаях, когда имеется достаточно четкий и ясный текст международного договора'.
520. To the opposite of 'caducidad', the 'prescripción' would allow the computation to be interrupted or suspended. *See*, Rodolfo González-Lebrero, *The Spanish Approach to the Limitation Period or Condition Precedent in the Montreal Convention on International Air Carriage of 28th May 1999*, 3 The Aviation & Space Journal 5 (2013); Belén Ferrer Tapia, *El contracto de transporte aéreo de pasajeros: sujetos, estatuto y responsabilidad* 323-326 (Dykinson, 2013).
521. Audiencia Provincial de Madrid, 18 May 2015, ECLI:ES:APM:2015:7272: 'En primer lugar, debemos analizar los cambios operados en su conjunto, porque la supresión del término "caducidad" no es la única modificación operada frente al anterior artículo 29 CV. [...] En segundo lugar, ya hemos señalado que la norma convencional, aplicable a Estados tan diversos como China, Qatar, los Estados Unidos de América, Perú o Pakistán, por poner algunos ejemplos, no puede interpretarse adaptándola al Derecho interno, fijando plazos como de

Taking an opposite view, other Courts still consider that the time limitation set out in the 1999 Montreal Convention may be suspended or interrupted pursuant to domestic law. This is the case, for instance, in Portugal, where the Court of Appeal of Lisbon held in 2017 that the time limits of the 1999 Montreal Convention could be subject to suspension or interruption in accordance with the Portuguese Civil Code.[523]

3.2.5.4 *Concluding Remarks*

The preceding analysis demonstrates yet again that an unclear structure of provisions, notably between uniform rules and referrals to domestic law, may sometimes lead to distinct interpretations, which are not necessarily in line with the content of the *Travaux Préparatoires*, and which erode the aim of the uniform rules. A clearer demarcation between what constitutes a uniform rule and what is subject to domestic law would have prevented such fragmentation of the Conventions from occurring.

3.2.6 Confidence in a Uniform Interpretation: The Example of Multiple Possible Fora

3.2.6.1 *Preliminary Remarks*

An additional source of fragmentation may come from the possibility of claims related to the same event being simultaneously heard by Courts in different jurisdictions. The

prescripción o de caducidad, refiriéndose a la habitual aplicación en el Derecho español de plazos prescriptivos a las acciones indemnizatorias, o poniendo como ejemplo los plazos de prescripción de la Ley de Navegación Aérea (por cierto, mucho más breves). En todo caso la interpretación debe efectuarse conforme a las reglas establecidas en la Convención de Viena sobre el Derecho de los Tratados (artículos 31 y 32). Para la interpretación del Convenio de Montreal resulta especialmente relevante el análisis de los criterios jurisprudenciales elaborados en relación al Convenio de Varsovia. [...] En la actual aplicación del Convenio de Montreal en otros países, como los Estados Unidos de América, se mantiene que el plazo fijado por el artículo 35 CM no es susceptible de suspensión [...] y se destaca como objetivo del Convenio de Montreal la necesidad de lograr uniformidad en su aplicación, de manera que atender a la suspensión de los plazos en función de la legislación de cada Estado Parte desvirtúa por completo dicho objetivo, concluyendo que el texto del Convenio resulta perfectamente claro en cuanto el periodo de dos años para solicitar cualquier indemnización, establecido como condición previa, no puede resultar desvirtuado por la aplicación de criterios suspensivos [...]'. The case went up to the Supreme Tribunal, which sought a preliminary ruling before the Court of Justice of the European Union (Tribunal Supremo, 19 July 2019, ECLI:ES:TS:2018:8522A). However, the parties agreed to withdraw the case. *See*, Tribunal Supremo, 29 January 2019, ECLI:EC:TS:2019:442A.

522. Audiencia Provincial de Tarragona, 26 July 2018, ECLI:ES:APT:2018:1024: '[...] estamos ante un plazo de caducidad y no de prescripción [...]'.
523. Tribunal da Relação de Lisboa, 11 May 2017, ECLI:PT:TRL:2017:1704.15.9T8AMD.L1.8.1E: 'Destarte, tendo a presente acção com fundamento a responsabilidade civil contratual (resultante da recusa de embarque) é aplicável o prazo de dois anos de prescrição, a contar da data de chegada ao destino, da data em que a aeronave deveria ter chegado ou da data da interrupção do transporte, nos termos do artigo 35° da Convenção. [...] Deste modo, caso não viesse a ocorrer qualquer circunstância que suspendesse ou interrompesse o prazo de dois anos, a prescrição ocorreria no dia [...] (artigo 279°, alínea c) do Código Civil)'.

following sections will examine decisions under the 1929 Warsaw Convention and 1999 Montreal Convention.

3.2.6.2 Prior to the 1999 Montreal Convention

The 1929 Warsaw Convention set forth that an action for damage can be brought, at the option of the plaintiff, before several determined fora. Article 28 of the 1929 Warsaw Convention provides that:

> 1. An action for damages must be brought, at the option of the plaintiff, in the territory of one of the High Contracting Parties, either before the Court having jurisdiction where the carrier is ordinarily resident, or has his principal place of business, or has an establishment by which the contract has been made or before the Court having jurisdiction at the place of destination.
> 2. Questions of procedure shall be governed by the law of the Court seised of the case.[524]

The draft text submitted to the 1929 Warsaw Conference was slightly different.[525] As explained in 1928 by the Rapporteur, in case of death, any action should have been brought before the first Court regularly seized of the case.[526] The issue was delicate: on the one hand, it was feared that the maximum liability limit would not be respected if the case was brought before several jurisdictions; on the other hand, a situation where a decision had been delivered but could not be enforced in another jurisdiction needed to be avoided.[527]

The proposal for a single jurisdiction in the case of death was abandoned because it was held to be rather theoretical.[528] This being said, it was discarded only insofar as

524. The French version reads: '1. L'action en responsabilité devra être portée, au choix du demandeur, dans le territoire d'une des Hautes Parties Contractantes, soit devant le tribunal du domicile du transporteur, du siège principal de son exploitation ou du lieu où il possède un établissement par le soin duquel le contrat a été conclu, soit devant le tribunal du lieu de destination. 2. La procédure sera réglée par la loi du tribunal saisi'.

525. ICAO Doc 7838, II Conférence Internationale de Droit Privé Aérien, 4-12 Octobre 1929, *Procès-Verbaux*, Varsovie, 1930, p. 172: 'L'action en responsabilité devra être portée, au choix du demandeur, dans un des Etats Contractants soit devant le tribunal du siège principal de l'exploitation ou du lieu où celui-ci possède un établissement par le soin duquel le contrat a été conclu, soit devant celui du lieu de destination ou, en cas de non arrivée de l'aéronef, du lieu de l'accident. En cas de mort, toutes actions devront être portées devant le premier tribunal qui aura été régulièrement saisi. La procédure sera réglée par la loi du tribunal saisi; toutefois, aucune formalité particulière ou caution ne peut être exigée du demandeur à raison de sa nationalité'.

526. *Ibid.*, pp. 165-166: 'En ce qui concerne la compétence du tribunal, le projet retient le tribunal du siège de l'exploitation ou du lieu où celle-ci possède un établissement par les soins duquel le contrat a été conclu, et le lieu de destination. En cas de non arrivée de l'aéronef, le tribunal du lieu de l'accident peut également être rendu compétent. La compétence du domicile du défendeur a donc été remplacée par une formule plus pratique pour l'exploitation de l'entreprise de transports. Le projet précise d'ailleurs que l'action doit être portée devant un tribunal d'un des Etats Contractants. Il prévoit en outre qu'en cas de mort, toutes actions devront être portées devant le premier tribunal qui aura été régulièrement saisi'.

527. *Ibid.*, pp. 79-85.

528. *Ibid.*, pp. 84-85.

the drafters contemplated the case of litigation before several fora in the case of death of a single specific passenger.

This possibility of having several competent fora in a scenario with multiple deaths was raised by the delegate for Japan:

> On dit dans le texte 'toutes actions'; ce texte n'est pas très clair. Est-ce que vous voulez dire 'toutes actions relatives à un seul décès'? s'il y a trois décès de personnes appartenant à trois nationalités différentes: un Américain, un Japonais, un Suisse, est-ce que quand une action a été introduite dans un pays, comme la France, je suppose, tous les ayants-droit devront aller en France?[529]

This remark promptly led to negative reactions from several delegations.[530] The above position can be understood – bearing in mind that at this time it was impractical for the family of the victim to litigate abroad and to enforce a foreign decision –[531] even if it theoretically allowed a possible fragmentation of the not yet born uniform regime.

Things have changed since then, and a typical example[532] of such fragmentation can be found in the opposing ways the French *Cour de cassation*[533] and the English House of Lords[534] treated the claims of victims of British Airways Flight 149, which landed in Kuwait at the time of hostilities with Iraq and were held hostage during several weeks in Baghdad. Whereas passengers were indemnified in France, their claims were dismissed in the UK.

3.2.6.3 Under the 1999 Montreal Convention

The 1999 Montreal Convention, after keeping the four fora agreed upon in the 1929 Warsaw Convention, and the two adopted in the 1961 Guadalajara Convention,[535] established one additional jurisdiction known as the 'fifth jurisdiction'.[536] This newcomer[537] permits, under limited conditions, to bring action in a territory where, at the time of the accident, the passenger holds principal and permanent residence. The United States strongly advocated for such an additional jurisdiction, arguing, among other things, that it would bring passengers further legal certainty.[538]

---

529. *Ibid.*, p. 83.
530. *Ibid.*
531. This point was also discussed at the 1955 Hague Conference, *see*, ICAO Doc 7686, International Conference on Private Air Law, The Hague, September 1955, volume I, *Minutes*, Montreal September 1956, pp. 259-261.
532. There are many others, *see*, for example, Michel Pourcelet, *The International Element in Air Transport*, 33 Journal of Air Law and Commerce 83 and the references (1967).
533. Cass, 15 July 1999, 97-10268.
534. *Sidhu and Others v. British Airways Plc; Abnett (Known as Sykes) v. Same* (1996) UKHL 5.
535. *See*, section 4.2.1.2.
536. 1999 Montreal Convention, Articles 33 and 46.
537. Although already discussed in the 1971 Guatemala City Protocol.
538. ICAO Doc 9775, International Conference on Air Law (Convention for the Unification of Certain Rules for International Carriage by Air), Montreal, 10-28 May 1999, volume II, *Documents*, Montreal 1999, p. 102: 'The passenger's home State is where most claimants are located, and that country's courts would usually apply the laws and standards of recovery that would be anticipated by such passengers or claimants.'

During the 1999 Montreal Conference, the delegate for Egypt noted that a fifth jurisdiction was not needed, explaining that:

> In the case of an accident, a carrier could be subjected to appear before many courts in different jurisdictions, [...].[539]

The delegate for France highlighted that the coexistence of parallel proceedings increased the risk of ending up with opposite decisions:

> [...] rather than advancing the unification and internationalization of law with a view to ensuring the identical treatment of persons under a single worldwide legal system, the result would be the further fragmentation of international law.[540]

Intense discussions continued around the adoption of this new forum.[541] There was a fear that a practice of forum shopping would develop. It was suggested that the doctrine forum non conveniens, a domestic procedure law standard in many common law jurisdictions, could mitigate this risk.[542]

Practice shows that the application of this doctrine did not bring the anticipated enhanced certainty. In 2005, a West Caribbean Airways flight from Panama to Fort-de-France in the French West Indies crashed in Venezuela. Several actions were introduced before American jurisdictions, which denied competence on the grounds of the doctrine forum non conveniens and, in substance, referred the case to the Courts of Fort-de-France. The French *Cour de cassation* eventually held that, given that Article 33(1) of the 1999 Montreal Convention provided that the action had to be brought 'at the option of the plaintiff', the French jurisdictions were not competent insofar as they were not the claimants' choice.[543]

Another example can be taken from litigations that followed the disappearance in 2014 of Malaysia Airlines flight MH370, which led to several actions being introduced in tandem before American and Malaysian Courts. As the action in Malaysia was said to be a protective measure in the event American jurisdictions denied competence,

539. ICAO Doc 9775, International Conference on Air Law (Convention for the Unification of Certain Rules for International Carriage by Air), Montreal, 10-28 May 1999, volume I, *Minutes*, Montreal 1999, p. 143.
540. *Ibid.*, p. 105.
541. *Ibid.*, pp. 143-187, 205, 235.
542. *See, Ibid.*, p. 108. The Chairman also wondered whether it would be appropriate to codify and incorporate such doctrine in the convention. *See, Ibid.*, pp. 148,149 and 158. The American delegate expressed concerns in this regard as it could raise ratification issues in jurisdictions where the doctrine was unknown. He also underscored that a codification might have altered existing jurisprudence. *See, Ibid.*, p. 159.
543. Cass., 7 December 2011, 10-30919: 'Attendu que l'option de compétence ouverte au demandeur par les textes susvisés s'oppose à ce que le litige soit tranché par une juridiction, également compétente, autre que celle qu'il a choisie; qu'en effet, cette option, qui a été assortie d'une liste limitative de fors compétents afin de concilier les divers intérêts en présence, implique, pour satisfaire aux objectifs de prévisibilité, de sécurité et d'uniformisation poursuivis par la Convention de Montréal, que le demandeur dispose, et lui seul, du choix de décider devant quelle juridiction le litige sera effectivement tranché, sans que puisse lui être opposée une règle de procédure interne aboutissant à contrarier le choix impératif de celui-ci; [...]'. *See also*, Sandra Adeline, *The Forum Non Conveniens Doctrine Put to the Test of Uniform Private International Law in Relation to Air Carrier's Liability: Lack of Harmony Between US and French Decision Outcomes*, 18 Uniform Law Review 313-328 (2013).

claimants requested to stay the Malaysian proceedings pending American litigation. With regard to the specific elements of the matter, the Court of Appeal of Malaysia considered that there were not sufficient grounds to justify putting the Malaysian suit on hold.[544]

3.2.6.4 Concluding Remarks

The existence of multiple possible fora in the Conventions shows that the intent to achieve a uniform application of the Conventions was once again met with obstacles from the drafting stage.

3.3 OTHER FACTORS CAUSING FRAGMENTATION

3.3.1 Preliminary Remarks

Next to the drafting elements examined above, factors which are not based on semantic choices have also limited the ability of the Conventions to fully deploy and realize their aim of uniformity from the time of their signing.

The Conventions, singular in their nature of being international public instruments regulating private law relations, face typical international public law limits, such as reservations and declarations, while, at the same time, are deprived of the possibility that their uniform application could be ensured by a single common Court or by clear specific interpretation mechanisms.

3.3.2 Reservations and Declarations

The first non-drafting elements that may limit the uniform application of the Conventions are reservations and declarations.

Reservations are defined by the 1969 Vienna Convention as:

> [...] a unilateral statement, however phrased or named, made by a State, when signing, ratifying, accepting, approving or acceding to a treaty, whereby it purports to exclude or to modify the legal effect of certain provisions of the treaty in their application to that State.[545]

In substance, reservations allow each State to be part of an international convention with certain ad hoc adjustments. Declarations are not defined in the 1969 Vienna Convention. However, as discussed above,[546] they can be considered as either

544. Court of Appeal of Malaysia, 5 July 2017, *Huang Min & orz v. MAS & orz*, W-01 (IM)(NCVC)-330-08/2016, ASEAN Legal Information Portal, Source, https://www.aseanlip.com/malaysia/general/judgments/huang-min-and-31-others-v-malaysian-airline-system-berhad-and-6-others/AL17593 (accessed 2019).
545. 1969 Vienna Convention, Article 2(1)(d).
546. *See*, section 3.2.4.3(4).

disguised reservations or political statements with limited impact in international public law.

It follows that if many different reservations and declarations were made admissible, they would undermine the whole purpose of the Conventions.[547]

During the 1929 Warsaw Conference, the possibility of allowing reservations in the text was discussed. The delegate for Italy voiced the concern that such an inclusion would jeopardize the envisaged uniformity:

> Il reste dans le procès-verbal que la Délégation italienne considère qu'une Convention pour unifier certaines règles ne peut insérer des réserves qui troublent précisément l'unification. En effet, s'il s'agit d'unifier on ne peut admettre que cette unification n'existe pas ou que cette unification soit boiteuse.[548]

It was however decided, given the purpose of uniformity, to refuse on principle any reservations unless specially allowed.[549] Thus, the Additional Protocol to the 1929 Warsaw Convention only authorizes reservations with respect to State flights. Article 40 of the 1929 Warsaw Convention also authorizes High Contracting Parties to declare that said convention does not apply to all or any of its overseas territories. Similar provisions are found in the 1955 Hague Protocol.[550]

In the same vein, Article 56 of the 1999 Montreal Convention provides that States can submit a declaration if they have two or more territorial units in which different systems of law are applicable in relation to matters dealt with by the convention. If submitted by a State, such declaration would have then to indicate whether the convention extends to all its territorial units, or to only to one or more of them.[551] With respect to reservations per se, Article 57 of the 1999 Montreal Convention specifies that:

> No reservation may be made to this Convention except that a State Party may at any time declare by a notification addressed to the Depositary that this Convention shall not apply to:
>
> (a) international carriage by air performed and operated directly by that State Party for non-commercial purposes in respect to its functions and duties as a sovereign State; and/or
> (b) the carriage of persons, cargo and baggage for its military authorities on aircraft registered in or leased by that State Party, the whole capacity of which has been reserved by or on behalf of such authorities.

547. On the effect of reservations, *see*, Malcolm Shaw, *International Law* 693 (8th edition, Cambridge University Press, 2017); Patrick Daillier, Mathias Forteau, Alain Pellet, *Droit International Public* 195-203 (8th edition, LGDJ, 2009).
548. ICAO Doc 7838, II Conférence Internationale de Droit Privé Aérien, 4-12 Octobre 1929, *Procès-Verbaux*, Varsovie, 1930, p. 152.
549. *Ibid.*, pp. 122-124.
550. Articles XXV and XXVI. This last article is more limited than the reservation authorized in the Additional Protocol to the 1929 Warsaw Convention, as it only permits States to declare that the Protocol shall not apply to the carriage of persons, cargo and baggage for its military authorities on aircraft, registered in that State, where the whole capacity has been reserved by or on behalf of such authorities.
551. Several declarations were submitted.

Theoretically, one could be satisfied with the limits imposed on the type of declarations and reservations allowed in the 1999 Montreal Convention. However, despite their limitations,[552] they have not prevented Argentina from submitting an interpretative declaration with respect to the term 'bodily injury' in Article 17 of the 1999 Montreal Convention, as discussed earlier.[553]

This might be an isolated case; however, it may be viewed as a precedent for others to further depart from the text, which, as regularly stated above, is designed to create uniformity.

3.3.3 The Lack of Uniform Jurisdiction and Interpretation Mechanisms

3.3.3.1 Preliminary Remarks

As the question of reservations is nevertheless very limited in practice, the genuine non-semantic flaw of the Conventions stands in the absence of common jurisdiction and/or specific interpretation mechanisms.

3.3.3.2 Lack of Uniform Jurisdiction

At the time of the 1929 Warsaw Conference, the possibility of enforcing a decision in another jurisdiction was discussed. The drafters of the 1929 Warsaw Convention were aware that sometimes an action would have to be introduced in a certain jurisdiction, but that the final decision would have to be enforced in another one, for example, where the debtor's assets could be found.[554] This situation was explored when the competence of the place of the accident was contemplated as a possible forum. The existence of different fora is a response to this lack of automatic recognition of foreign decisions, as the plaintiffs would then have a greater chance to introduce their action in a State where a final decision could easily be enforced.

Notwithstanding the above, the creation of an international specialized Court would have had the advantage of solving this question, but more essentially, would have prevented the existence of conflicting, or at least opposing decisions. Another substantial advantage of a common global Court would have been to provide a uniform interpretation of the Conventions.[555] Such a common global Court would have indeed prevented, or at least mitigated, what Professor Michel Pourcelet named in 1964 the 'désunification judiciaire'.[556]

552. There were suggestions to introduce opt-out provisions, which eventually were not accepted. *See*, ICAO Doc 9775, International Conference on Air Law (Convention for the Unification of Certain Rules for International Carriage by Air), Montreal, 10-28 May 1999, volume I, *Minutes*, Montreal 1999, p. 105.
553. *See*, section 3.2.4.3(4).
554. *See*, for example, ICAO Doc 7838, II Conférence Internationale de Droit Privé Aérien, 4-12 Octobre 1929, *Procès-Verbaux*, Varsovie, 1930, pp. 79-80.
555. Suggestions will be made in these regards below. *See*, section 5.3.1.
556. Michel Pourcelet, *Transport Aérien International et Responsabilité* 222 (Les Presses de l'Université de Montréal, 1964).

The idea of such a common global Court is not new, but has always been thwarted by national resistance. As a matter of fact, an international aviation Court for private law matters[557] was already discussed at the time of the negotiations of the 1952 Rome Convention, but no common agreement was reached at this stage. Since none of the delegates were willing to risk delaying the signing of the agreed-upon text, the 1952 Rome Conference merely made the following recommendation to the ICAO to examine this question:

> (a) instruct the Secretariat and the Legal Committee to study a system of settlement, at least in appeal proceedings, of international private law disputes that may arise either from the Convention signed this date, or from any other aviation convention either by the establishment of a special permanent tribunal, or by establishment of a special *ad hoc* tribunal, or by arbitrators acting under uniform rules of procedure to be developed, or by resorting to any other existing international institution;
>
> (b) make an immediate enquiry from States to ascertain the objections that may exist against such systems of settlement of disputes arising in connexion with international civil aviation.[558]

During the preparation of the 1955 Hague Conference, despite efforts made by the Netherlands to insist on the recommendation made in 1952,[559] no such recommendation was submitted to the 1955 Hague Conference. As pointed out by the Dutch delegate, such an idea created nervousness:

557. For public law matters, by 1919 the International Commission for Air Navigation already had a certain judicial role with respect to disputes on technical annexes. Later, the ICAO Council was vested with quasi-judiciary powers with respect to certain disputes. *See*, René Mankiewicz, *L'organisation international de l'aviation civile*, 3 Annuaire Français de Droit International 383-417 (1957); Bin Cheng, *The Law of International Air Transport* 100-105 (Stevens & Sons Limited, 1962); Paul Dempsey, *Public International Air Law* 666-740 (Institute and Center for Research in Air & Space Law, McGill University, 2008). The role of the International Court of Justice has also been confirmed with regard to the interpretation of the 1971 Montreal Convention for the Suppression of Unlawful Acts against the Safety of Civil Aviation, *see*, ICJ, *Questions of Interpretation and Application of the 1971 Montreal Convention arising from the Aerial Incident at Lockerbie (Libyan Arab Jamahiriya v. United Kingdom), Preliminary Objections, Judgment, I.C.J. Reports 1998*, p. 9; *ICJ, Questions of Interpretation and Application of the 1971 Montreal Convention arising from the Aerial Incident at Lockerbie (Libyan Arab Jamahiriya v. United States of America), Preliminary Objections, Judgment, I.C.J. Reports 1998*, p. 115. For a commentary of this decision, *see*, Peter Bekker, *Questions of Interpretation and Application of the 1971 Montreal Convention arising from the Aerial Incident at Lockerbie (Libyan Arab Jamahiriya v. United Kingdom) and (Libyan Arab Jamahiriya v. United States), Preliminary Objections, Judgements*, 92 The American Journal of International Law 503-508 (1998). For a confirmation of the ICAO Council's quasi-judicial role, *see*, International Court of Justice, *Appeal Relating to the Jurisdiction of the ICAO Council under Article II, Section 2, of the 1944 International Air Services Transit Agreement (Bahrain, Egypt and United Arab Emirates v. Qatar)*, 14 July 2020. *See also*, section 5.3.1.

558. ICAO Doc 7379, Conference on Private International Air Law, Rome, September-October 1952, volume II, *Documents*, Montreal April 1953, p. 278.

559. ICAO Doc 7686, International Conference on Private Air Law, The Hague, September 1955, volume II, *Documents*, Montreal September 1956, p 272.

> As soon as the word 'international' was pronounced, there were a number of countries which became nervous and thought that their sovereign rights might be endangered.[560]

The possibility and feasibility of a common jurisdiction, which the ICAO Council declined to investigate a few months earlier,[561] were, however, brought up again during the debates. A division appeared between civil law jurisdictions, which were mostly in favour, and common law jurisdictions.[562] As a result, no major steps were taken in that direction, with the notable exception that, in the Final Act of the 1955 Hague Conference, it was agreed, as cited below, to lay out in the resolutions and recommendations that the question of enforcement of judgments deserved further consideration:

> The Conference, Considering that neither the Convention Warsaw nor the Protocol to amend the said Convention signed at The Hague on 28 September 1955, contains rules relating to the execution of judgments rendered under the Convention or the Protocol, Invites the International Civil Aviation Organization to consider whether it is desirable to include, in the Warsaw Convention, rules relating to procedure in cases arising under the Convention, including the execution of judgments.[563]

The idea of creating an international Court never again reached such a high political level. Professor Paul Chauveau, when preparing a draft convention for the establishment of an aviation-specific dispute resolution body before the 1955 Hague Conference, took into consideration the arguments which he considered as generally voiced against the project of a global aviation Court.[564] These arguments can be summarized as follows:

(1) inadmissible substitution to national competent Courts;
(2) pragmatic difficulties due to the geographical distance between the Court and the plaintiff, witnesses and, generally speaking, actors in the litigation;
(3) Constitutional barriers; and
(4) lack of an automatic enforcement of foreign decisions.

560. ICAO Doc 7686, International Conference on Private Air Law, The Hague, September 1955, volume I, *Minutes*, Montreal September 1956, p. 264.
561. ICAO Doc 7379, Conference on Private International Air Law, Rome September-October 1952, volume II, *Documents*, Montreal, 1953, pp. 277-278. The ICAO Legal Committee requested the Council to include the subject in the work programme. On 31 March 1955, the Council decided to not comply with this request, *see*, ICAO Doc 7686, International Conference on Private Air Law, The Hague, September 1955, volume II, *Documents*, Montreal September 1956, p. 272.
562. ICAO Doc 7686, International Conference on Private Air Law, The Hague, September 1955, volume I, *Minutes*, Montreal, September 1956, pp. 264-268 and 342-343.
563. ICAO Doc 7686, International Conference on Private Air Law, The Hague, September 1955, volume II, *Documents*, Montreal, September 1956, pp. 30-31.
564. *See*, Paul Chauveau, *Rapport sur la création d'une Cour internationale pour la solution des difficultés nées de l'interprétation et de l'application des conventions internationales en matière de Droit aérien*, Revue Française de Droit Aérien et Spatial 465-481 (1955).

In a detailed analysis of the interest in the establishment of a common jurisdiction, Professor Otto Riese noted that said draft convention encountered strong opposition, notably by the ICAO Legal Committee.[565] Despite the optimism of many authors,[566] the idea never succeeded in surmounting national resistance.

3.3.3.3 *The Lack of Common Interpretation Mechanisms*

After the adoption of the 1929 Warsaw Convention, the IATA – which was in charge of the preparation of uniform documents of carriage – asked the CITEJA[567] in 1933 to give its interpretation on the concept of 'arrêts prévus' under Article 3 of the convention.[568]

Following the IATA question, the Third Conference – which led notably to the adoption of the 1933 Rome Convention – expressed the wish that an analysis be conducted on the potential role of the CITEJA as an advisory source of interpretation on private air law conventions.[569] From that perspective, the Rapporteur Albert de la Pradelle suggested amending the CITEJA internal rules,[570] and, during the XII session of the CITEJA in 1937, submitted a draft convention which would have given the CITEJA the option of providing interpretative advice with respect to private air law conventions if so required by governments, international Courts or other international official bodies. This preliminary draft convention regarding the role of the CITEJA in the interpretation and enforcement of private air law conventions was as follows:

> Avant-Projet de Convention relatif à la collaboration du C.I.T.E.J.A. à l'interprétation et à l'exécution des Conventions internationales de Droit Privé Aérien

565. *See*, Otto Riese, *Une juridiction supranationale pour l'interprétation du droit unifié?*, 13 Revue Internationale de Droit Comparé 717-735 (1961).
566. *See*, for example, Nicolas Mateesco Matte, *Traité de droit aérien-aéronautique* 59 (2nd edition, Pedone, 1964); Huib Drion, *Towards a Uniform Interpretation of the Private Air Law Conventions*, 19 Journal of Air Law and Commerce 423 (1952).
567. For a detailed description of its working methodology, *see*, Le Comité International Technique d'Experts Juridiques Aériens, *Son origine, son but, son oeuvre* (Publications du Comité International Technique d'Experts Juridiques Aériens, 1931); Stephen Latchford, *The Warsaw Convention and the CITEJA*, 6 Journal of Air Law and Commerce 79 (1935).
568. Albert de la Pradelle, *L'interprétation des Conventions Internationales de droit privé aérien à titre d'avis consultatif par le C.I.T.E.J.A.*, Revue Générale de Droit Aérien 456 (1934).
569. 'C) La Conférence, Considérant l'intérêt pour tous les usagers de l'aéronautique de pouvoir être, le cas échéant, éclairés sur les textes élaborés par les Conférences Internationales de Droit Privé Aérien; Prie le C.I.T.E.J.A. d'examiner, en vue de la Quatrième Conférence de Droit Privé, si, dans quelle mesure et de quelle manière, il pourra donner son avis sur l'interprétation des textes de Conventions Internationales de Droit Privé Aérien lorsqu'il en sera sollicité par une administration publique ou un organisme international sans qu'il soit porté atteinte au droit du pouvoir judiciaire saisi d'un différend', quoted in Albert de la Pradelle, *L'interprétation des Conventions Internationales de droit privé aérien à titre d'avis consultatif par le C.I.T.E.J.A.*, Revue Générale de Droit Aérien, 459 (1934).
570. For proposed changes in 1934, *see*, Albert de la Pradelle, *Rapport relatif à l'interprétation des Convention de droit privé aérien*, Revue Générale de Droit Aérien 793 (1934); Michel Smirnoff, *La Comité International Technique d'Experts Juridiques Aériens, Son Activité, Son Organisation* 139-145 and 227-229 (Pierre Bossuet, 1936).

I. Interprétation

Article Premier - Au cas où l'un des Etats représentés au C.I.T.E.J.A. ou l'un des tribunaux internationaux ou tout autre organisme officiel à caractère international qui aurait à connaître d'une Convention de Droit Privé Aérien aurait demandé au C.I.T.E.J.A. son opinion sur le sens à donner aux termes et dispositions de cette Convention, le C.I.T.E.J.A. est autorisé à fournir tous éclaircissements à titre purement consultatif en utilisant les travaux préparatoires des Avants-Projets de Convention, ainsi que tous éléments d'interprétation.

Article 2 - (1) La demande adressée au Comité est transmise par les soins du Secrétariat Général à une Commission permanente désignée par le C.I.T.E.J.A. Celle-ci prépare le projet de réponse.
(2) Le Comité, sur le Rapport de cette Commission, se prononce à la majorité des membres présents.
(3) La réponse est motivée; elle est transmise non seulement à l'auteur de la demande, mais à tous les Etats représentés au C.I.T.E.J.A. auxquels il appartient de la rendre publique.
(4) Toute opinion dissidente, également motivée, peut, si son auteur le désire, être jointe à la réponse.

II. Exécution

Article 3 - (1) Si la Conférence, au cours de laquelle est adoptée une Convention Internationale de Droit Privé Aérien, confie au C.I.T.E.J.A. la préparation de tout texte d'exécution commun à tous les Etats parties à la Convention pour aider à la mise en vigueur de cette Convention, le C.I.T.E.J.A. procède de la manière suivante: le Secrétariat Général saisit de la question la Commission chargée de l'élaboration de la Convention; celle-ci arrête à la majorité un projet de texte qu'elle soumet au C.I.T.E.J.A., qui l'adopte à la majorité sans qu'il soit fait mention autre part qu'aux procès-verbaux de toute opinion dissidente.
(2) Le texte ainsi préparé par le C.I.T.E.J.A. doit être accepté par chacun des Etats parties à la Convention pour avoir force obligatoire à son égard.

Article 4 - Si le gouvernement chargé de recueillir les signatures et de recevoir le dépôt des ratifications d'une Convention Internationale de Droit Privé Aérien croit devoir, dans le silence de la Conférence, confier au C.I.T.E.J.A. la mission prévue à l'article 3, il appartient au C.I.T.E.J.A. d'y procéder de même manière que suivant cet article et avec les mêmes effets.

Vœu

Pour permettre de suivre l'exécution des Conventions Internationales de Droit Privé Aérien, tout Etat partie à la Convention est prié de communiquer au Secrétariat Général du C.I.T.E.J.A., aussitôt que possible, tout document législatif, réglementaire, administratif ou judiciaire, relatif à cette exécution.[571]

Given the resistance mounted by a number of States such as the United States and the UK, and internal procedure points, the preliminary draft convention did not make it as far as a diplomatic conference.[572]

571. Report of the session published in the Revue Générale de Droit Aérien 605-617 (1937).
572. For a detailed description of the evolution of the draft text, *see*, Stephen Latchford, *Pending Projects of the International Technical Committee of Aerial Legal Matters*, 40 The American Journal of International Law 280-302 (1946).

However, in 1946, the plenary session of the CITEJA adopted two new projects of conventions, conferring upon it certain powers in connection to the interpretation of private air law convention. These draft conventions were referred in vain to the PICAO Secretariat for further action.[573]

According to Professor Huib Drion, during the preparation of the 1955 Hague Conference, the ICAO 'Warsaw' Subcommittee suggested in 1952 the insertion into Article 25 of the following provision:

> Contracting States shall co-operate to secure, as far as possible, a uniform interpretation of this Convention.[574]

This provision did not pass different tests and was not reflected in the draft proposal submitted to the 1955 Hague Conference.

During the 1955 Hague Conference, while considering the topic of international dispute settlement, negotiators finally agreed to revert the question back to the general terms of international bodies and organizations responsible or interested in the development of international private air law. The Final Act of the 1955 Hague Conference indeed provides, among the different resolutions and recommendations, that:

> The Conference,
>
> Considering that the uniform interpretation of the Warsaw Convention and of the Protocol to amend the said Convention as well as of other existing private air law conventions, is of vital importance for the unification of private air law aimed at by these conventions,
>
> Considering Also that the international nature of the situations to which these conventions apply, especially in connection with the distribution of the amounts to which liability is limited in some of these conventions, raises certain serious problems which cannot easily be solved otherwise than by means of some international legal forum,
>
> Considering Further that the problems envisaged in the foregoing are complicated that a complete study will require much time,
>
> Recommends that such international bodies and organizations, as are responsible for or interested in the development of private air law, commence as soon as possible to study the problems involved in the promotion of uniform interpretation of the international private air law conventions and in the international settlement of disputes arising under said conventions.[575]

Since then, the 1969 Vienna Convention has been adopted. It contained several provisions regarding the way international conventions must be interpreted.[576] The

573. *See*, Stephen Latchford, *Pending Projects of the International Technical Committee of Aerial Legal Matters*, 40 The American Journal of International Law 299-300 (1946).
574. Huib Drion, *Towards a Uniform Interpretation of the Private Air Law Conventions*, 19 Journal of Air Law and Commerce 423 (1952).
575. ICAO Doc 7686, International Conference on Private Air Law, The Hague, September 1955, volume II, *Documents*, Montreal September 1956, pp. 31-32.
576. *See*, section 1.3.1.2(2).

next chapter will explore whether the principles of interpretation of said convention are sufficient to ensure a uniform interpretation of the Conventions.

3.4 CONCLUSIONS

This chapter questioned the existence of factors that could have prevented, or still prevent, the Conventions from being uniformly applied from the moment of their signing. The analysis carried out confirmed the existence of such obstacles and identified them.

The major drafting factors examined prevent the Conventions from being uniformly applied and occasionally enable domestic law to sneak in. Non-drafting factors, such as reservations, declarations and the absence of a specific uniform jurisdiction or at the latest common interpretation mechanisms, may also be seen as impediments to a uniform application from an early stage after the signing of the Conventions.

Whereas the aim of uniformity of the 1929 Warsaw Convention suffered from shortcomings, these were understandable given the fact that the text adopted in 1929 had been discussed rather rapidly and was not deemed to last many decades.[577] At that time, it was above all a question of letting the practice develop before improving provisions. The successive waves of modifications after the Second World War, including the 1999 Montreal Convention, only partially improved these internal factors of fragmentation. As a matter of fact, other needs appeared to be more urgent, such as revisions to monetary limits, to the detriment of overall improvements in the name of uniformity. The ambition of the pioneers, particularly of the CITEJA – which had projects aiming at the creation of a fully efficient legal environment for international private air law – was thus thwarted.

The effectiveness of the uniform application of the Conventions essentially depends, therefore, on the behaviour of those having ratified the Conventions and the Courts which, despite the obstacles described, have to ensure their uniform application.

The next chapter will examine how such missions have been carried out, and other pitfalls on the road of the Conventions.

577. ICAO Doc 7838, II Conférence Internationale de Droit Privé Aérien, 4-12 Octobre 1929, *Procès-Verbaux*, Varsovie, 1930, pp. 62, 85, 104.

CHAPTER 4

External Factors of Fragmentation

4.1 INTRODUCTION

Alongside internal factors preventing a uniform application of the Conventions from an early stage, this analysis has yet to indicate whether other factors, which only appeared during the lifespan of the Conventions, may have created hurdles to their aim of uniformity.

With this in mind, this chapter will examine the behaviour of ratifying Parties in order to determine whether a modification of the regulatory environment might have affected the aim of uniformity (section 4.2). Subsequently, it will scrutinize the behaviour of Courts that have to apply the Conventions, in order to ascertain how they have responded to the characteristics described in Chapter 2, that is to say, exclusivity and autonomy (section 4.3). Finally, this chapter will explore whether the existence of various linguistic versions of the Conventions may have impacted their aim of uniformity (section 4.4).

4.2 REGULATORY MODIFICATIONS

4.2.1 Evolution of the Regime

4.2.1.1 A Multilayered System

Uniform rules are the outcome of compromise, and can easily be affected through a modification to the regulatory environment. In the case of the Conventions, modifications notably occurred when decisions were made to successively amend the original text.

The major role of revisions is to modernize the text in order to fit actual needs. This task is an opportunity for adapting provisions of the initial text when their substantive aspect was too fragmented across jurisdictions, and a common need for further reunification was expressed. However, revisions have a double impact. While they may proceed to necessary adjustments to respond to technical, social and/or legal needs,[578] the coexistence of rival texts attacks the effectiveness of unification.[579]

The international air carrier liability regime as established by the Conventions was modified on numerous occasions on the initiative of States, via protocols or a supplementary convention,[580] as well as through private initiatives and domestic/regional interventions. These modifications will be discussed in the next sections against the backdrop of the principal research question, the envisaged uniformity in private international air law.

4.2.1.2 *International Conventions*

(1) Numerous Modifications

The 1929 Warsaw Convention was first amended by the 1955 Hague Protocol. Through this, passengers were offered a greater protection with new provisions. As an example, their ticket would no longer contain a mere 'statement'[581] of their rights, but from that point onwards would include a 'notice'[582] informing them that their journey was regulated by the uniform rules. The carriers also saw their situation improve. For example, the 1955 Hague Protocol authorized carriers to alleviate their liability with respect to inherent defects to cargo.[583] In addition to these changes, former controversies, such as the negotiability of the airway bill, were also solved.[584]

Moreover, the concepts of 'dol'[585] and 'faute équivalente',[586] which were used in the 1929 text,[587] and which had given rise to many misunderstandings in common law jurisdictions, were redrafted to lower the potential connections with domestic law and therefore enhance the autonomy of the concepts. While the idea remained the same, the two concepts were respectively redrafted as follows: '[...] done with intent to cause damage [...]' and '[...] recklessly and with knowledge that damage would probably

578. *See*, Otto Riese, *Une juridiction supranationale pour l'interprétation du droit unifié?*, 13 Revue Internationale de Droit Comparé 717-735 (1961).
579. *See*, Barry Spitz, *Assessment of the Unification of Private International Air Law by Treaty*, 83 South African Law Journal 179 (1966).
580. For a description of the relationship between these instruments and the 1999 Montreal Convention, *see*, section 1.3.1.1(2).
581. 1929 Warsaw Convention, Articles 3 and 4.
582. 1955 Hague Protocol, Articles III and IV.
583. *Ibid.*, Article XII.
584. *Ibid.*, Article IX: 'Nothing in this Convention prevents the issue of a negotiable air waybill.' In practice, however, they are generally not negotiable instruments. *See*, Marc Godfroid, 'Transport aérien', in Jacques Libouton (ed.), *Traité Pratique de Droit Commercial: Transport de marchandises* 173 (Wolters Kluwer, 2015).
585. Translated as 'willful misconduct' in the English translation.
586. Translated as 'default equivalent to' in the English translation.
587. 1929 Warsaw Convention, Article 25.

result'.[588] This redrafting towards further autonomy faced resistance as references to concepts known under domestic law were preferred by certain negotiators, particularly when it came to matters of translation. The *Travaux Préparatoires* report, to that effect, that the delegate for Belgium expressed the view that it was important to have a French text which would be absolutely clear for French-speaking jurisdictions. He noted that the suggested word 'recklessly' could not be satisfyingly translated into French with the word 'témérairement', as recklessly would refer, in his understanding, to a 'total lack of care', which would correspond more closely in French to 'insouciance totale'.[589] But as pointed out above, this comment did not result in any changes.[590]

Although the 1955 Hague Protocol improved the text of the 1929 Warsaw Convention in many ways, delegates were aware that the new text could not depart too drastically from the original one insofar as ratifiability was at stake as underlined here by the Soviet delegation:

> [...] the introduction of a large number of amendments in the Warsaw Convention would make it very difficult to accept and ratify the Protocol which might be adopted by the Conference, and this would result in the destruction of the provisions of the Convention which brought about the unification of the rules of international air transport.[591]

Successive waves of improvements later occurred with the 1961 Guadalajara Convention, the 1971 Guatemala City Protocol, the 1975 Montreal Additional Protocols and the 1974 Montreal Protocol No 4, which all also contributed to the fragmentation of the uniform regime, although to a lesser extent.

The 1961 Guadalajara Convention supplemented the 1929 Warsaw Convention and, as such, did not substantially modify the existing uniform regime. The 1961 Guadalajara Convention organized the liability regime in the case of charter arrangements that were developing at the time.[592] It created a distinction between contractual and actual carriers. Most of its provisions were later reflected in the 1999 Montreal Convention.

Later, neither the 1971 Guatemala City Protocol, which had ambitions to modernize provisions of the system and to introduce unbreakable liability limits, nor the 1975 Additional Protocol No 3 entered into force.

The 1975 Additional Protocol Nos 1 and 2 and 1975 Montreal Protocol No 4 entered into force only a few years before the adoption of the 1999 Montreal Convention, and did not therefore have many opportunities to widely impact the existing system. These two Additional Protocols primarily aimed at replacing the

588. 1955 Hague Protocol, Article XIII. In the French version: 'avec l'intention de provoquer un dommage', 'soit témérairement et avec conscience qu'un dommage en résultera probablement'.
589. ICAO Doc 7686, International Conference on Private Air Law, The Hague, September 1955, volume I, *Minutes*, Montreal September 1956, p. 280.
590. On the linguistic issues, *see*, section 4.4.
591. ICAO Doc 7686, International Conference on Private Air Law, The Hague, September 1955, volume I, *Minutes*, Montreal September 1956, p. 56.
592. *See*, Isabella Diederiks-Verschoor, Pablo Mendes de Leon, *An Introduction to Air Law* 210 (9th edition, Wolters Kluwer, 2012).

currency unit established in francs in the prior instruments by Special Drawing Rights (hereinafter also referred to as 'SDRs') which had been recently created.[593] In parallel, the Montreal Protocol No 4 essentially aimed to modernize the provisions of the 1955 Hague Protocol regarding carriage of cargo and mail.[594]

(2) Consequences

In 2021, among States that have ratified the 1929 Warsaw Convention, twenty-two still have not ratified the 1955 Hague Protocol.[595] This shows the risk of having several acting liability regimes.[596] The absence of symmetrical ratifications creates a situation of fragmentation of the uniform regime.

Although the goal of the successive changes was to improve the liability regime set forth in the 1929 Warsaw Convention – in order among other things, to more adequately respond to the interests of the travelling public – these changes resulted in a fragmentation of the rule due to the different levels of ratification.

An example of such fragmentation can be found in the litigation that followed the crash of Canadian Pacific Airlines flight CP 402 in Tokyo in 1966. The actions of two different families of deceased passengers went to the Supreme Court of Canada. The discussions essentially focused on the limit of liability of the carrier insofar as the reference to the applicable liability regime was drafted in small print on the ticket. With respect to one family, the Supreme Court held that the carrier was entitled to the limitation of liability, given that, in light of the passenger routing, only the 1929 Warsaw Convention applied.[597] With regard to the other family, it held that the carrier was not entitled to the limitation of liability given the passenger's specific routing triggered the application of the 1955 Hague Protocol. The consequence of the application of the 1955 Hague Protocol was that the carrier had to comply with the new

---

593. A Special Drawing Right is a unit of accounting created by the International Monetary Fund in 1969. Its value is based on the basket of several currencies used in international trade and finance, namely in 2021: US Dollar (41.73%), Euro (30.93%), Chinese Yuan (10.92%), Japanese Yen (8.33%), Pound Sterling (8.09%), Source: International Monetary Fund, https://www.imf.org/en/About/Factsheets/Sheets/2016/08/01/14/51/Special-Drawing-Right-SDR (accessed 17 February 2021).

594. *See*, ICAO Doc 9154, International Conference on Air Law, Montreal, September 1975, volume I, *Minutes*, Montreal, 1977, pp. 2, 250.

595. ICAO, https://www.icao.int/secretariat/legal/LEB%20Treaty%20Collection%20Documents/composite_table.pdf (accessed 5 January 2021).

Some have ratified the 1999 Montreal Conference. Five States have ratified only the 1929 Warsaw Convention, namely: Comoros, Liberia, Mauritania, Myanmar, and Turkmenistan; 24 States have not yet ratified neither the 1929 Warsaw Convention, the 1955 Hague Protocol or the 1999 Montreal Convention: Andorra, Antigua and Barbuda, Bhutan, Burundi, Central African Republic, Djibouti, Dominica, Eritrea, Guinea-Bissau, Haiti, Kiribati, Marshall Islands, Micronesia, Niue, Palau, Saint Kitts and Nevis, Saint Lucia, San Marino, Sao Tome and Principe, Somalia, South Sudan, Tajikistan, Timor-Leste and Tuvalu. In total, 152 States have ratified the 1929 Warsaw Convention, 137 the 1955 Hague Protocol and 137 (including the European Union) the 1999 Montreal Convention in 2021.

596. The 1955 Hague Protocol sets forth that its ratification or adherence by any State which is not a Party to the 1929 Warsaw Convention has the effect of adherence to the latter in its version amended by the Protocol. *See*, 1955 Hague Protocol, Articles XXI and XXIII.

597. *Ludecke v. Canadian Pacific Airlines* (1979) 2 SCR 63.

'notice' requirement,[598] which, in this case, was not considered as correctly fulfilled by the Court.[599] This example perfectly illustrates how different ratification stages may lead to undesirable fragmentation.

(3) Concluding Remarks

Despite the existence of specific provisions in the Conventions governing how they should interact, the various changes and disparities in the ratification's stages impacted the uniformity of the international air carrier regime established by the 1929 Warsaw Convention. The same is true for initiatives adopted by non-State actors, that is, private initiatives, which the next section will cover at greater length.

4.2.1.3 Private Initiatives

In parallel to the waves of international conventions unravelling the uniform system, carriers were developing many international private initiatives. Some tended to bring further uniformity, such as the IATA Recommended Practices, and particularly their recommended general conditions of carriage[600] that provided common definitions. But they did not modify the uniform regime established by the 1929 Warsaw Convention.

In contrast, right when the United States was dissatisfied with the low limits of the 1955 Hague Protocol and was about to denounce the 1929 Warsaw Convention, numerous international carriers agreed under the 1966 Montreal Agreement[601] to raise the limit of indemnification in case of death, wounding or other bodily injury up to USD 75,000 of proven damage for services to and from the United States.[602] This voluntary agreement entered into by air carriers to save as much as possible of the uniform regime was accepted by the American Civil Aeronautics Board,[603] and ultimately became domestic law.[604]

Two decades later, in Japan on 20 November 1992, ten Japanese airlines voluntarily relinquished the limits of the Warsaw Convention using Article 22(1) of the 1929 Warsaw Convention, which allowed them to opt for higher limits.[605]

---

598. *See*, section 4.2.1.2(1).
599. *Montreal Trust Company et al. v. Canadian Pacific Airlines* (1977) 2 SCR 793.
600. *See*, Rishiraj Baruah, *IATA Conditions of Contract and Carriage (Passengers And Baggage): A Constant Tussle Between Regulatory Authorities and Airlines*, Source: International Law Square, https://ilsquare.org/2016/03/25/iata-conditions-of-contract-and-carriage/ (accessed 22 August 2019).
601. Also known as CAB Agreement 18900. *See*, section 1.1.3.1.
602. *See*, Andreas Lowenfeld, Allan Mendelsohn, *The United States and the Warsaw Convention*, 80 Harvard Law Review 497-602 (1967).
603. *See*, Allan Mendelson, *Warsaw: In Transition or Decline?*, 21 Air & Space Law 183 (1996); Michael Milde, *International Air Law and ICAO* 275 (Eleven International Publishing, 2008).
604. *See*, US 14 CFR Part 203.
605. This modification was made with the approval of the Japanese government. *See*, Michael Milde, *International Air Law and ICAO* 280 (Eleven International Publishing, 2008); Naneen Baden, *The Japanese Initiative on the Warsaw Convention*, 61 Journal of Air Law and Commerce 437 (1995).

A few years later, on 30 and 31 October 1995 in Kuala Lumpur, an impressive number of international carriers also voluntarily modified the limits of the 1929 Warsaw Convention and 1955 Hague Protocol under the 1995 IATA Agreement.[606] This Agreement provides that:

> The undersigned carriers agree
> 1. To take action to waive the limitation of liability on recoverable compensatory damages in Article 22 paragraph 1 of the Warsaw Convention [the 1929 text or its version as amended in 1955 which ever may be applicable] as to claims for death, wounding or other bodily injury of a passenger within the meaning of Article 17 of the Convention, so that recoverable compensatory damages may be determined and awarded by reference to the law of the domicile of the passenger.
> 2. To reserve all available defences pursuant to the provisions of the Convention; nevertheless, any carrier may waive any defence, including the waiver of any defence up to a specified monetary amount of recoverable compensatory damages, as circumstances may warrant. [...].

In 1996, the Air Transport Association of America mirrored the changes made in 1995 in its own text, known as the 1996 ATA Intercarrier Agreement.[607]

Despite their necessity, and their provisions essentially targeting pecuniary measures,[608] all of these carrier initiatives gradually chipped away at the uniform regime initially established in a single instrument.[609] The next section will look at domestic and regional initiatives that created similar issues for the envisaged uniformity of rule-making.

4.2.1.4 Domestic and Regional Initiatives

Amendments were also adopted pursuant to domestic and regional initiatives. In 1988, the Italian government unilaterally enacted legislation that increased the liability limit in case of death or injury to SDR 100,000 for all Italian carriers and foreign carriers operating stopovers on the Italian territory.[610]

In 1997, the then European Community, developing its legal arsenal in the field of air transport, adopted Regulation 2027/97 on air carrier liability in the event of accidents (hereinafter the '**EU Regulation 2027/97**').[611] Said regulation modified the content of the existing Warsaw Instruments. On the grounds that the limit on liability

606. *See*, section 1.1.3.1.
607. Also known as 1996 IPA. This last text was modified after the adoption of the 1999 Montreal Convention. *See*, George Tompkins, *Liability Rules Applicable to International Air Transportation as Developed by the Courts in the United States: From Warsaw 1929 to Montreal 1999* 14 (Kluwer, 2010).
608. The 1929 Warsaw Convention authorizes higher limits of liability in the carriage of passengers under specific conditions. *See*, 1929 Warsaw Convention, Article 22(1).
609. *See*, with respect to the erosion of the uniform system by the 1966 Montreal Agreement, Michael Milde, *International Air Law and ICAO* 275 (Eleven International Publishing, 2008).
610. Legge 5 iuglio 1988 n. 274 – Limite di risarcimento nei trasporti aerei internazionali di persone, GU Serie Generale n. 168 del 19-07-1988.
611. Council Regulation (EC) No 2027/97 of 9 October 1997 on air carrier liability in the event of accidents, *Official Journal*, 17 October 1997, L 285/1.

in the case of accident in the 1955 Hague Protocol was too low with respect to European economic and social standards, EU Regulation 2027/97 set forth that the liability of a Community air carrier for damage sustained in the event of passenger death, wounding or any other bodily injury due to accident would not be subject to any financial limit.[612] For any damage up to SDR 100,000, the Community carrier would no longer be in a position to exclude or limit its liability[613] by proving that all necessary measures to avoid damage had been taken, or that it was impossible to take such measures.[614] As an innovative measure, EU Regulation 2027/97 also provided that 'immediate economic needs' should be rapidly covered. To that effect, Article 5 established that a Community air carrier should without delay, and in any event not later than fifteen days after the identity of the natural person entitled to compensation had been established, make advance payments, as may be required, of not less than SDR 15,000 per passenger in case of death,[615] in order to meet those needs on a basis proportional to the hardship suffered. Although advance payments are not a recognition of liability, they create some expectations from victims, which contributes to the destruction of the uniform regime.[616]

In 2002, EU Regulation 2027/97 was amended in consideration of the adoption of the 1999 Montreal Convention by Regulation (EC) No 889/2002 of the European Parliament and of the Council of 13 May 2002 on air carrier liability in the event of accidents (hereinafter the '**EU Regulation 889/2002**').[617]

Although the revision was not supposed to become a cause of fragmentation, the wording adopted by the European legislator is not exactly in line with that used in the 1999 Montreal Convention. For example, Article 17 of the 1999 Montreal Convention uses the following wording in its English version: '[...] upon condition only that the accident which caused the death or injury took place [...]'; and in the French version: '[...] par cela seul que l'accident qui a causé la mort ou la lésion s'est produit [...]'. In this abstract, the word 'injury' corresponds to 'lésion' in French. Notwithstanding this correspondence, EU Regulation 889/2002 does not use the term 'lésion' in its French version, but 'blessure', which is the term used in the 1929 Warsaw Convention and translated into English as 'wounding'. This discrepancy could be misleading, given that Article 1(3)(2) of Regulation 889/2002 provides that: 'Concepts contained in this Regulation which are not defined in paragraph 1 shall be equivalent to those used in the Montreal Convention.' Yet, the term 'blessure' is not defined in the European text and

612. EU Regulation 2027/97, Article 3(1)(a).
613. A defence grounded in passenger negligence still remains possible.
614. EU Regulation 2027/97, Article 3(2).
615. Following the adoption of the 1999 Montreal Convention, this amount was increased to SDR 16,000 in EU Regulation 889/2002.
616. Recital 4 of EU Regulation 2027/97 indicates that one of the aims of the regulation is indeed to have the 'same level and nature of liability in both national and international transport'. This stems from the fact that Member States have variously increased the liability limits with the consequence that different limits existed in the European internal market. This vow of further uniformity within the European Community was indeed a positive step, but again participated in the unravelling of the system.
617. Regulation (EC) No 889/2002 of the European Parliament and of the Council of 13 May 2002 amending Council Regulation (EC) No 2027/97 on air carrier liability in the event of accidents, *Official Journal*, 30 May 2002, L 140/2.

has ceased to be used following the adoption of the 1999 Montreal Convention. This is the example of a text too hastily adopted without due consideration for changes made in the 1999 Montreal Convention.

4.2.1.5 Concluding Remarks

All of these successive modifications to the uniform regime adopted in the 1929 Warsaw Convention, and their coexistence, be it through international instruments, carrier initiatives or domestic/regional law, appear to have eroded the uniformity of the international air carrier regime itself.[618] As argued in Chapter 2 above, the coexistence of various regimes is exactly what the drafters of the 1929 Warsaw Convention wanted to avoid.

4.2.2 The Development of Consumer Rights at Regional and Domestic Levels

4.2.2.1 Preliminary Remarks

Only a few years after the signing of the 1999 Montreal Convention, legislators in several parts of the world decided to increase general consumer protection. Among other concerns, this extended to the improvement of air passenger protection.

The following analysis will look at whether the development of air passengers' rights at regional and domestic levels potentially conflicted with the uniform regime established by the Conventions. If so, it will explore to what extent these regional and domestic laws might have affected the uniformity of the 1999 Montreal Convention.

4.2.2.2 European Union

(1) Introduction to EU Regulation 261/2004

(i) Scope

After the adoption of the 1999 Montreal Convention, the *credo* of protecting air passengers took new shape in the EU. Recognizing the improvements made in case of air accidents, the European Parliament and Council acknowledged that denied boarding and cancellation as well as long flight delays caused serious troubles, and were an inconvenience to passengers that had to be addressed. The solutions proposed were translated into EU Regulation 261/2004, which entered into force in 2005.[619]

---

618. *See*, Bin Cheng, *A New Era in the Law of International Carriage by Air: From Warsaw (1929) to Montreal (1999)*, 53 International & Comparative Law Quarterly 858 (2004).
619. For a detailed description of EU Regulation 261/2004, *see*, Michal Bobek, Jeremias Prassl (eds), *Air Passenger Rights: Ten Years On* (Hart Publishing, 2016); Jeremy Heymann (ed.), *Règlement (CE) n°261/2004 sur la protection des passagers aériens: Commentaire article par article* (Bruylant, 2021). Because a substantial number of claims are introduced daily against air

EU Regulation 261/2004 governs situations of denied boarding, downgrading, flight cancellation and long delays. Most of these situations are not regulated by the Conventions. EU Regulation 261/2004 applies to passengers departing from an airport located in a Member State territory, whether they travel with a EU carrier or not, and to passengers departing from an airport in a non-EU State and travelling to an airport in a Member State territory, if they travel with a EU carrier and under the condition that they do not receive benefits, compensation or assistance from the third country.[620]

(ii) Denied Boarding and Downgrading

With respect to denied boarding,[621] EU Regulation 261/2004 provides that, when an operating carrier reasonably expects to deny boarding to a passenger, it will first call for volunteers to surrender their reservation in exchange for commonly agreed benefits, and at least a right to reimbursement or rerouting. If none or an insufficient number of passengers surrenders, the operating carrier may then deny boarding to passengers against their will.

In this situation, EU Regulation 261/2004 provides that the air carrier will have to compensate the concerned passengers according to the chart set out in Article 7, which sets a fixed compensation between EUR 250 and EUR 600, depending on the destination. The air carriers will also be required to offer reimbursement or rerouting to the passengers denied boarding, and to provide them with assistance, which may include food, hotel accommodation and communication tools such as calls. Passengers denied boarding are obviously those who are denied the right to board the aircraft against their will, but to fall within the definition of EU Regulation 261/2004, they should have a confirmed reservation on the flight and have presented themselves for check-in at the agreed time or, if no time was agreed, at least forty-five minutes before the published departure time.[622] Passengers without valid travel documentation or other related

carriers pursuant to EU Regulation 261/2004, it is worth noting that the case law is constantly developing. The reader is therefore invited to follow the evolution of judicial decisions with particular care.

620. In an early decision following the adoption of EU Regulation 261/2004, the Court of Justice of the European Union held (in a case involving a non-European air carrier) that said regulation, in opposition to the 1999 Montreal Convention, does not apply to the case of an outward and return journey in which passengers who have originally departed from an airport located in the territory of a Member State travel back to that airport on a flight from an airport located in a non-Member State. According to the Court, the fact that the outward and return flights are the subject of a single booking has no effect on the interpretation of that provision. *See*, CJEC, 10 July 2008, *Emirates Airlines – Direktion für Deutschland v. Diether Schenkel*, C-173/07, ECLI:EU:C:2008:400. Moreover, it should be underscored that EU Regulation 261/2004 also applies to any scheduled and non-scheduled flights, including package tours, except when the package tour is cancelled for reasons other than the cancellation of the flight.

621. In the United States, certain Courts have considered denied boarding as a form of delay. *See*, George Tompkins, *Bumping – Denied Boarding – And Article 19 of the 1999 Montreal Convention*, 32 Air & Space Law 231-232 (2007). *Contra*, Supreme Court of the Philippines, *Philippine Airlines, Inc. v. Simplicio Griño*, 579 Phil 344 (2008).

622. The CJEU held that the concept of 'denied boarding' included a situation where, in the context of a single contract of carriage involving a number of reservations on immediately connecting flights and a single check-in, an air carrier denied boarding to some passengers on the grounds

reasons exemplified in EU Regulation 261/2004 may be denied boarding without any rights to compensation.[623]

EU Regulation 261/2004 also provides that in the case of downgrading, the operating carrier shall reimburse the passenger from 30% to 75% of the price of the ticket, according to the flight distance.[624]

(iii) Cancellation

Regarding cancellation, which is not a situation regulated by the 1999 Montreal Convention,[625] EU Regulation 261/2004 provides that the affected passenger should be offered the choice between reimbursement and rerouting under comparable transport conditions, and the possibility to eat and place calls where appropriate. In the event of rerouting, when a stay of at least one night becomes necessary, the passenger should also be offered hotel accommodation and transport from and to the airport.

One particularity of this legislation is the automatic and standardized financial compensation offered to passengers whose flight was cancelled. Article 7 sets this

---

that the first flight included in their reservation was subject to a delay attributable to that carrier and that the latter mistakenly expected those passengers not to arrive in time to board the second flight. *See*, CJEU, 4 October 2012, *Germán Rodríguez Cachafeiro and María de los Reyes Martínez-Reboredo Varela-Villamor v. Iberia, Líneas Aéreas de España SA*, C-321/11, ECLI:EU:C:2012:609. On the same day, the CJEU considered in another case that this regime related not only to cases where boarding was denied because of overbooking but also to those where boarding is denied on other grounds, such as operational reasons. The Court noted that the occurrence of 'extraordinary circumstances' resulting in an air carrier rescheduling flights after those circumstances arose 'cannot give grounds for denying boarding on those later flights or for exempting that carrier from its obligation [...] to compensate a passenger to whom it denies boarding on such a flight'. *See*, CJEU, 4 October 2012, *Finnair Oyj v. Timy Lassooy*, C-22/11, ECLI:EU:C:2012:604. The regime described above does not apply when there are reasonable grounds to deny boarding, for instance, for health, safety, security or inadequate travel documentation reasons.

623. *See*, EU Regulation 261/2004, Article 2(j).

624. The CJEU ruled that where a passenger is downgraded on a flight, the price to be taken into account in determining the reimbursement for the passenger affected is the price of the flight on which he or she was downgraded, unless that price is not indicated on the ticket entitling him or her to transport on that flight, in which case, it must be based on the part of the price of the ticket corresponding to the quotient resulting from the distance of that flight and the total distance that the passenger is entitled to travel. The Court added that the price of the ticket to be taken into consideration for the purpose of determining the reimbursement is solely the price of the flight itself, with the exclusion of taxes and charges indicated on that ticket, as long as neither the requirement to pay those taxes and charges nor their amount depends on the class for which that ticket has been purchased. *See*, CJEU, 22 June 2016, *Steef Mennens v. Emirates Direktion für Deutschland*, C-255/15, ECLI:EU:C:2016:472.

625. *See*, section 1.1.3.2(4)(ii). EU Regulation 261/2004 gives the following definition of cancellation: 'non-operation of a flight which was previously planned and on which at least one place was reserved'. The CJEU ruled that the term 'cancellation' also covers cases in which a flight departs but then returns to the airport of departure and does not proceed further. *See*, CJEU, 13 October 2011, *Aurora Sousa Rodríguez and Others v. Air France SA*, C-83-10, ECLI:EU:C:2011:652. *Compare*, Audiencia Provincial de Madrid, 1 February 2008, ECLI:ES:APM:2008:10106, discussed in fn 495. The CJEU also ruled that a flight in respect of which the places of departure and arrival adhered to the planned schedule but during which an unscheduled stopover took place could not be regarded as cancelled. *See*, CJEU, 5 October 2016, *Ute Wunderlich v. Bulgarian Air Charter Limited*, C-32/16, ECLI:EU:C:2016:753 (Order).

compensation between EUR 250 and EUR 600, depending on travel distance. These amounts may, however, be decreased by 50% in a rerouting situation, when the arrival time does not exceed the scheduled arrival time originally booked by more than two to four hours, depending on the distance. This standardized compensation may nevertheless be avoided if the passenger is informed of the cancellation within a certain time limit[626] or if the cancellation results from 'extraordinary circumstances'.[627]

(iv) Delay

EU Regulation 261/2004 also sets forth specific provisions in case of long delay. Although it does not provide a definition of the concept of delay, it sets out that when an operating carrier reasonably expects a flight to be delayed beyond its scheduled time of departure by a certain time, which varies depending on the travel destination, passengers shall be offered meals and refreshments, the ability to place two calls and, accommodation and transfer between the airport and a hotel under certain conditions. If the delay is at least five hours, the concerned passengers should also be offered the choice of a reimbursement and, when relevant, of a return flight to the first point of departure.

(2) The Possible Overlap with the Principle of Exclusivity of the 1999 Montreal Convention

The existence of an additional European regime on delays, in parallel to that of the 1999 Montreal Convention, was immediately challenged before English Courts, which sought a preliminary ruling from the CJEU.

In the *IATA* decision,[628] the CJEU ruled, as reported below, that there was no overlap between the two instruments insofar as there existed two different kinds of damages in the case of delay. That is to say, one was general and one was more personal, and each was respectively regulated by EU Regulation 261/2004 and the 1999 Montreal Convention:

> First, excessive delay will cause damage that is almost identical for every passenger, redress for which may take the form of standardised and immediate assistance or care for everybody concerned [...] Second, passengers are liable to suffer individual damage, inherent in the reason for travelling, redress for which requires

626. *See*, EU Regulation 261/2004, Article 8(1)(c). The CJEU ruled that the operating air carrier was required to pay compensation when a flight was cancelled and that information was not communicated to the passenger at least two weeks before the scheduled time of departure, including in the case where the air carrier, at least two weeks before that time, communicated that information to the travel agent via whom the contract for carriage had been entered into with the passenger concerned and the passenger had not been informed of that cancellation by that agent within that period. *See*, CJEU, 11 May 2017, *Bas Jacob Adriaan Krijgsman v. Surinaamse Luchtvaart Maatschappij NV*, C-302/16, ECLI:EU:C:2017:359.
627. *See*, section 4.2.2.2(3).
628. *See also*, section 1.3.2.3(2)(vi).

> a case-by-case assessment of the extent of the damage caused and can consequently only be the subject of compensation granted subsequently on an individual basis.[629]

On these grounds, the Court affirmed the validity of EU Regulation 261/2004 with regard to European law and the 1999 Montreal Convention.

The adoption of EU Regulation 261/2004 and the confirmation of its validity had two major consequences. *First*, with regard to the vow of uniformity of the 1999 Montreal Convention, the jurisprudence of the CJEU departs from the general interpretation given by the highest Courts in other jurisdictions regarding the principle of exclusivity.[630] *Second*, this deviation from foreign jurisprudence opened the door to further erosion of the uniformity of the 1999 Montreal Convention.

The CJEU later ruled in *Sturgeon* that passengers whose flight was delayed by three or more hours were in a position comparable to those whose flight had been cancelled, with the consequence that they could also obtain standard compensation.[631] This unexpected interpretation was later reaffirmed by the Grand Chamber of the CJEU on 23 October 2012 in *Nelson*.[632] The argument of the primacy of the 1999 Montreal Convention over European secondary legislation,[633] despite being acknowledged by the Court,[634] could not have been of great assistance once the Court had previously ruled in *IATA* that two different kinds of damage could exist in case of delay. The potential violation of the principle of legal certainty[635] was also rejected by the Court on the grounds that, in its view, the preamble of the 1999 Montreal Convention recognized the importance of ensuring consumer protection.[636]

(3) The Potential Impact of EU Regulation 261/2004 on the Autonomy of the Terms in the 1999 Montreal Convention

The carriers' means of defence granted by the 1999 Montreal Convention may also be affected by European case law interpreting EU Regulation 261/2004. Indeed, the 1999 Montreal Convention provides that, under Article 19:

629. CJEC, 10 January 2006, *The Queen, on the application of International Air Transport Association and European Low Fares Airline Association v. Department for Transport*, C-344/04, ECLI:EU:C:2006:10, point 43.
630. *See*, section 4.3.2.2.
631. CJEC, 19 November 2009, *Christopher Sturgeon, Gabriel Sturgeon and Alana Sturgeon v. Condor Flugdienst GmbH and Stefan Böck and Cornelia Lepuschitz v. Air France SA*, Joined Cases C-402/07 and C-432/07, ECLI:EU:C:2009:716. *See*, for commentary, Robert Lawson, Tim Marland, *The Montreal Convention 1999 and the Decisions of the ECJ in the Cases of IATA and Sturgeon: In Harmony or Discord?*, 36 Air & Space Law 99-108 (2011); Cyril-Igor Grigorieff, *Arrêts Condor et Air France: une protection accrue des passagers aériens*, 165 Journal de Droit Européen 7-9 (2010).
632. CJEU, 23 October 2012, *Emeka Nelson e.a. v. Deutsche Lufthansa AG and TUI Travel plc and Others v. Civil Aviation Authority*, C-581/10 and C-629/10, ECLI:EU:C:2012:657.
633. *See*, section 2.5.3.2.
634. CJEC, 22 December 2008, *Friederike Wallentin-Hermann v. Alitalia – Linee Aeree Italiane SpA*, C-549/07, ECLI:EU:C:2008:771, point 28: '[...] it must be stated that that convention forms an integral part of the Community legal order. Moreover, it is clear from Article 300(7) EC that the Community institutions are bound by agreements concluded by the Community and, consequently, that those agreements have primacy over secondary Community legislation [...]'.
635. *See*, section 2.3.2.
636. *See*, section 2.3.3.

> [...] the carrier shall not be liable for damage occasioned by delay if it proves that it and its servants and agents took all measures that could reasonably be required to avoid the damage or that it was impossible for it or them to take such measures.

EU Regulation 261/2004 appears to offer the same means of defence to air carriers in case of flight cancellation, as its Article 5(3) provides that:

> An operating air carrier shall not be obliged to pay compensation in accordance with Article 7, if it can prove that the cancellation is caused by extraordinary circumstances which could not have been avoided even if all reasonable measures had been taken.

Recital 14 of EU Regulation 261/2004 also recalls that:

> *As under the Montreal Convention*, obligations on operating air carriers should be limited or excluded in cases where an event has been caused by extraordinary circumstances which could not have been avoided even if all reasonable measures had been taken (*italics added*).

The desire for EU Regulation 261/2004 to mirror the means of defence organized in the 1999 Montreal Convention is therefore unambiguously expressed.

However, the CJEU held in *Wallentin* that the 1999 Montreal Convention's rules on limitation and exclusion of liability were not decisive for the interpretation of liability provisions in EU Regulation 261/2004.[637]

The concept of 'extraordinary circumstances' has since then been widely interpreted by domestic Courts and the CJEU.[638] A few illustrations of interpretations given by the CJEU, also referred to as the 'EU Court' in this section, are given below.

On a restrictive side, the EU Court ruled in *Wallentin* that a technical problem with an aircraft that leads to the cancellation of a flight is not covered by the concept of extraordinary circumstances, unless that problem stems from events which, by their nature or origin, are not inherent to the normal exercise of the activity of the air carrier concerned and are beyond its actual control. The EU Court further held that the fact that an air carrier complied with minimum aircraft maintenance rules is not in itself sufficient to establish that the carrier had taken all reasonable measures.[639] Later, in *Eglītis*, the EU Court decided that, since an air carrier is obliged to implement all reasonable measures to avoid extraordinary circumstances, it must reasonably, when organizing the flight, take into account the risk of delay connected to the possibility of such circumstances arising and, consequently, must provide for a certain reserve time to make it possible for the flight to be operated in its entirety, if feasible, once the extraordinary circumstances have come to an end.[640] In *van der Lans*, the EU Court once again reduced the scope of the defence founded on 'extraordinary circumstances',

637. CJEC, 22 December 2008, *Friederike Wallentin-Hermann v. Alitalia – Linee Aeree Italiane SpA*, C-549/07, ECLI:EU:C:2008:771, point 33: '[...] the Montreal Convention cannot determine the interpretation of the grounds of exemption under that Article 5(3)'.
638. Since it may be used also for flight delays.
639. CJEC, 22 December 2008, *Friederike Wallentin-Hermann v. Alitalia – Linee Aeree Italiane SpA*, C-549/07, ECLI:EU:C:2008:771.
640. CJEU, 12 May 2011, *Andrejs Eglītis and Edvards Ratnieks v. Latvijas Republikas Ekonomikas ministrija*, C-294/10, ECLI:EU:C:2011:303.

ruling that a delay resulting from an unexpected technical problem that was not attributable to poor maintenance and that was also not detected during routine maintenance checks did not fall within the concept of 'extraordinary circumstances'.[641] In *McDonagh*, the EU Court also decided that even if circumstances such as the partial closure of European airspace as a result of an Icelandic volcano eruption constituted extraordinary circumstances, the concept of 'extraordinary circumstances' did not release air carriers from their obligation to provide care as described above, such as hotel accommodation in case of rerouting.[642] In *Siewert*, the EU Court held that mobile stairs colliding with an aircraft did not automatically constitute 'extraordinary circumstances'.[643] In *Krüsemann*, departing from the recital of EU Regulation 261/2004, the Court further held that a wildcat strike was not constitutive of an 'extraordinary circumstance'.[644] The Grand Chamber further held, in *Airhelp v. SAS*, that strike action entered into upon by a trade union of the staff of an operating air carrier, in compliance with the conditions laid down by domestic legislation, did not qualify as extraordinary circumstances.[645]

However, not all EU Court decisions have rejected the carrier's defence based on 'extraordinary circumstances'. The EU Court often recognized the existence of 'extraordinary circumstances' when the event's origins were external to the carrier. In *Pešková*, the EU Court ruled that a bird strike fell in that category, and when a delay resulted from both an extraordinary circumstance and another circumstance that did not qualify as extraordinary, the delay caused by the first event must be deducted from the total delay in arrival of the flight concerned before assessing whether compensation for the delay must be paid.[646] In the same vein, in *Pauels*, the EU Court held that damage to an aircraft tyre caused by a foreign object lying on an airport runway, such as loose debris, must also be considered as extraordinary circumstances.[647] In *TAP*, the EU Court admitted that a flight diversion to disembark an unruly passenger qualified as an extraordinary circumstance unless the carrier contributed to the occurrence of that behaviour or failed to take appropriate measures in the face of warning signs of such behaviour.[648] In *Airhelp v. Austrian Airlines*, the EU Court considered that a collision between the elevator of an aircraft in a parked position and the winglet of another

641. CJEU, 17 September 2015, *Corina van der Lans v. Koninklijke Luchtvaart Maatschappij NV*, C-257/14, ECLI:EU:C:2015:618.
642. CJEU, 31 January 2013, *Denise McDonagh v. Ryanair Ltd*, C-12/11, ECLI:EU:C:2013:43.
643. CJEU, 14 November 2014, *Sandy Siewert and Others v. Condor Flugdienst GmbH*, C-394/14, ECLI:EU:C:2014:2377 (Order).
644. CJEU, 17 April 2018, *Helga Krüsemann and Others v. TUIfly GmbH*, C-195/17, ECLI:EU:C:2018:258.
645. CJEU, 23 March 2021, *Airhelp Ltd v. Scandinavian Airlines System Denmark-Norway-Sweden*, C-28/20, ECLI:EU:C:2021:226. On strike, *see also*, CJEU, 6 October 2021, *CS v. Eurowings GmbH*, C-613/20, ECLI:EU:C:2021:820.
646. CJEU, 4 May 2017, *Marcela Pešková and Jiří Peška v. Travel Service a.s.*, C-315/15, ECLI:EU:C:2017:342.
647. CJEU, 4 April 2019, *Germanwings GmbH v. Wolfgang Pauels*, C-501/17, ECLI:EU:C:2019:288.
648. CJEU, 11 June 2020, *LE v. Transportes Aéreos Portugueses SA*, C-74/19, ECLI:EU:C:2020:460.

airline's aircraft, caused by the movement of the second aircraft, fell under the concept of extraordinary circumstances.[649]

In order to mitigate the risk of fragmentation from EU Regulation 261/2004, National Enforcement Bodies (in short 'NEBs'), created pursuant to EU Regulation 261/2004, established a non-exhaustive list[650] of what they considered to be 'extraordinary circumstances'.[651] The European Commission also tried to bring clarification in its Guidelines.[652]

The concept of 'extraordinary circumstances' and its various interpretations may affect the way Article 19 of the 1999 Montreal Convention is construed by domestic Courts. Some of them may be tempted to consider that the concept of 'extraordinary circumstances', as interpreted by the EU Court with respect to EU Regulation 261/2004, also applies in cases governed by the 1999 Montreal Convention, despite the fact that the distinction between the two had been made clear by the EU Court.

(4) Concluding Remarks

In conclusion, even if the decisions of the CJEU are consistent with European law, in *IATA*, the CJEU lost sight of the uniform ambition of the 1999 Montreal Convention and the crucial role of said Court in ensuring its uniform application by having due regards for foreign jurisprudence. The provisions of EU Regulation 261/2004 regarding delay, and its subsequent interpretations by the CJEU, harm the uniformity of the 1999 Montreal Convention.

The proposal to revise EU Regulation 261/2004 does not augur well for further uniformity.[653] The existence of parallel regimes set out in EU Regulation 261/2004 and in the 1999 Montreal Convention, particularly regarding compensation in case of delays, does not seem to raise concerns for the European legislators.

649. CJEU, 14 January 2021, *Airhelp Limited v. Austrian Airlines AG*, C-264/20, ECLI:EU:C:2021:26 (Order).
650. The list is no longer publicly available. A very similar one was established by the UK Civil Aviation Authority. *See*, United Kingdom Civil Aviation Authority, https://www.caa.co.uk/Commercial-industry/Airlines/Guidance-on-consumer-law-for-airlines/ (accessed 18 December 2020).
651. For an analysis of the concept of 'extraordinary circumstances' in the context of a pandemic, *see*, Chrystel Erotokritou, Cyril-Igor Grigorieff, *EU Regulation No 261/2004 on Air Passenger Rights: The Impact of the COVID-19 on Flight Cancellation and the Concept of Extraordinary Circumstances*, 45(Special Issue) Air & Space Law 123-142 (2020).
652. Commission Notice – Interpretative Guidelines on Regulation (EC) No 261/2004 of the European Parliament and of the Council establishing common rules on compensation and assistance to passengers in the event of denied boarding and of cancellation or long delay of flights and on Council Regulation (EC) No 2027/97 on air carrier liability in the event of accidents as amended by Regulation (EC) No 889/2002 of the European Parliament and of the Council, C/2016/3502, *Official Journal*, 15 June 2016, C 214/5.
653. Proposal for a Regulation of the European Parliament and of the Council amending Regulation (EC) No 261/2004 establishing common rules on compensation and assistance to passengers in the event of denied boarding and of cancellation or long delay of flights and Regulation (EC) No 2027/97 on air carrier liability in respect of the carriage of passengers and their baggage by air, 13 March 2013, COM (2013) 130 final. This proposal is still under discussion in 2021 despite several attempts to make it progress in the political agenda.

In a nutshell, the coexistence of parallel regimes in the case of delays creates a situation which favours a fragmentation of the uniform regime established at an international level in the 1999 Montreal Convention.

As the next section will analyse, other regional organizations have adopted specific consumer rights legislations that may also jeopardize the uniformity of the Conventions.

4.2.2.3 Other Regional Legislations

(1) The African Union

In order to boost the implementation of the 1999 Yamoussoukro Decision concerning the liberalization of air transport market access in Africa,[654] and to increase the protection of consumers on the African continent,[655] in 2018, the African Union adopted the Regulations on the Protection of Consumers of Air Transport Services.[656]

The Regulations established, among other points, that when the reasonably expected time of departure is at least six hours later than the previously announced time of departure, the airline must inform passengers of their right to obtain immediate reimbursement for the full cost of the ticket, if the flight is no longer serving any purpose.[657] It becomes immediately apparent that, depending on the reading of the exclusivity clause of the 1999 Montreal Convention,[658] such provisions potentially infringe the liability limit established by the Conventions in case of delays.

(2) The West African Economic and Monetary Union

The same risk of fragmentation also exists in the UEMOA. The UEMOA is an organization of eight States established in 1994 with the ambition of creating a common

654. Decision Relating to the Implementation of the Yamoussoukro Declaration Concerning the Liberalisation of Access to Air Transport Markets in Africa, 14 November 1999, Yamoussoukro, Source: African Civil Aviation Commission, https://afcac.org/en/images/Documentation/yd_eng.pdf (accessed 7 November 2020). *See*, for a commentary, Adejoke Adediran, *Implementation of the Single African Air Transport Market Legal Regime: Challenges of the Interface Between the Yamoussoukro Decision and Domestic Regimes*, 43 Annals of Air & Space Law 23-54 (2018).
655. For a detailed analysis of African air law, *see*, Hamadi Gatta Wagué, *Droit aérien africain* (Pedone, 2019).
656. African Union Regulations on the Protection of Consumers of Air Transport Services – Annex 6 to the Yamoussoukro Decision (Assembly/AU/Dec 676 (XXX) – Decision on Legal Instruments), adopted on 28-29 January 2018 at Addis Ababa.
657. Regulations on the Protection of Consumers of Air Transport Services, Article 11(c)(i): 'When an airline reasonably expects a flight to be delayed beyond its scheduled time of departure: when the reasonably expected time of departure is at least six hours after the time of departure previously announced, the airline shall: inform the passengers of their right to immediate reimbursement of the full cost of the ticket at the price at which it was bought, for the part or parts of the journey not made if the flight is no longer serving any purpose in relation to the passenger's original travel plan, together with, when relevant, a return flight to the first point of departure, at the earliest opportunity.'
658. *See*, sections 2.5.3.2 and 4.3.2.

market among its members. From an early stage, the UEMOA showed a deep interest in aviation policy.

On 20 March 2003, the UEMOA adopted a regulation establishing rules regarding compensation in the case of denied boarding, cancellation and long flight delays.[659] Although said UEMOA regulation has not yet been interpreted by the UEMOA Court, it would be interesting to observe whether this Court will rule any potential claim in the same direction as the CJEU or will adopt a different approach.

In parallel, the UEMOA also adopted another regulation that, on one side, reflects the content of EU Regulation 2027/97 and, on the other, supplements the 1929 Warsaw Convention insofar as said UEMOA regulation provides a definition[660] of 'accident' under its Article 1(1)(a) as follows:

> Accident: événement, lié à l'utilisation d'un aéronef, qui se produit entre le moment où une personne monte à bord de l'aéronef avec l'intention d'effectuer un vol et le moment où toutes les personnes qui sont montées dans cette intention sont descendues, et au cours duquel:
> 1) une personne est mortellement ou grièvement blessée du fait qu'elle se trouve:
>   - dans l'aéronef, ou
>   - en contact direct avec une partie quelconque de l'aéronef, y compris les parties qui s'en sont détachées, ou
>   - directement exposée au souffle des réacteurs, sauf s'il s'agit de lésions dues à des causes naturelles, de blessures infligées à la personne par elle-même ou par d'autres ou de blessures subies par un passager clandestin caché hors des zones auxquelles les passagers et l'équipage ont normalement accès, ou
> 2) l'aéronef subit des dommages ou une rupture structurelle:
>   - qui altèrent ses caractéristiques de résistance structurelle, de performances ou de vol, et
>   - qui devraient normalement nécessiter une réparation importante ou le remplacement de l'élément endommagé,
>   sauf s'il s'agit d'une panne de moteur ou d'avaries de moteur, lorsque les dommages sont limités au moteur, à ses capotages ou à ses accessoires ou encore de dommages limités aux hélices, aux extrémités d'ailes, aux antennes, aux pneumatiques, aux freins, aux carénages ou à de petites entailles ou perforations du revêtement ou
> 3) l'aéronef a disparu ou est totalement inaccessible.[661]

This definition is substantially similar to the one provided in Annex 13 of the 1944 Chicago Convention.[662] As a result, it is likely that said definition could be taken into

659. Règlement N° 03/2003/CM/UEMOA établissant les règles relatives aux compensations pour refus d'embarquement des passagers et pour annulation ou retard important d'un vol, fait à Ouagadougou le 20 mars 2003, *Bulletin Officiel*, n°31, premier trimestre 2003, pp. 12-14.
660. The same definition can also be found in the UEMOA Civil Aviation Code. *See*, Règlement N° 01/2007/CM/UEMOA portant adoption du Code communautaire de l'aviation civile des Etats membres de l'UEMOA, fait à Lomé le 6 avril 2007, *Bulletin Officiel*, n°56, premier trimestre 2007, pp. 1-36.
661. Règlement N° 02/2003/CM/UEMOA relatif à la responsabilité des transporteurs aériens en cas d'accident, fait à Ouagadougou le 20 mars 2003, *Bulletin Officiel*, n°31, premier trimestre 2003, pp. 10-12.
662. 'Accident. An occurrence associated with the operation of an aircraft which takes place between the time any person boards the aircraft with the intention of flight until such time as all such persons have disembarked, in which:

consideration where the term 'accident' under the Conventions would have to be interpreted.[663]

(3) *The Economic and Monetary Community of Central Africa*

The Economic and Monetary Community of Central Africa (hereinafter 'CEMAC') also expressed interest in passengers' rights and in 2007 developed its own piece of legislation. CEMAC Regulation No 06/07[664] foresees that, in the case of long delays, passengers should be offered the cost of a phone call, the option to eat, and accommodation if required.

So far, the provisions of this CEMAC Regulation have not been subject to any interpretation by the CEMAC Court. Again, it would be instructive to observe if any Court seized on this question would rely on existing foreign jurisprudence or would adopt a regional approach.

(4) *The Andean Community*

Latin America has also shown interest in developing its own regional air legislation. The wish to have common aviation rules in Latin America is not recent as several attempts have already been made in this regard, notably in 1985 with the *Proyecto Código Aeronáutico Latino Americano*.[665]

---

a) a person is fatally or seriously injured as a result of:
   - being in the aircraft, or
   - direct contact with any part of the aircraft, including parts which have become detached from the aircraft, or
   - direct exposure to jet blast,

   except when the injuries are from natural causes, self-inflicted or inflicted by other persons, or when the injuries are to stowaways hiding outside the areas normally available to the passengers and crew; or

b) the aircraft sustains damage or structural failure which:
   - adversely affects the structural strength, performance or flight characteristics of the aircraft, and
   - would normally require major repair or replacement of the affected component,

   except for engine failure or damage, when the damage is limited to the engine, its cowlings or accessories; or for damage limited to propellers, wing tips, antennas, tires, brakes, fairings, small dents or puncture holes in the aircraft skin; or

c) the aircraft is missing or is completely inaccessible.'

663. *See*, section 3.2.2.
664. Règlement N° 06/07-UEAC-082-CM15 du 11 mars 2007, signé à N'Djamena le 19 mars 2007, *Bulletin Officiel*, Source: Droit-Afrique, http://www.droit-afrique.com/upload/doc/cemac/CEMAC-Reglement-2007-06-responsabilite-transporteur-aerien.pdf (accessed 18 December 2020).
665. ALADA, https://alada.org/2017/04/27/proyecto-codigo-aeronautico-latino-americano/ (accessed 19 June 2019).
See, Mario Folchi, *El Proyecto Código Aeronáutico Latinoamericano y la uniformidad legislativa en la región*, 35 Revista Latino American de Derecho Aeronáutico (2017).

At a more intra-regional level, the Andean Community, which was created in 1969, voted on several pieces of legislation affecting its members' air transport industry.[666] The Andean Community *Decisión 619*[667] establishes several new passenger rights.[668] Its Article 8(e) provides, for instance, that in the case of delays of more than six hours, the carrier will have to compensate the passenger with a minimum of 25% of the value of the unfulfilled journey.[669] Again, such a provision may contradict those of the Conventions.

(5) The Association of Southeast Asian Nations

The Association of Southeast Asian Nations (hereinafter 'ASEAN'), created in 1967,[670] took measures to create a common aviation market among its members in 2010.[671] While public law integration is generally the first step of a deeper integration, at this stage, there is no common ASEAN air passenger legislation although common consumer protection rules are being developed.[672]

4.2.2.4 Domestic Legislations

The adoption of specific air passenger rights is not limited to regional organizations. Individual States have also adopted their own air passenger protection legislation. Certain of these domestic legislations set out specific provisions in the case of delays.

This is, for example, the case of Canada, which in 2019 adopted its own air passenger regulations. The Canadian Air Passenger Protection Regulations[673] provide, for instance, that if a delay is due to a situation outside the carrier's control, and passengers were informed fourteen days or less before departure time that the arrival

666. Namely: Bolivia, Colombia, Ecuador and Peru.
667. Decisión 619 – Normas para la Armonización de los Derechos y Obligaciones de los Usuarios, Transportistas y Operadores de los Servicios de Transporte Aéreo en la Comunidad Andina, 15 de Julio de 2005, dada en Lima, Source: Comunidad Andina, http://www.comunidadandina.org/StaticFiles/DocOf/DEC619.pdf (accessed 29 September 2020).
668. *See*, for instance, Manuel Guillermo Sarmiento García, *Los derechos del pasajero derivados del convenio de Montreal de 1999 y del derecho comunitario Andino*, 93 Revista Brasileira de Direito Aeronáutico e Especial 50-57 (2010).
669. 'El transportista aéreo deberá compensar al pasajero con una suma mínima equivalente al 25% del valor del trayecto incumplido [...]'.
670. Its members in 2021 include: Brunei, Cambodia, Indonesia, Laos, Malaysia, Myanmar, the Philippines, Singapore, Thailand and Vietnam.
671. ASEAN Multilateral Agreement on the Full Liberalisation of Passenger Air Services signed at Bandar Seri Begawan on 12 November 2010.
672. *See*, for example, Handbook on ASEAN Consumer Protection Laws and Regulations, Source: ASEAN, https://asean.org/wp-content/uploads/2021/01/Handbook-on-ASEAN-Consumer-Protection-Laws-and-Regulations.pdf (accessed 22 February 2022).
673. Air Passenger Protection Regulations, SOR/2019-150, *Canada Gazette*, Part II, volume 153, No 11. At the time of writing, these regulations are being challenged before the Canadian Federal Court of Appeal. *See*, the following press articles, Canadian Broadcasting Corporation, https://www.cbc.ca/news/business/canadian-airlines-fight-passenger-rights-bill-in-court-1.5201985 (accessed 22 March 2021); Le Devoir, https://www.ledevoir.com/economie/560781/la-cour-d-appel-federale-entendra-la-contestation-des-transporteurs-aeriens (accessed 22 March 2021).

of their flight at its final destination would be delayed, the carrier must offer a minimum compensation for the inconvenience.[674] This compensation varies between CAN 125 and CAN 1,000, depending on the duration of the delay, and on whether domestic legislation considers the carrier to be large or small.[675]

Other States have also adopted domestic legislation on air passenger rights,[676] such as: Algeria,[677] Brazil,[678] China,[679] India,[680] Indonesia,[681] the Philippines,[682] South Korea,[683] the UK[684] and Vietnam.[685]

This being said, each legislation deserves an ad hoc analysis as it cannot be assumed that all of them would necessarily be in contradiction with the principle of exclusivity of the 1999 Montreal Convention.[686]

674. Canadian Air Passenger Protection Regulations, section 12.
675. *Ibid.*, section 19.
676. For a description of several domestic legislations on air passenger rights, *see*, European Commission, *Study on the current level of protection of air passenger rights in the EU*, January 2020, 168-184, Source: Publications Office of the European Union, https://op.europa.eu/en/publication-detail/-/publication/f03df002-335c-11ea-ba6e-01aa75ed71a1 (accessed 29 September 2020). *See also*, the ICAO database on aviation specific consumer protection regulations, Source: ICAO, https://www.icao.int/sustainability/Pages/ConsumerProtectionRules.aspx (accessed 23 March 2021).
677. Décret exécutif No 16-175 du 9 Ramadhan 1437 correspondant au 14 juin 2016 fixant les conditions et les modalités d'application des droits des passagers de transport aérien public, *Journal Officiel de la République Algérienne*, No 36, p. 7.
678. Resolução No 400, de 13 de Dezembro de 2016, Diário Oficial da União, 14 Dezembro 2016, Pág. 104, *erratum* 15 Dezembro 2016, Pág. 111.
679. CCAR-300, 航班正常管理规定 (Provisions on the Management of Flight Regularity, 2016), Source: Civil Aviation Administration of China, http://www.caac.gov.cn/XXGK/XXGK/MHGZ/201706/t20170621_44917.html (accessed 6 January 2021).
680. CAR, section 3, Series M, Part IV, Source: India Directorate General of Civil Aviation, https://www.dgca.gov.in/digigov-portal/?dynamicPage=dynamicPdf/130576445&mainCivilAviationReqContent/6/211/viewDynamicRuleContLvl2/html&maincivilAviationRequirements/6/0/viewDynamicRulesReq (accessed 22 February 2022).
681. Ministerial Regulation No 89/2015, Source: Direktorat Jenderal Perhubungan Udara, http://hubud.dephub.go.id/hubud/assets/file/regulasi/permen/PM_89_Tahun_2015-1_$_1433827446_1078314159_$_.pdf (accessed 22 February 2022).
682. DOTC-DTI Joint Administrative Order No 1, s. 2012, Source: Philippines Official Gazette, https://www.officialgazette.gov.ph/2012/12/10/dotc-dti-joint-administrative-order-no-1-s-2012/ (accessed 20 June 2019), which also provides with the following definition of delay under section 2.8: '"delay" is the result of the deferment of a flight to a later time […]'.
683. 항공사업법 (Aviation Business Act), Article 61-2, Source: National Law Information Center, https://www.law.go.kr (accessed 6 January 2021). On the subject, *see*: Kyeong-Won Baeck, Ho-Won Hwang, *Article 61bis of the Aviation Business Act and the Legal Principles for the Aviation Consumers Protection: Comparison with the U.S. 'Tarmac Delay Rule'*, 35 The Korean Journal of Air & Space Law and Policy 169-195 (2020).
684. In the United Kingdom, after the Brexit, the provisions of EU Regulation 261/2004 were essentially retained but slightly amended in the new domestic regulations named the Air Passenger Rights and Air Travel Organisers' Licensing (Amendment) (EU Exit) Regulations 2019. For a description of the new regime and the value of the case law developed by the CJEU, *see*, *Lipton v. BA City Flyer Limited* (2021) EWCA Civ. 454.
685. Circular 14/2015/TT-BGTVT, Source: Civil Aviation Authority of Vietnam, https://caa.gov.vn/van-ban/14-2015-tt-bgtvt-68.htm (accessed 20 June 2019).
686. *See*, Vincent Correia, Noura Rouissi, *Global, Regional and National Air Passenger Rights: Does the Patchwork Work?*, 40 Air & Space Law 123-146 (2015).

4.2.2.5 Concluding Remarks

The development of consumer law led States and regional organizations to consider the adoption of an additional regime for the protection of their air passengers.

These regional and domestic legislations all create a risk of harming the uniform regime established in the Conventions either, with respect to their autonomous nature, by supplementing them with definitions or, with respect to their primacy and exclusivity, by creating competing regimes in the case of delay.

The somewhat disorganized emergence of various air passenger rights across the globe may echo the situation that existed prior to the adoption of the 1929 Warsaw Convention. Indeed, the existence of various domestic and regional legislations means that, on certain occasions, different domestic or regional legislations overlap in the patchwork of regulations.[687] Such a scenario would eventually require the application of conflict of laws rules, which do not exist on this matter at a global level. Consequently, both carriers and passengers could end up in a situation of legal uncertainty.

4.3 COURTS' RESPONSES TO UNIFORMITY

4.3.1 Preliminary Remarks

While it has been seen that modifications to the regulatory environment have caused a fragmentation to the uniformity wished by the drafters of the Conventions, it remains to be determined how Courts have responded, even in the absence of regulatory changes, to the specific features of the Conventions described in Chapter 2, namely the exclusivity of the Conventions and the autonomy of the terms used therein.

4.3.2 Exclusivity

4.3.2.1 A Large Spectrum of Variations

As discussed in Chapter 2, Article 24 of the 1929 Warsaw Convention and Article 29 of the 1999 Montreal Convention are supposed to ensure the primacy of the Conventions and their exclusivity vis-à-vis domestic law. Nevertheless, the exact extent of exclusivity may be subject to different views. The following developments will provide an overview of the different applications Courts made of these provisions.

687. *See*, European Commission, *Study on the current level of protection of air passenger rights in the EU*, January 2020, 177-178, Source: Publications Office of the European Union, https://op.europa.eu/en/publication-detail/-/publication/f03df002-335c-11ea-ba6e-01aa75ed71a1 (accessed 29 September 2020).

4.3.2.2 *A Strict Application*

Several Courts have retained a strict application of the principle of exclusivity as described earlier,[688] that is to say, they deemed that once the Conventions applied, they excluded the application of domestic law, even if the conditions set out in either Article 17, 18 or 19 of the Conventions were not met.

Such a perception was first endorsed by the highest Court of the UK. In 1997, the House of Lords was asked in *Sidhu*[689] to analyse the interaction between domestic remedies and the exclusivity of the 1929 Warsaw Convention as amended by the 1955 Hague Protocol. The question was to determine whether a passenger, who due to a potential fault of the carrier, sustained damage in the course of international carriage by air, but who had no claim against the carrier under its Article 17 was left without remedy or could still rely on domestic law. The response of the House of Lords was that the liability rules of the 1929 Warsaw Convention - in this case its Article 17 - were absolutely exclusive, as it held that:

> The language used and the subject matter with which it deals demonstrate that what was sought to be achieved was a uniform international code, which could be applied by the courts of all the high contracting parties without reference to the rules of their own domestic law. The Convention does not purport to deal with all matters relating to contracts of international carriage by air. But in those areas with which it deals - and the liability of the carrier is one of them - the code is intended to be uniform and to be exclusive also of any resort to the rules of domestic law. An answer to the question which leaves claimants without a remedy is not at first sight attractive. [...] Alongside these principles, however, there lies another great principle, which is that of freedom of contract. Any person is free, unless restrained by statute, to enter into a contract with another on the basis that his liability in damages is excluded or limited if he is in breach of contract.[690]

Later, under the wording of the 1999 Montreal Convention, the Supreme Court of the United Kingdom confirmed its earlier position. In *Stott*, the Court was asked whether a claimant could be awarded damages for discomfort and injury to feelings, caused by a breach of the UK Disability Regulations implementing EU Regulation 1107/2006[691] in light of the provisions of the 1999 Montreal Convention.[692] As the claimant argued that he suffered bad treatment both before and after boarding, the Court went even further in its strict application of the principle of exclusivity and ruled that:

---

688. *See*, section 3.2.2.
689. *Sidhu and Others v. British Airways Plc; Abnett (Known as Sykes) v. Same* (1996) UKHL 5.
690. *Ibid.*, conclusions.
691. Regulation (EC) No 1107/2006 of the European Parliament and of the Council of 5 July 2006 concerning the rights of disabled persons and persons with reduced mobility when travelling by air, *Official Journal*, 26 July 2006, L 204/1; *Corrigendum*, *Official Journal*, 26 January 2013, L 26/34.
692. *See*, Ingrid Koning, *The Disabling of the EC Disability Regulation: Stott v. Thomas Cook Tour Operators Ltd in the Light of the Exclusivity Doctrine*, 5 European Review of Private Law 786-796 (2014). *See also*, Andrea Buitrago Carranza, *Exploring the Compatibility Between the Air Carrier Liability Regime and International Human Rights Law*, 44 Annals of Air & Space Law 205-260 (2019).

> In the course of argument it was suggested that Mr Stott had a complete cause of action before boarding the aircraft based on his poor treatment prior to that stage. If so, it would of course follow that such a pre-existing claim would not be barred by the Montreal Convention, but that was not the claim advanced. Mr Stott's subjection to humiliating and disgraceful maltreatment which formed the gravamen of his claim was squarely within the temporal scope of the Montreal Convention. [...] Many if not most accidents or mishaps on an aircraft are capable of being traced back to earlier operative causes and it would distort the broad purpose of the Convention [...] to hold that it does not apply to an accident or occurrence in the course of international carriage by air if its cause can be traced back to an antecedent fault.[693]

A similar reasoning was adopted by the Supreme Court of the United States in 1999. In *Tseng*, the Court was asked to determine whether a passenger who could not fulfil the requirement of Article 17 of the 1929 Warsaw Convention, as her claim related to an allegedly traumatizing preboarding security check, could validly ground her claim against the carrier in domestic law, which in this case was tort under New York law. The Court dismissed the passenger's claim holding that:

> [...] the Warsaw Convention precludes a passenger from maintaining an action for personal injury damages under local law when her claim does not satisfy the conditions for liability under the Convention.[694]

The question of compatibility between provisions of the 1999 Montreal Convention and a domestic quasi-constitutional act was also analysed by the Supreme Court of Canada in *Thibodeau*.[695] The Canadian Supreme Court was seized by passengers who claimed compensation under domestic law for moral prejudice after they did not receive services in French on several Air Canada flights, allegedly in violation of the Canadian Official Languages Act.[696] The Canadian Supreme Court aligned itself with the American and English jurisprudence and held that:

> Permitting an action in damages to compensate for 'moral prejudice, pain and suffering and loss of enjoyment of [a passenger's] vacation' that does not otherwise fulfill the conditions of Article 17 of the *Montreal Convention* (because the action does not relate to death or bodily injury) would fly in the face of Article 29. It would also undermine one of the main purposes of the *Montreal Convention*, which is to bring uniformity across jurisdictions to the types and upper limits of claims for damages that may be made against international carriers for damages sustained in the course of carriage of passengers, baggage and cargo. As the international jurisprudence makes clear, the application of the *Montreal Convention* focuses on the factual circumstances surrounding the monetary claim, not the legal foundation of it. To decide otherwise would be to permit artful pleading to define the scope of the *Montreal Convention*.[697]

693. *Stott v. Thomas Cook Tour Operators Ltd* (2014) UKSC 15, point 60.
694. *El Al Israel Airlines, Ltd. v. Tsui Yuan Tseng*, 525 U.S. 155 (1999), at 176.
695. *See also*, section 2.5.3.3(3) regarding the autonomy of the terms of the 1999 Montreal Convention discussed in this decision.
696. *See*, Carlos Martins, *The 'Strong Exclusivity' Consensus Interpretation of the Montreal Convention*, 28(3) The Air and Space Lawyer 4-8 (2015).
697. *Thibodeau v. Air Canada* (2014) 3 SCR 340, point 64. On a side note, the plaintiffs continued their quest for the equal use of French. In a 2019 decision, the Federal Court of Canada ordered

In France, the interpretation of the principle of exclusivity has evolved. In 1981, the *Cour de cassation* held that any action against a carrier that fell within its scope was exclusive, with the consequence that a claim lodged by the pension fund of the victim of an air disaster was compelled by the two-year limitation.[698] In 1999, in the *Sidhu* mirroring case, the *Cour de cassation* adopted a different approach, which allowed passengers to be compensated under domestic law on the grounds that, in the Court's view, the 1929 Warsaw Convention did not apply since the damage occurred after disembarking.[699] In 2007, the *Cour de cassation* seemed to have endorsed a strict application of the principle of exclusivity when it essentially held that in the absence of an 'accident', the carrier could not be held liable.[700] This view was later implicitly confirmed in 2014, in a claim governed by the 1999 Montreal Convention.[701] Another important decision from the same Court regarding the scope of the principle of exclusivity, in the case of an action directed by a manufacturer against a carrier, will be discussed below.[702]

This strict application of the principle of exclusivity has been recognized in many other jurisdictions, such as in Australia,[703] China (Hong Kong),[704] Ireland,[705] New Zealand,[706] South Africa,[707] and Tonga.[708]

Air Canada to indemnify Mr and Ms Thibodeau for the violation of their rights established by the Canadian Official Languages Act. In substance, they claimed that some signs, such as the 'exit' sign, were not translated into French or were only indicated in smaller print. They also claimed that the boarding announcement at Fredericton Airport was shorter in French than in English. In this case, the question of the exclusivity of the 1999 Montreal Convention was not discussed. *See*, *Thibodeau c. Air Canada* (2019) CF 1102.

698. Cass., 2 July 1981, 80-11.234: '[...] que la responsabilité du transporteur de voyageurs par air ne pouvant être recherchée que dans les conditions et les limites prévues par la Convention de Varsovie, quelles que soient les personnes qui la mettent en cause et quel que soit le titre auquel elles prétendent agir'.
699. Cass., 15 July 1999, 97-10268: '[...] que la cour d'appel, qui a constaté que les dommages subis par les passagers s'étaient produits hors de l'aéronef et après leurs débarquement, alors qu'ils étaient regroupés dans un hôtel, en a exactement déduit que cette convention n'avait pas vocation à s'appliquer au litige'.
700. Cass., 14 June 2007, 05-17248: 'Mais attendu que la cour d'appel a, à bon droit, relevé qu'il résulte, tant de l'article 24 de la Convention de Varsovie que de l'article L. 322-3 du code de l'aviation civile, que toute action en responsabilité, à quelque titre que ce soit, à l'encontre du transporteur aérien de personnes, ne peut être exercée que dans les conditions et limites de la dite Convention qui, dans son article 17, déclare ce transporteur responsable de plein droit en cas de décès, de blessures ou de toute autre lésion corporelle subie par un voyageur, lorsque l'accident qui a causé le dommage s'est produit à bord de l'aéronef; que la cour d'appel a, à cet égard, constaté qu'il ne résultait d'aucun des éléments produits que l'embolie pulmonaire, survenue plusieurs jours après la fin du voyage, puisse être imputée à un événement extérieur à la personne de Mme Y ... qui se serait produit à bord de l'avion ou au cours des opérations d'embarquement ou de débarquement qui seul, serait de nature à faire jouer la présomption de responsabilité édictée par l'article 17 de la Convention de Varsovie; que dès lors, elle a pu en déduire, sans encourir les griefs du moyen, que la responsabilité du transporteur aérien ne pouvait être retenue'.
701. Cass., 14 January 2014, ECLI:FR:CCASS:2014:C100009.
702. *See*, section 5.2.2.
703. *Parkes Shire Council v. South West Helicopters Pty Limited* (2019) HCA 14.
704. *Ong v. Malaysian Airline System Berhad* (2008) HKCA 88.
705. *Hennessey v. Aer lingus Ltd* (2012) IEHC 124.
706. *Emery Air Freight Corp v. Nerine Nurseries Ltd* (1997) 3 NZLR 723.
707. *Potgieter v. British Airways plc* (2005) ZAWCH 5.

However, the cases listed in this section are mostly related to a combined interpretation of Article 17 of the Conventions. I am not aware of any final decision from a highest Court, with the exception of the decisions delivered by the CJEU, which would have been seized on the validity of coexisting regimes with respect to delays. A decision on this is, however, expected from the Canadian Federal Court.[709]

4.3.2.3 A Liberal Application

Alongside the strict application above, a more liberal approach has been adopted by the CJEU. Although the case concerned Article 19 of the 1999 Montreal Convention and not Article 17 of the Conventions as detailed above, the Court adopted a pro-consumer approach in *IATA* holding that, as discussed in section 4.2.2.2, the 1999 Montreal Convention and EU Regulation 261/2004 could validly coexist, in the Court's view, as each addressed different kind of damages.[710] This decision led to further flexibility permitting, in *Sturgeon*,[711] passengers whose flight has been delayed by three or more hours to claim standardized compensation pursuant to EU Regulation 261/2004. Invited to possibly overturn its position in *Nelson*, the Grand Chamber of the CJEU however reaffirmed the earlier point of view of the Court and held that:

> In paragraph 45 of *IATA and ELFAA*, the Court held that it does not follow from Articles 19, 22 and 29 of the Montreal Convention, or from any other provision thereof, that the authors of that convention intended to shield air carriers from any form of intervention other than those laid down by those provisions, in particular action which could be envisaged by the public authorities to redress, in a standardised and immediate manner, the damage that is constituted by the inconvenience that delay in the carriage of passengers by air causes, without the passengers having to suffer the inconvenience inherent in the bringing of actions for damages before the courts.[712]

The CJEU's stance is therefore clear. Without ruling on the possibility of applying domestic law when all conditions of Article 17 of the 1999 Montreal Convention are not met, the CJEU still held that parallel regimes could exist. As far as the Court held that the 1999 Montreal Convention and EU Regulation 261/2004 concerned different kinds of damages, the reasoning of the Court may be seen as coherent. Nevertheless, it seriously impairs the purposes and object of the 1999 Montreal Convention.

---

708. *Cauchi v. Air Fiji & Air Pacific Ltd* (2005) TOSC 7.
709. *See*, fn 673.
710. CJEC, 10 January 2006, *The Queen, on the application of International Air Transport Association and European Low Fares Airline Association v. Department for Transport*, C-344/04, ECLI:EU:C:2006:10.
711. CJEC, 19 November 2009, *Christopher Sturgeon, Gabriel Sturgeon and Alana Sturgeon v. Condor Flugdienst GmbH and Stefan Böck and Cornelia Lepuschitz v. Air France SA*, Joined Cases C-402/07 and C-432/07, ECLI:EU:C:2009:716.
712. CJEU, 23 October 2012, *Emeka Nelson e.a. v. Deutsche Lufthansa AG and TUI Travel plc and Others v. Civil Aviation Authority*, C-581/10 and C-629/10, ECLI:EU:C:2012:657, point 46.

4.3.2.4 A Defective Application

Other jurisdictions adopted an attitude which is different from the two priorly described and denied any primacy of the Conventions over domestic law.

For instance, in Brazil, judges admitted that the Consumer Defence Code prevailed over the 1999 Montreal Convention. It was only in 2017 that the Brazilian Federal Supreme Court held that the 1929 Warsaw Convention and 1999 Montreal Convention prevailed over domestic consumer protection legislation:

> Nos termos do art. 178 da Constituição da República, as normas e os tratados internacionais limitadores da responsabilidade das transportadoras aéreas de passageiros, especialmente as Convenções da Varsóvia e Montreal, têm prevalência em relação ao Código de Defesa do Consumidor.[713]

Another example of defective application of the principle of exclusivity of the Conventions may be found in India. In 2011, the Indian Supreme Court ruled that at least equal value should be granted to domestic consumer protection legislation and to the Carriage by Air Act, which incorporates the 1929 Warsaw Convention:

> In our view, the protection provided under the C[onsumer] P[rotection] Act to consumers is in addition to the remedies available under any other Statute.[714]

Other Courts have rejected the application of the Conventions, as illustrated by the decision of the 11th District Court of Panama. This Court disregarded the limitation of liability set in the 1999 Montreal Convention, with respect to damage to cargo, preferring to rule in favour of the claimant with an argument of equity.[715]

4.3.2.5 Conclusions

Although the predominant view seems to favour a strict application of the principle of exclusivity of the Conventions, these examples demonstrate that the diversity in interpretations of the exclusivity of the Conventions given by Courts weakens the aim of uniformity and undermines the purposes of the Conventions.

713. Supremo Tribunal Federal, 25 May 2017, RE 636331/RJ. *See*, Carolina Castro Costa Viegas, Marco Fábio Morsello, *Seguridad jurídica vs. nueva caja de Pandora: Breves apuntes acerca de la reciente sentencia del Supremo Tribunal Federal en Brasil*, 42 Revista Latino Americana de Derecho Aeronáutico (2018).

714. *Trans Mediterranean Airways v. M/s Universal Exports & Anr.* (2011) 10 SCC 316, at 32.

715. Juzgado Undécimo de Circuito de lo Civil del Primer Circuito Judicial de Panamá, 27 October 2017, *Caisa c. KLM*, Sentencia No 25-2017, not published. This decision was overruled in Appeal. *See*, Primer Tribunal Superior del Primer Distrito Judicial, 25 April 2019, *Caisa c. KLM*, 18SA.069, not published.

4.3.3 Autonomy

4.3.3.1 Preliminary Remarks

While the autonomy of the terms and concepts used in the Conventions was confirmed in Chapter 2, Chapter 3 showed that attempts made by Courts to give a definition to undefined terms and concepts resulted in divergent interpretations.

One could wonder whether the autonomy of the terms used in the Conventions entails that each term should be interpreted according to a 'special' meaning pursuant to Article 31 (4) of the 1969 Vienna Convention, or if the 'ordinary' meaning developed under its Article 31 (1) may be applicable.[716] I understand that a 'special' meaning is not only limited to terms that are defined in the Conventions, as exemplified in section 3.2.2.1, but also covers broader situations where the intent of the parties would have to be assessed and demonstrated.[717] I also understand that the reading of Article 31 (4) of said convention permits to consider that in a special regime, such as that of the Conventions, the 'special' meaning is essentially the 'ordinary meaning in the particular context'.[718] I think therefore that, in the case of the Conventions, the 'special' meaning may be limited to the terms that are defined, and to those whose meaning clearly transpires from the *Travaux Préparatoires*.

The following section will examine the different elements mostly used by Courts to interpret the terms and concepts of the Conventions, and will scrutinize the interpretative role of the preamble, *Travaux Préparatoires*, case law, external laws,[719] and literature. This analysis will hopefully permit an identification of the specific reasons why Courts adopted distinct interpretations. It may also allow us to verify whether the hermeneutical principles of the 1969 Vienna Convention are sufficient to interpret the Conventions in a uniform manner.

For the reasons explained in Chapter 1,[720] the examination of interpretation methods employed by Courts will be limited to those used by the highest Courts of Belgium, Canada, France, the EU, the UK and the United States. As a reminder, the Supreme Court of the United States has not yet handed down any decision interpreting the 1999 Montreal Convention. Therefore, this study will also refer to the most recent decision delivered by a Circuit Court in the United States at the time of writing.

716. *See*, section 1.3.1.2(2)(v).
717. *See*, United Nations Conferences on the Law of Treaties, First and second sessions, Vienna, 26 March-24 May 1968 and 9 April-22 May 1969, Official Records, *Documents of the Conference*, United Nations, New York, 1971, p. 42, Source: United Nations, https://treaties.un.org/doc/source/docs/A_CONF.39_11_Add.2-E.pdf (accessed 2 August 2019).
718. *See*, Oliver Dörr, Kristen Schmalenbach (eds), *Vienna Convention on the Law of Treaties: A Commentary* 613 (2nd edition, Springer, 2018). *See also*, Richard Gardiner, *Treaty Interpretation* 339 (2nd edition, The Oxford International Law Library, 2017).
719. As defined below in section 4.3.3.5(1).
720. *See*, section 1.3.2.3.

4.3.3.2 Preamble

As seen in Chapter 2, the preamble of the 1999 Montreal Convention makes reference to the concept of both 'balance of interests' and 'protection of the interests of consumers', and this created confusion as certain Courts read this introduction of the notion of consumer protection as a new, additional purpose to the 1999 Montreal Convention.[721]

Like most Courts, the Supreme Court of Canada considered in *Thibodeau* that the 'purposes' remained the same in both Conventions:

> The *Warsaw Convention* (and therefore its successor the *Montreal Convention*) had three main purposes: to create uniform rules governing claims arising from international air transportation; to protect the international air carriage industry by limiting carrier liability; and to balance that protective goal with the interests of passengers and others seeking recovery. These purposes responded to concerns that many legal regimes might apply to international carriage by air with the result that there could be no uniformity or predictability with respect to either carrier liability or the rights of passengers and others using the service. Both passengers and carriers were potentially harmed by this lack of uniformity.[722]

In contrast, the CJEU has adopted a different view and regularly considers consumer protection as an additional purpose of the 1999 Montreal Convention, which would supplement the purpose of achieving an 'equitable balance of interests'. In *Air Baltic Corporation*, the Court ruled that the reference to consumers in the preamble was distinct from the concept of passengers.[723] Later, in *Finnair*, the Court clearly admitted that both elements - that is to say, the balance of interests between carriers and passengers, and then, protection of consumers - had to be taken into consideration when interpreting the Convention.[724] Ultimately, this position was confirmed in *Guaitoli* as follows:

> However, the interpretation that the purpose of Article 33(1) of the Montreal Convention is to designate not only the State Party competent to hear the liability action concerned, but also the courts of that State before which the action is to be brought, is such as to contribute to attaining the objective of enhanced unification, as expressed in the preamble to that instrument, and to protect the interests of

721. *See*, sections 2.3.3.2 and 4.2.2.2(2).
722. *Thibodeau v. Air Canada* (2014) 3 SCR 340, at 41.
723. CJEU, 17 February 2016, *Air Baltic Corporation AS v. Lietuvos Respublikos specialiųjų tyrimų tarnyba*, C-429/14, ECLI:EU:C:2016:88, at 38: '[...] it being understood that the concept of "consumer" for the purposes of that convention should not be confused with the concept of "passenger", but may include persons who are not themselves carried and are therefore not passengers'.
724. CJEU, 12 April 2018, *Finnair Oyj v. Keskinäinen Vakuutusyhtiö Fennia*, C-258/16, ECLI:EU:C:2018:252, at 34: 'In addition, in the light both of the third paragraph of the preamble to the Montreal Convention, which emphasises the importance of ensuring protection of the interests of consumers in international carriage by air, and of the principle of "an equitable balance of interests" referred to in the fifth paragraph of the preamble of that convention, the requirement of being in a written form cannot have the effect of excessively limiting the specific way in which a passenger may choose to complain, provided that that passenger remains identifiable as the person who made the complaint.'

consumers, while at the same time ensuring a fair balance with the interests of air carriers. The direct appointment of the territorially competent court is likely to ensure, in the interests of both parties to the dispute, greater predictability and greater legal certainty.[725]

The fact that certain Courts judged that a difference could be discerned in the purposes of the Conventions caused serious concerns about Article 31 of the 1969 Vienna Convention and, consequently, the emergence of uniform autonomous definitions that ultimately would ensure a uniform application. The use of a vague concept such as 'protection of the interests of consumers' may also lead to an evolutionary interpretation[726] of the 1999 Montreal Convention that could potentially rewrite the text and further increase its fragmentation across ratifying Parties. Yet, as ruled in *Morris*, an evolutionary interpretation of the Conventions is not possible[727] as only an amendment can change them.[728]

Finally, assuming the Conventions have different purposes raises a question on the value of case law developed under the 1929 Warsaw Convention, as discussed below.[729]

4.3.3.3 Travaux Préparatoires

Although the 1969 Vienna Convention permits recourse to the *Travaux Préparatoires* as a supplementary interpretation aid in specific circumstances,[730] in many jurisdictions, the *Travaux Préparatoires* have regularly been considered as major interpretation tools.[731]

725. CJEU, 7 November 2019, *Adriano Guaitoli, e.a. v. easyJet Airline Co. Ltd*, C-213/18, ECLI: EU:C:2019:927, at 53-54.
726. *See*, section 3.2.4.3(5)(iv).
727. *Morris v. KLM Royal Dutch Airlines* (2002) UKHL 7, at 25: '[...] I accept that courts of law cannot ignore advances in scientific knowledge. [...] statutes are generally always speaking, and ought therefore to be interpreted in light of the contemporary social and scientific world. This is not a rule of law but a principle of construction [...] Given that the rationale of the principle is that statutes are generally intended to endure for a long time, one can readily accept that multilateral international trade conventions, which are by statute incorporated in our law, should be approached in a similar way.'
728. *Ibid.*, at 26: '[...] if cases of mental injuries and illnesses are to be brought within the Convention system, it must be done by amendment of the Convention system and not by judicial creativity'. *See also*, *Stott v. Thomas Cook Tour Operators Ltd* (2014) UKSC 15, at 63: 'The underlying problem is that the Warsaw Convention long pre-dated equality laws which are common today. There is much to be said for the argument that it is time for the Montreal Convention to be amended to take account of the development of equality rights, whether in relation to race (as in *King v American Airlines*) or in relation to access for the disabled, but any amendment would be a matter for the contracting parties.'
729. *See*, section 4.3.3.4(2).
730. 1969 Vienna Convention, Article 32. *See*, section 1.3.1.2(2)(ii).
731. This position may reflect the divergence of views in legal theory between a normative (*volontariste*) and a subjective (*objectiviste*) approach. The first is more inclined to interpret international conventions pursuant to the intentions of the States, and the latter is more favourable to a teleological interpretation. On this point, the 1969 Vienna Convention seems essentially to adopt a subjective approach.

In the United States, Justice O'Connor held in *Saks* that the *Travaux Préparatoires* were an important tool for clarification:

> In interpreting a treaty it is proper, of course, to refer to the records of its drafting and negotiations. [...] In part because the 'travaux préparatoires' of the Warsaw Convention are published and generally available to litigants, courts frequently refer to these materials to resolve ambiguities in the text.[732]

In *Chan*, Justice Brennan considered that the *Travaux Préparatoires* deserved attention when several readings of a provision were possible:

> But it is disingenuous to say that it is the only possible reading. Certainly it is wrong to disregard the wealth of evidence to be found in the Convention's drafting history on the intent of the governments that drafted the document.[733]

More importantly, he emphasized their importance even with respect to parties that did not participate in diplomatic conferences:

> Sometimes, of course, a state may become a party to an international convention only after it has entered into force, without having participated in its drafting. Thus, the United States was not represented at Warsaw and adhered to the Convention only in 1934. But to say that for that reason the drafting history of an international treaty may not be enlisted as an aid in its interpretation would be unnecessarily to forgo a valuable resource. We do not, after all, find it necessary to disregard the drafting history of our Constitution, notwithstanding that 37 of the 50 States played no role in the negotiations and debates that created it.[734]

The relevance of the *Travaux Préparatoires* was later reaffirmed in subsequent decisions, such as in *Zicherman* where Justice Scalia explained the reasons of their importance, as follows:

> Because a treaty ratified by the United States is not only the law of this land [...], but also an agreement among sovereign powers, we have traditionally considered as aids to its interpretation the negotiating and drafting history (*travaux préparatoires*) and the post-ratification understanding of the contracting parties.[735]

Historically in the UK, no substantial credit was granted to the *Travaux Préparatoires*, as they were generally not used under English law for interpretation purposes. However, this position changed in *Fothergill*. Lord Wilberforce submitted that it was in the interest of uniformity to not ignore them, given that international Courts used them as an aid, that the practice was endorsed by the 1969 Vienna Convention,[736] and that foreign Courts had recourse to them. He expressed his concern that their use, however, should be cautious and limited to conditions where they were publicly accessible and where they clearly and indisputably pointed to a definite legislative intention. He further noted that if these conditions were met, there would be no more room for the

732. *Air France v. Saks*, 470 U.S. 392 (1985), at 400.
733. *Chan et. al. v. Korean Air Lines, Ltd*, 490 U.S. 122 (1989), at 136.
734. *Ibid.*, at 137, fn 2.
735. *Zicherman, Individually and as Executrix of the Estate of Kole, et. al. v. Korean Air Lines Co, Ltd.*, 516 U.S. 217 (1996), at 226.
736. Which was not in force yet, as underlined by Lord Fraser of Tullybelton, at 112.

argument that the *Travaux Préparatoires* could not apply to acceding States, or more generally to individuals who might never have heard of them:

> My Lords, [...] the use of travaux préparatoires in the interpretation of treaties should be cautious, I think that it would be proper for us, in the same interest, to recognise that there may be cases where such travaux préparatoires can profitably be used. These cases should be rare, and only where two conditions are fulfilled: first, that the material involved is public and accessible, and, secondly, that the travaux préparatoires clearly and indisputably point to a definite legislative intention. [...] If the use of travaux préparatoires is limited in this way, that would largely overcome the two objections which may properly be made: first, that relating to later acceding states [...] and secondly, the general objection that individuals ought not to be bound by discussions or negotiations of which they may never have heard.[737]

The *Travaux Préparatoires* have since then occasionally been used by the highest English Court, such as in *Morris*.[738]

In France, it is generally standard to consult the *Travaux Préparatoires* when it comes to interpreting domestic legislation. However, when it comes to the interpretation of international conventions, the question is more delicate. As already discussed,[739] under the 1929 Warsaw Convention, several decisions were handed down regarding the possibility of interrupting the two-year limitation period established under Article 29. In a 1966 decision, the defendant argued that the time limitation foreseen in the 1929 Warsaw Convention was established 'sous peine de déchéance' and therefore required that any claim must be filed within said limit. The *Cour de cassation*, however, held that the time limitation only governed contractual liability and did not extend to criminal actions.[740] In a subsequent case, the fixed time limit was further discussed, as the claimant was a minor at the time of accident. This case came before the *Cour de cassation* twice, as the second Court of Appeal refused to follow the first position adopted by the *Cour de cassation*. On the second occasion, the Court of Appeal put forth that the claim was time-barred in light of the wording, purpose and *Travaux Préparatoires* of the 1929 Warsaw Convention.[741] However, the plenary

737. *Fothergill v. Monarch Airlines* (1980) UKHL 6, at 75.
738. *Morris v. KLM Royal Dutch Airlines* (2002) UKHL 7, at 103.
739. *See*, section 3.2.5.
740. Cass., 17 May 1966, 65-92986: 'Que dès lors l'action civile était régie par l'article 10 du Code de procédure pénale et, conformément au droit commun, pouvait être mise en œuvre tant que l'action publique n'était pas prescrite; qu'elle échappait à la forclusion prévue par la loi du 2 mars 1957 qui, par adoption expresse des règles de la Convention de Varsovie, limite à deux ans le délai pendant lequel la responsabilité du transporteur par air peut être recherchée; que ces dispositions qui régissent l'action contractuelle de la victime ou de ses ayants cause sont étrangères à l'exercice de l'action civile devant le juge répressif'. *See*, Jean-Pierre Tosi, *Responsabilité aérienne* 180 (Litec, 1978).
741. Cass., 14 January 1977, 74-15061: 'Attendu que, pour déclarer irrecevable comme tardive l'action en réparation engagée [...] au nom de son fils mineur [...] l'arrêt attaqué énonce que le délai de deux ans imparti sous peine de déchéance par l'article 2 de la loi du 2 mars 1957 comme par l'article 29 de la Convention de Varsovie pour intenter l'action en responsabilité contre le transporteur aérien est un délai préfix et que ce caractère résulte sinon de l'expression sous peine de déchéance, qui ne lui confère pas nécessairement, du moins de la finalité du texte telle que la révèle l'intention du législateur français qui s'est expressément référé aux seules

session of the *Cour de cassation* hearing the case the second time ruled that nothing in the explicit wording of said convention precluded the application of French law, and therefore implicitly rejected any reference to the content of the *Travaux Préparatoires*:

> Attendu, cependant, que si la Convention de Varsovie du 12 octobre 1929, à laquelle renvoie l'article L 322-3 du Code de l'aviation civile pour la détermination des règles de la responsabilité du transporteur aérien, prévoit que l'action en responsabilité doit être intentée à peine de déchéance dans un délai de deux ans, il n'existe dans ces textes aucune disposition expresse selon laquelle, par dérogation aux principes du droit interne français, ce délai ne serait susceptible ni d'interruption, ni de suspension.[742]

Since then, it still cannot be concluded with certainty that the French *Cour de cassation* always ignores the *Travaux Préparatoires* of the Conventions. As the decisions of this Court are quite succinct, it is impossible to say whether the *Travaux Préparatoires* of the Conventions are systematically considered by the Court.

In Belgium, it is general practice to refer to the *Travaux Préparatoires* in order to determine both domestic[743] and international legislators' intentions.[744] However, for the same reasons as those developed for the French *Cour de cassation*, it is not possible to assess whether they are automatically taken into consideration by the Belgian *Cour de cassation*.

In Canada, it appears that the Supreme Court clearly refers to the *Travaux Préparatoires*, as pointed out in *Thibodeau*,[745] when asked to interpret the 1999 Montreal Convention.

At the level of the CJEU, the Court did not expressly refer to the *Travaux Préparatoires* of the 1999 Montreal Convention until 2020. In the past, only the opinions of Advocates General have occasionally referred to them.[746] However, in 2020, the CJEU expressly referred to the *Travaux Préparatoires* in order to interpret the 1999 Montreal Convention in *Vueling*.[747]

In conclusion, despite some reluctance and uncertainty, most jurisdictions consider the *Travaux Préparatoires* as useful tools for interpreting the Conventions, even if references to them have not always been systematic. Despite being considered as supplementary means of interpretation by the 1969 Vienna Convention, their role in finding a definition that respects the autonomy of the Conventions should probably be accorded a higher value.

---

dispositions de la Convention de Varsovie dont les travaux préparatoires expriment nettement l'intention de ses auteurs de ne soumettre le délai à aucune cause de suspension'.

742. Cass., 14 January 1977, 74-15061. *See*, Jean-Pierre Tosi, *Responsabilité aérienne* 183 (Litec, 1978).
743. Axel de Theux, e. a., *Précis de méthodologie juridique: Les sources documentaires du droit* 164 (2nd edition, Publications des Facultés universitaires Saint-Louis, 2000).
744. *See*, Cass., 27 January 1977, 1 Pasicrisie 574 (1977); Cass., 30 March 2000, C.9.70.176.N.
745. *Thibodeau v. Air Canada* (2014) 3 SCR 340, at 38.
746. *See*, CJEU, 26 September 2019, *GN v. ZU acting for Niki Luftfahrt*, C-532/18, ECLI:EU:C:2019:788 (Opinion), at 38.
747. CJEU, 9 July 2020, *SL v. Vueling Airlines SA*, C-86/19, ECLI:EU:C:2020:538, at 32: 'Furthermore, it is apparent from the *travaux préparatoires* relating to the Montreal Convention that [...].'

4.3.3.4 *Case Law*

(1) Foreign Case Law

One of the most distinguishable elements dividing selected jurisdictions into two groups consists in the consideration given to foreign decisions.

In common law jurisdictions, as per the principle of stare decisis, there is a long-standing tradition to refer to foreign case law as an interpretation aid. It is therefore not a surprise that the highest Courts of the UK and the United States have regularly examined foreign jurisprudence. Furthermore, because the 1929 Warsaw Convention was written in French and originated from the French government, there was a trend to consider that French law carried substantial weight for interpretation purposes. In addition to these two reasons, common law jurisdictions have rapidly acknowledged the importance of having a uniform interpretation of the Conventions that required at least a review of foreign decisions. In the United States, Justice Ginsburg recalled in *Tseng* that:

> [I]t is our responsibility to give the specific words of the treaty a meaning consistent with the shared expectations of the contracting parties [...].[748]

The same view is reported in the UK as follows, in *Morris*:

> It really goes without saying that the international uniformity of interpretation of article 17 is highly desirable.[749]

However, the value credited to foreign decisions has not systematically been equal to that of domestic case law. In the UK, Lord Diplock ruled in *Fothergill* that the value of foreign decisions depended particularly on the Court's reputation, their binding nature and the reporting system in place. He held that:

> [...] the persuasive value of a particular court's decision must depend on its reputation and its status, the extent to which its decisions are binding on courts of co-ordinate or inferior jurisdiction in its own country and the coverage of the national law reporting system.[750]

In *Sidhu*, the House of Lords added that the extent of the analysis given by foreign Courts was also to be taken into consideration when assessing the value of their decisions.[751] In this respect, and in light of the importance of having a uniform application of the Conventions, the Supreme Court of the United States notably disregarded a decision delivered by a foreign Court, on the ground that the position

---

748. *El Al Israel Airlines, Ltd. v. Tsui Yuan Tseng*, 525 U.S. 155 (1999), at 167.
749. *Morris v. KLM Royal Dutch Airlines* (2002) UKHL 7, at 5.
750. *Fothergill v. Monarch Airlines* (1980) UKHL 6, at 96.
751. On this basis, in *Sidhu*, Lord Craighead denied substantial weight to a French decision, as he considered that the French decision of the *Tribunal de Grande Instance* of Paris: '[...] does not contain a close analysis of the Convention, nor is there any reference to previous decisions on the issue in the French courts or elsewhere'. *See*, *Sidhu and Others v. British Airways Plc; Abnett (Known as Sykes) v. Same* (1996) UKHL 5.

adopted by the latter created a potential source of divergence which was not compliant with the aim of uniformity.[752]

In civil law jurisdictions, there is no tradition to refer to foreign decisions or any compulsory duty to refer to domestic jurisprudence, given their relatively low legal value. In France, the rapprochement of the *Cour de cassation*, regarding the interpretation of the term 'accident' with respect to the one developed in other jurisdictions,[753] may lead us to believe that some consideration has been given to foreign law. In Belgium, equally, there is no clear evidence that any consideration would automatically be given to foreign case law.[754]

In Canada, the Supreme Court acted in a similar fashion as common law jurisdictions and confirmed in *Thibodeau* that the Court would be reluctant to depart from any 'strong international consensus'.[755]

The Advocates General of the CJEU may occasionally refer to foreign case law such as in *Niki*.[756] But none of the decisions of the European Court employ decisions delivered by other non-European jurisdictions for the sake of a uniform interpretation.

In conclusion, it seems that even if there could be a light general trend towards the perusal of foreign jurisprudence, many high Courts still do not systematically refer to the interpretations given abroad. This lack of interest undoubtedly hinders a uniform application of the Conventions.

(2) Case Law Developed Prior to the 1999 Montreal Convention

While the seventy years of existence of the 1929 Warsaw Convention have generated an impressive amount of case law, this study should verify whether Courts still rely on case law developed under previous instruments in cases governed by the 1999 Montreal Convention, in order to ascertain whether or not there is uniformity in the interpretation tools used by these Courts.

In the United States, the 6th District Court highlighted in *Doe* that the wording of the 1999 Montreal Convention was different to the one of the 1929 Warsaw Convention, with the consequence that previous case law did not have any authority:

> [...] the Montreal Convention is a new treaty that we interpret as a matter of first impression, and there is no legal authority that would require us to import *Erhlich*'s Warsaw Convention determination to govern this Montreal Convention claim.[757]

752. *Eastern Airlines, Inc. v. Floyd et al.*, 499 U.S. 530 (1991), at 551-552.
753. *See*, section 3.2.2.3.
754. However, more and more comparative analyses are being carried out by both *Cours de cassation*. *See*, Cour de cassation de Belgique, *Rapport annuel* 160 et seq. (2018), Source: Belgian Federal Public Service of Justice, https://justice.belgium.be/sites/default/files/downloads/20180321_jp_31.pdf (accessed 31 March 2020).
755. *Thibodeau v. Air Canada* (2014) 3 SCR 340, at 50.
756. CJEU, 26 September 2019, *GN v. ZU acting for Niki Luftfahrt*, C-532/18, ECLI:EU:C:2019:788 (Opinion), at 44.
757. *Doe v. Etihad Airways, P.J.S.C.*, 870 F.3d 406 (6th Cir. 2017), at 415.

The Court nevertheless admitted that domestic or foreign decisions rendered under the previous text were still valid precedent, insofar as they concerned similar provisions and were delivered before the ratification of the 1999 Montreal Convention:

> Because these Supreme Court cases analyzed aspects of the Warsaw Convention that we have no reason to believe have changed following the ratification of the Montreal Convention (and that neither party has argued have changed following the ratification of the Montreal Convention), it is reasonable to conclude that these cases form part of the 'precedent' consistent with which, according to the Explanatory Note [...], the drafters expected signatories to construe Article 17(1) of the Montreal Convention. Accordingly, we have adopted *Saks*' definition of 'accident', and our discussion of damages [...] will be guided by *Zicherman*'s deference to the forum jurisdiction's choice-of-law rules.[758]

The UK Supreme Court implicitly confirmed in *Stott* the continuity to a certain extent of the case law related to these instruments.[759] Interpreting the concept of exclusivity, Lord Toulson referred to jurisprudence established under the 1929 Warsaw Convention on the grounds particularly that Article 17 of both Conventions were formulated in materially identical terms.[760]

In Canada, Justice Cromwell in turn noted, in *Thibodeau*, that case law drawn up under the 1929 Warsaw Convention was only 'helpful' for interpretation purposes. He held that:

> The *Montreal Convention* was adopted in 1999 in Montreal and applies to all international carriage by aircraft of persons, baggage or cargo. It was the successor to the [Warsaw Convention] [...] and its purpose was 'to modernize and consolidate the Warsaw Convention and related instruments': preamble of the *Montreal Convention*. To understand the purposes of the *Montreal Convention*, we therefore must go back to its predecessor, the *Warsaw Convention* [...]. The purposes of the *Warsaw Convention* and of the *Montreal Convention* were the same and decisions and commentary respecting the *Warsaw Convention* are therefore helpful in understanding those purposes [...].[761]

Looking at the CJEU, the same prudent approach was adopted by Advocate General Henrik Saugmandsgaard Øe in *Niki*, where he considered that only inspiration could be taken from foreign case law, including decisions delivered under the Warsaw Convention:[762]

758. *Ibid.*, at 425-426. The temporal requirement (i.e., before the ratification) seems to have been given up by the 2nd Circuit in 2021. *See*, *Cohen v. American Airlines, Inc*, 13F.4th 240 (2nd Cir. 2021).
759. Later, in a case governed by the 1999 Montreal Convention, the High Court of England and Wales carefully confirmed the interpretation of the term 'accident' given under the 1999 Warsaw Convention. *See*, *Labbadia v. Alitalia* (2019) EWHC 2013 (QB).
760. *Stott v. Thomas Cook Tour Operators Ltd* (2014) UKSC 15, at 26.
761. *Thibodeau v. Air Canada* (2014) 3 SCR 340, at 31.
762. As a reminder, the Court of Justice of the European Union is not competent to interpret the 1929 Warsaw Convention. *See*, CJEC, 22 October 2009, *Irène Bogiatzi, married name Ventouras v. Deutscher Luftpool, Société Luxair, société luxembourgeoise de navigation aérienne SA, European Communities, Grand Duchy of Luxembourg, Foyer Assurances SA*, C-301/08, ECLI: EU:C:2009:649.

> In that regard, I consider, as have both the referring court and all the parties which have submitted observations in the present case, that it is appropriate to take into consideration the interpretation of that concept employed by various *courts of States Parties* to the Warsaw Convention and/or the Montreal Convention, in order to draw any inspiration from those judicial precedents, even though the Court is not bound by them.[763]

In a nutshell, Courts are in an uncomfortable position. They are supposed to consider the 1999 Montreal Convention as a new international instrument which prevails over prior instruments such as the 1929 Warsaw Convention,[764] but, at the same time, the connections between the Conventions are so numerous and important that they seem to be hesitant to depart from existing case law, except for a valid reason.

4.3.3.5 *Legal Instruments External to the 1929 Warsaw Convention and the 1999 Montreal Convention*

(1) *Preliminary Remarks*

During the interpretation process, Courts have also referred to domestic legislations and international agreements in order to interpret the terms of the 1999 Montreal Convention.

(2) *French Law*

As already mentioned,[765] the fact that the first legislative drive to regulate air carrier liability at an international level came from the French government, and especially that the only authentic language of the 1929 Warsaw Convention was French, led the American Supreme Court to consider the terms and concepts used therein were to be interpreted in accordance with French law to a certain extent. This was notably the case in *Saks*, where Justice O'Connor held that the term 'accident' was, in the absence of definition, to be examined for interpretation purposes in light of French law:

> To determine the meaning of the term 'accident' in Article 17 we must consider its French legal meaning. [...] it is our responsibility to give the specific words of the treaty a meaning consistent with the shared expectations of the contracting parties. [...] We look to the French legal meaning for guidance as to these expectations because the Warsaw Convention was drafted in French by continental jurists.[766]

763. CJEU, 26 September 2019, *GN v. ZU acting for Niki Luftfahrt*, C-532/18, ECLI:EU:C:2019:788 (Opinion), at 43.
764. *See*, section 1.3.1.1(2).
765. *See*, section 4.3.3.4(1).
766. *Air France v. Saks*, 470 U.S. 392 (1985), at 399. This position is not justified in the author's view, as the Convention was drafted not only by continental jurists but also by representatives of common law jurisdictions. In addition, continental law is not uniform, therefore what may be valid in one civil law jurisdiction is not necessarily the case in another.

Later in *Floyd*, Justice Marshall used the same interpretation method, referring to the French legal meaning of 'bodily injury'. But, not convinced by the elements found, he suggested that reference to French law should potentially be set aside:

> Since our task is to 'give the specific words of the treaty a meaning consistent with the shared expectations of the contracting parties' [...], we find it unlikely that those parties' apparent understanding of the term 'lésion corporelle' as 'bodily injury' would have been displaced by a meaning abstracted from the French law of damages. Particularly is this so when the cause of action for psychic injury that evidently was possible under French law in 1929 would not have been recognized in many other countries represented at the Warsaw Convention.[767]

Ultimately, in *Zicherman*, the question of whether damages for loss of society resulting from the death of a relative in a crash on high seas could be compensated was raised. In its interpretation of the word 'damage' under Article 17 of the 1929 Warsaw Convention,[768] Justice Scalia declined to adopt a solution that would be a mix of French and American law and stated that:

> When presented with an equally plausible reading of Article 24 that leads to a more comprehensible result – that the Convention left to domestic law the questions of who may recover and what compensatory damages are available to them – we decline to embrace a reading that would produce the mélange of French and domestic law proposed by petitioners.[769]

These examples demonstrate that the interpretation developed in American cases made under the 1929 Warsaw Convention was partly inspired by French law on the grounds that it would have been expected by the Parties in the concerned litigation.

(3) *Other Domestic Laws*

Several Courts have also considered that their domestic law could be a valid source of interpretation of the Conventions. For example, the French *Cour de cassation* ruled that the term 'act' described under 25 of the 1929 Warsaw Convention as amended by the

767. *Eastern Airlines, Inc. v. Floyd et al.*, 499 U.S. 530 (1991), at 540.
768. It is also interesting to compare how the term 'damage' was interpreted by the Supreme Court of the United States and the Court of Justice of the European Union. In *Zicherman*, the Supreme Court, asked to interpret the term 'damage' under Article 17 of the Warsaw Convention, held that this notion was to be interpreted pursuant to domestic law applicable under the forum's choice-of-law rules. In contrast, in *Walz*, the Court of Justice of the European Union held that the term 'damage', which underpinned Article 22(2) of the 1999 Montreal Convention, required an autonomous interpretation. The autonomous dimension was nevertheless left aside, as the Court eventually referred to a definition used in international law rather than trying to offer a genuine autonomous definition. This being said, the comparison between these two decisions is limited. First, they concern different provisions in different instruments. Second, they raise serious translation issues as the French translation of the word 'damage' is different. Under *Zicherman*, the sole authentic French text uses the word 'dommage', whereas under *Walz*, the non-exclusive authentic French version of the text uses, depending of the provision examined, either the word 'avarie', 'dommage' or 'préjudice'. For further discussions on linguistic issues, *see*, section 4.4.
769. *Zicherman, Individually and as Executrix of the Estate of Kole, et. al. v. Korean Air Lines Co, Ltd.*, 516 U.S. 217 (1996), at 225-226.

1955 Hague Protocol was identical to the inexcusable fault (*faute inexcusable*) set out in French legislation. This Court concluded that the interpretation of the inexcusable fault, which was previously given by the Court with respect to a labour accident, could be transposed into a case of aerial accident.[770] This reference to domestic legislation led to an objective appreciation of the fault, whereas in other jurisdictions a subjective appreciation was preferred[771] as more in line with the discussions reported in the *Travaux Préparatoires* of the 1955 Hague Protocol.[772]

In 2015, when the CJEU was asked to interpret the concept of 'passenger' under Article 17 of the 1999 Montreal Convention, it held an unclear reasoning in *Wurcher*. The Court mixed up the provisions of this Convention with EU law concepts when it concluded that:

> It follows from the foregoing that Article 17 of the Montreal Convention must be interpreted as meaning that a person who comes within the definition of 'passenger' within the meaning of Article 3 (g) of Regulation No 785/2004, also comes within the definition of 'passenger' within the meaning of Article 17 of that convention, once that person has been carried on the basis of a 'contract of carriage' within the meaning of Article 3 of that convention.[773]

This Court view is puzzling, given that it refers to other sources of inspiration for interpreting the 1999 Montreal Convention earlier in *Walz*.[774]

In any case, referring to domestic law as a source of inspiration for the interpretation of the Conventions infringes on the concept of autonomy of the Conventions and prevents their uniform application. This is especially true when these Conventions do not refer to the applicability of domestic regulations through a *renvoi*.[775]

(4) Other International Legislative Instruments

In 2005, the CJEU, seized on the interpretation of the word 'damage' under the 1999 Montreal Convention, ruled in *Walz* that this concept should be understood pursuant to an international law definition. In this case, the Court ruled that the word 'damage' under the 1999 Montreal Convention should be interpreted in light of the *Articles on Responsibility of States for Internationally Wrongful Acts*:[776]

770. Cass., 5 December 1967, volume II JCP 15350 (1967) – a case known in the English literature as *Emery v. Sabena*. This position was later reaffirmed in Cass., 24 June 1968 Revue Française de Droit Aérien et Spatial 453 (1968) – a case known in the English literature as *Air France v. Diop*.
771. *See*, René Mankiewicz, *L'origine et l'interprétation de la l'article 25 de la Convention de Varsovie amendée à La Haye en 1955*, 26 Zeitschrift für Luft- und Weltraumrecht 175 (1977).
772. ICAO Doc 7686, International Conference on Private Air Law, The Hague, September 1955, volume I, *Minutes*, Montreal September 1956, pp. 206 and 285.
773. CJEU, 26 February 2015, *Wucher Helicopter GmbH, Euro-Aviation Versicherungs AG v. Fridolin Santer*, C-6/14, ECLI:EU:C:2015:122, at 42.
774. *See*, section 4.3.3.5(4).
775. *See*, section 1.1.3.2(4)(iii).
776. International Law Commission, *Responsibility of States for Internationally Wrongful Acts (2001)*, Source: United Nations, https://legal.un.org/ilc/texts/instruments/english/draft_articles/9_6_2001.pdf (accessed 22 March 2021).

> Lastly, in order to determine the ordinary meaning to be given to the term 'damage' in accordance with the rule of interpretation referred to at paragraph 23 above, it should be recalled that there is a concept of damage which does not originate in an international agreement and is common to all the international law sub-systems. Thus, Article 31(2) of the Articles on Responsibility of States for Internationally Wrongful Acts, drawn up by the International Law Commission of the United Nations, and of which the General Assembly of that organisation took note in its Resolution 56/83 of 12 December 2001, provides that '[i]njury includes any damage, whether material or moral ...'.[777]

This decision is to be put in perspective with the reasoning of the Supreme Court of the United States, which in *Saks* expressly denied recourse to the definition of 'accident' established in another international instrument.[778]

In short, to guarantee the autonomy of the terms used in the Conventions, the incorporation of a definition given in another international instrument should be avoided.

4.3.3.6 Literature

Finally, Courts have regularly tried to seek confirmation of their views in books and articles written by esteemed authors.

Regular references to scientific literature may be found in decisions handed down by the highest Courts in Belgium,[779] Canada,[780] UK[781] and the United States.[782]

In France, despite that the *doctrine* is considered an important source of law, the decisions of the *Cour de cassation* do not generally refer to them. However, it is more than likely that these Courts refer to the literature, as the Advocates General to said Court and lower Courts do.

Equally, the decisions of the CJEU do not explicitly refer to relevant literature, but the Advocates General generally do in their opinions.[783]

A review of scientific literature is therefore one of the tools that is commonly used in the selected Courts.

4.3.3.7 Concluding Remarks

As seen in the preceding sections, a large variety of tools have been used across time by Courts in selected jurisdictions, and there is no perfect symmetry in the tools each uses.

777. CJEU, 6 May 2010, *Axel Walz v. Clickair SA.*, C-63/09, ECLI:EU:C:2010:251, at 27.
778. *Air France v. Saks*, 470 U.S. 392 (1985), at 407: 'The definition in Annex 13 and the corresponding Convention expressly apply to aircraft accident *investigations*, and not to principles of liability to passengers under the Warsaw Convention.'
779. For example, *see*, Cass., 10 April 2008, ECLI:BE:CASS:2008:ARR.20080410.10.
780. For example, *see*, *Thibodeau v. Air Canada* (2014) 3 SCR 340, at 368.
781. For example, *see*, *Fothergill v. Monarch Airlines* (1980) UKHL 6, at 62-65.
782. For example, *see*, *Air France v. Saks*, 470 U.S. 392 (1985), at 404.
783. For example, *see*, CJEU, 26 September 2019, *GN v. ZU acting for Niki Luftfahrt*, C-532/18, ECLI:EU:C:2019:788 (Opinion), at 29-30.

As each Court has developed its own mechanisms for interpreting the Conventions, which sometimes evolve across time, the fragmentation of the Conventions is therefore ineluctable. However, the analysis has highlighted elements that, in the absence of an international specialized Court, allow an interpretation of the Conventions with due respect to their autonomy.

It is not easy to determine whether the principles of interpretation laid down in the 1969 Vienna Convention have been, at least implicitly, applied by all selected Courts. However, it can be argued that all the elements described above may be considered as falling either under its Article 31 or 32.

This being said, the absence of a hierarchical order between the tools set out in Article 31[784] does not positively respond to the need for predictability of the Conventions. Moreover, the fact that Article 32 is non-exhaustive and that the review of *Travaux Préparatoires* is only supplementary means[785] do not provide for a consistent interpretation of unification rules, notably with regard to their uniform application. It can also be deplored that that perusal of foreign case law is not clearly encouraged by the 1969 Vienna Convention.

In short, the 1969 Vienna Convention is a useful general instrument, but it does not explicitly provide clear tools to ensure the uniform application of specific Uniform Instruments such as the 1999 Montreal Convention.

It may therefore be concluded that, despite efforts made by most Courts to recognize the specific nature of the Conventions, the lack of common and clear interpretation rules in the Conventions constitutes a serious obstacle to the aim of uniformity.

784. International Law Commission, *Draft conclusions on subsequent agreements and subsequent practice in relation to the interpretation of treaties, with commentaries* 7 (2018), Source: United Nations, https://legal.un.org/docs/?path=../ilc/texts/instruments/english/commentaries/1_11_2018.pdf&lang=EF (accessed 21 February 2020).

785. The *Travaux Préparatoires* of the 1969 Vienna Convention provide that: '*Ex hypothesi* this is not the case with preparatory work which does not, in consequence, have the same authentic character as an element of interpretation, however valuable it may sometimes be in throwing light on the expression of the agreement in the text. Moreover, it is beyond question that the records of treaty negotiations are in many cases incomplete or misleading, so that considerable discretion has to be exercised in determining their value as an element of interpretation', United Nations Conferences on the Law of Treaties, First and second sessions, Vienna, 26 March-24 May 1968 and 9 April-22 May 1969, Official Records, *Documents of the Conference*, United Nations, New York, 1971, p. 40, Source: United Nations, https://treaties.un.org/doc/source/docs/A_CONF.39_11_Add.2-E.pdf (accessed 2 August 2019). They also underline that: 'It also considered whether, in regard to multilateral treaties, the article should authorize the use of *travaux préparatoires* only as between States which took part in the negotiations or, alternatively, only if they have been published. [...] A State acceding to a treaty in the drafting of which it did not participate is perfectly entitled to request to see the *travaux préparatoires*, if it wishes, before acceding. [...] Accordingly, the Commission decided that it should not include any special provision in the article regarding the use of *travaux préparatoires* in the case of multilateral treaties', Source: United Nations Conferences on the Law of Treaties, First and second sessions, Vienna, 26 March-24 May 1968 and 9 April-22 May 1969, Official Records, *Documents of the Conference*, United Nations, New York, 1971, p. 43, Source: United Nations, https://treaties.un.org/doc/source/docs/A_CONF.39_11_Add.2-E.pdf (accessed 2 August 2019).

4.3.4 Concluding Remarks

The analysis carried out regarding Courts' responses to the aim of uniformity of the Conventions has demonstrated that they have not systematically succeeded in ensuring a uniform application of the Conventions.

The specific features of the Conventions, their principle of exclusivity and the autonomy of the terms used therein, may hence be regarded as insufficient as currently drafted, for achieving the desired uniformity.

This examination has also shown that the dichotomy, as discussed above,[786] between monist and dualist States does not seem to have had any influence on the achievement of this aim.

4.4 LINGUISTIC ELEMENTS

4.4.1 Preliminary Remarks

The third element that could create unwitting discrepancies and hence an additional source of fragmentation of the uniform regime envisaged by the drafters of the Conventions may be the existence of different linguistic versions of the Conventions.

As a reminder, the only authentic version of the 1929 Warsaw Convention is French, and the authentic versions of the 1999 Montreal Convention are Arabic, Chinese, English, French, Russian and Spanish.[787] The 1955 Hague Protocol was drafted in three authentic languages - English, French and Spanish - but its final clauses provide that in case of inconsistency, the French version shall prevail.

The following analysis will examine how the Conventions' translations and their drafting in multiple authentic versions potentially affected their uniformity.[788]

4.4.2 Translations

4.4.2.1 The Variety of Translation Issues

When applying the Conventions, one would expect Courts to refer to the authentic linguistic version to verify whether there is or not a discrepancy with their domestic translation. However, this is not always the case for several reasons.

First, Courts may not necessarily be fluent in any of the authentic versions of the text, with the consequence that they would limit the application of the Conventions to their own domestic translation.

Second, they may also be prevented from, or see no interest in, giving greater weight to authentic versions over their domestic text. This may potentially be more

786. *See*, section 1.3.2.2(5).
787. *See*, section 1.3.1.2(2)(ii).
788. This last point could have been discussed as an internal factor. But for the sake of clarity and consistency, the risks of having a text drafted in several authentic versions will be analysed in parallel to translation issues.

likely in dualist States that do not attach any authentic version of the Conventions to their domestic legislation.

Third, it may not occur to them to check for discrepancies between the different versions.

The following analysis will examine the major types of translation issues.

4.4.2.2 Inaccurate Translations

Sometimes a discussion may arise from a non-accurate transcription of the original version. This was notably the case in the UK, where the English version of the 1929 Warsaw Convention originally replaced a comma by a conjunction under Article 8(i). While the authentic French text provided: 'La lettre de transport aérien doit contenir les mentions suivantes: (i) le poids, la quantité, le volume ou les dimensions de la marchandise', the English version read as follows: 'The air consignment note shall contain the following particulars: (i) the weight, the quantity and the volume or dimensions of the goods.' The absence of comma, and the subsequent insertion of 'and', led to a dispute.

In *Corocraft*, the Court of Appeal of England and Wales, seized on the controversy, rightly held that in case of discrepancy, the French version should prevail.[789] If this is in line with the provisions of the Convention, the question nevertheless had to be confirmed by a senior Court.

4.4.2.3 Various Translations in the Same Language

One might assume that the translation into a non-authentic language would be identical in each State sharing that language. But this is not always the case. Taking the example of Portuguese, which is not an authentic language, Article 17(1) of the 1999 Montreal Convention[790] is translated differently in at least three jurisdictions. The domestic translations read as follows in the Brazilian version of this provision:

> O transportador é responsável pelo dano causado em caso de morte ou de lesão corporal de um passageiro, desde que o acidente que causou a morte ou a lesão haja ocorrido a bordo da aeronave ou durante quaisquer operações de embarque ou desembarque.[791]

789. *Corocraft Ltd v. Pan American Airways* (1969) 1 QB 616, at 653: 'The Warsaw Convention is an international convention which is binding in international law on all the countries who have ratified it; and it is the duty of these courts to construe our legislation so as to be in conformity with international law and not in conflict with it.'
790. 'The carrier is liable for damage sustained in case of death or bodily injury of a passenger upon condition only that the accident which caused the death or injury took place on board the aircraft or in the course of any of the operations of embarking or disembarking.'
791. Decreto N° 5.910, de 27 Setembro de 2006, Source: Brazilian Government, http://www.planalto.gov.br/ccivil_03/_Ato2004-2006/2006/Decreto/D5910.htm (accessed 20 June 2019).

Whereas the Portuguese version reads as follows:

> A transportadora só é responsável pelo dano causado em caso de morte ou lesão corporal de um passageiro se o acidente que causou a morte ou a lesão tiver ocorrido a bordo da aeronave ou durante uma operação de embarque ou desembarque.[792]

And the one of Macau presents this wording:

> O transportador só é responsável pelo dano verificado em caso de morte ou lesão corporal de um passageiro se o acidente que causou a morte ou a lesão tiver ocorrido a bordo da aeronave ou no decurso de quaisquer operações de embarque ou desembarque.[793]

The comparison between these three versions shows several variations.

First, grammatical distinctions are immediately apparent: with variations in the use of masculine and feminine words,[794] and the use of past subjunctive and future subjunctive tenses.[795]

Second, while these are only minor dissimilarities, some variations may have more significant differences. For instance, the translation of 'upon condition only that the accident' is expressed *as soon as the accident* in the Brazilian version, and *if the accident* in the Portuguese and Macau texts. In terms of causal effect, this may lead to distinct views. Equally, where the original English version provides that 'The carrier is liable for damage', the Portuguese and Macau versions add the adverb *only*, saying in substance that the carrier is only liable for damage. The liability for damage sustained in the Macau version is moreover translated as *verified damage*, adding a condition that was not textually foreseen by the original version.

Finally, where the Brazilian and Macau texts stick closely to the authentic passage of 'in the course of any of the operations of embarking or disembarking', the Portuguese merely mention one operation of embarking or disembarking, which could potentially lead to a stringent interpretation of this sentence.

4.4.2.4 Various Translations Within the EU

(1) The Example of the Use of the Dutch Language

Another example can be found within the EU where the 1999 Montreal Convention is part of Belgian, Dutch and EU law.[796] Each linguistic service has therefore translated the text into Dutch, as the latter is one of their official languages, but not an authentic

792. Decreto N° 39/2002, Diario da República N° 274/2002, Série I-A de 2002-11-27.
793. *B.O.* N°: 17, II Série, de 2006/04/26, Pág. 3412-3434.
794. Such as 'transportador' or 'transportadora'.
795. Such as 'haja ocorrido' or 'tiver ocorrido'.
796. *See*, in Belgium, loi du 13 mai 2003 portant assentiment à la Convention pour l'unification de certaines règles relatives au transport aérien international, faite à Montréal le 28 mai 1999, *Moniteur belge*, 18 mai 2004; in the Netherlands, Rijkswet van 3 februari 2004, *Staatsblad*, 21 juni 2004; in the European Union, Council Decision of 5 April 2001 on the conclusion by the

language of the 1999 Montreal Convention.[797] Each translation, however, is slightly different from the others.

Most of the differences essentially concern typography questions such as the use or lack of spaces,[798] capital letters,[799] and - perhaps more problematic - commas.[800]

Nevertheless, in the Belgian and Netherlands translations, differences are more obvious as totally different words are used. If the word 'omission' is translated as 'nalaten' in Belgium and 'nalatigheden' in the Netherlands, these would however be considered as synonyms. More strikingly, to translate the concept of 'servants or agents', the words 'ondergeschikten of lasthebbers' are used in Belgium, whereas a unique word, 'hulppersonen', is used in the Netherlands. Each expression refers to concepts known under domestic law.[801] The question becomes even more complicated, and a source of potential imbroglio, when reference is made to the translation made by the EU,[802] whose primacy may be questioned. The European translation appears to be a compromise between the versions of its Member States. In the European version, 'omission' is sometimes translated as 'nalatigheid'[803] or as

European Community of the Convention for the Unification of Certain Rules for International Carriage by Air (the Montreal Convention), 2001/539/EC, *Official Journal*, 18 July 2001, L 194/38.

797. Discrepancies also exist in other air law conventions, such as the 1948 Geneva Convention on the International Recognition of Rights in Aircraft, which is drafted in three authentic languages: English, French and Spanish. When the text needed to be translated into Dutch, the source text selected in the Netherlands was the English version. This led to controversies on the application of the accession rule to engines in light of Article XVI of said convention. Indeed, this article provides in its English version that: '"aircraft" shall include the airframe, engines, propellers, radio apparatus, and all other articles intended for use in the aircraft whether installed therein or temporarily separated therefrom'. The question as to what was included under the terms 'intended' had a significant importance on the application of the accession rule in the Netherlands. The difficulties would probably have been less important if the Dutch translators had looked to the French version which uses the term 'destinées', clearly indicating that this refers to plural and feminine words. *See*, Berend Crans, 'Aspect particuliers de la location de moteurs', in Cyril-Igor Grigorieff, Vincent Corriea (eds), *Le droit du financement des aéronefs* 115-142 (Bruylant, 2017).
798. 'voorzover' and 'plaatsvond' in Belgium, compared to 'voor zover' and 'plaats vond' in the Netherlands.
799. 'partij' and 'partijen' in Belgium, compared to 'Partij' and 'Partijen' in some cases in the Netherlands.
800. Article 3(2) last sentence: 'If any such other means is used, the carrier shall offer to deliver to the passenger a written statement of the information so preserved' is translated in Belgium as 'Indien een dergelijk ander middle wordt gebruitkt biedt de vervoerder aan de passagier een schrijftelijke verkaring te verstrekken van de aldus vastgelegde gegevens', and in the Netherlands as 'Indien een dergelijk ander middle wordt gebruitkt biedt de vervoerder aan, de passagier een schrijftelijke verkaring te verstrekken van de aldus vastgelegde gegevens'.
801. *See*, in the Netherlands, Burgerlijk Wetboek, Boek 6, Artikel 76. The situation in Belgium is less clear. The term 'ondergeschikten' is not defined in the Civil Code, but the word used in the authentic French version 'préposés' is also used under Article 1384 of said Code. The Dutch version of this article uses the expression 'aangestelden'. In contrast, the word 'lasthebbers' is known under Articles 1991 et seq. of the Civil Code and is translated in the French version of the Civil Code as 'mandataire' which corresponds to the word used in the authentic French version of the 1999 Montreal Convention.
802. *Official Journal*, 18 July 2001, L 194/39.
803. Article 21(2)(a).

'nalaten'[804] while the concept of 'hulppersonen', only known in the Netherlands, is used. This means, in practice, that in the Netherlands one may be tempted to refer to a domestically elaborated and interpreted concept, whereas in Belgium if priority is given to the European translation, the concept would be viewed as more autonomous.

(2) The Example of the Use of the Italian Language

Another European translation issue can be found in Italy. When the 1999 Montreal Convention was published in the *Official Journal of the European Communities*,[805] the Italian text translated Article 35 using the concept of 'prescrizione',[806] leading to the belief that the time limit could be interrupted or suspended.[807] This view could have been reinforced when the Italian 2004 Ratification Act[808] used the same translation. These translations raised concerns as the 1929 Warsaw Convention did not use this term.[809] Only in 2014 did the *Official Journal of the European Union*[810] publish a rectification that replaced the concept of 'precrizione' with the stricter one of 'decadenza'.[811]

As the national Italian version has not been amended since then, this situation may be a source of conflicting decisions.[812]

---

804. Article 41(2).
805. *Official Journal*, 18 July 2001, L 194/39.
806. 'Articolo 35
Prescrizione
1. Il diritto al risarcimento per danni si prescrive nel termine due anni decorrenti dal giorno di arrivo a destinazione o dal giorno previsto per l'arrivo a destinazione dell'aeromobile o dal giorno in cui il trasporto è stato interrotto.
2. Il metodo di calcolo del periodo di prescrizione è determinato in conformità dell'ordinamento del tribunale adito'.
807. On this topic, *see*, section 3.2.5.
808. Legge 10 gennaio 2004, n. 12 – Ratifica ed esecuzione della Convenzione per l'unificazione di alcune norme relative al trasporto aereo internazionale, con Atto finale e risoluzioni, fatta a Montreal il 28 maggio 1999, GU Serie Generale n.20 del 26-01-2004 – Suppl. Ordinario n. 11.
809. 1929 Warsaw Convention, Article 29: '1. L'azione per responsabilità dev'essere promossa, sotto pena di decadenza, entro il termine di due anni a contare dall'arrivo a destinazione o dal giorno in cui l'aeromobile avrebbe dovuto arrivare o da quello in cui il trasporto fu interrotto. 2. Il modo di calcolare il termine è determinato dalla legge del tribunale chiamato a giudicare', Source: Italian Civil Aviation Authority, https://www.enac.gov.it/la-normativa/normativa-internazionale/convenzioni-trattati-protocolli/convenzione-di-varsavia (accessed 21 August 2019).
810. *Official Journal*, 24 December 2014, L 369/79 (Italian version only).
811. 'Articolo 35
Decadenza
1. Il diritto al risarcimento del danno si estingue se non è proposta la relativa azione entro il termine di due anni decorrenti dal giorno di arrivo a destinazione, o dal giorno previsto per l'arrivo a destinazione, ovvero dal giorno in cui il trasporto è stato interrotto.
2. Il metodo di calcolo del predetto termine è determinato in conformità dell'ordinamento del tribunale adito'.
812. *See*, Enzo Fogliano, *L'art. 35 della Convenzione di Montreal: prescrizione o decadenza?*, 33 Diritto dei trasporti 115-117 (2020).

4.4.3 The Plurality of Authentic Versions

An even more difficult situation arises when there is a discrepancy between authentic versions. In this scenario, Article 33(3) of the 1969 Vienna Convention[813] sets out that unless otherwise provided, the terms must be presumed to have the same meaning in each language.

This principle is nevertheless not always applied. For example, in 2000, the *Cour de cassation* of Belgium delivered a decision in a CMR matter that can be explored for comparison purposes *mutatis mutandis*.[814] In this cargo case, where the carrier had indemnified the claimant according to limits set out in the CMR, the claimant argued he was entitled to full compensation on the grounds that the loss was caused by 'willful misconduct' as set out in the English authentic version of the CMR.[815] The plaintiff further contended that the definition of 'dol' in the French version used by the inferior Court was more restrictive than the 'willful misconduct' term used in the English version, which was also authentic. In that regard, the claimant submitted that the inferior Court infringed on the aim of uniformity of said convention. The *Cour de cassation* held in substance that the definition of 'dol' as used in the French version of the CMR and as known under Belgian law required an intentional element which was not present in this case. It further said that the fact that the English concept of 'willful misconduct' may not necessarily entail an intentional element, and that Article 29 was generally interpreted in that manner in other jurisdictions, made no difference.[816]

813. *See*, section 1.3.1.2(2)(ii).
814. Cass., 30 March 2000, C.9.70.176.N.
815. Compare the French version of Article 29(1) of the CMR Convention: 'Le transporteur n'a pas le droit de se prévaloir des dispositions du présent chapitre qui excluent ou limitent sa responsabilité ou qui renversent le fardeau de la preuve, si le dommage provient de son dol ou d'une faute qui lui est imputable et qui, d'après la loi de la juridiction saisie, est considérée comme équivalente au dol'; to the English text: 'The carrier shall not be entitled to avail himself of the provisions of this chapter which exclude or limit his liability or which shift the burden of proof if the damage was caused by his wilful misconduct or by such default on his part as, in accordance with the law of the court or tribunal seized of the case, is considered as equivalent to wilful misconduct.'
816. Cass., 30 March 2000, C.9.70.176.N., ECLI:BE:CASS:2000:ARR.20000330.4:'Attendu que le moyen reproche aux juges d'appel d'avoir incorrectement interprété la Convention CMR dès lors que, dans l'arrêt attaqué, ils excluent l'application de l'article 29.1 par le motif que le transporteur n'a pas commis de dol au sens d'intention méchante de causer un dommage, alors que le terme "dol" au sens de l'article 29.1 vise la notion de "wilful misconduct", qui vise tant l'intention méchante de causer un dommage ou une perte que l'intervention téméraire sans dessein réel de nuire; Attendu que les juges d'appel décident qu'à l'égard d'un juge belge, la faute grave ne peut être assimilée au dol et que, dès lors, ce juge est uniquement tenu d'examiner si le dol est requis; qu'ils décident ensuite "qu'il n'est pas contesté que le transporteur n'a pas commis de dol en l'espèce"; Qu'ils n'excluent pas que la faute intentionnelle puisse être une faute qui, dans les autres systèmes juridiques, correspondrait à une autre notion, telle que la notion de "wilful misconduct"; que, sans préciser davantage la notion de "dol", ils relèvent uniquement la nécessité d'un élément intentionnel qui, selon eux, fait défaut; Attendu que, dans la mesure où il invoque la violation des dispositions de la Convention CMR, le moyen est fondé sur la thèse que les juges d'appel ont appliqué une notion de "dol" qui déroge à la notion de "wilful misconduct"; que l'arrêt ne contient pas de décision de cette nature; Attendu que la violation des règles d'interprétation des traités ne donne lieu à cassation que si, ce faisant, le traité faisant l'objet de l'interprétation a été violé; [...] Par ces motifs, [...]

Moreover, Article 33(4) of the 1969 Vienna Convention sets out that the meaning that best reconciles the text must be adopted in the event of a discrepancy between different authentic versions. In *Air Baltic Corporation*, while trying to determine whether Article 19 of the 1999 Montreal Convention only applied to damage caused to passengers or also applied to damage suffered by an employer, the CJEU, referring to various authentic versions of the 1999 Montreal Convention, noted that the French version of Article 22(1) restricted the concept of damage occasioned by delay to damage to 'each passenger'; whereas the English, Spanish and Russian versions only referred to damage occasioned by delay without restricting it to damage suffered by passengers.[817] Following a further examination of this provision, the Court eventually rejected the meaning of the French version.

Although the 1969 Vienna Convention gives clear guidance on how to handle discrepancies between authentic versions, that the 1999 Montreal Convention does not give priority to any of its authentic versions, one could wonder whether priority should not be given to the French version, as the 1955 Hague Protocol did, given the historicity of the terms adopted.[818]

4.4.4 Concluding Remarks

The existence of various authentic versions of the 1999 Montreal Convention and its multiple translations constitute additional sources of potential fragmentation of the uniform regime. This phenomenon is particularly problematic when Courts are not composed of judges fluent in one of its authentic languages.

4.5 CONCLUSIONS

The analysis confirms the fragmentation of the contemplated uniform regime as was already acknowledged by authoritative literature on the 1929 Warsaw Convention.[819] As Professor Michel Pourcelet emphasized in 1973, real anarchy surrounded the international air carrier liability regime:

> L'anarchie la plus complète triomphe en matière de transport aérien international de passagers et de marchandises, tant en ce qui concerne la détermination de la loi

Rejette le pourvoi'. However, it is possible that the Court thought that the CMR offered a certain marge of manoeuvre for referring to domestic law.

817. CJEU, 17 February 2016, *Air Baltic Corporation AS v. Lietuvos Respublikos specialiųjų tyrimų tarnyba*, C-429/14, ECLI:EU:C:2016:88, at 29-34.

818. *See*, Bin Cheng, *The Labyrinth of the Law of International Carriage by Air: Has the Montreal Convention 1999 Slain the Minotaur?*, 50 Zeitschrift für Luft- und Weltraumrecht 172 (2001).

819. *See*, Peter Sand, *The International Unification of Air Law*, 30 Law and Contemporary Problems 400-424 (1965); Huib Drion, *Toward a Uniform Interpretation of the Private Air Law Conventions*, 19 Journal of Air Law and Commerce 423-442 (1952); Euthymene Georgiades, *De la méthodologie juridique pour l'unification du Droit aérien international privé*, Revue Française de Droit Aérien et Spatial 369-389 (1972); René Mankiewicz, *La Convention de Varsovie et le Droit Comparé*, Revue Française de Droit Aérien et Spatial 136-150 (1969).

applicable au litige soumis au tribunal [...] que l'interprétation donnée par les tribunaux des différents pays aux textes internationaux applicables.[820]

While, at the 1999 Montreal Conference, the President of the ICAO Council expressed the view that the adoption of a new convention would re-establish uniformity;[821] this analysis shows that the 1999 Montreal Convention is still subject to fragmentation by powerful external factors.

This study demonstrated that the successive waves of modifications of the Conventions by various international, regional and domestic instruments led to a fragmentation of the uniform regime. The emergence of regional and domestic consumer rights in parallel to the international air carrier liability regime also threatens the uniformity of the 1999 Montreal Convention and particularly with respect to the provisions governing delays.

Moreover, the exclusivity clause and the autonomy of the terms used in the Conventions, which were expected by their drafters to ensure their uniform application, did not fully achieve this aim. This chapter showed that the broadly formulated principle of exclusivity and the lack of clear indications as to how to apply undefined autonomous terms resulted in heterogeneous judicial decisions.

Lastly, the coexistence of various authentic versions of the 1999 Montreal Convention and its numerous translations in different languages participate in the fragmentation of the uniform regime.

Chapter 5 will discuss possible ways to enhance the uniformity of the 1999 Montreal Convention.

820. Michel Pourcelet, *A propos d'un accident d'avion: la diversité des solutions données par le tribunaux*, Revue Générale de l'Air 211 (1973).

821. ICAO Doc 9775, International Conference on Air Law (Convention for the Unification of Certain Rules for International Carriage by Air), Montreal, 10-28 May 1999, volume I, *Minutes*, Montreal 1999, p. 205: 'Since that time the Warsaw Convention had been fragmented into different protocols and into different views, interpretations and jurisdictions. The Conference was making history in consolidating, for the first time, what had been fragmented and by introducing new elements to cope with the vision for the 21st century.'

CHAPTER 5

Suggestions for Enhancing Uniformity

5.1 INTRODUCTION

In the previous chapters, the analysis has shown that the 1999 Montreal Convention had ambitions to offer a uniform legal regime that contributed to predictable interpretations. Several factors, from the drafting stage to the everyday application of the rules, have demonstrated that this aim has not been fully achieved.

This chapter is designed to provide proposals that could be implemented to enhance its uniform application. The analysis of these proposals is divided into three categories: substantive elements (section 5.2), procedural elements (section 5.3), and prospective elements using Artificial Intelligence (section 5.4).

The implementation of such proposals may require a revision of the 1999 Montreal Convention. Such a revision should not be a taboo. George Tompkins, who, at the conclusions of his analysis of the uniform effectiveness of the 1999 Montreal Convention, indicated that:

> As perhaps a last resort, ICAO should re-convene the Montreal Conference of 1999 to make even clearer the intent of the Parties to MC99 as to the meaning of those Articles of MC99 which have been misconstrued, misinterpreted and misread by courts when applying the liability rules of MC99 to actual cases.[822]

Nevertheless, a revision may also create risks. To be useful, an eventual revision would need therefore several components.

first, clear provisions based on a broad political consensus, which, as seen in this study, is a difficult task;[823]

822. George Tompkins, 'The Malaise Affecting the Global Uniform Effectiveness of the Montreal Convention, 1999 (MC99)', in Pablo Mendes de Leon (ed.), *From Lowlands to High Skies: A Multilevel Jurisdictional Approach Towards Air Law: Essays in Honour of John Balfour* 282 (Martinus Nijhoff Publishers, 2013).
823. *See*, section 3.2.4.3.

second, in order not to further increase fragmentation,[824] a universal ratification status.

Taking into account these risks, the elements described below will not all need to wait for a new diplomatic conference to be convened before being useful.

5.2 SUBSTANTIVE ELEMENTS

5.2.1 Enhancing Autonomy

5.2.1.1 A Double-Edged Mechanism

Symptomatically and ironically, the autonomy that was contemplated as a mechanism to ensure the uniform application of the Conventions is also a source of their fragmentation. Despite efforts to draft legal instruments, the vagueness of several terms and concepts has been identified as source of fragmentation.[825]

In addition, the 1999 Montreal Convention's negotiators' wish to stick as closely as possible to the wording of the Warsaw Instruments prevented the coherent application of the guidance generally used to draft clear treaties.[826] Whereas the text adopted in 1929 was voluntarily imperfect, its negotiators wished to test it before possibly improving it,[827] and it was not made to last for a very long time; these arguments are no longer valid.

The need for certainty in a globalized industry and the interest of achieving a homogenized passenger protection regime require that formulations be clearer. To this end, autonomy deserves further enhancement with, as a starting point, the elements developed below.

5.2.1.2 Elements Requiring Amendments of the 1999 Montreal Convention

(1) Amendments of the Preamble

The previous sections highlighted how the conceptual and hermeneutical ties between the Warsaw Instruments and the 1999 Montreal Convention were not properly addressed during the 1999 Montreal Conference,[828] despite the fact that the 1999 text took the form of a new convention supposed to prevail over prior instruments pursuant to its Article 55.[829] A clearer position could therefore be adopted, in the preamble, on the exact weight to be given to the jurisprudence of the Warsaw System when

824. *See*, section 4.2.1.
825. *See*, section 3.2.
826. *See*, section 3.2.1.
827. ICAO Doc 7838, II Conférence Internationale de Droit Privé Aérien, 4-12 Octobre 1929, *Procès-Verbaux*, Varsovie, 1930, p. 104: 'Je pense qu'il vaut mieux mettre des indications et laisser un peu la pratique se développer. Nous sommes en présence d'un mode de transport qui vient de naître, il faut laisser la pratique s'établir'.
828. *See*, sections 1.3.2.4 and 4.3.3.4(2).
829. *See*, section 1.3.1.1(2).

interpreting the 1999 Montreal Convention. One possibility could be to indicate that, while prior judicial decisions should be regarded as interpretation tools pursuant to Article 32 of the 1969 Vienna Convention, legal certainty recommends that an explanation be given as to why one would depart from them or not.

Furthermore, as divergences should be avoided with respect to the purposes of the 1999 Montreal Convention, particularly as to whether consumer protection is an additional purpose,[830] the preamble ought to be redrafted to clearly highlight its envisaged purposes and put an end to existing controversies.

(2) *The Incorporation of Definitions*

The inextricable links between the various texts also prevented the 1999 Montreal Convention from adopting new – ideally clearly autonomous – definitions, as reported in its *Travaux Préparatoires*:

> The Delegate of Cameroon proposed that the definitions in Article 1 be expanded to include 'combined carriage', 'intermodal carriage' and 'multi-modal carriage'. [...] However, the Delegate of Poland took the view that firstly, the introduction of further definitions should be avoided as the authors of the draft Convention had preserved much of the text from the Warsaw instruments in order to ease the transfer from one system to another and secondly, to avoid lengthy discussions by lawyers in the application of these definitions. The Delegate of Pakistan supported this view and added that as a general principle of law, when no definition is given of any term, the general meaning attached to the term was commonly used.[831]

The fact that it was suggested that undefined terms be understood under their 'general meaning' has been seen as insufficiently self-explanatory. Moreover, these reported statements must be read in conjunction with another one suggesting that reference may be sought in the ICAO documentation:

> The Delegate of Lebanon suggested that a unified concept be developed on the basis of ICAO documents which could be applied in all countries. In this connection, he was aware of the existence of an ICAO document which explained the definitions of certain terms that could be useful for the courts when considering these cases. The Delegate of Lebanon suggested that this be mentioned in the 'travaux préparatoires' of the Convention for easier application of Article 27.[832]

Practice shows that the drafters should not be reluctant to adopt specific autonomous definitions when unification is at stake. This was notably done in the 2001 Cape Town Convention[833] and in its 2001 Aircraft Protocol,[834] which respectively count

830. *See*, section 2.3.3.2.
831. ICAO Doc 9775, International Conference on Air Law (Convention for the Unification of Certain Rules for International Carriage by Air), Montreal, 10-28 May 1999, volume I, *Minutes*, Montreal 1999, p. 55.
832. *Ibid.*, p. 179. There is no clear indication of which ICAO Document the delegate referred to.
833. Convention on International Interests in Mobile Equipment, 16 November 2001, Cape Town, ICAO Doc 9793, entry in force 1 March 2006.

forty and sixteen specific definitions. Equally, the 2008 Rotterdam Rules count more than thirty definitions despite them only concerning carriage of goods by sea.[835]

In light of these elements, efforts should be made to adopt more definitions. These definitions should use neutral language, free from expressions used in specific legal systems or well known to practitioners,[836] and should be distinct from those used in other international instruments whenever possible.[837]

Back in 1929, legislators decided against producing a simple set of private international rules with a list of competent laws and jurisdictions with regard to an international air liability regime. Instead, they chose to adopt uniform rules. Therefore, negotiators should not be uncomfortable with what they are creating. The 1999 Montreal Convention is a sui generis private air law regime relying on autonomous terms and concepts, which can be compared to a certain extent to a domestic law in itself, or more accurately to an a-national law that would rank above pure domestic law. This autonomous dimension should be better reflected in the text. While it could be argued that, in the past, private initiatives, such as the IATA Recommended Practices,[838] may have partly filled the gaps, experience demonstrates that with respect to carrier liability towards passengers, Courts often deny legal value to industry standards such as the IATA's General Conditions of Carriage,[839] given that certain Courts reproach these private initiatives for lacking balance between the interests of passengers and air carriers. Therefore, such drafting missions can only be entrusted to international legislators.

Despite difficulties, the inclusion of new well-articulated definitions, clearly marked as autonomous, would limit the fragmentation of the 1999 Montreal Convention, particularly if the other suggestions made in this chapter were also adopted.

---

834. Protocol to the Convention on International Interests in Mobile Equipment on Matters Specific to Aircraft Equipment, 16 November 2001, Cape Town, ICAO Doc 9794, entry in force 1 March 2006.
835. United Nations Convention on the Contracts for the International Carriage of Goods Wholly or Partly by Sea, 11 December 2008, New York, not yet in force. Again, with respect to the law of the sea, on the public law side, the 1982 Montego Bay Convention has several specific definitions. *See*, United Nations Convention on the Law of the Sea, 10 December 1982, Montego Bay, UNTS, 1834, I-31363, entry in force 16 November 1994.
836. *See*, Silvia Ferreri, 'The Devil is in the Details: Undetected Differences in Projects to Harmonize the Law', in UNIDROIT (ed.), *Eppur si Muove: The Age of Uniform Law – Essays in Honour of Mickael Joachim Bonell to Celebrate His 70th Birthday* 318 (UNIDROIT, 2016). She however underlines that, as a downside, neutral language may be uncertain and ill-defined at the beginning, given the absence of case law. For example, she refers to the choice of using the concept of 'extraordinary circumstances' instead of 'force majeure' in EU Regulation 261/2004.
837. *See*, Camilla Andersen, *Defining Uniformity in Law*, 12 Uniform Law Review 53 (2007).
838. *See*, Lasantha Hettiarachchi, *The Quasi-Regulatory Regime of the International Air Transport Association (IATA) and Its Impact upon the Airline Industry and the Consumer* (Thesis McGill University, 2018).
839. Peter Sand, *The International Unification of Air Law*, 30 Law and Contemporary Problems 402 (1965).

(3) *The Identification of Uniform Rules*

The complexity of the 1999 Montreal Convention is also due to the fact that it contains both uniform rules and provisions referring to domestic law.[840]

In order to avoid the risk of divergent decisions, a clear distinction should always be made between what is governed by uniform rules[841] and what is subject to domestic law. The analysis showed that this distinction has not always been clearly acknowledged by Courts.[842] A clear demarcation between uniform rules and *renvois* will also be very important when Artificial Intelligence is at stake, as discussed below.[843]

5.2.1.3 *Elements Not Requiring an Amendment to the 1999 Montreal Convention*

(1) *The Dissemination of Knowledge*

As the ICAO vowed greater dissemination of air law in its 39th session,[844] further teaching of uniform law and particularly of international private air law instruments such as the 1999 Montreal Convention would hopefully lead Courts across its ratifying States to better appreciate its purposes and the function of autonomous terms.

Such endeavours may rely on new technologies, as pointed out by the HCCH and the European Commission in their joint conclusions on access to foreign law in commercial and civil matters.[845] For example, these new technologies now permit efficient distance learning and instantaneous document translation.

(2) *A Database of Judicial Decisions*

The 1999 Montreal Conference rightly pointed out that judges are not all aviation regulatory experts[846] with an aviation law background.[847] Even experts wishing to ensure a uniform application of the 1999 Montreal Convention through an analysis of foreign case law meet certain hindrances. Among various obstacles, one of the most regrettable is that, depending on the jurisdiction, not all decisions are published. The

840. *See*, section 1.1.3.2.
841. Despite this, an autonomous nature might have been (and might still be) unnatural for many.
842. *See*, sections 3.2.4.3(5) and 3.2.5.
843. *See*, section 5.4.
844. ICAO, Resolution A39-11: Consolidated Statement of Continuing ICAO Policies in the Legal Field, Appendix D, Assembly, 39th session (October 2016).
845. Hague Conference on Private and International Law and the European Commission, Joint Conclusions of the Hague Conference on Private and International Law and the European Commission, Access to Foreign Law in Commercial and Civil Matters, Conclusions and Recommendations, points 2 and 7, Source: Hague Conference on Private International Law, https://assets.hcch.net/upload/foreignlaw_concl_e.pdf (accessed 29 October 2019).
846. ICAO Doc 9775, International Conference on Air Law (Convention for the Unification of Certain Rules for International Carriage by Air), Montreal, 10-28 May 1999, volume I, *Minutes*, Montreal 1999, p. 154.
847. *Ibid.*, p. 144.

proliferation of different journals, reports and search engines also increases the difficulty for local Courts to have quick access to relevant foreign air law decisions.

Most of these hurdles were recognized from early on. For example, in 1977, Dr Georgette Miller noted that:

> A better diffusion of the judicial decisions interpreting the uniform law has been advocated as a means of lessening divergences by letting courts know of existing precedents adopted in other countries.[848]

In order to tackle this issue, one solution could be to gather relevant case law in a specific database.[849]

Certain Uniform Instruments already benefit from such centralization. The jurisprudence of the UNCITRAL conventions is, for instance, gathered on an online public platform.[850] The jurisprudence of certain Uniform Instruments related to transportation by sea also benefits from an online platform organized on the initiative of the *Comité Maritime International* and managed in cooperation with the National University of Singapore.[851] A database of decisions regarding the application of the CMR was also organized, in the past by UNIDROIT,[852] and now by the *Institut du Droit International des Transports*.[853]

With respect to air law instruments, and more particularly the 1999 Montreal Convention, this central database could be entrusted to the ICAO. Although it seems difficult to consider the ICAO the guardian of the application of the 1999 Montreal Convention,[854] being essentially its depositary,[855] there would not be too many hurdles to the ICAO serving as a central documentation point, to which the major case law of each ratifying Party could be sent, translated and made publicly available for free.[856] However, this role could be taken on by any trustworthy entity.

Beyond the costs associated with the creation and maintenance of such a database, its effectiveness would depend on the will of the ratifying Parties to

848. Georgette Miller, *Liability in International Air Transport* 366 (Kluwer, 1977). *See also*, Emmanuel du Pontavice, *L'interprétation des conventions internationals portant loi uniforme dans les rapports internationaux*, Annales de Droit Aérien et Spatial 30 (1982); Peter Sand, *The International Unification of Air Law*, 30 Law and Contemporary Problems 400-424 (Springer, 1965); Huib Drion, *Towards A Uniform Interpretation of the Private Air Law Conventions*, 19 Journal of Air Law and Commerce 423-424 (1952).
849. *See*, João Ribeiro-Bidaoui, *The International Obligation of the Uniform and Autonomous Interpretation of Private Law Conventions: Consequences for Domestic Courts and International Organisations*, 67 Netherlands International Law Review 148, 155-159 (2020).
850. *See*, UNCITRAL, https://www.uncitral.org/clout/ (accessed 8 April 2020).
851. National University of Singapore, https://law.nus.edu.sg/cmlcmidatabase/ (accessed 8 April 2020). *See also*, Patrick Griggs, *Obstacles to Uniformity of Maritime Law* 158-173 (CMI Yearbook, 2002).
852. However, the project was discontinued as it was too resource intensive. *See*, Lena Peters, *UNIDROIT* (Max Planck Encyclopedias of International Law, 2017).
853. *See*, Institut du Droit International des Transports, https://www.idit.fr/_private/moteur_cmr /jurisprudence/index.php (accessed 1 November 2019).
854. *See*, Michael Milde, *International Air Law and ICAO* 179 (Eleven International Publishing, 2008).
855. *See*, 1999 Montreal Convention, Article 53.
856. As the *Travaux Préparatoires* should be.

communicate decisions delivered by their Courts, ideally with a translation into at least one of the authentic languages of the 1999 Montreal Convention.

The implementation of such a database would not only enhance the uniform application of the 1999 Montreal Convention but also increase the visibility of judicial decisions delivered in less commented-on jurisdictions.

The importance of such a database managed by a trustworthy entity will be further examined below, in the section dedicated to Artificial Intelligence tools.[857]

5.2.2 Refining Exclusivity

The principle of exclusivity has been seen as a mechanism that, while envisaged as safeguarding the uniformity of the Conventions, unintentionally led to various divergent interpretations. Even if Professor Bin Cheng stated that Article 29 of the 1999 Montreal Convention was 'designed to protect both the objective of the Convention and the integrity of the rules drawn up to implement it',[858] the exact scope of this provision is still controversial as evidenced by this analysis[859] and reported in the literature.[860]

In the absence of a clear position on the exact extent of Article 29 of the 1999 Montreal Convention, the aim of uniformity suggests that the interpretation of this mechanism should be made along with the most cited decisions of Courts, which – depending on how they are looked at – essentially point in the direction of a strict application of the principle of exclusivity as understood in common law jurisdictions.

A clarification of the exact shape of said provision is important not only with respect to personal injury but also in light of the development of passenger rights at regional and domestic levels. The situation where Courts have strictly applied the principle of exclusivity, while governments enacted new passenger rights, is not sustainable in light of the uniformity of the 1999 Montreal Convention.[861]

The attempt made by the ICAO with the publication of Core Principles on Consumer Protection in 2015 could have been useful, as it insists on a respect for consistency with international law:

> Government authorities should have the flexibility to develop consumer protection regimes which strike an appropriate balance between protection of consumers and industry competitiveness and which take into account States' different social, political and economic characteristics, without prejudice to the safety and security of aviation. National and regional consumer protection regime should [...] iii) be consistent with the international treaty regimes on air carrier liability [...].[862]

857. *See*, section 5.4.
858. Bin Cheng, *A New Era in the Law of International Carriage by Air: From Warsaw (1929) to Montreal (1999)*, 53 International & Comparative Law Quarterly 846 (2004).
859. *See*, sections 2.5.3.2 and 4.3.2.
860. *See*, for example, Elmar Giemulla, e. a., *The Montreal Convention* 29-5 (Supplement 5, Kluwer, 2009); Marc McDonald, *The Montreal Convention and the Preemption of Air Passenger Harm Claims*, 44 The Irish Jurist 203-238 (2009).
861. *See*, section 4.2.2.
862. ICAO, Core Principles on Consumer Protection, Source: ICAO, www.icao.int/sustainability/SiteAssets/pages/eap_ep_consumerinterests/ICAO_CorePrinciples.pdf (accessed 27 October 2019). For a commentary, *see*, Steven Truxal, *Air Carrier and Air Passenger Rights: A Game of*

However, this timid step, together with the non-binding nature of these Core Principles, falls short of efficiently refining the principle of exclusivity.

A fine-tuning of Article 29 of the 1999 Montreal Convention would also be beneficial to resolving other controversies. In States who are parties to this Convention, and who host important aircraft manufacturers, victims of air disasters may consider initiating legal proceedings, pursuant to domestic law, against the manufacturer only, in order to avoid conditions and limits set out in Conventions that would have been applicable if they had sued the carrier. In this scenario, the manufacturer would likely request the carrier to indemnify it against any potential condemnation. As the Conventions do not explicitly address this situation, the question arises if the carrier could still benefit in this configuration from the limits provided by the Conventions.

In a decision made in 2015, the French *Cour de cassation* concluded that carriers were not allowed such a defence.[863] This decision was particularly unexpected, insofar as the Court had previously held that a manufacturer could not call in guarantee an airline before a jurisdiction not listed in the Conventions.[864]

On a more theoretical note, one wonders whether, in a situation of major loss where criminal investigations are carried out, Article 29 of the 1999 Montreal Convention would not preclude the possibility of enforcing criminal penalties, being understood as economic compensation in favour of collectivity, against air carriers.[865]

In order to clarify the exact scope of the principle of exclusivity, the best option would be to redraft Article 29 of the 1999 Montreal Convention. In the meantime, given the various interpretations of this principle in the Conventions, the aim of uniformity could be ensured if Courts followed the interpretation most regularly given by highly

Tug of War, 4 Journal of International and Comparative Law 103-122 (2017). In 2013, the IATA published its own Core Principles on Consumer Protection, which even went further, advocating that: 'Passenger rights legislation, in accordance with the Chicago Convention 1944, should only apply to events occurring within the territory of the legislating State, or outside that territory with respect to aircraft registered there. [...] Legislation should be clear and unambiguous', Source: IATA, www.iata.org/policy/Documents/consumer_protection_principles.pdf (accessed 29 October 2019).

863. Cass., 4 March 2015, ECLI:FR:CCASS:2015:C100327. In this case, passengers had already agreed on a settlement with the carrier but sought further compensation from the manufacturer. *See*, Pablo Mendes de Leon, 'Jurisdiction under and Exclusivity of Private International Air Law Agreements on Air Carrier Liability: The Case of Airbus versus Armavia Airlines (2013)', in Pablo Mendes de Leon (ed.), *From Lowlands to High Skies: A Multilevel Jurisdictional Approach Towards Air Law – Essays in Honour of John Balfour* 261-273 (Martinus Nijhoff Publishers, 2013); Laurent Chassot, *Le domaine de la responsabilité du transporteur aérien international à la lumière de deux décisions récentes*, Revue Française de Droit Aérien et Spatial 5-25 (2016). This position was later reaffirmed in another French decision. *See*, Cass., 14 April 2021, ECLI:FR:CCASS:2021:C100308.

864. Cass., 11 July 2006, 04-18.644. *See*, Gilbert Guillaume, *Du caractère impératif des dispositions de l'article 28 de la Convention de Varsovie*, Revue Française de Droit Aérien et Spatial 227-239 (2006).

865. A different approach is adopted in France, for instance, where there is a long-standing jurisprudence preventing passengers from seeking compensation against carriers in the course of criminal proceedings. One of the reasons for this prohibition stands in the clear distinction between civil and criminal actions. *See*, Jean-Pierre Tosi, *Responsabilité aérienne* 158 (Litec, 1978).

regarded Courts. As mentioned earlier,[866] it appears that the interpretation most regularly adopted by such Courts is a strict application of the principle of exclusivity.[867]

5.3 PROCEDURAL ELEMENTS

5.3.1 The Establishment of a Common Court

On the side of possible improvements at a procedural level, the question of having a common specialized Court has already been discussed, along with reasons why it has not yet been created.[868]

International dispute mechanisms already exist, however, with respect to international public law instruments. Next to the well-known ICJ, many other international remedies have been created and implemented. For instance, the uniform application of the 1982 Montego Bay Convention on the Law of the Sea[869] is safeguarded by the International Tribunal of the Law of the Seas sitting in Hamburg. Even in aviation, the 1947 Chicago Convention sets forth specific provisions under its Articles 84 et seq. in order to settle potential disputes between Contracting States on its interpretation or application.[870] Many other international public air conventions have also established specific dispute resolution mechanisms.[871]

With respect to international private law, and more particularly international transportation law, the CMR provides under its Article 47 that:

866. *See*, section 4.3.3.5.
867. Another option is suggested by John Balfour, at least with respect to the position adopted by the Court of Justice of the European Union regarding delays, and consists in requesting that the International Court of Justice settles opposing views. *See*, John Balfour, 'Luxembourg v Montreal: Time for The Hague to Intervene', in Michal Bobek, Jeremias Prassl (eds), *Air Passenger Rights: Ten Years On* 73 (Hart Publishing, 2016). However, such an action would have to be initiated by a State which is Party to the 1999 Montreal Convention but is not an EU Member State. Such a State must also be affected by case law developed by the Court of Justice of the European Union, despite it being in contradiction with its domestic interpretation of said convention. Without going into the procedural aspects and limits of such a claim, this endeavour would essentially depend on political will rather than constituting an option directly offered to Courts. However, this divergence of views could be more effectively settled through the adoption of international rules on passenger rights, which could take the form of a convention or a protocol to the 1999 Montreal Convention (depending on the compromise to be reached, the 1999 Montreal Convention being modified or not). *Contra*, Nicolas Bernard, *Taking Air Passenger Rights Seriously: The Case Against the Exclusivity of the Montreal Convention*, 23 International Community Law Review 1-31 (2021).
868. *See*, section 3.3.3.2.
869. United Nations Convention on the Law of the Sea, 10 December 1982, Montego Bay, UNTS, 1834, I-31363, entry in force 16 November 1994.
870. *See*, for instance, International Court of Justice, *Appeal Relating to the Jurisdiction of the ICAO Council under Article II, Section 2, of the 1944 International Air Services Transit Agreement (Bahrain, Egypt and United Arab Emirates v. Qatar)*, 14 July 2020. *See also*, section 5.3.3.
871. *See*, for example, 1963 Tokyo Convention on Offences and Certain Other Acts Committed on Board Aircraft, Article 24; 1971 Montreal Convention for the Suppression of Unlawful Acts against Safety of Civil Aviation, Article 14; 2010 Beijing Convention on the Suppression of Unlawful Acts Relating to International Civil Aviation, Article 20.

> Any dispute between two or more Contracting Parties relating to the interpretation or application of this Convention, which the parties are unable to settle by negotiation or other means may, at the request of any one of the Contracting Parties concerned, be referred for settlement to the International Court of Justice.[872]

Nevertheless, this provision has never been used in practice,[873] and the right to be heard is limited to Contracting Parties. But specific international Courts, open to private bodies, do exist in international law. For example, disputes arising out of the application of the World Trade Organization rules are heard by its Dispute Settlement Body.[874]

Many States have agreed to establish common, in some cases supranational, Courts at a regional level in order to ensure not only dispute resolution but also uniformity in matters relating to both public and private laws. This is notably the case of the CJEU.

There also exist many specifically orientated Courts, such as the Common Court of Justice and Arbitration of the OHADA acting as an ultimate jurisdiction on points of law only,[875] or the Unified Patent Court which will function with different First Instance Courts across the EU and with a single Court of Appeal.[876]

Furthermore, many arbitration mechanisms have also been implemented with respect to disputes arising between States, between States and private bodies, and between private bodies. The 1999 Montreal Convention even authorizes such recourse regarding cargo disputes.[877] However, notwithstanding the advantages of arbitration, the absence of a publication of awards does not assist in enhancing a uniform application of the 1999 Montreal Convention. This could be the case if there was a single arbitration Court for cargo claims, as a certain uniformity in the awards could be expected. Nevertheless, there could still be divergences in the interpretation of provisions of the 1999 Montreal Convention, as certain of its provisions deal with both cargo and passenger matters. The exclusion of arbitration to passenger-related claims[878] in the 1999 Montreal Convention finds an explanation in the wish to protect

872. Regarding the interpretation of the CMR Convention, *see*, Waldemar Czapski, *Application et interprétation de la Convention CMR à la lumière du droit international*, 9 Uniform Law Review 545 (2006); Cécile Legros, *Modalités de l'interprétation uniforme de la CMR: Quelles difficultés? Quels remèdes?*, 20 Uniform Law Review 426 (2016); Wouter Verheyen, *National Judges as Gatekeepers to the CMR Convention*, 21 Uniform Law Review 441 (2016).
873. *See*, Francisco Sánchez-Gamborino, *La llamada Culpa Grave en el transporte de mercancías por carretera* 434 and fn (Marge Books, 2016).
874. *See*, WTO Secretariat, *A Handbook on the WTO Dispute Settlement System* (2nd edition, Cambridge University Press, 2017).
875. *See*, Eugène Assepo Assi, *La Cour commune de justice et d'arbitrage de l'OHADA: un troisième degré de juridiction?*, 57 Revue Internationale de Droit Comparé 943-955 (2005).
876. *See*, Clement Petersen, Jens Schovsbo, 'Decision-Making in the Unified Patent Court: Ensuring a Balanced Approach', in Geiger Christophe, e. a. (eds), *Intellectual Property and the Judiciary* 231-254 (Edward Elgar Publishing, 2019).
877. 1999 Montreal Convention, Article 34.
878. However, nothing seems to prevent a passenger claim from being subject to arbitration, provided the arbitration clause be agreed a posteriori. *See*, ICAO Doc 9775, International Conference on Air Law (Convention for the Unification of Certain Rules for International Carriage by Air), Montreal, 10-28 May 1999, volume I, *Minutes*, Montreal 1999, p. 188.

passengers from expensive technical procedures, as noted in the *Travaux Préparatoires* of the 1929 Warsaw Conference:

> L'arbitrage commercial s'adresse à des personnes expérimentées qui savent ce qu'elles font, qui ont les moyens de choisir un arbitre; tandis que quand une compagnie de navigation aérienne met au bas du billet: toutes les difficultés seront réglées par arbitrage, le voyageur ne sait même pas ce que cela veut dire. Il est obligé d'aller chercher un arbitre. Les tribunaux sont institués pour la sauvegarde des gens; s'il est permis à des commerçants de régler entre eux leurs affaires, il faut, pour protéger les individus, qu'il ne soit pas possible de déroger à la protection judiciaire par un simple arbitrage.[879]

The more likely reason to justify the absence of a common Court for litigation relating to the 1999 Montreal Convention is that it is politically difficult to imagine depriving a consumer of his or her right of action before domestic Courts, which are his or her natural jurisdiction. Moreover, it cannot be expected that judges sitting in such a common Court be familiar with every possible domestic legislation.

Nonetheless, these arguments do not prevent the creation of a common Court that could be seized on a preliminary ruling basis, as the analysis will examine below.[880] But, to fully achieve the purposes of the Conventions, specific interpretation rules must still be agreed upon.

5.3.2 The Formulation of Interpretation Rules

While a common Court would undoubtedly promote the uniform interpretation of the provisions of the 1999 Montreal Convention, this scenario appears unlikely to happen. In terms of common interpretation rules, the examination and conclusions made in the previous chapter show that the formulation of the principles of interpretation of the 1969 Vienna Convention is not sufficiently self-explanatory to fully ensure a uniform application of the 1999 Montreal Convention.[881]

In order to achieve the envisaged uniformity, clear interpretation rules should be added to the 1999 Montreal Convention.

This idea is not revolutionary: many international instruments have already set out hermeneutical provisions.[882] For example, Protocol No 2 to the 1988 Lugano Convention on Jurisdictions and the Enforcement of Judgments in Civil and Commercial Matters[883] sets out under its Article 1 that:

879. ICAO Doc 7838, II Conférence Internationale de Droit Privé Aérien, 4-12 Octobre 1929, *Procès-Verbaux*, Varsovie, 1930, p. 86.
880. *See*, section 5.3.3.
881. *See*, section 4.3.3.7.
882. *See*, João Ribeiro-Bidaoui, *The International Obligation of the Uniform and Autonomous Interpretation of Private Law Conventions: Consequences for Domestic Courts and International Organisations*, 67 Netherlands International Law Review 142 (2020).
883. Convention on Jurisdictions and the Enforcement of Judgements in Civil and Commercial Matters, 16 September 1988, Lugano, UNTS, 1659, I-28551, entry in force 1 January 1992. This Convention was recast in 2007 and kept this provision.

> The courts of each Contracting State shall, when applying and interpreting the provisions of the Convention, pay due account to the principles laid down in any relevant decision delivered by courts of the other Contracting State concerning provisions of this Convention.

The 2016 UNIDROIT Principles of International Commercial Contracts[884] provide under their Article 1(6)(1) that:

> In the interpretation of these Principles, regard is to be had to their international character and to their purposes including the need to promote uniformity in their application.

The 1980 CISG also provides under its Article 7(1) that:

> In the interpretation of this Convention, regard is to be had to its international character and to the need to promote uniformity in its application and the observance of good faith in international trade.[885]

In terms of interpretation guidance, this Convention is also supplemented by an Explanatory Note prepared by the UNCITRAL Secretariat.[886] Its uniform application is also reinforced by a dedicated case law database, publicly available on the UNCITRAL website.[887]

Professor Olivier Cachard underlined that the absence of similar provisions for the 1999 Montreal Convention notably stems from the fact that the CISG Convention is applied by international arbitrators without a specific *forum*, whereas, in the case of the 1999 Montreal Convention, such a uniform interpretation would be implicit and would not require special inclusion.[888] However, contrary to his view, in other Uniform Instruments in the transport sector, such an inclusion was made. For example, Article 2 of the Rotterdam Rules provides that:

> In the interpretation of this Convention, regard is to be had to its international character and to the need to promote uniformity in its application and the observance of good faith in international trade.

Article 8(1) of the COTIF, as amended by the 1999 Vilnius Protocol, provides that:

> When interpreting and applying the Convention, its character of international law and the necessity to promote uniformity shall be taken into account.

---

884. UNIDROIT, https://www.unidroit.org/instruments/commercial-contracts/unidroit-principles-2016 (accessed 1 October 2020). On this topic, *see*, Jürgen Basedow, *Uniform Law and Conventions and the UNIDROIT Principles of International Commercial Contracts*, 5 Uniform Law Review 129 (2000); Christina Ramberg, *The UNIDROIT Principles as a Means of Interpreting Domestic Law*, 9 Uniform Law Review 669 (2014); Olaf Meyer, *The UNIDROIT Principles as a Means to Interpret or Supplement Domestic Law*, 21 Uniform Law Review 559 (2016).

885. United Nations Convention on Contracts for International Sale of Goods, 11 April 1980, Vienna, UNTS, I-25567, 1489, entry in force 1 January 1988.

886. On this topic, *see*, Paul Schiff Berman, *The Inevitable Legal Pluralism Within Harmonization Regimes: The Case of the CISG*, 21 Uniform Law Review 23 (2016); Martin Gebauer, *Uniform Law, General Principles and Autonomous Interpretation*, 5 Uniform Law Review 683 (2000).

887. UNCITRAL, https://www.uncitral.org/clout/ (accessed 29 October 2019).

888. Olivier Cachard, *Le transport international aérien de passager* 169 (Les livres de Poche des l'Académie de droit international de La Haye, 2015).

This is also the case in other private air law conventions, such as under Article 5(1) of the 2001 Cape Town Convention:

> In the interpretation of this Convention, regard is to be had to its purposes as set forth in the preamble, to its international character and to the need to promote uniformity and predictability in its application.[889]

This crafty idea, with respect to the interpretation of this Convention, is that it also receives assistance from Official Commentaries[890] published regularly and from a dedicated online journal.[891] Such additional help may also become useful for interpreting the 1999 Montreal Convention.

Formal inclusion of specific interpretative guidance will obviously not solve every difficulty that a uniform application of the 1999 Montreal Convention raises, but it would be a useful tool for Courts. As a reminder, the pioneers of air law had a clear intention to adopt a specific international convention on the interpretation of private international air law conventions.[892]

In the absence of the adoption of common specific interpretation rules, Courts should be encouraged, when interpreting Uniform Instruments such as the 1999 Montreal Convention, to further detail their reasoning and the interpretation mechanisms they used, in order to assist other Courts seeking guidance. They are also strongly invited to refer to foreign case law when interpreting the Conventions. Recourse to foreign case law when interpreting international instruments has indeed been endorsed by the ICJ in *Ahmadou Sadio Diallo*.[893]

5.3.3 Intermediary Solutions

Another approach could be for any specialist in the area to intervene in foreign Court proceedings – whenever the jurisdiction seized allows it – as an amicus curiae to defend the aim of uniformity of the Conventions.[894] Without a designated effective guardian of the 1999 Montreal Convention, each ratifying States should be the watchdog of its ambition. But, aside from being utopian, this would raise other issues,

889. On this subject, *see*, Thomas Traschler, *A Uniform Application of Article 13 of the Cape Town Convention via an Autonomous Interpretation*, 21 Uniform Law Review 640 (2016).
890. *See*, for example, Roy Goode, *Cape Town Convention and Aircraft Protocol Official Commentary* (4th edition, UNIDROIT, 2019).
891. *See*, Cape Town Convention Journal, https://ctcjournal.net/index.php/ctcj (accessed 29 October 2019).
892. *See*, section 3.3.3.3.
893. International Court of Justice, *Ahmadou Sadio Diallo (Republic of Guinea v. Democratic Republic of the Congo), Merits, Judgements*, I.C.J. Reports 2010, p. 639, at 66: '[...] Although the Court is in no way obliged, in the exercise of its judicial functions, to model its own interpretation of the Covenant on that of the Committee, it believes that it should ascribe great weight to the interpretation adopted by this independent body that was established specifically to supervise the application of that treaty. The point here is to achieve the necessary clarity and the essential consistency of international law, as well as legal security, to which both the individuals with guaranteed rights and the States obliged to comply with treaty obligations are entitled.'
894. Such a mechanism is already implemented in certain jurisdictions, such as in the United States before the Supreme Court.

such as the awareness of the existence of litigation and linguistic issues resulting from the lack of a common mutual language.

Nevertheless, in the absence of a common Court, common specific interpretation rules, or even the possibility to act as an amicus curiae, an official body of experts[895] could be created to act as a *collegium jurisconsultorum* and deliver advisory opinions.[896] Should the ICAO[897] or any other entity be prepared to assume this new function, the question would remain how to determine the value of these opinions.

Additionally, mechanisms should be found to encourage Courts to seize, on a preliminary basis, such *collegium jurisconsultorum*. Linguistic issues, as well as a vision of national centrism, could constitute strong barriers to its materialization, and it would therefore require communication campaigns to be implemented across ratifying States. The creation of such an advisory body could, however, be implemented without needing to amend the 1999 Montreal Convention, as it could exist in parallel to it and be open to other private air law instruments. The non-binding nature of these opinions would permit a strong and smooth adherence of Courts in this endeavour of uniformity. The composition of such an advisory body might however raise difficulties, particularly if decided at a political level.

In the case where no official public body could establish such an advisory body, initiatives could also potentially come from the private sector. Taking again the example of the CISG, upon the initiative of various academics, the CISG Advisory Council[898] was established in 2001. This informal Advisory Council aims to promote a uniform interpretation of the CISG by delivering opinions upon request. Its members are scholars fluent in different languages that do not represent a specific legal culture or governments. Since its establishment in 2001, it has already delivered twenty opinions. Depending on possibilities offered by each domestic law, certain Courts have expressly relied on their opinion in their decisions.[899]

---

895. *See*, Euthymène Georgiades, *De la méthodologie juridique pour l'unification du Droit aérien international privé*, Revue Française de Droit Aérien et Spatial 379 (1972).

896. A similar approach was adopted by the Hague Conference on Private International Law. Article 8(1) of the Statute of the Hague Conference on Private International Law provides that: 'The Sessions and, in the interval between Sessions, the Council, may set up Special Commissions to prepare draft Conventions or to study all questions of private international law which come within the purpose of the Conference', Source: Hague Conference on Private International Law, https://www.hcch.net (accessed 30 October 2019). On this basis, interpretative 'Conclusions and Recommendations' have occasionally been published.

897. Technically, the Council of the ICAO may provide advisory opinions on any matter related to civil aviation on the grounds of its Resolution A1-23. *See*, ICAO, Resolution A1-23: Authorization to the Council to Act as an Arbitral Body, ICAO Doc 10140. But to our knowledge, such a mechanism was never used and only States can seize this arbitral body. *See*, Michael Milde, *International Air Law and ICAO* 184 (Eleven International Publishing, 2008). Moreover, the composition of this arbitral body does not appear to include independent experts in air law, but rather essentially delegates of States who are expected to respect the instructions given from their capital. *See*, Paul Dempsey, *Public International Air Law* 734 (Institute and Center for Research in Air & Space Law, McGill University, 2008).

898. CISG Advisory Council, www.cisgac.com (accessed 29 October 2019).

899. *See*, Olivier Deshayes, *L'amélioration de l'application et de l'interprétation uniforme des conventions internationales relative au contrat de transport: le cas de la faute qualifiée* 293 (Thesis, Université de Rouen Normandie, 2018).

As academics have already expressed an interest for this type of *collegium jurisconsultorum* with respect to the CMR,[900] the uniform application of the 1999 Montreal Convention could also be widely improved through such an advisory body, be it of a public or private nature, as long as it were independent and composed of highly esteemed legal professionals.

5.4 PROSPECTIVE ELEMENTS USING ARTIFICIAL INTELLIGENCE

5.4.1 A Proposal for a Robotic Court

In her remarkable work on the way the Warsaw Instruments were interpreted in various jurisdictions, Dr Georgette Miller concluded in 1977 that:

> Pushing this to the absurd, the only tribunal qualified to apply a uniform law would be a kind of robot programmed solely with the uniform law.[901]

More than forty years later, her conclusion may no longer be so absurd or unrealistic. It is impossible to ignore the current evolution of technology and particularly that of Artificial Intelligence, which some believe heralds the fourth industrial revolution.[902]

While communication speed has tremendously increased in the last decades, research and development programmes have made a step further in calculation capacity, offering new technologies that are capable of learning and reasoning in a way close to humans, as further explained in the Appendix to this study.[903] As the whole process of litigation may already be partly dematerialized through online Courts,[904] the development of Artificial Intelligence mechanisms suggests that particular software could, in the future, act as a substitute for judges, or at least, could pre-draft a Court decision based on a rapid analysis of the different sources of law and interpretation tools available.

The following analysis will examine the potential benefits and risks of these new software with respect to the quest for further uniformity in the application of the 1999 Montreal Convention.

---

900. *See*, Cécile Legros, *The CISG Advisory Council: A Model to Improve Uniform Application of CMR?*, 9 European Journal of Commercial Contract Law 27 (2017).
901. Georgette Miller, *Liability in International Air Transport* 351 (Kluwer, 1977).
902. *See*, Nicolás Lozanda-Pimiento, *AI Systems and Technology in Dispute Resolution*, 24 Uniform Law Review 350 (2019).
903. The reader unfamiliar with Artificial Intelligence mechanisms is invited to read this Appendix before continuing any further in this chapter.
904. For example, the British Columbia Civil Resolution Tribunal is an online dispute resolution (ODR) forum incorporated in the public judicial system. *See*, British Columbia Civil Resolution Tribunal, www.civilresolutionbc.ca (accessed 19 February 2021). Said online Court has notably confirmed its competence to hear certain air passengers' claims. *See*, *Serbinenko v. Air Canada* (2020) BCCRT 1330.

5.4.2 Benefits

The benefits of recourse to such mechanisms are obvious and numerous. As no judge can pretend to have an exhaustive knowledge of the law, particularly when it comes to air law and foreign case law, such software would provide an immediate solution inspired by all available case law and interpretation tools. For the law consumers, such as passengers, air carriers and insurers, this would also give an insight into the forecast decision without having to await the outcome of litigation proceedings.

It would also achieve the aim of predictability to the highest extent possible, insofar as a common solution could be obtained at pre-litigation level. The remaining degree of unpredictability would be due to the possibility of the human judge deviating from the precomposed decisions of the machine. Finally, in terms of uniformity, the aim would be reached, as the machine would take into consideration all possible sources of law available and each interpretation tool that may exist.

5.4.3 Risks

5.4.3.1 A Multiplicity of Risks

Next to the feasibility of such software and the benefits that could be gained from it, such recourse to machines might pose several risks with respect to the improvement of the uniformity of the 1999 Montreal Convention.

5.4.3.2 Software Design

The first category of risk lies with the software design. In order to be acceptable, the software using Artificial Intelligence mechanisms should be unique and designed by a public body, such as the ICAO, or during a diplomatic conference. This would avoid disputes over the nature of the algorithm used, given that, as explained by Adrien van den Branden, algorithms are opinions integrated into code.[905] It would also guarantee that the algorithm was publicly known, with the consequence that its application could be verified at any time in order to detect any possible corruption.[906] Therefore, to avoid these risks, each State would have to play three active roles in this process.

905. Adrien van den Branden, *Les robots à l'assaut de la justice: L'intelligence artificielle au service des justiciables* 107 (Bruylant, 2019).

906. This risk was emphasized by the Council of the European Union as follows: '[...] in certain cases, outcomes of artificial intelligence systems based on machine learning cannot be retraced, leading to a black-box-effect that prevents adequate and necessary responsibility and makes it impossible to check how the result was reached and whether it complies with relevant regulations. This lack of transparency could undermine the possibility of effectively challenging decisions based on such outcomes and may thereby infringe the right to a fair trial and an effective remedy, and limits the areas in which these systems can be legally used', Council of the European Union, Council Conclusions, "Access to justice – seizing the opportunity of digitalization", *Official Journal*, 14 October 2020, C-342 I/1, at 41.

First, all States should participate in this project. Otherwise, there would be a risk of not having a full picture of existing case law and of having a multispeed decision-making process, where certain States would use one system and others would rely on another. This situation would eventually lead to disproportionated inputs into the software if decisions delivered in non-participating States artificially nourished the system. The challenge, however, would be to allow less-developed countries to be able to feed into the system, which would probably require a modernization of their judiciary system in order to use the software and deliver decisions that were readable by the machine.

Second, participants should play an active role in ensuring that every decision and official comment is made publicly available for free in a machine-readable format, in order to ensure every decision can be analysed.

Third, the major risk with respect to uniformity and global predictability would consist in the failure to mutually agree on a common algorithm. As a reminder, the drafting of an international convention faces many hurdles, and sometimes the outcome of mutual concessions leads to a lack of clarity. When it comes to the creation of an algorithm, a lack of clarity cannot be tolerated. While the general architecture of the common algorithm may reasonably be accepted by all participants pursuant to the interpretation tools described in the 1969 Vienna Convention, the discussions might still be endless with regard to the actual value to be allocated to each parameter. The elements of fragmentation analysed earlier show indeed that there remain many divergent views that would need to be reconciled. Here is a sample of various questions that would have to be answered.

- What value, for example, out of ten, should be allocated to Supreme Court decisions in comparison to inferior Courts? Should the value allocated to Supreme Court decisions be equal to those delivered by the French *Cour de cassation*, knowing that French domestic law allows a higher percentage of decisions to pass its filter?

- Should some jurisdictions be given a higher credit than others based on the degree of independence of their judiciary system or on the degree of corruption? What factors should be taken into consideration in this deliberation?

- Should recent case law receive a higher score than the older one? Should Warsaw case law be integrated, and if so, should it receive the same consideration as Montreal case law?

- Should decisions delivered in one of the authentic languages of the 1999 Montreal Convention be granted a higher score? Should decisions delivered in French, or having been cross-checked against the French version, regarding provisions that have not changed since 1929, receive a higher score?

- Should the decisions that have insisted on a specific purpose of the Convention be considered as equal to those that have taken into consideration all the purposes of the Convention?

This list of examples demonstrates that many delicate questions would have to be raised and solved if a single software using a common algorithm were to be adopted.

5.4.3.3 *Software Use by Courts*

The next category of risks appears in the use that could be made of such software.

First, there is an initial risk of dominance of common law jurisprudence, given that dissident opinions are equally published, and that the interpretative reasoning behind the highest Court's decision in civil law jurisdictions is for the time being less detailed.

Second, there is a high risk of crystallization of *proforma* solutions if Courts tend to always stick to suggested decisions without deviating from them, and consequently do not feed the system with new decisions.

5.4.3.4 *Software Use by Law Consumers*

The last category of risks consists in law consumers' attitude.

The highest variation in the predictability of a case outcome might result, at least at the beginning of its implementation, from an increase in forum shopping. However, this risk might be mitigated by the existence of more uniformly applied terms and concepts.

In addition, the use of such software by passengers, air carriers and their insurers may lead to a substantial rise in amicable out-of-Court settlements or recourses to alternative dispute resolution mechanisms. The risk is again that, by avoiding Court proceedings, the machine will not be fed with new and divergent decisions.

5.4.4 Concluding Remarks

The question of whether the implementation and the use of machines using Artificial Intelligence are desirable or not should not be assessed given that technologies do not await general acceptance, and no one has ever succeeded in prohibiting new technologies in the long run.

Machines using Artificial Intelligence are already in use in many industries such as: finance, leisure, sports, medicine, arts, air transport, and the legal sector.[907]

Smart Contracts are increasingly employed.[908] Software aiming at facilitating legal research using Artificial Intelligence is already in use in different jurisdictions.[909]

---

907. For several examples in the air transport sector, *see*, Ruwantissa Abeyratne, *Legal Priorities in Air Transport* (Springer, 2019); European Aviation Artificial Intelligence High Level Group, *The Fly AI Report: Demystifying and Acceleration AI in Aviation/ATM*, 5 March 2020, Source: Eurocontrol, https://www.eurocontrol.int/sites/default/files/2020-03/eurocontrol-fly-ai-report-032020.pdf (accessed 9 March 2020). *See also*, Appendix.

908. *See*, Riccardo De Caria, *The Legal Meaning of Smart Contracts*, 27 European Review of Private Law 731 (2018). The author acknowledged the existence of myriad possible definitions of smart contracts. He suggests the following definition of 'decentralized smart contract', at 737: '[...] any digital agreement which is (a) written in computer code (thus, a piece of software), (b) run on blockchain or similar distributed ledger technologies (thus, decentralized) and (c) automatically executed without any need for human intervention (thus, smart)'.

909. *See*, for example, in the United States, Ross, www.rossintelligence.com (accessed 31 October 2019).

Air law is also already impacted by these new technologies. Some programmes developed by claims agencies have already automated the production of their Court documents and the extraction of data from third-party websites in order to evidence, for example, the reality of weather conditions at a specific airport.[910] In a 2019 interview with a French financial newspaper, a company specializing in European air passenger right claims reported the use of several machines using Artificial Intelligence to, among other things, identify the most appropriate Court on the grounds of tens of thousands of legal proceedings and to analyse the legal aspects of each claim.[911]

More is then to come. And it is therefore not a surprise that UNCITRAL and UNIDROIT, both known to be active in international law, have jointly initiated an examination of legal issues arising from the use of these technologies.[912]

5.5 CONCLUSIONS

The variety of tools that could be implemented to enhance the uniformity of the 1999 Montreal Convention demonstrates that the fragmentation factors examined in Chapters 3 and 4 could be mitigated. Among the possible proposals for enhancing uniformity, some do require heavy machinery that would entail a revision of the 1999 Montreal Convention. Such proposals pertain to redrafting points discussed regarding the autonomy and exclusivity mechanisms. Other suggestions could, however, be implemented without amending the current text, although their efficiency would be improved if they were integrated therein. This is particularly the case of the procedural elements examined and the implementation of a centralized database.

A robotic Court would also improve the uniformity of the 1999 Montreal Convention without any changes being made to its provisions, but would only be efficient if a single algorithm was used worldwide.

In the meantime, in order to adhere as much as possible to the aim of the Conventions, Courts should bear in mind that the terms and concepts therein are distinct from those that could possibly exist under domestic law or in other international instruments.

In addition, while recourse should be made to the hermeneutical canons of the 1969 Vienna Convention, significant value should be granted to foreign case law and, as a corollary, eventual deviation from widespread jurisprudence should be well reasoned.[913]

---

910. On this topic, *see*, Paul Fitzgerald, *Automating the Process of Passenger Claims under the EU Passenger Rights Regime*, The Aviation & Space Journal 2 (October 2018).
911. Les Echos, https://business.lesechos.fr/directions-juridiques/droit-des-affaires/contentieux/0601825123420-l-intelligence-artificielle-se-met-au-service-des-juristes-d-airhelp-331496.php (accessed 31 October 2019).
912. UNIDROIT, https://www.unidroit.org/english/news/2019/190506-unidroit-uncitral-workshop/conclusions-e.pdf (accessed 31 October 2019).
913. *See*, João Ribeiro-Bidaoui, *The International Obligation of the Uniform and Autonomous Interpretation of Private Law Conventions: Consequences for Domestic Courts and International Organisations*, 67 Netherlands International Law Review 149 (2020).

CHAPTER 6

General Conclusions and Recommendations

6.1 GENERAL CONCLUSIONS

The purpose of the analysis carried out in this study was to determine whether the regime for international air carrier liability established by the 1999 Montreal Convention could be uniform. Three sub-questions were posed in order to reply to this question.

First, it was necessary to analyse whether uniformity was a predominant aim of the 1999 Montreal Convention. The examination carried out highlighted that the purpose of the treaty was dual. On the one hand, it had ambitions to solve the lack of legal certainty generated by the existence of parallel, and occasionally conflicting, regimes. On the other hand, its negotiators, updating pre-existing treaties, wished to adopt rules that would simultaneously create a level playing field among airlines and would reflect a balance between carrier and passenger rights. Such purposes had to be achieved through a unification process. However, unification under a single common text could either have materialized through common rules of conflict of laws or through uniform rules. As the purposes of the 1999 Montreal Convention and its predecessors could not have been satisfied with rules of conflict of laws only, the choice was therefore made to unify, as far as possible, the contemplated international regime through uniform rules. In this regard, this study has demonstrated that these uniform rules were expected to be uniformly applied in order to ensure the effectiveness of the purposes of the treaty, with the assistance of features such as the principle of exclusivity and the concept of autonomy.

Second, with the assistance of the *Travaux Préparatoires* and judicial decisions, the study examined whether there were any factors that would constitute obstacles to this aim of uniformity. The analysis highlighted that factors both internal and external to the treaty prevented this aim from being achieved, and led to a fragmentation of the 1999 Montreal Convention. Designated as internal factors, that is to say, factors that stemmed from the text itself, the analysis demonstrated that several drafting factors contributed to fragmentation. These included:

- the lack of definition of key terms and concepts used;
- the transfer of concepts used in other Uniform Instruments;
- the admissibility of variations in interpretations of the terms and concepts used, to the extent that a certain significance is given to the *Travaux Préparatoires*;
- the unclear division between uniform rules and referrals to domestic rules; and
- finally, the inclusion of a provision that would potentially allow different Courts to be seized with respect to the same event.

All of these internal factors could have however been mitigated if the treaty had included specific common specific interpretation rules or had created a dedicated Court.

Despite the existence of long-standing warnings, and some of which being raised during the 1999 Montreal Conference, none of these mitigating measures were adopted.

Moreover, external factors to the Conventions have also participated in the fragmentation of the uniform regime. Regulatory changes disturbed the autonomy and exclusivity of the treaty. These include rules adopted at regional and domestic levels that supplement or compete with the uniform regime of the 1999 Montreal Convention. In parallel, Courts have also not always uniformly understood the nature of the autonomy of the terms and of the principle of exclusivity, which has resulted in divergent interpretations of the 1999 Montreal Convention. In addition, linguistic variations of the uniform rules have been seen as a source of fragmentation of the uniform regime. This study also demonstrated that despite being useful tools, the principles of interpretation laid down in the 1969 Vienna Convention were not always helpful for ensuring a uniform application of the uniform rules.

Third, having acknowledged the existence of a fragmentation of the international air carrier liability regime which is in contradiction with its aim of uniformity, the study tried to assess whether certain elements could be developed to improve the uniform application of the 1999 Montreal Convention. To do so, this study examined solutions adopted in other international instruments and discussed the possibilities offered by Artificial Intelligence. The outcome of this analysis was particularly promising.

In light of all these elements, the recommendations that follow appear reasonably useful for further improving the uniformity of the 1999 Montreal Convention.

6.2 RECOMMENDATIONS

6.2.1 Preliminary Remarks

I suggest implementing the recommendations laid out in this study in three phases. The first and second phases could start rapidly.

Certain recommendations do not need a modification to the 1999 Montreal Convention, while others require the political commitment to set up a new diplomatic conference. Although the third phase could be initiated in parallel with the first two, it would only be truly useful once the second phase had been completed.

6.2.2 The First Phase

The choice of the subject matter of this study, along with the conclusions drawn, demonstrates that the aim of uniformity of the 1999 Montreal Convention deserves to be constantly recalled. Therefore, in light of the purposes and object of the 1999 Montreal Convention, *Recommendation No 1* would be that, with immediate effect, whenever one of the terms or concepts thereof needs to be interpreted, the persons in charge of the interpretation give due respect to the principles set out in the 1969 Vienna Convention, together with significant weight to the dominant jurisprudence developed by Courts in other ratifying States.

6.2.3 The Second Phase

The second phase requires little more than mere goodwill, as most of the following recommendations entail amending the 1999 Montreal Convention. On a cosmetic side, given the variations in terminology used regarding the different techniques of approximation of legislations, *Recommendation No 2* would be to redraft the preamble in order to clearly distinguish harmonization from unification. On this occasion, the wish for a uniform application should be underlined.

Moreover, as the examination carried out also showed that the combination of uniform rules and *renvois* has led to undesirable situations, *Recommendation No 3* would be to proceed with a clear drafting separation between uniform rules and non-uniform rules. The implementation of this would avoid leaving to the Courts the task of determining whether a provision must be regarded as autonomous or subject to domestic law. Such a redrafting would also be of paramount importance to the implementation of the third phase, where an algorithm would have to be commonly developed.

During the redrafting process, discussions should also take place on the exact intended scope of the exclusivity principle. As different views exist on the matter, *Recommendation No 4* would be to consider a redrafting of Article 29 of the 1999 Montreal Convention for further clarity. This discussion should ideally include the possibility of solving any difficulties that arose in connection with the emergence of consumer rights.

In light of this element, *Recommendation No 5* would therefore be to include, in a revised version of the 1999 Montreal Convention, new uniform rules on the matter, which would replace the existing regional and domestic legislations on air passengers' rights. This recommendation is also grounded in the fact that the current situation with respect to consumer rights shares many similarities with the one that concurred with the adoption of the first uniform rules in 1929.

As the autonomous nature of the uniform rules also generated misunderstandings and conflicting views, *Recommendation No 6* would be to insert a provision into the revised version that would clearly indicate that uniform rules are autonomous, and that the treaty establishes a sui generis regime, with the consequence that terms and concepts therein should not be interpreted pursuant to domestic law or other international instruments. This being said, even in the case where autonomy was rightly acknowledged, there still remains a question of how to validly interpret autonomous terms and concepts in the absence of definitions and/or prior judicial decisions.

Recommendation No 7 would therefore be to add more definitions and to include a dedicated provision in the revised text that would provide that uniform rules should be interpreted pursuant to the principles of interpretation laid down in the 1969 Vienna Convention with, when existing, the necessity to pay due consideration to foreign judicial decisions and to depart from dominant jurisprudence only on reasonable grounds. On this occasion, delegates should also take the opportunity to reformulate the purposes and object of the 1999 Montreal Convention, in order to avoid divergent decisions on this basis. They should also firmly stipulate the value they intend to give to judicial decisions handed down on the grounds of previous instruments.

As a review of foreign decisions would become mandatory, *Recommendation No 8* would be to implement a common database of all related decisions delivered in each ratifying State. Such a database would have to include a description of the judiciary system in place in each State, in order to determine the domestic value of the decisions uploaded in the database, and a translation of the decisions submitted in at least one of the official languages of the 1999 Montreal Convention.

All of the above Recommendations do not anticipate solving every potential issue regarding a uniform application of the 1999 Montreal Convention, but they are expressed as means to achieve a less fragmented application. The ideal solution to ensure the full effectiveness of the purposes and object of the treaty would obviously be the establishment of a common Court, endowed with complete jurisdictional competencies. As one should not be too naive regarding the tensions that such a transfer of competence would generate, *Recommendation No 9* would be to establish a public or private *collegium jurisconsultorum* that could be seized by any domestic Court on a point of law to ensure, through the mechanism of a preliminary ruling, a highly regarded interpretation made by recognized law professionals. In the situation where the opinions to be handed down by such *collegium jurisconsultorum* would not be binding, Recommendation No 7 should be supplemented in order to guarantee a certain value to these opinions for interpretation purposes.

6.2.4 The Third Phase

The third phase aims to apply Artificial Intelligence software in a coordinated manner to the 1999 Montreal Convention. The recommendations included hereinafter are ready to be discussed at a political level, as they do not require per se a modification of the current version of the 1999 Montreal Convention. However, most of the points raised in the second phase and in section 5.4 would ideally need to be addressed before expecting a useful software that would guarantee a uniform application of the Conventions.

As different software products relying on Artificial Intelligence technology are being developed, *Recommendation No 10* would be to ensure that as many ratifying Parties as possible gather to decide together on a common algorithm that would be used to interpret the 1999 Montreal Convention. To this end, the project should ideally be organized under the auspices of an international organization such as the ICAO, in order to guarantee public access to the algorithm and to avoid unnecessary copyright issues. The international organization would then have to appoint a dedicated team composed of legal experts, computer scientists, Artificial Intelligence scientists and data protection officers to enact this goal. This team would have to make specific suggestions as to who could benefit from the software, and who would potentially be able to amend the algorithm.

6.3 CLOSING WORDS

Despite numerous remarks made in the course of this study, the 1999 Montreal Convention is a remarkable achievement and an undisputed success. It is one of the most unique instruments to cover both business and consumer law provisions under a single text. Its application may have resulted in few weaknesses but also confirms its strength.

As carriage by air grows and improves, thanks to the continuing development of new technologies, the uniformity of the 1999 Montreal Convention also profits from the development of technologies such as the internet, which enables judicial decisions and commentaries to easily cross borders. But in this world where technology enables the possibility of a very high degree of predictability and uniformity in Court decisions, now may be the right moment to consider whether such a promise is still desirable. A few years after the adoption of the 1929 Warsaw Convention, Professor Karl Wieland expressed the view that: '[...] the future uniform world law remains a utopia, it is a dream and not even a beautiful one'.[914] Is it really not a beautiful dream? A certain degree of flexibility is probably a shadow component to what might be considered a right decision. There is little doubt that once Artificial Intelligence software is implemented to assist Courts, the next generation of judges will have to be particularly creative about finding the appropriate balance between uniformity and flexibility.

914. Karl Wieland, 'Rechtsquellen und Weltrech', in *Recueil d'études sur les sources du droit en l'honneur de François Gény*, t. 3, 473 (Sirey, 1934): 'Allein das künftige einheitliche Weltrecht bleibt eine Utopie, ist ein Traum und nicht einmal ein schöner'.

APPENDIX

Artificial Intelligence as an Aid in the Decision-Making Process

A.1 INTRODUCTION

The purpose of this Appendix is to provide a primary introduction to Artificial Intelligence technologies, with a particular focus on their expected capabilities when it comes to a uniform application of the 1999 Montreal Convention.

From this perspective, this primer will start with a description of what Artificial Intelligence consists of and what its applications could be in the field of Justice (section A.2). Once the main features of Artificial Intelligence have been examined, this Appendix will look at how the principles of interpretation of the 1969 Vienna Convention may be converted into an algorithm (section A.3).

A.2 ARTIFICIAL INTELLIGENCE AND PREDICTIVE JUSTICE

A.2.1 The Role of the Machine

We have arrived at a stage where humans are able to create machines with computing capabilities far superior to our own, with almost instantaneous results. In order to proceed with a complex calculation, the machine follows a mathematical logic that is essentially translated into algorithms.[915] An algorithm can be compared to a cooking

915. The online *Oxford University Press Dictionary* gives the following definition: 'A process or set of rules to be followed in calculations or other problem-solving operations, especially by a computer', Source: Lexico, https://www.lexico.com/en/definition/algorithm (accessed 31 October 2019); The European Commission for the Efficiency of Justice in its 2018 'European ethical Charter on the use of Artificial Intelligence in judicial systems and their environment' gave the following definition: 'Finite sequence of formal rules (logical operations and instructions) making it possible to obtain a result from the initial input of information. This sequence may be part of an automated execution process and draw on models designed through machine

recipe, where the procedure is described step by step in detail, with possible alternatives. For example, in the case of lack of wheat flour, the algorithm might recommend other flours.

While the process can be translated into a mathematical language, the choice of recipe is still human. These human factors, known as 'proxies',[916] present the risk of possibly forgetting important data or incorporating biases into the coding.

Thanks to the intervention of statisticians, an algorithm can be continually improved by so-called 'feedback loops'. In other words, they will award bonus points when the solution proposed by the algorithm is ultimately adopted, or to stay with the cooking example, when the dish made according to the recipe only is considered satisfactory without any personal changes. Technology improvement, known as 'machine learning',[917] means that sometimes the machine no longer requires external intervention from statisticians to assign bonus points. There are different levels of machine learning.

The current most advanced level is known as 'deep learning'. It allows, for example, for facial recognition and permits instant translations that are not on the basis of simple dictionaries, but from learning of millions of examples and deducing context.[918] Reference can be made to the concept of Artificial Intelligence,[919] when it

---

learning', Source: Council of Europe, https://rm.coe.int/ethical-charter-en-for-publication-4-december-2018/16808f699c (accessed 31 October 2019). UNIDROIT and UNCITRAL are working on a common list of definitions relating to Artificial Intelligence. For an in-depth presentation of these mechanisms and their role, *see*, Adrien van den Branden, *Les robots à l'assaut de la justice: L'intelligence artificielle au service des justiciables* (Bruylant, 2019).

916. The online *Oxford University Press Dictionary* gives, among other things, the following definition: 'A figure that can be used to represent the value of something in a calculation', Source: Lexico, https://www.lexico.com/en/definition/proxy (accessed 31 October 2019).

917. The online *Oxford University Press Dictionary* gives the following definition: 'The use and development of computer systems that are able to learn and adapt without following explicit instructions, by using algorithms and statistical models to analyse and draw inferences from patterns in data', Source: Lexico, https://www.lexico.com/en/definition/machine_learning (accessed 23 December 2020); The European Commission for the Efficiency of Justice in its 2018 'European ethical Charter on the use of Artificial Intelligence in judicial systems and their environment' gave the following definition: 'Machine learning makes it possible to construct a mathematical model from data, incorporating a large number of variables that are not known in advance. The parameters are configured gradually during the learning phase, which uses training data sets to find and classify links. The different methods of machine learning are chosen by the designers depending on the nature of the tasks to be completed (grouping). These methods are usually classified into three categories: (human) supervised learning, unsupervised learning and reinforcement learning. These three categories group together different methods including neural networks, deep learning, etc', Source: Council of Europe, https://rm.coe.int/ethical-charter-en-for-publication-4-december-2018/16808f699c (accessed 31 October 2019).

918. *See*, for example, Google, https://ai.google/research/pubs/pub45610 (accessed 31 October 2019).

919. The online *Oxford University Press Dictionary* gives the following definition: 'The theory and development of computer systems able to perform tasks normally requiring human intelligence, such as visual perception, speech recognition, decision-making, and translation between languages', Source: Lexico, https://www.lexico.com/en/definition/artificial_intelligence (accessed 31 October 2019); The European Commission for the Efficiency of Justice in its 2018 'European ethical Charter on the use of Artificial Intelligence in judicial systems and their environment' gave the following definition: 'A set of scientific methods, theories and techniques whose aim is to reproduce, by a machine, the cognitive abilities of human beings.

becomes difficult for a human to distinguish if a reasoning was elaborated by a human or a machine.[920] There would be three different stages in its evolution: the weak level, where the machine only reproduces human behaviour; the strong level, where it thinks and acts like a human; and finally, the ultimate level of superintelligence where the machine would be radically more intelligent than humans.[921] This last stage is still far from being reached. However, these Artificial Intelligence technologies have already found some application in different fields of our everyday life, including in justice.[922]

Indeed, these technologies allow an instant analysis of a huge amount of data, such as legislation, judicial decisions and literature, and suggest a possible legal solution in light of given factual elements.[923] This application, known as 'predictive justice',[924] has proven efficiency in cases which did not require human emotion[925] such

Current developments seek to have machines perform complex tasks previously carried out by humans. However, the term artificial intelligence is criticised by experts who distinguish between "strong" AIs (yet able to contextualise specialised and varied problems in a completely autonomous manner) and "weak" or "moderate" AIs (high performance in their field of training). Some experts argue that "strong" AIs would require significant advances in basic research, and not just simple improvements in the performance of existing systems, to be able to model the world as a whole. [...]', Source: Council of Europe, https://rm.coe.int/ethical-charter-en-for-publication-4-december-2018/16808f699c (accessed 31 October 2019).

920. A test was first introduced by Alan Turing in 1950. *See*, Alan Turing, *Computing Machinery and Intelligence*, 59 Mind 433-460 (1950).

921. *See*, Adrien van den Branden, *Les robots à l'assaut de la justice: L'intelligence artificielle au service des justiciables* 81-82 (Bruylant, 2019).

922. *See*, European Commission, *Study on the Use of Innovative Technologies in the Justice Field*, final report, Source: Publications Office of the European Union, https://op.europa.eu/en/publication-detail/-/publication/4fb8e194-f634-11ea-991b-01aa75ed71a1/language-en (accessed 17 September 2020).

923. In 2020, the Council of the European Union acknowledged that: '[...] artificial intelligence systems in the justice sector may in the future be capable of performing increasingly complex tasks – within the legal framework of a Member State – such as analysing, structuring and preparing information on the subject matter of cases, automatically transcribing records of oral hearings, offering machine translation, supporting the analysis and evaluation of legal documents and court/tribunal judgements, estimating the chances of success of a lawsuit, automatically anonymising case law and providing information via legal chatbots', Council of the European Union, Council Conclusions, Access to justice – seizing the opportunity of digitalization, *Official Journal*, 14 October 2020, C-342 I/1, at 35.

924. The European Commission for the Efficiency of Justice in its 2018 'European ethical Charter on the use of Artificial Intelligence in judicial systems and their environment' gave the following definition: 'Predictive justice is the analysis of large amounts of judicial decisions by artificial intelligence technologies in order to make predictions for the outcome of certain types of specialised disputes (for example, redundancy payments or alimentary pensions). The term "predictive" used by legal tech companies comes from the branches of science (principally statistics) that make it possible to predict future results through inductive analysis. Judicial decisions are processed with a view to detecting correlations between input data (criteria set out in legislation, the facts of the case and the reasoning) and output data (formal judgment such as the compensation amount). Correlations deemed to be relevant make it possible to create models which, when used with new input data (new facts or precisions described as a parameter, such as the duration of the contractual relationship), produce according to their developers a prediction of the decision (for example, the compensation range). Some authors have criticised both the form and substance of this approach. They argue that, in general, the mathematical modelling of certain social phenomena is not a task comparable to other more easily quantifiable activities (isolating the really causative factors of a court decision is infinitely more complex than playing the game of Go or recognising an image for example): here, there is a much higher risk of false correlations. In addition, in legal theory, two

as equity.[926] While legal professionals spend a lot of time consulting books or in search of the right case law in libraries and databases with limited keywords, Predictive Justice software uses a semantic field of research. It means that not only keywords but also the contextual environment, occurrence of commentaries, and so forth are used. The number of research parameters can therefore be largely extended.[927]

Nevertheless, to achieve this mission, the machine needs to have access to a considerable amount of data.[928] The collection of this data in a machine-readable format is complex. While some data is not collectable for free, such as commentaries, the *Travaux Préparatoires* of the 1999 Montreal Convention or some judicial decisions, other is known to be 'open access', that is to say, publicly available for free in a full version, and some is even called 'open data'[929] once it is in 'open access' and in a machine-readable format.

In light of the improvement of translation systems, Predictive Justice software will be able to suggest a *proforma* decision after an examination of existing domestic and foreign jurisprudence, legislation, *Travaux Préparatoires*, dictionaries, or any other parameter included in the applicable algorithm. This instantaneous analysis of existing knowledge would not only improve the predictability of a Court decision, as the system would have analysed the way equal facts have been treated in the past, but also bring

contradictory decisions can prove to be valid if the legal reasoning is sound. Consequently, making predictions would be a purely informative exercise without any prescriptive claim', Source: Council of Europe, https://rm.coe.int/ethical-charter-en-for-publication-4-december-2018/16808f699c (accessed 31 October 2019).

925. *See*, Adrien van den Branden, *Les robots à l'assaut de la justice: L'intelligence artificielle au service des justiciables* 27 (Bruylant, 2019). A further step was taken in 2016 when a research team observed that Artificial Intelligence could predict the outcome of decisions of the European Court of Human Rights with 79% accuracy. *See*, Nikolaos Aletras, e. a., *Predicting Judicial Decisions of the European Court of Human Rights: A Natural Language Processing Perspective*, PeerJ Computer Science (24 October 2016), Source: PeerJ, https://peerj.com/articles/cs-93 (accessed 12 May 2020).

926. There are other Artificial Intelligence-based applications used in the Justice environment, such as one that predetermines recidivism risk in criminal proceedings, but these go beyond the scope of this book. Moreover, the concept of 'predictive justice' should not be confused with any sort of mechanism allowing criminals to be arrested prior to offences being committed, a concept popularized in Science Fiction movies and known as 'predicative justice'.

927. Adrien van den Branden, *Les robots à l'assaut de la justice: L'intelligence artificielle au service des justiciables* 84 (Bruylant, 2019).

928. *See*, Council of the European Union, Council Conclusions, 'Access to justice – seizing the opportunity of digitalization', *Official Journal*, 14 October 2020, C-342 I/1, at 36.

929. The European Commission for the Efficiency of Justice in its 2018 'European ethical Charter on the use of Artificial Intelligence in judicial systems and their environment' gave the following definition: 'The term refers to making structured databases available for public download. These data can be inexpensively re-used subject to the terms of a specific licence, which can, in particular, stipulate or prohibit certain purposes of re-use. Open data should not be confused with unitary public information available on websites, where the entire database cannot be downloaded (for example, a database of court decisions). Open data do not replace the mandatory publication of specific administrative or judicial decisions or measures already laid down by certain laws or regulations. Lastly, there is sometimes confusion between data (strictly speaking open data) and their processing methods (machine learning, data science) for different purposes (search engines, assistance in drafting documents, analysis of trends of decisions, predicting court decisions, etc.)', Source: Council of Europe, https://rm.coe.int/ethical-charter-en-for-publication-4-december-2018/16808f699c (accessed 31 October 2019).

further uniformity as the decision suggested would ideally have analysed all available case law and would be the same across all ratifying jurisdictions using and/or feeding the same software.

A.2.2 The Role of Humans

The emerging reliance on Artificial Intelligence-designed software in the sphere of Justice will undoubtedly change the role of legacy actors. With a decision in hand prepared by a machine whose legal skills are not disputed, judges would be likely to adhere to it once the litigious factual elements had been proven. The judge may, however, consider the decision suggested by the machine as not in line with his or her personal understanding of the case. In this scenario, they would have to justify in writing – probably more explicitly than what they are currently required to in many jurisdictions – the reasons why they deviated from the suggested decision.

Depending on how the suggested decisions are provided, such a deviation may require that the judges have some coding skills in order to be able to explain the reasons why they believe the algorithm used did not fit in a particular case. Lawyers as well would have to demonstrate, if they are not satisfied with the suggested decision, that the algorithm used did not fit the particulars of the case. This could happen, for instance, if they deemed factual elements to have been incorrectly filled in, or if the weight given to certain elements in the algorithm were not consistent with the case. With respect to the Conventions, such scenarios could occur, for example, if a lawyer believed that too much credit had been granted to Warsaw Instruments case law while litigating a Montreal case.

In order to be able to dispute the suggested decisions, the algorithm used must obviously be known.[930] As copyright issues may prevent full transparency, such algorithms should be established by States, and more specially by all States that have ratified the 1999 Montreal Convention. This would also have the benefit, in terms of uniformity, of the existence of a unique algorithm shared by all.

930. In a case involving Artificial Intelligence in criminal proceedings, the algorithm used to help determine the risk of recidivism was neither communicated to the judge nor the defendant. The possibility of challenging this computer-based decision was hence very limited. The Supreme Court of Wisconsin held, however, that such a risk assessment, based on a computerized tool developed by a private company, could still validly be used, provided it was not determinative. *See*, *State of Wisconsin v. Eric L. Loomis*, 2016 WI 68, cert. denied. For a commentary of the decision, *see*, Adrien van den Branden, *Les robots à l'assaut de la justice: L'intelligence artificielle au service des justiciables* 5-6 (Bruylant, 2019); Anonymous, *State v. Loomis*, 130 Harvard Law Review 1530-1537 (2017).

A.3 ARTIFICIAL INTELLIGENCE AND INTERPRETATION

A.3.1 Researching a Coherent Algorithm

However, in order to suggest decisions in line, not only with existing international case law but also with the 1999 Montreal Convention itself, a coherent algorithm translating common interpretation rules should be found.

A.3.2 Translating a Hermeneutical Methodology into an Algorithm

The question is therefore to determine whether the process of interpretation can be translated into an algorithm. In a 2018 study, Professor Luigi Viola took up the challenge.[931] He used as an example the Italian interpretation rules set out in Article 12 of the Preliminary Provisions (*Preleggi*) of the Italian Civil Code, assuming this methodology would be universal, being an expression for the natural need for legal certainty,[932] and similar to the one established by the 1969 Vienna Convention.[933] Article 12 of the Preliminary Provisions of the Italian Civil Code, giving priority to literal interpretation over any other methodology, provides that:

> In applying the law, one cannot attribute to it any other meaning other than that made evident by the particular meaning of the words and the connection between them, and by the intention of the lawmaker. If a dispute cannot be decided by a specific provision, reference shall be made to provisions governing similar cases or similar matters. If the doubt persists, the decision shall be made according to the general principles of the legal system of the State.[934]

The author saw in this provision an algorithm insofar as it provided for a sequenced operation to arrive at an outcome.[935] He also considered the trial itself to be an algorithm insofar as:

> [...] a judicial measure (PG) is determined by a series of operations predetermined by law, arising from the composition of proven facts (FP) and the law as it is interpreted (IP), namely PG = FP Λ[936] IP.[937]

---

931. Luigi Viola, *Interpretation of the Law Through Mathematical Models: Trial, A.D.R., Predictive Justice* (Diritto Avanzato, 2018).
932. *Ibid.*, p. 55.
933. *Ibid.*, p. 61.
934. Translation provided at *Ibid.*, p. 44. The original text reads: 'Nell'applicare la legge non si può ad essa attribuire altro senso che quello fatto palese dal significato proprio delle parole secondo la connessione di esse, e dalla intenzione del legislatore. Se una controversia non può essere decisa con una precisa disposizione, si ha riguardo alle disposizioni che regolano casi simili o materie analoghe; se il caso rimane ancora dubbio, si decide secondo i principi generali dell'ordinamento giuridico dello Stato'.
935. Luigi Viola, *Interpretation of the Law Through Mathematical Models: Trial, A.D.R., Predictive Justice* 116 (Diritto Avanzato, 2018).
936. This symbol means 'union'. *See*, *Ibid.*, p. 36.
937. *Ibid.*, pp. 35-36.

He further noted that:

> In essence, Article 12 highlights the fact that to understand the meaning of a text of law we must start from what is written (IL), together with the reason for which it was written (IR) [...]. Only if what is written, which is the clear starting point, does not produce a sufficiently certain meaning, do we then look for a similar situation in the legal system (AL) that can help us solve a practical case. If we do not find a situation similar to the proposed case anywhere in the legal system, then we apply general principles (AI).[938]

Would there be any difference between a literal interpretation and a teleological one, a greater weight or at least equal value weight should be given to literal interpretation. In a mathematical language, this would be translated as: $(IP) = IL \geq IR$.[939]

The next step, recourse to an interpretation by *analogia legis* (AL), could be translated as follows:

> Consequently: the interpretation of a law provision can derive from *analogia legis* if and only if a precise provision cannot be found, namely if $IL = 0$ (IR normally depends on the presence of IL). Thus, interpretation $(IP) = AL <=> IL = 0$; if it is used despite being unusable, where a 'precise provision' exists, then $IL \geq IR > AL$ (literal interpretation is greater or equal to teleological interpretation, which, in turn is greater than *analogia legis*, only when $IL > 0$, $IR > 0$, $AL > 0$).[940]

The same reasoning applies with respect to interpretation by *analogia iuris* (AI).

Professor Luigi Viola considered that Article 12 does not prevent other types of interpretation, such as evolutionary, systematic or constitutional-orientated interpretations from being used.[941] The value of these could be summarized as follows: $IL \wedge IR \circ$[942] $AL \circ AI$.[943] Other tools should also be considered such as *ad absurdum*, equitable and through combined provisions interpretations. As these would be considered as a union of a literal and a teleological interpretation, they would be translated as: $IL \wedge IR$.[944]

Acknowledging that the same type of interpretation may lead to opposite outcomes, he noted that an interpretation, pursuant to each mechanism, may either be positive (+), negative (–) or indirect (being ultimately negative in terms of logical incompatibility).[945] He suggested therefore that:

> If a literal interpretation (+IL) affirms a *quid*, but the latter is neutralised by another literal interpretation (–IL), then no literal interpretation can prevail ($+IL - IL = 0$) over the other because it has, in effect, been neutralised. Consequently, other interpretative instruments must be used, such as *analogia legis* (AL),

938. *Ibid.*, p. 56.
939. *Ibid.*, p. 73.
940. *Ibid.*, pp. 79-80.
941. *Ibid.*, p. 89.
942. This symbol means that the composition must be understood as a merger or synthesis of non-homogeneous data. *See*, *Ibid.*, p. 35.
943. *Ibid.*, pp. 93, 95, 98.
944. *Ibid.*, pp. 99, 100, 101.
945. *Ibid.*, p. 119.

> legitimised by the absence of a precise literal interpretation ($+IL - IL = 0$), and, as an *ultima ratio* (should *analogia legis* 'fail' - AL ≈[946] 0), an interpretation based on general principles (AI).[947]

In light of the above, he considered that the content of Article 12 of the Italian law could be summarized as follows:

> The interpretation of law (IP) equals (=) the union (Λ) of positive or negative literal interpretations ($IL \pm ILn$) with positive or negative teleological interpretations ($IR \pm IR$); in the absence of a precise provision of law ($IL = 0$), interpretations by *analogia legis* are added or subtracted ($=> (AL \pm ALn)$); in the event that the case is still dubious ($AL \approx 0$), interpretations by *analogia iuris* are added or subtracted ($=> (AI \pm AIn)$).[948]

> In short:

> IP = (IL ± IL*n*)[949] Λ (IR ± IR*n*) ° [IL = 0 = >[950] (AL ± AL*n*)] ° [AL ≈ 0 = > (AI ± AI*n*)] or **IP = Σi(n)**.[951]

The perfect adequacy of such a formula with the requirements of the 1969 Vienna Convention and the specificities of a uniform instrument such as the 1999 Montreal Convention must, of course, be discussed and decided by the ratifying Parties of the 1999 Montreal Convention, and was introduced here only as an example of the possibility of translating interpretation rules into an algorithm. Again, alongside the structure of the formula, ratifying Parties should also agree on the weight to be given to several parameters, as discussed in Chapter 5.

A.4 THE DAWN OF ARTIFICIAL INTELLIGENCE LAW

The potentialities of Artificial Intelligence mechanisms are promising. However, the ability of machines to reason and make decisions impacting human life will require the creation of new liability rules and the adoption of strict measures to safeguard our human rights.[952]

Interesting legal discussions on all these topics are yet to come, but go beyond the scope of the present study.

---

946. This symbol means 'approximately', *see, Ibid.*, p. 125.
947. *Ibid.*, p. 119.
948. *Ibid.*, p. 125.
949. This symbol means 'a variable denoting the number of possible interpretations of the same type', *see, Ibid.*, p. 125.
950. This symbol means 'if … then', *see, Ibid.*, p. 125.
951. *Ibid.*, pp. 124-126.
952. *See*, for example, European Commission, Proposal for a Regulation of the European Parliament and the Council laying down harmonised rules on Artificial Intelligence (Artificial Intelligence Act) and amending certain Union legislative Acts, 21 April 2021, COM (2021) 206 final.

Bibliography

Books, Monographs and Thesis

General International Law

Boele-Woelki Katharina, *Unifying and Harmonizing Substantive Law and the Role of Conflict of Laws* (Pocketbooks of The Hague Academy of International Law, 2010).

Cheng Bing, *General Principles of Law as Applied by International Courts and Tribunals* (Cambridge University Press, 1953).

Corten Olivier, *Méthodologie du droit international public* (Editions de l'Université de Bruxelles, 2017).

Craig Paul, Búrca (de) Gráinne, *EU Law: Text, Cases and Material* (7th edition, Oxford University Press, 2020).

Daillier Patrick, Forteau Mathias, Pellet Alain, *Droit International Public* (8th edition, LGDJ, 2009).

Decaux Emmanuel, Frouville (de) Olivier, *Droit international public* (11th edition, Dalloz, 2018).

Delmas-Marty Mireille, *Trois défis pour un droit mondial* (Seuil, 1998).

Dörr Oliver, Schmalenbach Kristen (eds), *Vienna Convention on the Law of Treaties: A Commentary* (2nd edition, Springer, 2018).

Evans Malcolm (ed.), *International Law* (3rd edition, Oxford University Press, 2010).

Fogt Morten (ed.), *Unification and Harmonization of International Commercial Law: Interaction or Deharmonization* (Wolters Kluwer, 2012).

Gardiner Richard, *Treaty Interpretation* (2nd edition, The Oxford International Law Library, 2017).

Lenaerts Koen, Gutiérrez-Fons José, *Les méthodes d'interprétation de la Cour de justice de l'Union européenne* (Bruylant, 2020).

Martineau Anne-Charlotte, *Une analyse critique du débat sur la fragmentation du droit international* (Thesis, Université Panthéon-Sorbonne, 2013).

Merkouris Panos, *Article 31(3)(c) VCLT and the Principle of Systemic Integration* (Brill, 2015).

Parrot Karine, *L'interprétation des conventions de droit international privé* (Dalloz, 2006).

Rigaux François, Fallon Marc, *Droit international privé* (Larcier, 2005).

Shaw Malcolm, *International Law* (8th edition, Cambridge University Press, 2017).

UNIDROIT (ed.), *Eppur si Muove: The Age of Uniform Law – Essay in Honour of Michael Joachim Bonell to Celebrate His 70th Birthday* (UNIDROIT, 2016).

Van Meerbeeck Jeremy, *Le principe de sécurité juridique dans la jurisprudence de la Cour de justice de l'Union européenne: de la certitude à la confiance* (Thesis, UCLouvain, 2013).

WTO Secretariat, *A Handbook on the WTO Dispute Settlement System* (2nd edition, Cambridge University Press, 2017).

TRANSPORTATION LAW (EXCLUDING AIR LAW)

Bokareva Olena, *Uniformity of Transport Law Through International Regimes* (Edward Elgar Publishing, 2019).

Bon-Garcin Isabelle, e. a., *Droit du transport de passagers: Droits français et de l'Union européenne* (Larcier, 2016).

Deshayes Olivier, *L'amélioration de l'application et de l'interprétation uniforme des conventions internationales relative au contrat de transport: le cas de la faute qualifiée* (Thesis, Université de Rouen Normandie, 2018).

Lamy, *Transport* (Wolters Kluwer, 2015).

Libouton Jacques (ed.), *Traité Pratique de Droit Commercial: Transport de marchandises* (Wolters Kluwer, 2015).

Mercadal Barthélémy, *Droit des transports terrestres et aériens* (Dalloz, 1996).

Nanassy (de) Bela, *Le droit international des transports par chemin de fer* (Rösch, 1946).

Paulin Christophe, *Droit des transports* (Litec, 2005).

Putzeys Jacques, *Droit des transports et droit maritime* (Bruylant, 1993).

Rimaboschi Massimiliano, *L'unification du droit maritime: Contribution à la construction d'un ordre juridique maritime* (Presses Universitaires d'Aix-Marseille, 2006).

Rodière René, *Droit des transports* (Sirey, 1977).

Sánchez-Gamborino Francisco, *La llamada Culpa Grave en el transporte de mercancías por carretera* (Marge Books, 2016).

AIR LAW

Abeyratne Ruwantissa, *Convention on International Civil Aviation* (Springer, 2014).

Abeyratne Ruwantissa, *Rulemaking in Air Transport: A Deconstructive Analysis* (Springer, 2016).

Abeyratne Ruwantissa, *Legal Priorities in Air Transport* (Springer, 2019).

Bergamasco Federico, *The ITU and ICAO Regulating Aeronautical Safety Services and Related Radio Spectrum* (Thesis, Université de Luxembourg, 2021).

Blanc-Dannery Yvonne, *La Convention de Varsovie et les règles du transport aérien international* (Pedone, 1933).

Bobek Michal, Prassl Jeremias (eds), *Air Passenger Rights: Ten Years On* (Hart Publishing, 2016).

Cachard Olivier, *Le transport international aérien de passager* (Les livres de Poche de l'Académie de droit international de La Haye, 2015).
Cartou Louis, *Le droit aérien* (Presses Universitaires de France, 1963).
Cartou Louis, *Le droit aérien* (Presses Universitaires de France, 1981).
Chami Diego, *La protesta aeronáutica: Teoría y práctica* (Abeledo-Perrot, 1988).
Chassot Laurent, *Les sources de la responsabilité du transporteur aérien international: entre conflit et complémentarité: La Convention de Montréal et son interaction avec le droit européen et national* (Schulthess, 2012).
Cheng Bin, *The Law of International Air Transport* (Stevens & Sons Limited, 1962).
Clarke Malcolm, Yates David, *Contracts of Carriage by Land and Air* (2nd edition, Informa Law from Routledge, 2008).
Coquoz Rafaël, *Le Droit Privé International Aérien* (Les Editions Internationales, 1938).
Constantinoff Jean, *Le droit aérien français et étranger: droit interne et droit international* (Librairie de Jurisprudence Ancienne et Moderne, 1932).
Correia Vincent, *L'Union européenne et le droit international de l'aviation civile* (Bruylant, 2013).
Diarra Souleymane, *La responsabilité contractuelle du transporteur aérien en droit malien* (L'Harmattan, 2021).
Diederiks-Verschoor Isabella, Mendes de Leon Pablo, *An Introduction to Air Law* (9th edition, Wolters Kluwer, 2012).
Dempsey Paul, Milde Michael, *International Air Carrier Liability: The Montreal Convention of 1999* (Centre for Research in Air & Space Law, McGill University, 2005).
Dempsey Paul, *Public International Air Law* (Institute and Center for Research in Air & Space Law, McGill University, 2008).
Drion Huib, *Limitation of Liabilities in International Air Law* (Springer, 1954).
Dupont Pascal, *Manuel de droit aérien: souveraineté et libertés dans la troisième dimension* (Pedone, 2015).
Ferrer Tapia Belén, *El contracto de transporte aéreo de pasajeros: sujetos, estatuto y responsabilidad* (Dykinson, 2013).
Folchi Mario, *Tratado de derecho aeronáutico y política de la aeronáutica civil* (Astrea, 2015).
Folliot Michel, *Les relations aériennes internationales* (Pedone, 1985).
Gates Sean (ed.), *The Aviation Law Review* (5th edition, The Law Reviews, 2017).
Giemulla Elmar, e. a., *The Montreal Convention* (Kluwer, regularly updated).
Goedhuis Daniel, *National Airlegislations and the Warsaw Convention* (Springer, 1937).
Goldhirsch Lawrence, *The Warsaw Convention Annotated: A Legal Handbook* (Kluwer Law International, 2000).
Goode Roy, *Cape Town Convention and Aircraft Protocol Official Commentary* (4th edition, UNIDROIT, 2019).
Grigorieff Cyril-Igor, Correia Vincent (eds), *Le droit du financement des aéronefs* (Bruylant, 2017).
Guerrero Lebrón María Jesús, *Los seguros aéreos: Los seguros de aerolíneas y operadores aéreos* (Marcial Pons, 2009).

Harakas Andrew (ed.), *Litigating the Aviation Case* (4th edition, American Bar Association, 2017).

Hatri Fayçal, *Droit du contentieux international aérien* (L'Harmattan, 2021).

Havel Brian, Sanchez Gabriel, *The Principles and Practice of International Aviation Law* (Cambridge University Press, 2014).

Hettiarachchi Lasantha, *The Quasi-Regulatory Regime of the International Air Transport Association (IATA) and Its Impact upon the Airline Industry and the Consumer* (Thesis, McGill University, 2018).

Heymann Jeremy (ed.), *Règlement (CE) n°261/2004 sur la protection des passagers aériens: Commentaire article par article* (Bruylant, 2021).

Hobe Stephan, von Ruckteschell Nicolai, Heffernan David (eds), *Cologne Compendium on Air Law in Europe* (Carl Heymanns Verlag, 2013).

Juglart (de) Michel, *Traité élémentaire de droit aérien* (LGDJ, 1952).

Juglart (de) Michel, du Pontavice Emmanuel, Dutheil de la Rochère Jacqueline, Miller Georgette, *Traité de droit aérien* (2nd edition, LGDJ, 1989).

Kazemi Hamid, *Carrier's Liability in Air Transport with Particular Reference to Iran* (Thesis, Universiteit Leiden, 2012).

Kiyana Maxence, *La responsabilité du transporteur aérien en droit positif congolais* (Editions Universitaires Européennes, 2018).

Le Comité International Technique d'Experts Juridiques Aériens, *Son origine, son but, son oeuvre* (Publications du Comité International Technique d'Experts Juridiques Aériens, 1931).

Leloudas Georges, *Risk and Liability in Air Law* (Informa Law from Routledge, 2009).

Litvine Max, *Précis élémentaire de droit aérien* (Bruylant, 1953).

Litvine Max, *Droit aérien: notions de droit belge et de droit international* (Bruylant, 1970).

Lobianco Rocco, *Compedio di Diritto Aeronautico* (Giuffrè, 2009).

Magdelénat Jean-Louis, *Le fret aérien: réglementation – responsabilités* (Pedone, 1979).

Mankiewicz René, *The Liability Regime of the International Air Carrier: A Commentary on the Present Warsaw Convention System* (Kluwer, 1981).

Martínez Sanz Fernando, Petit Lavall María Victoria (eds), *Estudios de Derecho aéreo: Aeronave y liberalización* (Marcial Pons, 2009).

Masutti Anna, *Il Diritto Aeronautico: Lezioni, casi e materiali* (2nd edition, Giappichelli, 2009).

Mateesco Matte Nicolas, *Traité de droit aérien-aéronautique* (2nd edition, Pedone, 1964).

Mendes de Leon Pablo (ed.), *From Lowland to High Skies: A Multilevel Jurisdictional Approach Towards Air Law – Essays in the Honour of John Balfour* (Martinus Nijhoff Publishers, 2013).

Mendes de Leon Pablo, *Introduction to Air Law* (10th edition, Wolters Kluwer, 2017).

Mendes de Leon Pablo, Buissing, Niall (eds), *Behind and Beyond the Chicago Convention: The Evolution of Aerial Sovereignty* (Wolter Kluwer, 2019).

Menéndez Adolfo (ed.), *Régimen Jurídico del Transporte Aéreo* (Thomson Civitas, 2005).

Milde Michael, *International Air Law and ICAO* (Eleven International Publishing, 2008).

Miller Georgette, *Liability in International Air Transport* (Kluwer, 1977).

Morillas Jarillo María José, Petit Lavall María Victoria, Guerrero Lebrón María Jesús, *Derecho Aéreo y del Espacio* (Marcial Pons, 2014).

Moura Vicente Dário (ed.), *Estudos de Direito Aéreo* (Coimbra Editora, 2012).

Naveau Jacques, Godfroid Marc, *Précis de droit aérien* (Bruylant, 1988).

Naveau Jacques, Godfroid Marc, Fruhling Pierre, *Précis de droit aérien* (2nd edition, Bruylant, 2006).

Ponet Frans, *Le transport aérien* (Story-Scientia, 1986).

Pourcelet Michel, *Transport Aérien International et Responsabilité* 222 (Les Presses de l'Université de Montréal, 1964).

Riese Otto, Lacour Jean, *Précis de droit aérien* (LGDJ, 1951).

Shawcross Christopher, Beaumont Kenneth, *Air Law* (LexisNexis, loose leaf, regularly updated).

Singamsetty Sagar (ed.), *Contemporary Issues and Future Challenges in Air and Space Law* (Airandspacebooks, 2011).

Smirnoff Michel, *Le Comité International Technique d'Experts Juridiques Aériens (CITEJA): Son Activité – Son Organisation* (Pierre Bossuet, 1936).

The International Bureau of the Permanent Court of Arbitration (ed.), *Arbitration in Air, Space and Telecommunications Law* (Kluwer Law International, 2002).

Tompkins George, *Liability Rules Applicable to International Air Transportation as Developed by the Courts in the United States: From Warsaw 1929 to Montreal 1999* (Kluwer, 2010).

Tosi Jean-Pierre, *Responsabilité aérienne* (Litec, 1978).

Tran Laurent, *Le régime uniforme de responsabilité du transporteur aérien de personnes* (Schultess, 2013).

Wagner Wenceslas, *International Air Transportation as affected by State Sovereignty* (Bruylant, 1970).

Wagué Hamadi Gatta, *Droit aérien africain* (Pedone, 2019).

Wassenbergh Henri, van Fenema Peter (eds), *International Air Transport in the Eighties* (Kluwer, 1981).

Artificial Intelligence

Abeyratne Ruwantissa, *Megatrends and Air Transport* (Springer, 2017).

Ashley Kevin, *Artificial Intelligence and Legal Analytics: New Tools for Law Practice in the Digital Age* (Cambridge University Press, 2017).

Hubin Jean-Benoît, e. a. (eds), *Le juge et l'algorithme: juges augmentés ou justice diminuée?* (Larcier, 2020).

Navas Navarro Susana (ed.), *Inteligencia Artificial: Tecnología – Derecho* (Tirant Lo Blanch, 2017).

Prévost Stéphane, Royer Erwan (eds), *Intelligence artificielle* (Grand angle, Dalloz, 2019).

van den Branden Adrien, *Les robots à l'assaut de la justice: L'intelligence artificielle au service des justiciables* (Bruylant, 2019).

Viola Luigi, *Interpretation of the Law Through Mathematical Models: Trial, A.D.R., Predictive Justice* (Diritto Avanzato, 2018).

MISCELLANEOUS

Boussofara Anissa, *Le principe d'interprétation autonome dans la Convention de Vienne sur les contrats de vente internationale de marchandises* (Thèse, Université Côte d'Azur, 2019).

Frydman Benoit, *Le sens des lois* (2nd edition, Bruylant, 2007).

Ost François, van de Kerchove Michel, *De la pyramide au réseau: pour une théorie de la dialectique du droit* (Publication des Facultés Universitaires Saint-Louis Bruxelles, 2002).

Pescatore Pierre, *Introduction à la science du droit* (reprint, Bruylant, 2009).

Theux (de) Axel, e. a., *Précis de méthodologie juridique: Les sources documentaires du droit* (2nd edition, Publications des Facultés universitaires Saint-Louis, 2000).

Thomasset Claude, Bourcier Danièle (eds), *Interpréter le droit: le sens, l'interprète, la machine* (Bruylant, 1997).

Articles and Book Chapters

GENERAL INTERNATIONAL LAW

Ancel Marcel, *From the Unification of the Law to Its Harmonization*, 51 Tulane Law Review 108-118 (1976-1977).

Andersen Camilla, *Defining Uniformity in Law*, 12 Uniform Law Review 5-54 (2007).

Assepo Assi Eugène, *La Cour commune de justice et d'arbitrage de l'OHADA: un troisième degré de juridiction?*, 57 Revue Internationale de Droit Comparé 943-955 (2005).

Attal Michel, *The Interpretation of Treaty by a National Jurisdiction (France and the United States)*, 28 Whittier Law Review 817-836 (2007).

Aust Helmut, e. a., *Unity or Uniformity? Domestic Courts and Treaty Interpretation*, 27 Leiden Journal of International Law 75-112 (2014).

Basedow Jürgen, *Uniform Law and Conventions and the UNIDROIT Principles of International Commercial Contracts*, 5 Uniform Law Review 129-152 (2000).

Basedow Jürgen, *Uniform Private Law Conventions and the Law of Treaties*, 11 Uniform Law Review 731-746 (2006).

Basedow Jürgen, *Antitrust or Competition Law, International*, Max Planck Encyclopedias of International Law (2014).

Baud William, Sachs Stephen, *The Law of Interpretation*, 130 Harvard Law Journal 1079-1147 (2017).

Bederman David, *Revivalist Canons and Treaty Interpretation*, 41 UCLA Law Review 953-1034 (1994).

Bonell Michael, *International Uniform Law in Practice: Or Where the Real Trouble Begins*, 38 American Journal of Comparative Law 865-888 (1990).

Cameron Iain, *Treaties, Declarations of Interpretation*, Max Planck Encyclopedias of International Law (2007).

Conforti Benedetto, *Unité et Fragmentation du Droit International: 'Glissez, Mortels, N'Appuyez pas!'*, 111 Revue Générale de Droit International Public 5-18 (2007).

Correia Vincent, 'L'adage lex specialis derogat generali: Réflexions générales sur sa nature, sa raison d'être et ses conditions d'application', in Muriel Ubéda-Saillard (ed.), *La mise en œuvre de la lex specialis dans le droit international contemporain* 27-47 (Pedone, 2017).

Correia Vincent, Trigeaud Béatrice, 'Transport, navigation et sources du droit international: Remarques générales', in Saïda El Bouhoudi (ed.), *Les transports au prisme du droit international public* 37-60 (Pedone, 2019).

David René, *The Methods of Unification*, 16 American Journal of Comparative Law 13-27 (1968).

De Brabandere Eric, *International Dispute Settlement: From Practice to Legal Discipline*, 31 Leiden Journal of International Law 459-468 (2018).

Deleau Olivier, *Les positions françaises à la Conférence de Vienne sur le droit des traités*, 15 Annuaire français de droit international 7-23 (1969).

Deumier Pascale, *Les principes UNIDROIT comme cadre de référence pour l'interprétation uniforme des droits nationaux*, 24 Revue Internationale de Droit Comparé 413-430 (2019).

Dubinsky Paul, *International Law in the Legal System of the United States*, 58 (Supplement) The American Journal of Comparative Law 455-478 (2010).

Ferreri Silvia, 'The Devil Is in the Details: Undetected Differences in Projects to Harmonize the Law', in UNIDROIT (ed.), *Eppur si Muove: The Age of Uniform Law – Essays in Honour of Mickael Joachim Bonell to Celebrate His 70th Birthday* 316-323 (UNIDROIT, 2016).

Gatsi Eric-Adol, *L'espace judiciaire commun CEMAC en matière civile et commerciale*, 21 Uniform Law Review 101-119 (2016).

Gebauer Martin, *Uniform Law, General Principles and Autonomous Interpretation*, 5 Uniform Law Review 683-704 (2000).

Gebauer Martin, *Unification and Harmonization of Laws* (Max Planck Encyclopedias of International Law, 2009).

Graveson Ronald, *The International Unification of Law*, 16 American Journal Comparative Law 4-12 (1968).

Helmersen Sondre, *Finding 'the Most Highly Qualified Publicists': Lessons from the International Court of Justice*, 30 European Journal of International Law 509-535 (2019).

Hendrikse Marc, Margetson Nick, *Uniform International Commercial Law: The Phenomena of Unification, Uniform Construction and Uniform Application*, 1 European Journal of Commercial Law 72-90 (2009).

Higgins Rosalyn, *The ICJ, the ECJ, and the Integrity of International Law*, 52 International and Comparative Law Quarterly 1-20 (2003).

Kamdem Innocent Fetze, *Harmonisation, unification et uniformisation en droit des contrats: plaidoyer pour un discours affiné sur les moyens d'intégration juridique*, 13 Uniform Law Review 709-744 (2008).

Kennedy William, *The Unification of Law*, 10 Journal of the Society of Comparative Legislation 212-219 (1909).

Kirchner Christian, *Evolution of Law: Interplay Between Private and Public Rule-Making – A New Institutional Economics-Analysis*, 4 Erasmus Law Review 161-171 (2011).

Klein Eckart, *Self-Contained Regime* 2 (Max Planck Encyclopedias of International Law, 2006).

Kono Toshiyuki, Kagami Kazuaki, *Is a Uniform Law Always Preferable to Private International Law: A Critical Review of the Conventional Debate on Uniform Law and Private International Law from the Viewpoint of Economic Analysis*, 56 Japanese Yearbook of International Law 314-337 (2013).

Koskenniemi Martii, Leino Päivi, *Fragmentation of International Law? Postmodern Anxieties*, 15 Leiden Journal of International Law 553-579 (2002).

Malaurie Philippe, *Loi uniforme et conflits de loi*, 1964-1966 Travaux du Comité français de droit international privé 83-109 (1967).

Malintoppi Antonio, *Droit uniforme et droit international privé*, 116 Recueil des cours de l'Académie de droit international 5-87 (1965).

Maxeiner James, *Legal Certainty and Legal Methods: A European Alternative to American Indeterminacy?*, 15 Tulane Journal of International & Comparative Law 541-607 (2007).

Maxeiner James, *Some Realism about Legal Certainty in the Globalization of the Rule of Law*, 31 Houston Journal of International Law 27-46 (2008).

McRae Donald, *The Legal Effect of Interpretative Declarations*, 49 British Yearbook of International Law 155-173 (1978).

Meyer Olaf, *The UNIDROIT Principles as a Means to Interpret or Supplement Domestic Law*, 21 Uniform Law Review 599-611 (2016).

Mola Lorenza, Poncibò Cristina, *The Autonomous Interpretation of International Uniform Private Law: A Dialogue on Methods of Interpretation from the Perspectives of Comparative Private Law and International Public Law*, 29 European Business Law Review 851-883 (2018).

Mutz Gerfried, *Objectifs et moyens de l'harmonisation juridique, illustrés d'après le droit de transport ferroviaire*, 8 Uniform Law Review 289-297 (2003).

Opperti Badán Didier, *Conflit de lois et droit uniforme dans le droit international privé contemporain: dilemme ou convergence?*, 359 Recueil des cours de l'Académie de droit international 9-86 (2012).

Pasquet Luca, *De-Fragmentation Techniques* (Max Planck Encyclopedias of International Law, 2018).

Pauwelyn Joost, *Fragmentation of International Law* (Max Planck Encyclopedias of International Law, 2006).

Peters Lena, *UNIDROIT* (Max Planck Encyclopedias of International Law, 2017).

Petersen Clement, Schovsbo Jens, 'Decision-Making in the Unified Patent Court: Ensuring a Balanced Approach', in Christophe Geiger, e. a. (eds), *Intellectual Property and the Judiciary* 231-254 (Edward Elgar Publishing, 2019).

Picker Colin, *International Law's Mixed Heritage: A Common/Civil Law Jurisdiction*, 41 Vanderbilt Journal of Transnational Law 1083-1140 (2008).

Popa Liliana, *The Holistic Interpretation of Treaties at the International Court of Justice*, 87 Nordic Journal of International Law 249-343 (2018).

Raban Offer, *The Fallacy of Legal Certainty: Why Vague Legal Standards May Be Better for Capitalism and Liberalism*, 19 Public Interest Law Journal 175-191 (2010).

Ramberg Christina, *The UNIDROIT Principles as a Means of Interpreting Domestic Law*, 19 Uniform Law Review 669-675(2014).

Ribeiro-Bidaoui João, *The International Obligation of the Uniform and Autonomous Interpretation of Private Law Conventions: Consequences for Domestic Courts and International Organisations*, 67 Netherlands International Law Review 139-168 (2020).

Rosett Arthur, *Unification, Harmonization, Restatement, Codification and Reform in International Commercial Law*, 40 American Journal of Comparative Law 683-697 (1992).

Roth Marianne, Happ Richard, *Interpretation of Uniform Law Instruments According to Principles of International Law*, 2 Uniform Law Review 700-710 (1997).

Schiff Berman Paul, *The Inevitable Legal Pluralism Within Harmonization Regimes: The Case of the CISG*, 21 Uniform Law Review 23-40 (2016).

Stephan Paul, *The Futility of Unification and Harmonization in International Commercial Law*, 39 Virginia Journal of International Law 743-797 (1999).

Sundberg Jacob, *A Uniform Interpretation of Uniform Law*, 10 Scandinavia Studies in Law 221-238 (1966).

Tomka Peter, *The Rule of Law and the Role of the International Court of Justice in Word Affairs*, Inaugural Hilding Eek Memorial Lecture, Stockholm Centre for International Law and Justice, 2 December 2013, https://www.icj-cij.org/public/files/press-releases/8/17848.pdf (accessed 29 May 2019).

Triantafilou Epaminontas, *Contemporary and Evolutive Interpretation under the Vienna Convention on the Law of Treaties*, 32 International Centre for Settlement of Investment Disputes Review 138-169 (2017).

van Ert Gib, *Dubious Dualism: The Reception of International Law in Canada*, 44 Valparaiso University Law Review 927-934 (2010).

Van Raepenbusch Sean, *Quelques réflexions sur l'autonomie de l'ordre juridique de l'Union européenne par rapport au droit international*, 622 Revue de l'Union Européenne 542-555 (2018).

Verhoeven Joe, *Jurisprudence belge relative au droit international*, 19 Revue belge de droit international 645-696 (1974).

Wieland Karl, 'Rechtsquellen und Weltrecht', *Recueil d'études sur les sources du droit en l'honneur de François Gény*, t. 3, 471-473 (Sirey, 1934).

Zeller Bruno, Andersen Camilla, *The Transnational Dimension of Statutory Interpretation: Tragically Overlooked in a Global Commercial Environment*, Nordic Journal of Commercial Law 6-19 (2019).

TRANSPORTATION LAW (EXCLUDING AIR LAW)

Czapski Waldemar, *Application et interprétation de la Convention CMR à la lumière du droit international*, 9 Uniform Law Review 545-567 (2006).

Griggs Patrick, *Obstacles to Uniformity of Maritime Law* 158-173 (CMI Yearbook, 2002).

Legros Cécile, *Modalités de l'interprétation uniforme de la CMR: Quelles difficultés? Quels remèdes?*, 21 Uniform Law Review 426-433 (2016).

Legros Cécile, *The CISG Advisory Council: A Model to Improve Uniform Application of CMR?*, 9 European Journal of Commercial Contract Law 27-30 (2017).

Ngnintedem Jean-Claude, *La réception des normes conventionnelles du droit du transport dans les Etats de la CEMAC*, 20 Uniform Law Review 325-360 (2015).

Putzeys Jacques, *Les tendances unificatrices et désunificatrices dans le droit des transports de marchandises: perspectives*, 8 Uniform Law Review 233-240 (2003).

Ramberg Jan, *Global Unification of Transport Law: A Hopeless Task?*, 27 Pennsylvania State International Law Review 851-858 (2009).

Verheyen Wouter, *National Judges as Gatekeepers to the CMR Convention*, 21 Uniform Law Review 441-456 (2016).

AIR LAW

Abeyratne Ruwantissa, *Morris v. KLM Royal Dutch Airlines: At the Crossroads of Warsaw and Montreal*, 26 Annals of Air & Space Law 283-302 (2001).

Adediran Adejoke, *Implementation of the Single African Air Transport Market Legal Regime: Challenges of the Interface Between the Yamoussoukro Decision and Domestic Regimes*, 43 Annals of Air & Space Law 23-54 (2018).

Adeline Sandra, *The Forum Non Conveniens Doctrine Put to the Test of Uniform Private International Law in Relation to Air Carrier's Liability: Lack of Harmony Between US and French Decision Outcomes*, 18 Uniform Law Review 313-328 (2013).

Aragone Coppola Augusto, *La Convención de Montreal 1999: ¿La Nueva Convención de Varsovia?*, 94 Revista Brasileira de Direito Aeronáutico e Espacial 39-56 (2012).

Baden Naneen, *The Japanese Initiative on the Warsaw Convention*, 61 Journal of Air Law and Commerce 437-466 (1995).

Baeck Kyeong-Won, Hwang, Ho-Won, *Article 61bis of the Aviation Business Act and the Legal Principles for the Aviation Consumers Protection: Comparison with the U.S. 'Tarmac Delay Rule'*, 35 The Korean Journal of Air & Space Law and Policy 169-195 (2020).

Balfour John, *Airline Liability for Delay: The Court of Justice of the EU Rewrites EC Regulation 261/2004*, 35 Air & Space Law 71-75 (2010).

Balfour John, 'Luxembourg v Montreal: Time for The Hague to Intervene', in Michal Bobek, Jeremias Prassl (eds), *Air Passenger Rights: Ten Years On* 65-73 (Hart Publishing, 2016).

Baruah Rishiraj, *IATA Conditions of Contract and Carriage (Passengers And Baggage): A Constant Tussle Between Regulatory Authorities and Airlines*, https://ilsquare.org/2016/03/25/iata-conditions-of-contract-and-carriage/ (accessed 22 August 2019).

Beaumont Kenneth, *The Warsaw Convention of 1929, as Amended by the Protocol Signed at The Hague, on September 28, 1955*, 22 Journal of Air Law and Commerce 414-433 (1955).

Bechky Perry, *Mismanagement and Misinterpretation: U.S. Judicial Implementation of the Warsaw Convention in Air Disaster Litigation*, 60 Journal of Air Law and Commerce 455-531 (1994).

Bekker Peter, *Questions of Interpretation and Application of the 1971 Montreal Convention arising from the Aerial Incident at Lockerbie (Lybian Arab Jamahiriya v. United Kingdom) and (Lybian Arab Jamahiriya v. United States), Preliminary Objections, Judgements*, 92 The American Journal of International Law 503-508 (1998).

Bernard Nicolas, *Taking Air Passenger Rights Seriously: The Case Against the Exclusivity of the Montreal Convention*, 23 International Community Law Review 1-31 (2021).

Bokareva Olena, *Air Passenger's Rights in the EU: International Uniformity Versus Regional Harmonization*, 41 Air & Space Law 3-24 (2016).

Buitrago Carranza Andrea, *Exploring the Compatibility Between the Air Carrier Liability Regime and International Human Rights Law*, 44 Annals of Air & Space Law 205-260 (2019).

Carvallo Javier, *Evaluation of Aviation Cases in Central and South America: A South American Perspective*, 83 Revista Brasileira de Direito Aerospacial 1728 (2001).

Castro Costa Viegas Carolina, Fábio Morsello Marco, *Seguridad jurídica vs. nueva caja de Pandora: Breves apuntes acerca de la reciente sentencia del Supremo Tribunal Federal en Brasil*, 42 Revista Latino Americana de Derecho Aeronáutico (2018).

Chappez Jean, *Questions d'interprétation et d'application de la Convention de Montréal de 1971 résultant de l'incident aérien de Lockerbie (Jamahiriya Arabe Libyenne c. Royaume-Unis) (Jamahiriya Arabe Libyenne c. Etats-Unis) Mesures Conservatoires, Ordonnance du 14 avril 1992*, 38 Annuaire Français du Droit International 468-479 (1992).

Chassot Laurent, *Le domaine de la responsabilité du transporteur aérien international à la lumière de deux décisions récentes*, Revue Française de Droit Aérien et Spatial 5-25 (2016).

Chauveau Paul, *Rapport sur la création d'une Cour internationale pour la solution des difficultés nées de l'interprétation et de l'application des conventions internationales en matière de Droit aérien*, Revue Française de Droit Aérien et Spatial 465-481 (1955).

Chaveau Paul, *Interprétation Judiciaire des Conventions Portant Loi Uniforme*, 2 Annals Air & Space Law 47-54 (1977).

Cheng Bin, *Wilful Misconduct: From Warsaw to The Hague and from Brussels to Paris*, 2 Annals of Air & Space Law 55-102 (1977).

Cheng Bin, *The Labyrinth of the Law of International Carriage by Air: Has the Montreal Convention 1999 Slain the Minotaur?*, 50 Zeitschrift für Luft- und Weltraumrecht 155-172 (2001).

Cheng Bin, *A New Era in the Law of International Carriage by Air: From Warsaw (1929) to Montreal (1999)*, 53 International & Comparative Law Quarterly 833-859 (2004).

Ciobanu Andrei, *Saving the Airlines: A Narrower Interpretation of the Term 'Accident' in Article 17 of the Montreal Convention*, 31 Annals of Air & Space Law 1-35 (2006).

Cluxton David, *The West Caribbean Conundrum: The United States Versus France on the Availability of Forum Non Conveniens under the Montreal Convention of 1999*, 85 Journal of Air Law and Commerce 3-104 (2020).

Correia Vincent, *Air Passengers' Rights, 'Extraordinary Circumstances', and General Principles of EU Law: Some Comments after the McDonagh Case*, 13 Issues in Aviation Law and Policy 245-278 (2014).

Correia Vincent, Rouissi Noura, *Global, Regional and National Air Passenger Rights: Does the Patchwork Work?*, 40 Air & Space Law 123-146 (2015).

Coultas Edward, *Interpretation of the Three Day Notice Requirement of Article 26(2) of the Warsaw Convention*, 39 Journal of Air Law and Commerce 251-266 (1973).

Crans Berend, *Article 28 of the Warsaw Convention*, 12 Air & Space Law 178-186 (1987).

Crans Berend, 'Aspect particuliers de la location de moteurs', in Cyril-Igor Grigorieff, Vincent Corriea (eds), *Le droit du financement des aéronefs* 115-142 (Bruylant, 2017).

Cunningham Mckay, *The Montreal Convention: Can Passengers Finally Recover for Mental Injuries?*, 41 Vanderbilt Journal of Transnational Law 1043-1081 (2008).

Devianikovaité Ieva, *The Montreal Convention of 1999 and Regulation No 261/2004 in the EUCJ and National Case Law*, 11 Baltic Journal of Law and Politics 21-47 (2018).

Drion Huib, *Towards A Uniform Interpretation of the Private Air Law Conventions*, 19 Journal of Air Law and Commerce 423-442 (1952).

Drion Huib, *Vers une interprétation uniforme des conventions de droit aérien privé*, Revue Française de Droit Aérien et Spatial 299-323 (1953).

Erotokritou Chrystel, Grigorieff Cyril-Igor, *EU Regulation No 261/2004 on Air Passenger Rights: The Impact of the COVID-19 on Flight Cancellation and the Concept of Extraordinary Circumstances*, 45(Special Issue) Air & Space Law 123-142 (2020).

Fitzgerald Gerald, *The Judgement of the International Court of Justice in the Appeal Relating to the Jurisdiction of the ICAO Council*, 12 Canadian Yearbook of International Law 153-185 (1974).

Fitzgerald Paul, *Automating the Process of Passenger Claims under the EU Passenger Rights Regime*, 4 The Aviation & Space Journal 2-14 (October 2018).

Fogliano Enzo, *L'art. 35 della Convenzione di Montreal: prescrizione o decadenza?*, 33 Diritto dei trasporti 115-117 (2020).

Folchi Mario, *El Proyecto Código Aeronáutico Latinoamericano y la uniformidad legislativa en la región*, 35 Revista Latino American de Derecho Aeronáutico (2017).

Fox Sarah, Martín-Domingo Luis, *EU Air Passengers' Rights Past, Present, and Future: In an Uncertain World (Regulation (EC) 261/2004 – Evaluation and Case Study)*, 85 Journal of Air Law and Commerce 271-308 (2020).

Freidenberg Elizabeth, *Quinta Juridicción*, 91 Revista Brasileira de Direito Aeronáutico e Espacial 40-55 (2008).

Gates Sean, *La Convention de Montréal de 1999*, Revue Française de Droit Aérien et Spatial 439-446 (1999).

Georgiades Euthymène, *De la méthodologie juridique pour l'unification du Droit aérien international privé*, Revue Française de Droit Aérien et Spatial 369-389 (1972).

Godfroid Marc, *Vers une autre interprétation de l'article 25 du Protocole de La Haye*, Revue Française de Droit Aérien et Spatial 467-475 (1982).

González-Lebrero Rodolfo, *The Spanish Approach to the Limitation Period or Condition Precedent in the Montreal Convention on International Air Carriage of 28th May 1999*, 3 The Aviation & Space Journal 5 (2013).

Gordilho Pedro, *O Dano Moral em Direito Aeronáutico (Panorama da Jurisprudência Brasileira)*, 73 Revista Brasileira de Direito Aeronáutico e Espacial 1618 (1997/1998).

Guillaume Gilbert, *La destruction, le 1er septembre 1983, de l'avion des Korean Airlines (vol KE 007)*, Revue Française de Droit Aérien et Spatial 215-226 (1984).

Guillaume Gilbert, *Du caractère impératif des dispositions de l'article 28 de la Convention de Varsovie*, Revue Française de Droit Aérien et Spatial 227-239 (2006).

Guinchard Michel, *L'influence de la convention de Varsovie sur les règles de droit interne relatives à la responsabilité du transporteur aérien*, Revue Française de Droit Aérien et Spatial 191-212 (1957).

Haanappel Peter, *The Right to Sue in Death in Cases under the Warsaw Convention*, 6 Air & Space Law 66-78 (1981).

Hammarskjöld Knut, *One World or Fragmentation: The Toll of Evolution in International Air Transport*, 9 Annals of Air & Space Law 79-106 (1984).

Havel Brian, Sanchez Gabriel, *The Emerging Lex Aviatica*, 42 Georgetown Journal of International Law 639-672 (2011).

Hempel Heinrich, *Keine Ausgleichsleistungen gemäss Fluggastrerechteverordnung bei Verspätung: Urteil des Bezirksgerichts Bülach vom 2. Februar 2016 mit Anmerkungen*, 148 Schweizerische Vereinigung für Luft- und Raumrecht 52-65 (2016).

Hiller William, *An Interpretation of the Embarking and Disembarking Requirements of Article 17 of the Warsaw Convention*, 16 Columbia Journal of Transnational Law 105-137 (1977).

Knauth Arnold, *The Citeja Meeting in Paris in January, 1939*, 10 Journal of Air Law and Commerce 167-175 (1939).

Koning Ingrid, *The Disabling of the EC Disability Regulation: Stott v. Thomas Cook Tour Operators Ltd in the Light of the Exclusivity Doctrine*, 5 European Review of Private Law 786-796 (2014).

Krueger David, *Mental Distress for Airlines Lawyers: The Sixth Circuit's Decision in Doe v. Etihad*, 31(2) The Air and Space Lawyer 4-7 (2018).

Latchford Stephen, *The Warsaw Convention and the CITEJA*, 6 Journal of Air Law and Commerce 79-93 (1935).

Latchford Stephen, Joseph Fennell, *The International Conventions on Private Aerial Law*, 8 Journal of Air Law and Commerce 298-357 (1937).

Latchford Stephen, *Pending Projects of the International Technical Committee of Aerial Legal Matters*, 40 The American Journal of International Law 280-302 (1946).

Lawson Robert, Marland Tim, *The Montreal Convention 1999 and the Decisions of the ECJ in the Cases of IATA and Sturgeon: In Harmony or Discord?*, 36 Air & Space Law 99-108 (2011).

Lawson Robert, *The Montreal Convention 1999 at 21: Has It Come of Age or Passed Its Sell-by Date?*, 45 Air & Space Law 265-284 (2020).

Lee Jae Woon, Wheeler Joseph, *Air Carrier Liability for Delay: A Plea to Return to International Uniformity*, 77 Journal of Air Law and Commerce 43-103 (2012).

Lemoine Maurice, *A la recherche du Droit international aérien*, Revue Française de Droit Aérien et Spatial 1-17 (1955).

Lowenfeld Andreas, Mendelsohn Allan, *The United States and the Warsaw Convention*, 80 Harvard Law Review 497-602 (1967).

Macara Peter, *The Brazilian Supreme Court Upholds the Application of the Warsaw and Montreal Conventions*, 43 Air & Space Law 505-513 (2018).

Mankiewicz René, *L'organisation international de l'aviation civile*, 3 Annuaire Français de Droit International 383-417 (1957).

Mankiewicz René, *La Convention de Varsovie et le Droit Comparé*, Revue Française de Droit Aérien et Spatial 136-150 (1969).

Mankiewicz René, *Conflicting Interpretations of the Warsaw Air Transport Treaty*, 18 The American Journal of Comparative Law 177-194 (1970).

Mankiewicz René, *L'Unification du Droit aérien: Organes et Techniques de l'Unification du Droit aérien (public et privé)*, 16 McGill Law Journal 419-459 (1970).

Mankiewicz René, *The Judicial Diversification of Uniform Private Law Conventions*, 21 International & Comparative Law Quarterly 718-757 (1972).

Mankiewicz René, *Vers la Refonte de la Convention de Varsovie et la Révision de la Convention de Rome?*, 11 European Transport Law 854-861 (1976).

Mankiewicz René, *L'origine et l'interprétation de la l'article 25 de la Convention de Varsovie amendée à La Haye en 1955*, 26 Zeitschrift für Luft- und Weltraumrecht 175-190 (1977).

Mankiewicz René, *The Application of Article 17 of the Warsaw Convention to Mental Suffering Not Related to Physical Injury*, 4 Annals of Air & Space Law 187-212 (1979).

Mankiewicz René, *Application of Article 26(2) of the Warsaw Convention as Amended at The Hague to Partial Loss of Contents of Registered Baggage: The House of Lords' New Standards for the Interpretation of Uniform Law Conventions*, 30 Zeitschrift für Luft- und Weltraumrecht 119-136 (1981).

Mapelli Lopez Enrique, *Air Carriers Liability in Cases of Delay*, 1 Annals of Air & Space Law 109-132 (1976).

Markhvida Kate, 'Antitrust and Competition Law', in Paul Dempsey, Ram Jakhu (eds), *Routledge Handbook of Public Aviation Law* 308-329 (Routledge, 2017).

Martins Carlos, *The 'Strong Exclusivity' Consensus Interpretation of the Montreal Convention*, 28(3) The Air and Space Lawyer 4-8 (2015).

McDonald Marc, *The Montreal Convention and the Preemption of Air Passenger Harm Claims*, 44 The Irish Jurist 203-238 (2009).

McKay Jennifer, *The Refinement of the Warsaw System: Why the 1999 Montreal Convention Represents the Best Hope for Uniformity*, 34 Case Western Reserve Journal International Law 73-101 (2002).

Mendelson Allan, *Warsaw: In Transition or Decline?*, 21 Air & Space Law 183-187 (1996).

Mendes de Leon Pablo, Eyskens Werner, *The Montreal Convention: Analysis of Some Aspects of the Attempted Modernization and Consolidation of the Warsaw System*, 66 Journal of Air Law and Commerce 1155-1185 (2001).

Mendes de Leon Pablo, *International Civil Aviation Organization* (Max Planck Encyclopedias of International Law, 2007).

Mendes de Leon Pablo, 'Jurisdiction under and Exclusivity of Private International Air Law Agreements on Air Carrier Liability: The Case of Airbus Versus Armavia Airlines (2013)', in Pablo Mendes de Leon (ed.), *From Lowlands to High Skies: A Multilevel Jurisdictional Approach towards Air Law – Essays in Honour of John Balfour* 261-273 (Martinus Nijhoff Publishers, 2013).

Mendes de Leon Pablo, *National Reflexes Following the COVID-19 Outbreak: Is Sovereignty Back in the Air?*, 45(Special Issue) Air & Space Law 17-38 (2020).

Mercer Antony, *Liability of Air Carriers for Mental Injury under the Warsaw Convention*, 28 Air & Space Law 147-187 (2003).

Müller-Rostin Wolf, *Article 50 Montreal Convention: A Provision with Considerable Consequences*, 53 Zeitschrift für Luft- und Weltraumrecht 551-557 (2004).

Naboush Eman, *The Meaning of 'Bodily Injury' in Air Passenger Litigation*, 39 Annals of Air & Space Law 39-73 (2014).

Neenan Peter, *The Damaged Quilt: Inadequate Coverage of the Montreal Convention*, 37 Air & Space Law 51-64 (2012).

Paliwal Nandini, *Interpretation of the Term 'Bodily Injury' in International Air Transportation: Whether Recovery for Mental Injury Is Tenable under the Warsaw System and Montreal Convention*, The Aviation & Space Journal 2 (April 2018).

Pradelle (de la) Albert, *L'interprétation des Conventions Internationales de droit privé aérien à titre d'avis consultatif par le C.I.T.E.J.A.*, Revue Générale de Droit Aérien 455-463 (1934).

Pradelle (de la) Albert, *Rapport sur la XII session du CITEJA*, Revue Française de Droit Aérien et Spatial 605-617 (1937).

Pontavice (du) Emmanuel, *L'interprétation des conventions internationales portant loi uniforme dans les rapports internationaux*, 7 Annals of Air & Space Law 3-40 (1982).

Pourcelet Michel, *The International Element in Air Transport*, 33 Journal of Air Law and Commerce 75-85 (1967).

Pourcelet Michel, *A propos d'un accident d'avion: la diversité des solutions données par le tribunaux*, Revue Générale de l'Air 211-215 (1973).

Radoševic Sonja, *CJEU's Decision in Nelson and Others in Light of the Exclusivity of the Montreal Convention*, 38 Air & Space Law 95-110 (2013).

Rafael Gema Díaz, *Forum Non Conveniens: Los Casos Spanair y Air France*, 8 Revista Latino Americana de Derecho Aeronáutico (2012).

Ravaud Didier, *La notion d'établissement au sens de l'article 28 de la convention de Varsovie*, Revue Française de Droit Aérien et Spatial 159-162 (1985).

Riese Otto, *Réflexions sur l'unification internationale du Droit aérien, sa situation actuelle, ses perspectives*, Revue Française de Droit Aérien et Spatial 131-148 (1951).

Riese Otto, *Une juridiction supranationale pour l'interprétation du droit unifié?*, 13 Revue Internationale de Droit Comparé 717-735 (1961).

Ripert Georges, *L'Unification du droit aérien*, Revue Française de Droit Aérien et Spatial 251-267 (1932).

Robins John, *The Montreal Convention of 1999 and the Smoking Wreckage of Accident*, 32 Annals of Air & Space Law 1-27 (2007).

Rodière René, *La faute inexcusable du transporteur aérien: Appréciation concrète ou abstraite*, 13 European Transport Law 24-30 (1978).

Sand Peter, *The International Unification of Air Law*, 30 Law and Contemporary Problems 400-424 (1965).

Sarmiento García Manuel Guillermo, *Los derechos del pasajero derivados del convenion de Montreal de 1999 y del derecho comunitario Andino*, 93 Revista Brasileira de Direito Aeronáutico e Especial 50-57 (2010).

Smithies Richard, *Regulatory Convergence: Extending the Reach of EU Aviation Law*, 72 Journal of Air Law and Commerce 3-20 (2007).

Spitz Barry, *Assessment of the Unification of Private International Air Law by Treaty*, 83 South African Law Journal 176-184 (1966).

Stewart Allison, *The Montreal Convention's Statute of Limitations: A Failed Attempt at Consistency*, 80 Journal of Air Law and Commerce 267-275 (2015).

Sundberg Jacob, *La jurisprudence des pays scandinaves sur la Convention de Varsovie*, Revue Française de Droit Aérien et Spatial 349-373 (1974).

Tompkins George, *Bumping: Denied Boarding – And Article 19 of the 1999 Montreal Convention*, 32 Air & Space Law 231-232 (2007).

Tompkins George, 'The Malaise Affecting the Global Uniform Effectiveness of the Montreal Convention, 1999 (MC99)', in Pablo Mendes de Leon (ed.), *From Lowlands to High Skies: A Multilevel Jurisdictional Approach Towards Air Law – Essays in Honour of John Balfour* 275-282 (Martinus Nijhoff Publishers, 2013).

Tompkins George, *Are the Objectives of the 1999 Montreal Convention in Danger of Failure?*, 39 Air & Space Law 203-214 (2014).

Traschler Thomas, *A Uniform Application of Article 13 of the Cape Town Convention via an Autonomous Interpretation*, 21 Uniform Law Review 640-662 (2016).

Truxal Steven, *Air Carrier and Air Passenger Rights: A Game of Tug of War*, 4 Journal of International and Comparative Law 103-122 (2017).

Villeneuve (de) Jacques, *Compétence Juridictionnelle et Lex Fori dans la Convention de Varsovie*, 8 Revue de droit de McGill 284-299 (1961-1962).

Visscher (de) Fernand, *Les conflits de loi en matière de droit aérien*, 48 Recueil des cours de l'Académie de droit international 279-385 (1934).

Warner Edward, *PICAO and the Development of Air Law*, 14 Journal of Air Law and Commerce 1-10 (1947).

West Alexa, *Defining Accidents in the Air: Why Tort Law Principles Are Essentials to Interpret the Montreal Convention's Accident Requirement*, 85 Fordham Law Review 1465-1496 (2016).

Zampone Alessandro, *La Convenzione di Montreal del 1999 sul trasporto aereo nell'interpretazione della Corte di Giustizia europea*, Diritto dei trasporti 1-35 (2020).

Zhang Luping, *Introduction to the Forums in Resolving International Aviation Disputes*, 25 Australian International Law Journal 195-212 (2018).

ARTIFICIAL INTELLIGENCE

Alarie Benjamin, e. a., *Law in the Future*, 66 University of Toronto Law Journal 423-428 (2016).

Alarie Benjamin, e. a., *How Artificial Intelligence Will Affect the Practice of Law*, 68 University of Toronto Law Journal 106-125 (2018).

Aletras Nikolaos, e. a., *Predicting Judicial Decisions of the European Court of Human Rights: A Natural Language Processing Perspective*, PeerJ Computer Science (24 October 2016), https://peerj.com/articles/cs-93 (accessed 12 May 2020).

Anonymous, *State v. Loomis*, 130 Harvard Law Review 1530-1537 (2017).

Buat-Ménard Eloi, *La justice dite 'prédictive': prérequis, risques et attentes: l'expérience française*, 2 Revue trimestrielle de l'Ecole nationale de la magistrature 269-276 (2019).

Cannarsa Michel, *Interpretation of Contracts and Smart Contracts: Smart Interpretation or Interpretation of Smart Contracts*, 27 European Review of Private Law 773-786 (2019).

De Caria Riccardo, *The Legal Meaning of Smart Contracts*, 27 European Review of Private Law 731-752 (2018).

Fitzgerald Paul, *Automating the Process of Passenger Claims under the EU Passenger Rights Regime*, 4 The Aviation & Space Journal 2-15 (2018).

Gobeil Gabriel, *When Artificial Intelligence Renders Lawyers Obsolete: Proposing a Legal Framework of AI-Assisted Unmanned Aerial Vehicles in American Counter-terrorism*, 43 Annals of Air & Space Law 127-166 (2018).

Kolain Michael, *Artificial Intelligence, Robotics and the Law: Current Research Projects and Unsolved Legal Questions – Report of the First RAILS-Conference on 23 March 2018 in Hamburg*, 27 European Review of Private Law 647-656 (2019).

Kozuka Souichirou, *A Governance Framework for the Development and Use of Artificial Intelligence: Lessons from the Comparison of Japanese and European Initiatives*, 24 Uniform Law Review 315-329 (2019).

Licoppe Christian, Dumoulin Laurence, *Le travail des juges et les algorithmes de traitement de la jurisprudence. Premières analyses d'une expérimentation de 'justice prédictive' en France*, 103 Droit et Société 535-554 (2019).

Linarelli John, *Artificial Intelligence and Contract*, 24 Uniform Law Review 330-347 (2019).

Lippi Marco, e. a., *Consumer protection requires artificial intelligence*, 1 Nature Machine Intelligence 168-169 (2019).

Lozanda-Pimiento Nicolás, *AI Systems and Technology in Dispute Resolution*, 24 Uniform Law Review 348-366 (2019).

Meyerowitz Glen, *Lawyers, Here's How to Begin Learning about Artificial Intelligence*, 1 Robotics, Artificial Intelligence & Law 261-266 (2018).

Poullet Yves, Jacquemin Hervé, *Blockchain: une révolution pour le droit*, Journal des Tribunaux 801-819 (2018).

Reiling Dory, *Quelle place pour l'intelligence artificielle dans le processus de décision d'un juge?*, 2 Revue trimestrielle de l'Ecole nationale de la magistrature 221-228 (2019).

Tajti Tibor, *The Impact of Technology on Access to Law and the Concomitant Repercussions: Past, Present, and Future (from 1980s to the Present Time)*, 24 Uniform Law Review 396-429 (2019).

Turing Alan, *Computing Machinery and Intelligence*, 59 Mind 433-460 (1950).

Walton Douglas, e. a., *An Argumentation for Contested Cases of Statutory Interpretation*, 24 Artificial Intelligence Law 51-91 (2016).

MISCELLANEOUS

Cote Pierre-André, *Le souci de la sécurité juridique dans l'interprétation de la loi au Canada*, 110 Revue du notariat 685-692 (2008).

Dumont Hugues, Horevoets Christine, 'L'interprétation des droits constitutionnels', in Marc Verdussen, Nicolas Bonbled (eds), *Les droits constitutionnels en Belgique. Les enseignements jurisprudentiels de la Cour constitutionnelle, du Conseil d'Etat et de la Cour de cassation* 1:147-244 (Bruylant, 2011).

Other Sources

ALADA, *Proyecto Código Aeronáutico Latino Americano* (version 1985), https://alada.org/2017/04/27/proyecto-codigo-aeronautico-latino-americano/ (accessed 19 June 2019).

Berchi Mauro, *La inteligencia artificial se asoma a la justicia*, 25 El Pais Retina 61-65 (2020).

Broc Numa, *Les voyageurs français et la connaissance de la Chine (1860-1914)*, t. 276, Fasc. 1 (559) Revue Historique 90 (Presses Universitaires Françaises, Juillet – Septembre 1986).

Canadian Broadcasting Corporation, https://www.cbc.ca/news/business/canadian-airlines-fight-passenger-rights-bill-in-court-1.5201985 (accessed 22 March 2021).

Conseil d'Etat, *Principes de techniques législatives: Guide de rédaction des textes législatifs et réglementaires* (2008).

Council of Europe, The European Commission for the Efficiency of Justice – 'European ethical Charter on the use of Artificial Intelligence in judicial systems and their environment' https://rm.coe.int/ethical-charter-en-for-publication-4-december-2018/16808f699c (accessed 31 October 2019).

Council of the European Union, Council Conclusions, Access to justice – seizing the opportunity of digitalization, *Official Journal*, 14 October 2020, C-342 I/1.

Cour de cassation, *Rapport de la Commission Réflexion sur la Réforme de la Cour de cassation* (April 2017) https://www.courdecassation.fr/files/files/R%C3%A9forme/Archives/Synth%C3%A8se%20introductive%20de%20la%20Commission%20de%20r%C3%A9flexion.pdf (accessed 22 January 2021).

Cour de cassation, *Note relative à la structure des arrêts et avis et à leur motivation en forme développée* (December 2018) https://www.courdecassation.fr/IMG///NOTE%20MOTIVATION%2018%2012%202018.pdf (accessed 22 January 2021).

Cour de cassation de Belgique, *Rapport annuel* (2018) https://justice.belgium.be/sites/default/files/downloads/20180321_jp_31.pdf (accessed 31 March 2020).

Documentation française, *Guide de Légistique* (3rd edition, 2017).

Expert Groups – European Commission, *Liability for Artificial Intelligence and other emerging technologies*, 2019 https://ec.europa.eu/transparency/regexpert/index.cfm?do=groupDetail.groupMeetingDoc&docid=36608 (accessed 27 October 2020).

European Aviation Artificial Intelligence High Level Group, *The Fly AI Report – Demystifying and Accelerating AI in Aviation/ATM, 5 March 2020*, https://www.eurocontrol.int/sites/default/files/2020-03/eurocontrol-fly-ai-report-032020.pdf (accessed 9 March 2020).

European Commission, Commission Notice – Interpretative Guidelines on Regulation (EC) No 261/2004 of the European Parliament and of the Council establishing common rules on compensation and assistance to passengers in the event of denied boarding and of cancellation or long delay of flights and on Council Regulation (EC) No 2027/97 on air carrier liability in the event of accidents as amended by Regulation (EC) No 889/2002 of the European Parliament and of the Council, C/2016/3502, *Official Journal*, 15 June 2016, *C 214/5*.

European Commission, Communication from the Commission to the European Parliament, the European Council, the Council, the European Economic and Social Committee of the Regions, Artificial Intelligence for Europe, 25 April 2018, COM (2018) 237 final.

European Commission, Communication from the Commission to the European Parliament, the European Council, the Council, the European Economic and Social Committee of the Regions, Coordinated Plan on Artificial Intelligence, 7 December 2018, COM (2018) 795 final.

European Commission, *Study on the current level of protection of air passenger rights in the EU*, January 2020, https://op.europa.eu/en/publication-detail/-/publication/f03df002-335c-11ea-ba6e-01aa75ed71a1 (accessed 29 September 2020).

European Commission, *Study on the Use of Innovative Technologies in the Justice Field*, September 2020, https://op.europa.eu/en/publication-detail/-/publication/4fb8e194-f634-11ea-991b-01aa75ed71a1/language-en (accessed 17 September 2020).

European Union, *Joint Practical Guide of the European Parliament, the Council and the Commission for persons involved in the drafting of European Union legislation*, July 2016, https://op.europa.eu/en/publication-detail/-/publication/3879747d-7a3c-411b-a3a0-55c14e2ba732 (accessed 22 December 2020).

Hague Conference on Private International Law, *Enhancing Access to Foreign Law and Case Law – Presentation of Solutions by the European Union*, April 2014 www.hcch.net.

International Air Transport Association, *The Liability Reporter*, annual publication.

International Air Transport Association, *Core Principles on Consumer Protection*, https://www.iata.org/contentassets/2e46aace261040b9a47fb7b9da18efc9/consumer_protection_principles.pdf (accessed 29 October 2019).

International Civil Aviation Organization, *Database on Aviation Specific Consumer Protection Regulations*, https://2001-2009.state.gov/r/pa/prs/ps/2003/23851.htm (accessed 23 March 2021).

Le Devoir, https://www.ledevoir.com/economie/560781/la-cour-d-appel-federale-entendra-la-contestation-des-transporteurs-aeriens (accessed 22 March 2021).

Le Figaro, http://www.lefigaro.fr/histoire/archives/2017/06/09/26010-20170609ARTFIG00288-pekin-paris-en-automobile-un-prodigieux-defi-en-1907.php (accessed 28 May 2019).

Les Echos, https://business.lesechos.fr/directions-juridiques/droit-des-affaires/contentieux/0601825123420-l-intelligence-artificielle-se-met-au-service-des-juristes-d-airhelp-331496.php (accessed 31 October 2019).

United States, *Statistical Abstract of the United States*, volume 125, Part 2006, p. 699 quoting ICAO, Civil Aviation Statistics of the World, https://www2.census.gov/library/publications/2005/compendia/statab/125ed/tables/trans.pdf (accessed 29 May 2019).

Table of Cases

International Courts

Permanent Court of Arbitration, *The Island of Palmas Case (Or Miangas)*, 4 April 1928

International Court of Justice, *Arbitral Award of 31 July 1989, Judgement, I.C.J. Reports 1991*, p. 53

International Court of Justice, *Questions of Interpretation and Application of the 1971 Montreal Convention arising from the Aerial Incident at Lockerbie (Libyan Arab Jamahiriya v. United Kingdom), Preliminary Objections, Judgment, I.C.J. Reports 1998*, p. 9

International Court of Justice, *Questions of Interpretation and Application of the 1971 Montreal Convention arising from the Aerial Incident at Lockerbie (Libyan Arab Jamahiriya v. United States of America), Preliminary Objections, Judgment, I. C.J. Reports 1998*, p. 115

International Court of Justice, *Ahmadou Sadio Diallo (Republic of Guinea v. Democratic Republic of the Congo), Merits, Judgements*, I.C.J. Reports 2010, p. 639

International Court of Justice, *Appeal Relating to the Jurisdiction of the ICAO Council under Article II, Section 2, of the 1944 International Air Services Transit Agreement (Bahrain, Egypt and United Arab Emirates v. Qatar)*, 14 July 2020

Regional Courts

European Court of Human Rights

ECHR, 26 April 1979, *Sunday Time v. United Kingdom (No 1)*, ECLI:CE:ECHR:1979:0426JUD000653874

Inter-American Court of Human Rights

ICHR, 3 February 1993, *Cayara v. Perú (Excepciones Preliminares)*, Serie C No 14

COURT OF JUSTICE OF THE EUROPEAN UNION

CJEC, 6 April 1962, *Kledingverkoopbedrijf de Geus en Uitdenbogerd v. Robert Bosch GmbH and Maatschappij tot voortzetting van de zaken der firma Willem van Rijn*, C-13/61, ECLI:EU:C:1962:11

CJEC, 5 February 1963, *NV Algemene Transport en Expeditie Onderneming van Gend & Loos v. Nederlandse Administratie der Bestelingen*, C-26/62, ECLI:EU:C:1963:1

CJEC, 27 March 1963, *Da Costa en Schaake NV, Jacob Meijer NV, Hoechst-Holland NV v. Nederlandse Belastingadministratie*, Joined Cases C-28/62, 29/62, 30/62, ECLI:EU:C:1963:6

CJEC, 15 July 1964, *Flaminio Costa v. E.N.E.L.*, C-6/64, ECLI:EU:C:1964:66

CJEC, 39 April 1974, *R. & V. Haegeman v. Belgian State*, C-181/73, ECLI:EU:C:1974:41

CJEC, 5 March 1986, *Wünsche Handelsgesellschaft GmbH & Co v. Federal Republic of Germany*, C-69/85, ECLI:EU:C:1986:104 (Order)

CJEC, 22 October 1987, *Foto-Frost v. Hauptzollamt Lübeck-Ost*, C-314/85, ECLI:EU:C:1987:452

CJEC, 19 June 1990, *The Queen v. Secretary of State for Transport, ex parte: Factortame Ltd*, C-213/89, ECLI:EU:C:1990:257

CJEC, 10 January 2006, *The Queen, on the application of International Air Transport Association and European Low Fares Airline Association v. Department for Transport*, C-344/04, ECLI:EU:C:2006:10

CJEC, 10 July 2008, *Emirates Airlines – Direktion für Deutschland v. Diether Schenkel*, C-173/07, ECLI:EU:C:2008:400

CJEC, 22 December 2008, *Friederike Wallentin-Hermann v. Alitalia – Linee Aeree Italiane SpA*, C-549/07, ECLI:EU:C:2008:771

CJEC, 2 July 2009, *Christopher Sturgeon, Gabriel Sturgeon and Alana Sturgeon v. Condor Flugdienst GmbH* and *Stefan Böck and Cornelia Lepuschitz v. Air France SA*, Joined Cases C-402/07 and C-432/07, ECLI:EU:C:2009:416 (Opinion)

CJEC, 22 October 2009, *Irène Bogiatzi, married name Ventouras v. Deutscher Luftpool, Société Luxair, société luxembourgeoise de navigation aérienne SA, European Communities, Grand Duchy of Luxembourg, Foyer Assurances SA*, C-301/08, ECLI:EU:C:2009:649

CJEC, 19 November 2009, *Christopher Sturgeon, Gabriel Sturgeon and Alana Sturgeon v. Condor Flugdienst GmbH* and *Stefan Böck and Cornelia Lepuschitz v. Air France SA*, Joined Cases C-402/07 and C-432/07, ECLI:EU:C:2009:716

CJEU, 6 May 2010, *Axel Walz v. Clickair SA.*, C-63/09, ECLI:EU:C:2010:251

CJEU, 12 May 2011, *Andrejs Eglītis and Edvards Ratnieks v. Latvijas Republikas Ekonomikas ministrija*, C-294/10, ECLI:EU:C:2011:303

CJEU, 13 October 2011, *Aurora Sousa Rodríguez and Others v. Air France SA*, C-83-10, ECLI:EU:C:2011:652

CJEU, 21 December 2011, *Air Transport Association of America e.a. v. Secretary of State for Energy and Climate Change*, C-366/10, ECLI:EU:C:2011:864

CJEU, 4 October 2012, *Finnair Oyj v. Timy Lassooy*, C-22/11, ECLI:EU:C:2012:604

CJEU, 4 October 2012, *Germán Rodríguez Cachafeiro and María de los Reyes Martínez-Reboredo Varela-Villamor v. Iberia, Líneas Aéreas de España SA*, C-321/11, ECLI:EU:C:2012:609

CJEU, 23 October 2012, *Emeka Nelson e.a. v. Deutsche Lufthansa AG and TUI Travel plc and Others v. Civil Aviation Authority*, C-581/10 and C-629/10, ECLI:EU:C:2012:657

CJEU, 22 November 2012, *Pedro Espada Sánchez, Alejandra Oviedo Gonzáles, Lucía Espada Oviedo, Pedro Espada Oviedo v. Iberia Líneas Aéreas de España SA*, C-410/11, ECLI:EU:C:2013:747

CJEU, 31 January 2013, *Denise McDonagh v. Ryanair Ltd*, C-12/11, ECLI:EU:C:2013:43

CJEU, 14 November 2014, *Sandy Siewert and Others v. Condor Flugdienst GmbH*, C-394/14, ECLI:EU:C:2014:2377 (Order)

CJEU, 26 February 2015, *Wucher Helicopter GmbH, Euro-Aviation Versicherungs AG v. Fridolin Santer*, C-6/14, ECLI:EU:C:2015:122

CJEU, 17 September 2015, *Corina van der Lans v. Koninklijke Luchtvaart Maatschappij NV*, C-257/14, ECLI:EU:C:2015:618

CJEU, 28 January 2016, *Heli Flight v. EASA*, C-61/15, ECLI:EU:C:2016:59

CJEU, 17 February 2016, *Air Baltic Corporation AS v. Lietuvos Respublikos specialiųjųtyrimų tarnyba*, C-429/14, ECLI:EU:C:2016:88

CJEU, 6 June 2018, *Flightright GmbH v. Iberia Express SA*, C-186/17, ECLI:EU:C:2018:399 (Opinion)

CJEU, 22 June 2016, *Steef Mennens v. Emirates Direktion für Deutschland*, C-255/15, ECLI:EU:C:2016:472

CJEU, 5 October 2016, *Ute Wunderlich v. Bulgarian Air Charter Limited*, C-32/16, ECLI:EU:C:2016:753 (Order)

CJEU, 4 May 2017, *Marcela Pešková and Jiří Peška v. Travel Service a.s.*, C-315/15, ECLI:EU:C:2017:342

CJEU, 11 May 2017, *Bas Jacob Adriaan Krijgsman v. Surinaamse Luchtvaart Maatschappij NV*, C-302/16, ECLI:EU:C:2017:359

CJEU, 12 April 2018, *Finnair Oyj v. Keskinäinen Vakuutusyhtiö Fennia*, C-258/16, ECLI:EU:C:2018:252

CJEU, 17 April 2018, *Helga Krüsemann and Others v. TUIfly GmbH*, C-195/17, ECLI:EU:C:2018:258

CJEU, 22 November 2018, *Germanwings GmbH v. Wolfgang Pauels*, C-501/17, ECLI:EU:C:2018:945 (Opinion)

CJEU, 4 April 2019, *Germanwings GmbH v. Wolfgang Pauels*, C-501/17, ECLI:EU:C:2019:288

CJEU, 26 September 2019, *GN v. ZU acting for Niki Luftfahrt*, C-532/18, ECLI:EU:C:2019:788 (Opinion)

CJEU, 7 November 2019, *Adriano Guaitoli, e.a. v. easyJet Airline Co. Ltd*, C-213/18, ECLI:EU:C:2019:927

CJEU, 19 December 2019, *GN v. ZU acting for Niki Luftfahrt*, C-532/18, ECLI:EU:C:2019:1127

CJEU, 11 March 2020, *GDVI Verbraucherhilfe GmbH v. Swiss International Air Lines AG*, C-918/19, ECLI:EU:C:2020:281 (Order)

CJEU, 11 June 2020, *LE v. Transportes Aéreos Portugueses SA*, C-74/19, ECLI:EU:C:2020:460
CJEU, 9 July 2020, *SL v. Vueling Airlines SA*, C-86/19, ECLI:EU:C:2020:538
CJEU, 14 January 2021, *Airhelp Limited v. Austrian Airlines AG*, C-264/20, ECLI:EU:C:2021:26 (Order)
CJEU, 23 March 2021, *Airhelp Ltd v. Scandinavian Airlines System Denmark-Norway-Sweden*, C-28/20, ECLI:EU:C:2021:226
CJEU, 12 May 2021, *YL v. Altenrhein Luftfahrt GmbH*, C-70/20, ECLI:EU:C:2021:379
CJEU, 6 October 2021, *CS v. Eurowings* GmbH, C-613/20, ECLI:EU:C:2021:820

National Courts

Argentine

Supreme Court of Justice, 16 October 2002, *Natasi Grace Jane E. c. Aerolineas Argentinas S.A. s/Daños y Perjuicios*, N. 148. XXXVII. REX

Australia

Pel-Air Aviation Pty v. Casey (2017) NSWCA 32
Bhatia v. Malaysian Airline System Berhad (2018) FCA 1471
Di Falco v. Emirates (No 2) (2019) VSC 654
Parkes Shire Council v. South West Helicopters Pty Limited (2019) HCA 14

Austria

Oberster Gerichthof, 2 July 2015, 2 Ob 58.15s

Belgium

Cass., 27 May 1971, Pasicrisie 886 (1971), ECLI:BE:CASS:1971:ARR.19710527.16
Cass., 4 May 1972, 1 Pasicrisie 806 (1972), ECLI:BE:CASS:1972:ARR.19720504.5
Cass., 27 January 1977, 1 Pasicrisie 574 (1977), ECLI:BE:CASS:1977:ARR.19770127.2
Cass., 18 September 1978, Pasicrisie 66 (1979), ECLI:BE:CASS:1978:ARR.19780918.1
CA Bruxelles, 2 May 1984, Journal des Tribunaux 550 (1984), ECLI:BE:CA-BRL:1984:19840502.2
Cass., 3 November 1986, Pasicrisie 285 (1987), ECLI:BE:CASS:1986:ARR.19861103.9
Cass., 30 March 2000, C.9.70.176.N, ECLI:BE:CASS:2000:ARR.20000330.4
Cass., 10 April 2008, C.07.0074.N, ECLI:BE:CASS:2008:ARR.20080410.10

Brazil

Supremo Tribunal Federal, 25 May 2017, RE 636331/RJ

Canada

Montreal Trust Company et al. v. Canadian Pacific Airlines (1977) 2 SCR 793
Ludecke v. Canadian Pacific Airlines (1979) 2 SCR 63
R. v. Daoust (2004) 1 SCR 217
Thibodeau v. Air Canada (2014) 3 SCR 340
Thibodeau c. Air Canada (2019) CF 1102

Serbinenko v. Air Canada (2020) BCCRT 1330

China (Hong Kong)

Ong v. Malaysian Airline System Berhad (2008) HKCA 88

France

Cass., 17 May 1966, 65-92986
Cass., 5 December 1967, vol. II JCP 15350 (1967)
Cass., 24 June 1968, Revue Française de Droit Aérien et Spatial 453 (1968)
Cass., 24 May 1975, 73-13.556
Cass., 14 January 1977, 74-15061
Cass., 1 July 1977, 75-15443
CA Paris, 19 June 1979, Revue Française de Droit Aérien et Spatial 327 (1979)
Cass., 2 July 1981, 80-11.234
Cass., 16 February 1982, 80-17009
Cass., 26 April 1984, 82-12048
CE, 20 October 1989, No 108243
Cass., 6 October 1992, 90-19667
Cass, 15 July 1999, 97-10268
Cass., 8 July 2003, 99-10590
CE, 24 March 2006, ECLI:FR:CEASS:2006:288460.20060324
Cass., 11 July 2006, 04-18.644
Cass., 14 June 2007, 05-17248
Cass., 7 December 2011, 10-30919
Cass., 16 October 2012, 11-13658
Cass., 15 January 2014, ECLI:FR:CCASS:2014:C100009
Cass., 15 January 2014, ECLI:FR:CCASS:2014:C100011
Cass., 8 July 2014, ECLI:FR:CCASS:2014:CO00655
Cass., 8 October 2014, ECLI:FR:CCASS:2014:C101159
Cass., 4 March 2015, ECLI:FR:CCASS:2015:C100327
CE, 9 October 2019, 430538, ECLI:FR:CECHR:2019:430538.20191009
CC, 25 October 2019, No 2019-810, ECLI:FR:CC:2019:2019.810.QPC
Cass., 14 April 2021, ECLI:FR:CCASS:2021:C100308

Germany

Bundesgerichtshof, 2 April 1974, 9 European Transport Law 777 (1974)
Amstgericht Frankfurt am Main, 5 September 1997, 47 Zeitschrift für Luft- und Weltraumrecht 247-249 (1998)
Bundesgerichthof, 21 November 2017, X ZR 30/15, ECLI:DE:BGH:2017:211117 IXZR30.15.0

India

Trans Mediterranean Airways v. M/s Universal Exports & Anr. (2011) 10 SCC 316

Ireland

AHP Manufacturing B.V. t/a Wyeth Medica Ireland v. DHL Worldwide Network N.V., DHL Worldwide Express GmbH, DHL International (Ireland) Limited (2001) IESC 71

Hennessey v. Aer lingus Ltd (2012) IEHC 124

Israel

Supreme Court, 22 October 1984, Revue Française de Droit Aérien et Spatial 232 (1985) – (French Translation)

Italy

Cass., 14 July 2015, ECLI:IT:CASS:2015:14666CIV

Luxembourg

Tribunal d'arrondissement, 27 March 2012, 1344/12
CA, 29 January 2013, 61/13
CA, 21 January 2014, 44/14 V
Cass., 21 May 2015, 27/2015

Madagascar

CA Tananarive, 9 March 1972, Revue Française de Droit Aérien et Spatial 325 (1972)

Malaysia

Court of Appeal of Malaysia, 5 July 2017, *Huang Min & orz v. MAS & orz*, W-01 (IM) (NCVC)-330-08/2016

Netherlands

Gerechtshof Amsterdam, 3 May 2016, ECLI:NL:GHAMS:2016:1750

New Zealand

Emery Air Freight Corp v. Nerine Nurseries Ltd (1997) 3 NZLR 723

Panama

Juzgado Undécimo de Circuito de lo Civil del Primer Circuito Judicial de Panamá, 27 October 2017, *Caisa c. KLM*, Sentencia No 25-2017

Primer Tribunal Superior del Primer Distrito Judicial, 25 April 2019, *Caisa c. KLM*, 18SA.069

Philippines

Philippine Airlines, Inc. v. Simplicio Griño, 579 Phil 344 (2008)

Portugal

Tribunal da Relação de Lisboa, 11 May 2017, ECLI:PT:TRL:2017:1704.15.9T8AMD.L1.8.1E

RUSSIA

Moscow City Court (**Московский городской суд**), 15 May 2017, N 4Г/ 10-1239/2017

SOUTH AFRICA

Potgieter v. British Airways plc (2005) ZAWCH 5

SPAIN

Audiencia Provincial de Madrid, 1 February 2008, ECLI:ES:APM:2008:10106
Audiencia Provincial de Madrid, 18 May 2015, ECLI:ES:APM:2015:7272
Tribunal Supremo, 19 July 2018, ECLI:ES:TS:2018:8522A
Audiencia Provincial de Tarragona, 26 July 2018, ECLI:ES:APT:2018:1024
Tribunal Supremo, 29 January 2019, ECLI:EC:TS:2019:442A

SWITZERLAND

Federal Court, 10 May 1982, Revue Française de Droit Aérien et Spatial 365 (1983)
Bezirksgericht Bülach, 2 February 2016, 148 Schweizerische Vereinigung für Luft- und Raumrecht 52-65 (2016)

TONGA

Cauchi v. Air Fiji & Air Pacific Ltd (2005) TOSC 7

TURKEY

Supreme Court of Appeals, 11th Chamber, 19 April 2018, quoted in: International Air Transport Association, 22 *The Liability Reporter* 8 (2019)

UNITED KINGDOM

Stag Line Ltd v. Foscolo Mango & Co Ltd (1932) AC 328
Corocraft Ltd v. Pan American Airways (1969) 1 QB 616
Fothergill v. Monarch Airlines (1980) UKHL 6
Sidhu and Others v. British Airways Plc; Abnett (Known as Sykes) v. Same (1996) UKHL 5
Fellowes or Herd and another v. Clyde Helicopters Ltd (1997) UKHL 6
Morris v. KLM Royal Dutch Airlines (2002) UKHL 7
Re Deep Vein Thrombosis and Air Travel Group Litigation (2005) UKHL 72
Golden Straight Corporation v. Nippon YKK (2007) UKHL 12
Barclay v. British Airways (2008) EWCA Civ 1419
Laroche v. Spirit of Adventure (UK) Limited (2009) EWCA Civ 12
Ford v. Malaysian Airline System Berhad (2013) EWCA Civ 1163
Stott v. Thomas Cook Tour Operators Ltd (2014) UKSC 15
Labbadia v. Alitalia (2019) EWHC 2103 (QB)
Lipton v. BA City Flyer Limited (2021) EWCA Civ. 454

UNITED STATES OF AMERICA

Husserl v. Swiss Air Transport Company Ltd., 388 F. Supp. 1238 (S.D.N.Y. 1975)
Trans World Airlines, Inc. v. Franklin Mint Corp. et. al., 466 U.S. 243 (1984)
Air France v. Saks, 470 U.S. 392 (1985)
Chan et. al. v. Korean Air Lines, Ltd, 490 U.S. 122 (1989)
Eastern Airlines, Inc. v. Floyd et al., 499 U.S. 530 (1991)
Zicherman, Individually and as Executrix of the Estate of Kole, et. al. v. Korean Air Lines Co, Ltd., 516 U.S. 217 (1996)
Fishman v. Delta Air Lines Inc, 132 F. 3d 138 (1998)
El Al Israel Airlines, Ltd. v. Tsui Yuan Tseng, 525 U.S. 155 (1999)
In re Air Crash at Little Rock Arkansas, on June 1, 1999, 291 F.3d 503 (8th Cir. 2002)
Olympic Airways v. Husain, Individually, and as Personal Representative of the Estate of Hanson, Deceased, et al., 540 U.S. 644 (2004)
Ehrlich v. American Airlines, Inc., 360 F.3d 366 (2nd Cir. 2004)
Bassam v. American Airlines, Inc., 287 F. App'x 309, 317 (5th Cir. 2008)
Dickinson v. American Airlines, Inc., 685 F. Supp. 2d 623 (N.D. Tex. 2010)
Jacob v. Korean Air Lines Co. Ltd, 606 F. App'x 478 (11th Cir. 2015)
Narayanan v. British Airways, 747 F.3d 1125 (9th Cir. 2014)
State of Wisconsin v. Eric L. Loomis, 2016 WI 68, cert. denied
Von Schoenebeck v. Koninklijke Luchtvaart Maatschappij N.V., 659 F. App'x 392 (9th Cir. 2016)
Doe v. Etihad Airways, P.J.S.C., 870 F.3d 406 (6th Cir. 2017)
Cohen v. American Airlines, Inc, 13F.4th 240 (2nd Cir. 2021)

Table of Legislation

International Law

Treaties

International Convention concerning the Carriage of Goods by Rail, 14 October 1890, Bern

Convention Relating to the Regulation of Aerial Navigation, 13 October 1919, Paris, LNTS, 11, p. 173, entry in force 29 March 1922

International Convention concerning the Carriage of Goods by Rail, 23 October 1924, Bern

International Convention concerning the Carriage of Passengers and Luggage by Rail, 23 October 1924, Bern

Convention for the Unification of Certain Rules Relating to International Carriage by Air, 12 October 1929, Warsaw, LNTS, 137, p. 11, entry in force 13 February 1933

Convention for the Unification of Certain Rules relating to Damage caused by Aircraft to Third Parties on the Surface, 29 May 1933, Rome

Convention on International Civil Aviation, 7 December 1944, Chicago, ICAO Doc 7300, entry in force 4 April 1947

Convention on the International Recognition of Rights in Aircraft, 19 June 1948, Geneva, ICAO Doc 7620, entry in force 17 September 1953

Convention on Damage Caused by Foreign Aircraft to Third Parties on the Surface, 7 October 1952, Rome, ICAO Doc 7364, entry in force 4 February 1958

Protocol to Amend the Convention for the Unification of Certain Rules Relating to International Carriage by Air signed at Warsaw on 12 October 1929, 28 September 1955, The Hague, ICAO Doc 7632, entry in force 1 August 1963

Convention on the Contract for the International Carriage of Goods by Road (CMR), 19 May 1956, Geneva, UNTS, 399, p. 189, entry in force 2 July 1961

Convention Supplementary to the Warsaw Convention for the Unification of Certain Rules Relating to International Carriage by Air Performed by a Person other than the Contracting Carrier, 18 September 1961, Guadalajara, ICAO Doc 8181, entry in force 1 May 1964

Convention on Offences and Certain Other Acts Committed on Board Aircraft, 14 September 1963, Tokyo, ICAO Doc 8364, entry in force 4 December 1969

Vienna Convention on the Law of Treaties 1969, 23 May 1969, Vienna, UNTS, 1155, I-18232, entry in force on 27 January 1980

Protocol to Amend the Convention for the Unification of Certain Rules Relating to International Carriage by Air signed at Warsaw on 12 October 1929 as Amended by the Protocol done at The Hague on 28 September 1955, 8 March 1971, Guatemala City, ICAO Doc 8932, not in force

Convention for the Suppression of Unlawful Acts against Safety of Civil Aviation, 23 September 1971, Montreal, ICAO Doc 8966, entry in force 26 January 1973

Athens Convention relating to the Carriage of Passengers and their Luggage by Sea (PAL), 13 December 1974, Athens, UNTS, 1463, I-24817, entry in force 28 April 1987

Additional Protocol No 1 to Amend Convention for the Unification of Certain Rules Relating to International Carriage by Air Signed at Warsaw on 12 October 1929, 25 September 1975, Montreal, ICAO Doc 9145, entry in force 15 February 1996

Additional Protocol No 2 to Amend Convention for the Unification of Certain Rules Relating to International Carriage by Air Signed at Warsaw on 12 October 1929, as Amended by the Protocol done at The Hague on 28 September 1955, 25 September 1975, Montreal, ICAO Doc 9146, entry in force 15 February 1996

Additional Protocol No 3 to Amend Convention for the Unification of Certain Rules Relating to International Carriage by Air Signed at Warsaw on 12 October 1929, as Amended by the Protocol done at The Hague on 28 September 1955 and at Guatemala City on 8 March 1971, 25 September 1975, Montreal, ICAO Doc 9147, not in force

Montreal Protocol No 4 to Amend Convention for the Unification of Certain Rules Relating to International Carriage by Air Signed at Warsaw on 12 October 1929, as Amended by the Protocol done at The Hague on 28 September 1955, 25 September 1975, Montreal, ICAO Doc 9148, entry in force 14 June 1998

United Nations Convention on the Carriage of Goods by Sea, 31 March 1978, Hamburg, UNTS, 1695, I-29215, entry in force 1 November 1992

Convention concerning International Carriage by Rail (COTIF), 9 May 1980, Bern, UNTS, 1396, I-23353, entry in force 1 May 1985

United Nations Convention on Contracts for the International Sale of Goods, 11 April 1980, Vienna, UNTS, 1489, I-25567, entry in force 1 January 1988

United Nations Convention on the Law of the Sea, 10 December 1982, Montego Bay, UNTS, 1834, I-31363, entry in force 16 November 1994

Vienna Convention on the Law of Treaties between States and International Organizations or between International Organization, 21 March 1986, Vienna, not in force

Convention on Jurisdiction and the Enforcement of Judgements in Civil and Commercial Matters, 16 September 1988, Lugano, UNTS, 1659, I-28551, entry in force 1 January 1992

Convention for the Unification of Certain Rules for International Carriage by Air, 28 May 1999, Montreal, UNTS, 2242, I-39917, entry in force 4 November 2003

Protocol for the modification of the Convention concerning International Carriage by Rail (COTIF) of 9 May 1980 (Protocol 1999), 3 June 1999, Vilnius, UNTS, 2828, I-23353, entry in force 1 July 2006

Agreement between the European Community and the Swiss Confederation on Air Transport, 21 June 1999, Luxembourg, *Official Journal*, L 114/73 (regularly amended)

Convention on International Interests in Mobile Equipment, 16 November 2001, Cape Town, ICAO Doc 9793, entry in force 1 March 2006

Protocol to the Convention on International Interests in Mobile Equipment on Matters Specific to Aircraft Equipment, 16 November 2001, Cape Town, ICAO Doc 9794, entry in force 1 March 2006

Protocol of 2002 to the Athens Convention relating to Carriage of Passengers and their Luggage by Sea, 1974, 1 November 2002, London, UNTS, A-24817, entry in force 23 April 2014

Air Transport Agreement between the United States of America and the European Community and its Member States, 25-30 April 2007, Brussels and Washington, *Official Journal*, 25 May 2007, L 134/4

United Nations Convention on the Contracts for the International Carriage of Goods Wholly or Partly by Sea, 11 December 2008, New York, not yet in force

Convention on Compensation for Damage Caused by Aircraft to Third Parties, 2 May 2009, Montreal, ICAO Doc 9919, not in force

Convention on Compensation for Damage to Third Parties, Resulting from Acts of Unlawful Interference Involving Aircraft, 2 May 2009, Montreal, ICAO Doc 9920, not in force

Protocol to amend the Air Transport Agreement between the United States of America and the European Community and its Member States signed at Brussels and Washington on 25 and 30 April 2007, 24 June 2010, Luxembourg, *Official Journal*, 25 August 2010, L 223/3

Treaty on the Functioning of the European Union (2016 version), *Official Journal*, 7 June 2016, C 202/1

Convention on the Suppression of Unlawful Acts Relating to International Civil Aviation, 10 September 2010, Beijing, ICAO Doc 9960, entry in force 1 July 2018

TRAVAUX PRÉPARATOIRES

Conférence Internationale de Droit Privé Aérien, 27 Octobre – 6 Novembre 1925, Paris, 1926

ICAO Doc 7838, II Conférence Internationale de Droit Privé Aérien, 4-12 Octobre 1929, *Procès-Verbaux*, Varsovie, 1930

ICAO Doc 7379, Conference on Private International Air Law, Rome, September-October 1952, volume I, *Minutes*, Montreal April 1953

ICAO Doc 7379, Conference on Private International Air Law, Rome, September-October 1952, volume II, *Documents*, Montreal April 1953

ICAO Doc 7686, International Conference on Private Air Law, The Hague, September 1955, volume I, *Minutes*, Montreal September 1956

ICAO Doc 7686, International Conference on Private Air Law, The Hague, September 1955, volume II, *Documents*, Montreal September 1956

ICAO Doc 9040, International Conference on Air Law, Guatemala City, February-March 1971, volume II, *Documents*, Montreal 1972

ICAO Doc 9154, International Conference on Air Law, Montreal, September 1975, volume I, *Minutes*, Montreal, 1977

ICAO Doc 9154, International Conference on Air Law, Montreal, September 1975, volume II, *Documents*, Montreal, 1977

ICAO Doc 9775, International Conference on Air Law (Convention for the Unification of Certain Rules for International Carriage by Air), Montreal, 10 – 28 May 1999, volume I, *Minutes*, Montreal 1999

ICAO Doc 9775, International Conference on Air Law (Convention for the Unification of Certain Rules for International Carriage by Air), Montreal, 10 – 28 May 1999, volume II, *Documents*, Montreal 1999

ICAO Doc 9775, International Conference on Air Law (Convention for the Unification of Certain Rules for International Carriage by Air), Montreal, 10 – 28 May 1999, volume III, *Preparatory Material*, Montreal 1999

United Nations, Conferences on the Law of Treaties, First and second sessions, Vienna, 26 March – 24 May 1968 and 9 April – 22 May 1969, Official Records, *Documents of the Conference*, United Nations, New York, 1971, https://treaties.un.org/doc/source/docs/A_CONF.39_11_Add.2-E.pdf (accessed 2 August 2019)

OTHERS

Hague Conference on Private International Law and the European Commission, Joint Conclusions of the Hague Conference on Private and International Law and the European Commission, Access to Foreign Law in Commercial and Civil Matters, Conclusions and Recommendations, https://assets.hcch.net/upload/foreignlaw_concl_e.pdf (accessed 29 October 2019)

Hague Conference on Private International Law, Statute of the Hague Conference on Private International Law, https://www.hcch.net (accessed 30 October 2019)

ICAO, Annex 13 to the Convention on International Civil Aviation – International Standards and Recommended Practices – Aircraft Accident and Incident Investigation

ICAO, Resolution A1-23: Authorization to the Council to Act as an Arbitral Body

ICAO, Resolution A39-11: Consolidated Statement of Continuing ICAO Policies in the Legal Field, Assembly, 39th session (October 2016)

ICAO, Legal Committee, Constitution – Procedure for Approval of Draft Conventions – Rules of Procedure, Doc 7669-LC/139/6 (2018)

ICAO, Core Principles on Consumer Protection, www.icao.int/sustainability/SiteAssets/pages/eap_ep_consumerinterests/ICAO_CorePrinciples.pfd (accessed 27 October 2019)

International Court of Justice, Statute of the International Court of Justice, 24 October 1945, San Francisco https://legal.un.org/avl/pdf/ha/sicj/icj_statute_e.pdf (accessed 6 September 2020)

International Law Commission, Statute of the International Law Commission, adopted by the General Assembly of the United Nations, Resolution 174 (II) of 21 November 1947, regularly amended https://legal.un.org/ilc/texts/instruments/english/statute/statute.pdf (accessed 21 February 2020)

International Law Commission, *Responsibility of States for Internationally Wrongful Acts (2001)* https://legal.un.org/ilc/texts/instruments/english/draft_articles/9_6_2001.pdf (accessed 22 March 2021)

International Law Commission, 'Fragmentation of International Law: Difficulties Arising from the Diversification and Expansion of International Law', in *Report of the International Law Commission on the Work of Its Fifty-Eighth Session*, II(2) Yearbook of the International Law Commission 179 (2006)

International Law Commission, *Draft conclusions on subsequent agreements and subsequent practice in relation to the interpretation of treaties, with commentaries* (2018) https://legal.un.org/docs/?path=../ilc/texts/instruments/english/commentaries/1_11_2018.pdf&lang=EF (accessed 21 February 2020)

UNIDROIT, Statute of the International Institute for the Unification of Private Law, 15 March 1940, regularly amended, https://www.unidroit.org/english/presentation/statute.pdf (accessed 12 February 2020)

UNIDROIT, UNIDROIT Principles of International Commercial Contracts 2016, https://www.unidroit.org/instruments/commercial-contracts/unidroit-principles-2016 (accessed 27 October 2020)

United Nations, General Assembly, Resolution 2205 (XXI) of 17 December 1966 on the Establishment of the United Nations Commission on International Law https://undocs.org/en/A/RES/2205(XXI) (accessed 21 February 2020)

United Nations, *The rule of law and transitional justice in conflict and post-conflict societies*, Report of the Secretary General, UN Doc. S/2004/616 (23 August 2004)

Regional Law

Africa

Decision Relating to the Implementation of the Yamoussoukro Declaration Concerning the Liberalisation of Access to Air Transport Markets in Africa, 14 November 1999, Yamoussoukro, https://afcac.org/en/images/Documentation/yd_eng.pdf (accessed 7 November 2020)

Règlement N° 02/2003/CM/UEMOA relatif à la responsabilité des transporteurs aériens en cas d'accident, fait à Ouagadougou le 20 mars 2003, *Bulletin Officiel*, n°31, premier trimestre 2003, 10-12

Règlement N° 03/2003/CM/UEMOA établissant les règles relatives aux compensations pour refus d'embarquement des passagers et pour annulation ou retard important d'un vol, fait à Ouagadougou le 20 mars 2003, *Bulletin Officiel*, n°31, premier trimestre 2003, 12-14

Règlement N° 06/07-UEAC-082-CM15 du 11 mars 2007, signé à N'Djamena le 19 mars 2007, *Bulletin Officiel*, http://www.droit-afrique.com/upload/doc/cemac/CEMAC-Reglement-2007-06-responsabilite-transporteur-aerien.pdf (accessed 18 December 2020)

Règlement N° 01/2007/CM/UEMOA portant adoption du Code communautaire de l'aviation civile des États membres de l'UEMOA, fait à Lomé le 6 avril 2007, *Bulletin Officiel*, n°56, premier trimestre 2007, 1-36

African Union Regulations on the Protection of Consumers of Air Transport Services – Annex 6 to the Yamoussoukro Decision (Assembly/AU/Dec 676 (XXX) – Decision on Legal Instruments), adopted on 28-29 January 2018 at Addis Ababa, https://au.int/en/treaties/regulatory-and-instutional-texts-implementation-yamoussoukro-decision-and-framework-towards (accessed 27 October 2020)

AMERICAS

Comunidad Andina, Decisión 619 – Normas para la Armonización de los Derechos y Obligaciones de los Usuarios, Transportistas y Operadores de los Servicios de Transporte Aéreo en la Comunidad Andina, 15 de Julio de 2005, dada en Lima, https://www.comunidadandina.org/DocOficialesFiles/Gacetas/Gace1221.pdf (accessed 27 October 2020)

ASIA

ASEAN, Multilateral Agreement on the Full Liberalisation of Passenger Air Services, 12 November 2010, Bandar Seri Begawan, https://asean.org/wp-content/uploads/images/archive/transport/Agreement-101112.pdf (accessed 27 October 2020)

EUROPE

Council Regulation (EC) No 2027/97 of 9 October 1997 on air carrier liability in the event of accidents, *Official Journal*, 17 October 1997, L 285/1

Council Decision of 5 April 2001 on the conclusion by the European Community of the Convention for the Unification of Certain Rules for International Carriage by Air (the Montreal Convention), 2001/539/EC, *Official Journal*, 18 July 2001, L 194/38

Regulation (EC) No 889/2002 of the European Parliament and of the Council of 13 May 2002 amending Council Regulation (EC) No 2027/97 of 9 October 1997 on air carrier liability in the event of accidents, *Official Journal*, 30 May 2002, L 140/2

Regulation (EC) No 261/2004 of the European Parliament and of the Council of 11 February 2004 establishing common rules on compensation and assistance to passengers in the event of denied boarding and of cancellation or long delay of flights, and repealing Regulation (EEC) No 295/91, *Official Journal*, 17 February 2004, L 046/1

Regulation (EC) No 1107/2006 of the European Parliament and of the Council of 5 July 2006 concerning the rights of disabled persons and persons with reduced mobility when travelling by air, *Official Journal*, 26 July 2006, L 204/1; *Corrigendum*, *Official Journal*, 26 January 2013, L 26/34

Proposal for a Regulation of the European Parliament and of the Council amending Regulation (EC) No 261/2004 establishing common rules on compensation and assistance to passengers in the event of denied boarding and of cancellation or long delay of flights and Regulation (EC) No 2027/97 on air carrier liability in respect of the carriage of passengers and their baggage by air, 13 March 2013, COM (2013) 130 final

Proposal for a Regulation of the European Parliament and of the Council laying down harmonised rules on Artificial Intelligence (Artificial Intelligence Act) and amending certain Union legislative Acts, 21 April 2021, COM (2021) 206 final

Domestic Law

Algeria

Décret exécutif no 16-175 du 9 Ramadhan 1437 correspondant au 14 juin 2016 fixant les conditions et les modalités d'application des droits des passagers de transport aérien public, *Journal Officiel de la République Algérienne*, no 36, p. 7

Australia

Explanatory Memorandum to the Australian Civil Aviation Legislation Amendment (1999 Montreal Convention and Other Measures) Bill 2008, Australia Federal Register of Legislation, www.legislation.gov.au/Details.C2008B00098/Explanatory%20Memorandum/Text (accessed 19 February 2019)

Brazil

Decreto N° 5.910, de 27 Setembro de 2006 Brazilian Government, http://www.planalto.gov.br/ccivil_03/_Ato2004-2006/2006/Decreto/D5910.htm (accessed 20 June 2019)

Resolução No 400, de 13 de Dezembro de 2016, Diário Oficial da União, 14 Dezembro 2016, Pág. 104, *erratum* 15 Dezembro 2016, Pág. 111

Canada

Air Passenger Protection Regulations, SOR/2019-150, *Canada Gazette*, Part II, Volume 153, Number 11

China (Macao)

Convenção para a Unificação de Certas Regras Relativas ao Transporte Aéreo Internacional, *Feita em Montreal, em 28 de Maio de 1999*, *B.O.* n.°: 17, II Série, de 2006/04/26, Pág. 3412-3434

China (Mainland)

CCAR-300, 航班正常管理规定 (Provisions on the Management of Flight Regularity), Civil Aviation Administration of China, http://www.caac.gov.cn/XXGK/XXGK/MHGZ/201706/t20170621_44917.html (accessed 6 January 2021)

INDIA

CAR, Section 3, Series M, Part IV India Directorate General of Civil Aviation, https://www.dgca.gov.in/digigov-portal/?dynamicPage=dynamicPdf/130576445&mainCivilAviationReqContent/6/211/viewDynamicRuleContLvl2/html&maincivilAviationRequirements/6/0/viewDynamicRulesReq (accessed 22 February 2022)

INDONESIA

Ministerial Regulation No 89/2015 Direktorat Jenderal Perhubungan Udara, http://hubud.dephub.go.id/hubud/assets/file/regulasi/permen/PM_89_Tahun_2015-1_$_1433827446_1078314159_$_.pdf (accessed 22 February 2022)

ITALY

Regio Decreto 16 marzo 1942, n. 262, Approvazione del testo del Codice civile, GU Serie Generale n. 79 del 04-04-1942

Legge 5 iuglio 1988 n. 274 – Limite di risarcimento nei trasporti aerei internazionali di persone, GU Serie Generale n. 168 del 19-07-1988

Legge 10 gennaio 2004, n. 12 – Ratifica ed esecuzione della Convenzione per l'unificazione di alcune norme relative al trasporto aereo internazionale, con Atto finale e risoluzioni, fatta a Montreal il 28 maggio 1999, GU Serie Generale n.20 del 26-01-2004 – Suppl. Ordinario n.11

PHILIPPINES

DOTC-DTI Joint Administrative Order No 1, s. 2012, Philippines Official Gazette, https://www.officialgazette.gov.ph/2012/12/10/dotc-dti-joint-administrative-order-no-1-s-2012/ (accessed 20 June 2019)

PORTUGAL

Decreto n.° 39/2002, Diario da República n.° 274/2002, Série I-A de 2002-11-27

SOUTH KOREA

항공사업법 (Aviation Business Act), Article 61-2, National Law Information Center, https://www.law.go.kr (accessed 6 January 2021)

THE NETHERLANDS

Burgerlijk Wetboek, Boek 6, Artikel 76

UNITED KINGDOM

Carriage by Air Act 1932

The Carriage by Air Acts (Implementation of the Montreal Convention 1999) Order 2002

The Air Passenger Rights and Air Travel Organisers' Licensing (Amendement) (EU Exit) Regulations 2019

United States

US 14 CFR Part 203

Vietnam

Circular 14/2015/TT-BGTVT, Civil Aviation Authority of Vietnam, https://caa.gov.vn/van-ban/14-2015-tt-bgtvt-68.htm (accessed 20 June 2019)

Index

AEROSPACE LAW AND POLICY SERIES

1. Erwin von den Steinen, *National Interest and International Aviation*, 2006 (ISBN 90-411-2455-1).
2. Ludwig Weber, *International Civil Aviation Organisation: An Introduction*, 2007 (ISBN 978-90-411-2622-1).
3. Niels van Antwerpen, *Cross-Border Provision of Air Navigation Services with Specific Reference to Europe: Safeguarding Transparent Lines of Responsibility and Liability*, 2008 (ISBN 978-90-411-2688-7).
4. Brian F. Havel, *Beyond Open Skies: A New Regime for International Aviation*, 2009 (ISBN 978-90-411-2389-3).
5. Jiefang Huang, *Aviation Safety through the Rule of Law: ICAO's Mechanisms and Practices*, 2009 (ISBN 978-90-411-3115-7).
6. Marian Hoeks, *Multimodal Transport Law: The Law Applicable to the Multimodal Contract for the Carriage of Goods*, 2010 (ISBN 978-90-411-3246-8).
7. George N. Tompkins, Jr., *Liability Rules Applicable to International Air Transportation as Developed by the Courts in the United States: From Warsaw 1929 to Montreal 1999*, 2010 (ISBN 978-90-411-2646-7).
8. Daniel Calleja Crespo and Pablo Mendes de Leon (eds), *Achieving the Single European Sky: Goals and Challenges*, 2011 (ISBN 978-90-411-3730-2).
9. Donal Patrick Hanley, *Aircraft Operating Leasing: A Legal and Practical Analysis in the Context of Public and Private International Air Law, Third Edition*, 2022 (ISBN 978-94-035-4030-6).
10. Mikołaj Ratajczyk, *Regional Aviation Safety Organisations: Enhancing Air Transport Safety through Regional Cooperation*, 2015 (ISBN 978-90-411-5861-1).
11. Benjamyn I. Scott (ed.), *The Law of Unmanned Aircraft Systems: An Introduction to the Current and Future Regulation under National, Regional and International Law*, 2016 (ISBN 978-90-411-6126-0).
12. Stamatis Varsamos, *Airport Competition Regulation in Europe*, 2016 (ISBN 978-90-411-6831-3).
13. Katarzyna Malinowska, *Space Insurance: International Legal Aspects*, 2017 (ISBN 978-90-411-6784-2).
14. John Milligan, *European Union Competition Law in the Airline Industry*, 2017 (ISBN 978-90-411-6618-0).

15. Dejian Kong, *Civil Liability for Damage Caused by Global Navigation Satellite System*, 2019 (ISBN 978-94-035-1171-9).
16. Pablo Mendes de Leon and Niall Buissing (eds), *Behind and Beyond the Chicago Convention: The Evolution of Aerial Sovereignty*, 2019 (ISBN 978-94-035-1131-3).
17. Neta Palkovitz, *Regulating a Revolution: Small Satellites and the Law of Outer Space*, 2019 (ISBN 978-94-035-1762-9).
18. Federico Bergamasco, Roberto Cassar, Rada Popova & Benjamyn I. Scott, *Cybersecurity: Key Legal Considerations for the Aviation and Space Sectors*, 2020 (ISBN 978-94-035-0110-9).
19. Luis Fernando Fiallos Pazmiño, *The International Civil Operations of Unmanned Aircraft Systems under Air Law*, 2021 (ISBN 978-94-035-2854-0).
20. Merinda E. Stewart, *Freedom of Overflight: A Study of Coastal State Jurisdiction in International Airspace*, 2021 (ISBN 978-94-035-3804-4).
21. Cyril-Igor Grigorieff, *Uniformity and Fragmentation of the 1999 Montreal Convention on International Air Carrier Liability*, 2022 (ISBN 978-94-035-3732-0).

www.ingramcontent.com/pod-product-compliance
Ingram Content Group UK Ltd.
Pitfield, Milton Keynes, MK11 3LW, UK
UKHW020844290926
15470UKWH00004B/1549

9 789403 537320